MW00341615

PHOENIX

TAMAS I. GOMBOSI

ISBN-13: 978-0-9912873-0-7

Cover image: Allen OPatka (©2013 Photobucket)

To my children and grandchildren, and to the generations to come, so the Phoenix can fly high and proud.

Phoenix by Friedrich Johann Justin Bertuch (1747-1822).

A phoenix is a mythical bird with a colorful plumage and a tail of gold and scarlet (or purple, blue, and green according to some legends). It has a 1000 year life-cycle, near the end of which it builds itself a nest of twigs that then ignites; both nest and bird burn fiercely and are reduced to ashes, from which a new, young phoenix arises, reborn anew to live again. The new phoenix is destined to live as long as its old self.

Wikipedia

Contents

Appendices

Preface

Phoenix tells the story of several generations. It spans from the 1800s through the period of two world wars, the Holocaust, The Cold War and the start of the "new world order" (or disorder I would say) to the 21st century. It is based on historical facts and documents about our families. As we go back in time, however, there are gaping holes in the documents and I used family legends and my own imagination to fill in these gaps. I am sure that I got some things wrong. This is unavoidable in a story based on incomplete evidence.

The book is my own interpretation of events. Occasionally I go to historical asides. These, again, are my own opinions, sometimes completely contradicting interpretations widely accepted by historians. After all, this is my story of our family history and not an historical study.

My main purpose with this book is to leave the next generations my children, my grandchildren and the generations that come after them with some sense of their roots, and the way we burned and raised from the ashes. I hope you will find the story interesting.

I appreciate the help of my editor, Ms. Hope Burwell, who made this book more organized and readable. Her contribution really made a big difference.

TAMAS I GOMBOSI
Ann Arbor, MI
November 2013

Part I

Roots

The Gombosi (Glauber) Branch

1

1.1. To America and Back

My paternal grandfather, Dezső Glauber, was born in 1881 in Bojt, a small village in the Hungarian province of Bihar. His parents were Ignác (Yitzhak) Glauber (1851–1910) and Záli (Sarah) Erber. He was the second of five children and probably the most ambitious one. The extended Glauber and Erber families lived in the small area of Berettyóujfalu, Váncsód and Bojt, all within a radius of about five miles. In the late 1800s there were about a thousand Jews living in this area (comprising approximately 10% of the population). In addition to the Glaubers and Erbers, other large families were the Herskovics and Farkas "clans." These families regularly intermarried and it was not unusual to marry second or third cousins. Occasionally, even first cousins married each other. These families also extended to nearby Nagyvárad which at the time had a Jewish population of about 12,000. After World War I Nagyvárad became part of Romania. Its name was officially changed to Oradea and it still belongs to that country. In order to make it easier to understand family relations I

Záli Erber and Ignác Glauber in 1905. Ignác was a peddler in the Bojt area.

show family trees in Appendix C. The relevant family trees are shown in Fig. C.3 and in Fig. C.4.

Dezső was smart and ambitious and wanted to move to the big cities. This was the time of Hungarian industrialization and many young people moved from the villages to the emerging population centers. Moving to the cities also meant that Dezső needed to learn a trade so he could make a better living. Around 1900 he attended trade school and was trained as a joiner, a word not used much in modern American English, essentially referring to a finish carpenter, one who does fine carpentry, such as furniture making and model building, or other carpentry where exact joints and minimal margins of error are

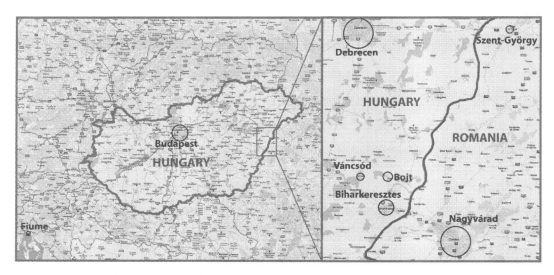

Present-day Hungary and the places of origin of the Gombosi (Glauber) family.

important. Dezső became a master joiner and was quite experienced in furniture and high-end picture frame making. It is my suspicion that this trade school was in Budapest, since this kind of highly specialized training probably could not have been obtained in smaller towns.

The wedding photo of Hani Herskovics and Dezső Gombosi (December 27, 1904).

Either during his trade school years, or shortly afterwards, Dezső Glauber changed his last name to the Hungarian sounding Gombosi. This was quite typical among Hungarian Jewry at this time.

I think that by the time he finished trade school Dezső decided to emigrate to America. This decision was probably influenced by his old friend and fellow finish carpenter, János Elbogen, who moved to New York in 1900. This was the peak of Hungarian emigration to the U.S.: during the "Great Economic Immigration" – between 1880 and 1914 – about a million Hungarians of all religions moved to the U.S., where they mainly settled in the New York, Chicago and Cleveland areas. It is interesting to note that around this time Cleveland was the second most populous Hungarian city. Only Budapest had more Hungarians in one place.

Dezső was concerned about finding an appropriate spouse in a new and unfamiliar country and wanted to get married before moving to America. In this situation the old Jewish tradition of turning to a matchmaker (shadkhin) was very useful. After getting engaged in June 1904 Dezső married a girl from the next village, Váncsód, on 27 December 1904. Hani Herskovics was 26 years old, an "old maid" by the social norms of the times. Officially, her name was Fáni but everyone called her Hani. Hani had two brothers and three sisters and I think she was the youngest child of Lőrincz (Lawrence) Herskovics. The family was not well-to-do and Hani did not have a dowry to speak of. Dezső was 23 years old, a bit young for marriage at a time when men usually waited until they reached some kind of economic stability. Between her age and Dezső's plan to embark on a risky adventure, each Hani and Dezső was less than a "prized catch."

The wedding was held in December 1904 in Hani's home village of Váncsód. Soon after the wedding the newlyweds applied for passports and took care of the necessary paperwork to go to America. In August of 1905 my paternal grandparents finally set sail for a new life together in the land of opportunities.

✂ ✂

It was a typical muggy hot day in New York in August 1905 when the passenger ship *SS Slavonia* operated by the British Cunard Line arrived from Trieste (today part of Italy) after a seventeen day voyage during which she stopped in several European ports before crossing the ocean. The new immigrants were processed at Ellis Island and released to the city. In the Ellis Island records Hani's name is recorded as Fany, probably because the American immigration officer used the English spelling. Soon after their arrival Dezső started to use Didier as his first name. Today it is unclear why he switched his Hungarian name to French instead of a more English sounding version, like Dennis. My guess is that he was under French cultural influence and thought that a French sounding name would make him more employable. He may have been right.

The passenger records reveal some interesting facts. The Gombosis listed Budapest as their last residence, indicating that they lived in this city before departure. They carried a relatively large amount of money, $382 (in 2013 dollars this would be around $10,000). Finally, they listed Hani's brother-in-law, János (John) Elbogen as the relative they wished to join.

The Gombosis were also accompanied on their journey by Hani's older sister, Eszter (or Eszti as the family called her). My best guess is that János was the brother of Eszti's deceased husband, whose name I don't know. Her immigration form indicates she was born

Name:	Gombosi, Dezso		Name:	Gombosi, Fany
Ethnicity:	Hungary, Magyar		Ethnicity:	Hungary, Magyar
Place of Residence:	Budapest		Place of Residence:	Budapest
Date of Arrival:	20 Aug 1905		Date of Arrival:	20 Aug 1905
Age on Arrival:	23y		Age on Arrival:	27y
Gender:	M		Gender:	F
Marital Status:	M		Marital Status:	M
Ship of Travel:	Slavonia		Ship of Travel:	Slavonia
Port of Departure:	Carnaro, Triest, Austria		Port of Departure:	Carnaro, Triest, Austria

The Ellis Island immigration records of Dezső and Fany Gombosi.

in 1863 (some 15 years before Hani) and was a widow. Upon arrival she had $30 (in 2013 dollars about $750). For her occupation she gave "dom. serv.," surely an abbreviation for domestic servant or service. She too listed János Elbogen as the relative she wished to join in the U.S.

When they arrived in New York, Hani was seven months pregnant. Two months later she gave birth to their first child, Róza (Rose). Rózsi, as the family called her, brought a lot of joy to her parents' lives.

✂ ✂

Starting a new life in a strange country is not easy for anyone. Surely the Gombosis would have had help and advice from János Elbogen who was born in 1873 and arrived in New York in December 1900. His last residence in Hungary was Szent-György, also known as Érmihályfalva. (Today it is part of Romania and is called Valea Lui Mihai.) Interestingly, he also gave "joiner" as his occupation to the U.S. immigration authorities. Thus, I suspect that Dezső and János were close acquaintances, or even friends, before János moved to New York. It looks very likely that they stayed in touch after János' immigration and János eventually persuaded Dezső to come to New York, the land of opportunities. The immigration record gives János Elbogen's address as 92 E. 40th St, New York.

By the time the Gombosis arrived five years later, Janos was married and had a two year old son, Nicholas. His wife, Sarah, was also from Hungary. She was born in 1880 and immigrated to America in 1902. It is not clear if they knew each other before their immigration, but János and Sarah married sometime in 1902 or early 1903. Nicholas was born in September 1903 and they had a second child, Elizabeth, who was about half a year younger than Rózsi.

Shortly after their arrival Dezső found work at the famous Steinway company, already a world reknown piano maker with a factory at 82–88 Walker Street in lower Manhattan.

Dezső Gombosi's postcard from New York to his wife, Hani.

With his background in precision woodwork Dezső was probably a sought after skilled worker.

A few months after the birth of their first child, Dezső and Hani decided that mother and daughter should return to Hungary to show Rózsi to the family. According to passenger records Hani and the five month old Rózsi left New York in April 2006 and a few weeks later arrived at Hani's parents' home in Váncsód.

Miraculously, a postcard written by Dezső to Hani survived all the turmoil of the last century. It was written in September 1906, five months after Hani's departure. There is no stamp on the card, so it is very likely that it was hand carried by someone traveling from New York to Váncsód (or some neighboring village). The photo on the postcard shows Eszter Herskovics with Rózsi.

The text on the postcard reads:

> *New York, 16 Sep 1906*
>
> *My Beloved Dearest Hanika,*
>
> *First of all, I inform you that thanks God I am well and I wish to hear the same from you. How is our sweet little Rózsi? Does she like the Grandparents? What is new at home? Here everything is the same as before. I am sending this bad picture to you because Eszti did not want to give it to anybody else. Last Sunday I visited Eszti. She is well and Szerén's folks are well too and they are sending kisses to all of you. I kiss you sweetie and the little darling Rózsika too. Dezső*

Unfortunately, it is unclear who "Szeréna" was. My best guess is that this name refers to Sarah Elbogen. If this assumption is correct then Sarah (Szeréna) Elbogen was well known to Hani and Sarah and János must have been already engaged before János left for New York.

By the middle of 1907 Dezső was living in a nice apartment in a middle class neighborhood on the East Side of Manhattan (417 E. 64th Street). It was about 4 miles from the Steinway factory on Walker Street, about half an hour by public transportation. On June 21, 1907 Hani and Rózsi got a new emigration passport in Nagyvárad and shortly thereafter boarded the *SS Carpathia* in Fiume (today Rijeka). After a ten day long journey they arrived in New York City on 14 August 1907. Apparently Dezső was eagerly waiting for them; nine months later (almost to the day) their son was born. I think that they named him János in honor of János Elbogen. I note that Hungarian Jews traditionally do not name children after ancestors who are still alive, so that the Angel of Death doesn't mistake the child for the adult. This, however, does not apply to distant relatives, so Dezső and Hani probably had no concern about naming the baby János.

✂ ✂

During the era of mass immigration evening schools for immigrants aimed at language and civic education were quite common and Dezső attended Evening School No 70 in Manhattan during the 1907-08 academic year. On November 21, 1907 and April 2, 1908 Didier Gombosi was given certificates "for faithfulness and proficiency as a pupil" by the New York Board of Education. It is interesting to note that the last name seems to be

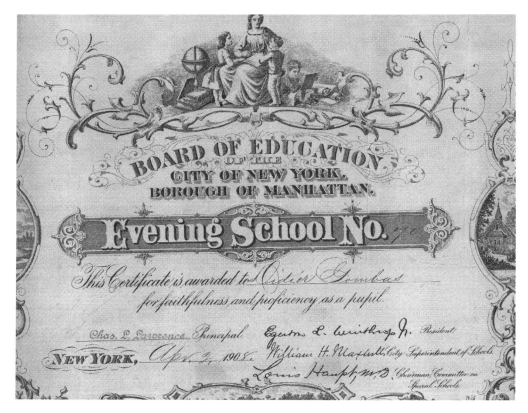

Dezső Gombosi's certificate from the New York Board of Education.

spelled as "Gombas" indicating the beginning of "Americanization" of the family. It was quite common at this time (even today) that difficult to spell names were distorted and eventually changed. One can also conclude from the fact that Dezső was making a serious effort to learn the language and assimilate to the new world that they were not planning to return to Hungary.

The early 1900s was a very active period of left wing, social democratic movements all over the world. The skilled worker Hungarian immigrants were no exception. The first Hungarian socialist club was organized in New York City in 1894. In 1900 the "Workers Sick Benefit and Educational Federation" was founded. At some point it had over 60 active branches. In May 1903 this organization launched a new periodical called "Népakarat" (Will of the People). Following several splits in the Hungarian-American social democratic

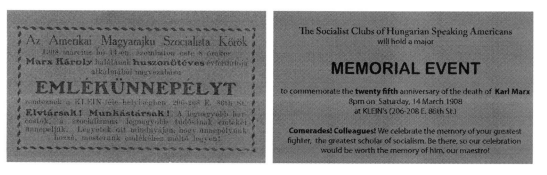

Invitation to commemorate the 25th anniversary of Karl Marx's death.

movement the publication "Előre" (Forward) was launched in 1904. Entering the country in 1905, Dezső would have had access to this paper which became a daily publication in 1907. This was the general situation of the leftist Hungarian-American movement when Dezső was actively participating in its activities.

It seems that Dezső was quite active in the socialist movement. This is indicated by an invitation to attend an event commemorating the 25th anniversary of Karl Marx's death. The text of the invitation is very interesting. The translation is shown next to the Hungarian text.

✂ ✂

During this period Dezső regularly sent money to his parents in Hungary. According to receipts that survived the times, in 1907 he sent $51, $12 and $41 to his father, Ignác Glauber in Bojt, Hungary in August, September and November. In 2013 dollars this corresponds to a total of approximately $3,000. On the receipts the last name is once again misspelled, this time to "Gombos." Ignác Glauber died in 1910 and it is reasonable to assume that by late 1907 his health was declining and he was unable to work and provide for his family. Since Dezső was quite successful in New York he was able to help his parents.

Caring for the two year old Rózsi while expecting her second child was not easy for Hani. My guess is that during this period she received a lot of help from her older sister, Eszter. It is not clear where Eszter worked after her arrival

The Gombosi family in late 1907 or early 1908. Left to right: Hani, Rózsi, Dezső and Eszter Herskovics.

to New York, but an old photograph showing the Gombosi family sometime in late 1907 or early 1908 shows Hani, Dezső, the two year old Rózsi and Eszter Herskovics. The fact that Eszter is part of a family picture implies that she played an important role in the life of the Gombosi family – perhaps as a caretaker for Rózsi and possibly for Hani as well.

As it was explained to me by my pulmonologist high school friend, Dr. Péter Kardos, early in the 20th century many people carried tuberculosis bacteria for most of their lives without knowing about their infection. However, when their immune system weakened for some reason, the latent infection could suddenly evolve into full-blown tuberculosis. It is well known that pregnancy weak-

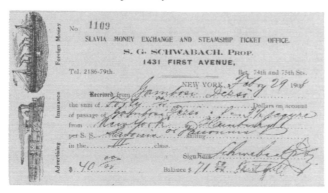

The receipt for three and a half tickets from New York to Hamburg.

ens the immune system because a somewhat foreign entity needs to grow inside the woman's body. It is, therefore, quite reasonable to assume that Hani's second pregnancy triggered her tuberculosis and the symptoms started to show up, eventually leading to medical diagnosis.

At the end of February 1908, Dezső purchased three and a half tickets for a Cunard line ship (*SS Slavonia* or *SS Pannonia*) for $40 (in 2013 dollars about $1,000). It is interesting that the tickets were for the New York – Hamburg route and not for the more direct New York – Fiume (Rijeka) one. It is possible that this was a cheaper route, but we will never know the real reason for traveling through Hamburg.

In April the Gombosi family returned to Hungary. It is obvious that Rózsi was the "half" person on the journey, but the identity of the third adult traveling with Dezső and Hani is not so clear. It is very likely that Eszter returned to Hungary with her pregnant younger sister.

The details of their trip from New York to Hamburg, to Budapest and eventually to Váncsód are lost. I am sure, however, that the travel from New York to Váncsód was long and exhausting. On May 14, 1908 their son, János was born in Hani's home town, Váncsód.

1.2. Tragic Lives

The Gombosi family settled in Váncsód where they bought two large parcels of land. It is not clear what Dezső was doing, but my guess is that he started his own business. Hani's parents were very helpful in caring for the children and Hani herself. Still, Hani's health deteriorated and she passed away on December 5, 1910 at the age of 32. Dezső was not even 30 years old when he became a widower with two small children. Hani's death was a huge trauma for the entire family. For over a year, the Herskovics grandparents took care of János. Rózsi moved in with Eszter so that Dezső could work to support his family.

My aunt, Rózsi and my father, János in 1909.

Sometime in 1911 Dezső sold the property in Váncsód. Since the property was originally purchased with help from Hani's parents, the proceeds were placed in a trust in the names of Rózsi and János. They were supposed to receive their inheritance when they reached 18. However, during the hyperinflation following World War I, the money lost all of its value and the children ended up getting nothing.

It was obvious to everyone that Dezső needed to remarry. The two kids needed a mother and Dezső had to earn a living. It was quite customary at this time that widowers married a sister of their deceased wife, but Hani's sisters were either already married or deemed too old to marry Dezső. Since Dezső – once again – was not a desirable "catch" he was eventually brought together with "old maid," Matild Farkas.

The extended Farkas "clan" was also from the Berettyóujfalu, Bojt, Nagyvárad region and they were extensively intermarried with the Glauber and Erber families. Shortly after the customary year of mourning, Matild and Dezső, both 31 years old, were married. Unfortunately, no details are known about their 1912 wedding.

On May 16, 1913 Dezső's third child was born. Júlia (or as the family called her, Juci) was seven and a half years younger than Rózsi and almost exactly five years younger than János. As the youngest child of the family and the only biological offspring of Matild she was pampered and spoiled.

✂ ✂

Dezső moved to Pestujhely (16 Adria Street), a northern suburb of Budapest. Today Pestujhely is part of the XVth district of Budapest, but at that time it was outside the city limits. It is not known where he found work at first, but it is likely that he worked for a joinery company. In March 1912 he started a joint venture with Olivér Kónya. Their joinery workshop was at 22 Molnár Street in downtown Budapest. This joint venture lasted about a year. For reasons we don't know, they closed shop in 1913.

A year later Dezső opened his own business, a small joinery workshop that remained in the family for over 70 years. It was always referred

Location of the Gombosi workshop (Műhely) in Budapest.

to only as the "Műhely" (Hungarian for workshop). It was located at 5 Cukor Street. This three-story building had its main entrance on 16 Veres Pálné Street and its back looked at the narrow Cukor Street. On the Cukor Street side were three ground floor units specifically designed for small businesses with their back doors connected to the inner courtyard of the building. These units did not have their own toilet facilities, the tenants had to use the communal bathroom in the courtyard.

The location was in the commercial center of Pest, just a few steps from major shopping streets. On the other side of Cukor Street was (and still is) a high school that today is occupied by one of the premier high schools of Hungary, the János Apáczai Csere high school. About a hundred yards away is the Law School of Loránd Eötvös University. A couple of hundred yards in the other direction is Ferenciek tere (Franciscan Square), a major commercial center of the city.

The Műhely remained in the family for two generations. Dezső operated it with the help of an employee until the 1940s when the war and the ever stricter anti-Jewish laws forced him to close. After World War II my father, János (Dezső's and Hani's son), reopened the workshop and operated it until the late 1980s, when his health did not allow him to work anymore. At that point János' only two children, my sister Éva and I, lived in the U.S.A., so the workshop was sold.

Matild Farkas and her two-year-old daughter Juci Gombosi in 1914.

My grandfather, Dezső Gombosi, in 1914.

✂ ✂

World War I started in 1914 when my grandfather Dezső had three young children between the ages of 18 months and 9 years. Since he was already 33 years old and the sole supporter of a family he was not conscripted to the army. During World War I business in the Műhely was quite sluggish. People had bigger problems than ordering picture frames or new furniture. The financial situation of the Gombosi family was challenging, but they were able to afford a modest lifestyle.

The "Spanish" influenza pandemic of 1918–1919 infected about a third of the planet's population and killed around 50 million people. It killed more people than World War I and mostly infected the 15 to 35 year old generation. Most victims died of complications, primarily of pneumonia. In Budapest, the pandemic peaked between October 1918 and February 1919 with a mortality rate approaching 10%. Unfortunately Matild was one of its victims. She died toward the end of 1918 at the age of 37, leaving Dezső and the three children behind: Rózsi was 13, János 10 and Juci 5 years old.

Matild's death deeply shook the entire family and a period of temporary solutions followed. They moved from apartment to apartment until they finally settled in a small rental apartment in 16 Királyi Pál Street. It was about 1/4 mile from the Műhely and provided adequate accommodation for the family.

Thirty-seven years old, widowed for a second time, with three small children, Dezső had to think about remarrying. Sometime around 1920 he married Szeréna Schwarcz, eleven years his junior. She was about 28 years old and also came from the Bojt area. Just like Dezső's previous wives, Szeréna was considered an old maid. According to my Aunt Juci,

János' bar mitzvah took place on May 14, 1921. This picture was probably taken on this occasion. Left to right: Rózsi, Szeréna, Juci, Dezső and János.

her father Dezső was deeply in love with Szeréna. She was a caring stepmother for the three Gombosi children.

World War I was long, bloody and dramatically changed Hungary and the lives of Hungarian Jews. Over 70% of Hungary was lost to neighboring countries by the 1920 Trianon Peace Treaty that also ended the rule of the Hapsburg dynasty. These changes impacted the life of most Hungarians, including the Gombosi family. For one thing, the province of Bihar, from which our family came, was divided between Hungary and Romania. Bojt, Berettyóujfalu, and Váncsód remained in Hungary. On the other hand, Nagyvárad (Oradea), where a large fraction of the extended family lived, was given to Romania. Travel between the hostile countries was quite limited. It took a long time to obtain a Romanian visa and even family visits were made difficult. Thus, it now took quite a bit of effort for Szeréna to visit her family in Nagyvárad.

But this loss of land didn't affect the Gombosis only in terms of inconvenience. Losing such a large part of her territories generated a huge wave of dissatisfaction in humiliated Hungary which gave rise to a Communist Revolution (Tanácsköztársaság) on March 21, 1919. Most of the leaders of the Communist Revolution were of Jewish origin and the presence of Jews in positions of revolutionary leadership helped foster the notion of a "Judeo-Communist" conspiracy. The Communist regime lasted only three months, but it greatly contributed to the resurfacing of anti-semitism in post World War I Hungary. This was reinforced by wide-spread resentment of Jewish successes.

In 1921, 88% of the members of the stock exchange and 91% of the currency brokers in Hungary were Jews, many of them ennobled. In interwar Hungary, more than half and perhaps as much as 90% of Hungarian industry was owned or operated by a few closely related Jewish banking families. Jews represented one-fourth of all university students and

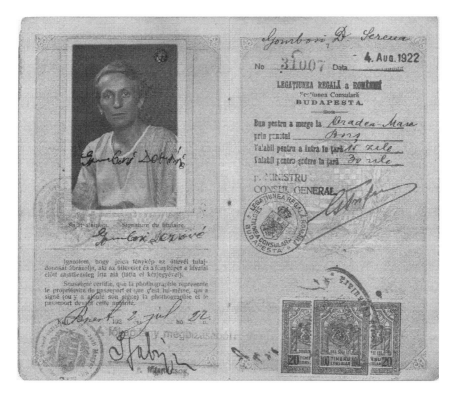

Szeréna Gombosi's passport with Romanian visa.

43% at Budapest Technical University. In 1920, 60% of Hungarian doctors, 51% of lawyers, 39% of all privately employed engineers and chemists, 34% of editors and journalists, and 29% of musicians identified themselves as Jews by religion.

Thus, in the new Hungary, Jews became the most visible minority remaining in Hungary. The other large "non-Hungarian" populations (including Slovaks, Slovenes, Croats, and Romanians, among others) were removed from Hungary by the territorial losses at Trianon leaving Hungary's Jews as the one ethnically separate group which could serve as a scapegoat for the nation's ills. The scapegoating began shortly after the defeat of the short-lived Communist regime.

Hungary was the first European country after World War I to introduce Jewish Laws. The first of these restrictive laws was the "*numerus clausus*" (limited number) of 1920. The law specifically stated that no new students should be accepted by universities unless they were "loyal from the national and moral standpoint," and that "the proportion of members of the various ethnic and national groups in the total number of students should amount to the proportion of such ethnic and national groups in the total population." In effect, *numerus clausus* primarily impacted the Jewish population who comprised about 6% of the population but was greatly overrepresented among university students (and faculty). Jewish students who were not admitted to Hungarian universities were forced to go abroad to study in Germany, Austria, Czechoslovakia, Italy, France, and Belgium. The Jewish students who were admitted despite the restrictions were often insulted and sometimes beaten up by right-wing students, whose "ideal" was to achieve a "numerus nullus" (no Jews).

✂ ✂

Reáliskolai érettségi bizonyítvány

Certificate of Matriculation from Reáliskola

János Gombosi

born on May 14, 1908 in Váncsód (Bihar province) of Jewish religion has completed grades I through VIII at the József Eötvös Reáliskola between the 1918/19 and 1925/26 academic years with exemplary moral behavior and he passed his matriculation examination with the following results:

Hungarian language and literature:	*satisfactory*
German language and literature:	*satisfactory*
History:	*good*
Mathematics:	*good*
Physics:	*satisfactory*

His grades in the other subjects are the following:

Religious studies:	*excellent*
French language and literature:	*satisfactory*
Philosophy:	*good*
Geography:	*good*
Science:	*excellent*
Chemistry:	*good*
Descriptive geometry:	*good*
Freehand drawing:	*good*

Based on these results he *satisfied* all requirements of matriculation.

János Gombosi's certificate of graduation from the József Eötvös Reáliskola.

Between the two World Wars Hungary had a tiered educational system. Everyone had to finish four years of elementary school, but the mandatory education pretty much ended here. After elementary school most middle-class girls attended four years of "polgári" (civic school). These schools prepared the students for middle-class life and not for higher education. Subjects included bookkeeping, home economics, sewing and other homemaking studies. The Gombosi girls attended civic school and finished their education at the age of 14. After this they worked as "office girls" doing clerical work at small companies.

There were two types of high schools that prepared one for university education: gimnázium and Reáliskola. Both of these schools provided eight years of education after elementary school and students took a final exam at graduation. The "gimnázium" focused more on humanities and languages and it mainly preparing students for careers in law, journalism, philosophy, classics, history – and needless to say – politics.

"Reáliskola,[1]" on the other hand, focused on mathematics, physics, chemistry and other physical sciences and prepared students for careers in science, engineering and other technical areas. A diploma of graduation from either a gimnázium or Reáliskola was a very big accomplishment for the sons of typical middle-class families. There were a few all-girls gimnáziums (mainly run by nuns) and, to the best of my knowledge, there was not a single Reáliskola for girls.

János was talented, diligent and ambitious. After finishing elementary school in 1922 he entered the József Eötvös Reáliskola located less than half a mile from the Királyi Pál Street apartment. The school was named after Baron József Eötvös who was Secretary of Education after the Compromise (see Appendix A.9) and who is credited with creating

---

[1]In modern American English I would call this STEM high school, where STEM stands for science, technology, engineering and mathematics.

the "Reáliskola" system. To the best of my knowledge, János was the first member of the extended family to graduate from high school.

János Gombosi's French ID card.

When he graduated in 1928 his dream was to attend the Technical University of Budapest and become a professional engineer. This dream, however, was crushed by the Hungarian reality. His grades were not good enough to be admitted to a Hungarian university due to "numerus clausus" limitations. At the same time, the financial situation of the Gombosi family did not allow him to continue his studies abroad. The fact that he was unable to obtain a university education was one of the biggest disappointments in János' life. Even toward the end of his life he sometimes lamented about this. Lacking other opportunities, he decided to continue in his father's footsteps and learn the trade of furniture design and manufacturing. In 1926 he started a year-long apprenticeship in the workshop of Sándor Pukanszky, located at 80 Baross Street. In parallel, he entered evening school at the Institute for Industrial Design (Iparművészeti Iskola) and specialized in furniture drawing. In the summer of 1929 he graduated with a three-year degree in industrial design.

Shortly after finishing his industrial design degree my father left for Paris where he obtained a "Master" certificate in fine furniture making. He really enjoyed Paris and never stopped talking about his exciting life there. I always had the feeling that if it had not been for his father and sisters he would have stayed in Paris.

In the meantime, tragedy did not spare the Gombosi family. Sometime in the late 1920s Szeréna was diagnosed with liver cancer and in the fall of 1929 she passed away of "severe jaundice." She was 38 years old. By this time Rózsi was 24, János 21 and Juci 16 years old. Dezső was devastated and he never married again. At the time of Szeréna's death he was 48 years old and was considered to be an old man. Malicious gossip said that he had married three old maids and buried all of them. During the last period of Szeréna's life János was in Paris and most of the emotional trauma fell on Dezső and the two girls.

✄ ✄

In the Fall of 1930 János returned from Paris. He found his father depressed and the financial situation of the family unstable. The world was in the middle of the Great Depression and the economic situation in Hungary was quite bleak. János was planning to join the family business, but due to the low profitability of the Műhely he had to look for an external income. He opened his own fine furniture and frame-making business, but it was a short-lived enterprise and he closed it within a year. János was a talented craftsman, but

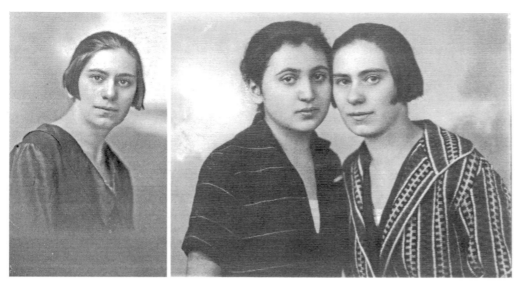

Very few pictures remained of the adult Rózsi. She was very low key and, according to my Aunt Juci, "not a beauty." I found the picture shown above among the old family photos. Left: Rózsi Gombosi. Right: Juci and Rózsi Gombosi. Both pictures were taken sometime in second part of the 1920s.

had no talent for business.

After the closure of his own workshop János found work at a fine furniture making company. The job was poorly paid, but it was an extra income that helped the family greatly. János and Dezső, however, never gave up the idea of working together in the Műhely. The business card shown here was printed around this time. The card is for the "Gombosi joiner-

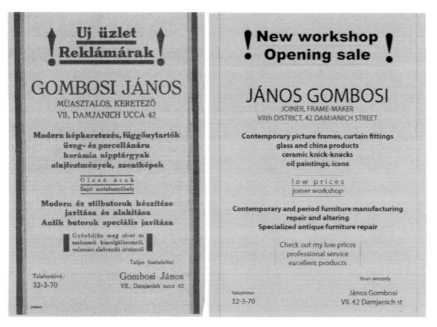

János Gombosi's "Grand Opening" announcement (left) and its translation (right). It advertises the fine furniture and frame-making workshop he opened at 42 Damjanich Street.

The business card of the Gombosi workshop from the 1930s.

The front entrance of the Műhely around 1930.

frame-maker" business and it has the description "Contemporary and classic-style furniture making, modernization of old furniture, specialized repair of antique furnitures, cornice boards." The card also lets the reader know that the Gombosis speak German and French. It is interesting that it does not mention English in spite of the fact that Dezső spent years in New York. This implies that there were very few potential customers who spoke English. Another interesting feature of the card is that it only uses the last name of the family. To me this indicates that Dezső and János were actively thinking about joining forces when the economy turned around.

Portrait of Dezső Gombosi around 1930 (by Árpád Szenes).

During the difficult economic times of the first part of the 1930s not only did the Gombosi enterprise struggle, but its customer base was also having difficulties. In particular, the Műhely had a number of painters among its patrons who still needed picture frames for their exhibitions. Since most people did not have much money some of the artists paid with pictures. This way the Műhely ended up with a sizable collection of contemporary Hungarian art. In the latter part of the 1920s, for example, one of Dezső's regular costumers was a young painter, Árpád Szenes. Sometime around 1930 he made a charcoal picture of Dezső.

The most interesting part of this picture is the artist himself. Árpád Szenes (1897–1985) was a Jewish Hungarian artist who spent most of his life in Paris. In 1930 he married Vieira da Silva, a well-known Portuguese painter. Over the years the couple had several joint exhibitions in the most prestigious venues, including the Hôtel de Ville in Paris.[2] In fact, many of the artists became quite well known and their paintings became quite valuable. Unfortunately Dezső was unable to enjoy the fruits of his art collection, but the paintings significantly contributed to the retirement security of János and his wife.

Another interesting angle of Árpád Szenes is his relation to Hannah Szenes.[3] Árpád Szenes' niece, Anikó Szenes (1921–1944) immigrated to Palestine (present day Israel) in 1929 where she took the name Hannah Szenes.

✂ ✂

Rózsi developed full-blown tuberculosis sometime in the first half of the 1930 when she was in her late twenties. It is very likely that she had been infected by her mother when she was a young child and carried tuberculosis bacteria most of her life. Like her mother, most probably a temporary weakening of the immune system resulted in the development of full-blown tuberculosis. Rózsi's illness devastated Dezső who had already lost a wife to tuberculosis and now had to watch their young daughter's decline. He was the main caretaker of Rózsi, since János was already married (see Section 3.1) and Juci was so worried about getting infected that she refused to go close to Rózsi.

Rózsi passed away in October 1936, one week before her 31st birthday. This devastated the entire family and especially Dezső who turned 55 the same month. Around this time Dezső started to show signs of coronary disease. He hired an assistant in the Műhely and gradually gave up the furniture making side of the business. From this time he (and later János) primarily focused on picture frame making which was physically less demanding. Dezső and Juci stayed in the Királyi Pál Street apartment until they were forced to move to the Ghetto.

---

[2]There is a permanent Szenes-Silva exhibition in Lisbon
(see http://www.golisbon.com/sight-seeing/vieira-da-silva-museum.html).

[3]During World War II the British actively recruited Jews in Palestine to be trained as guerillas and sent them behind enemy lines. In 1944 Hannah Szenes parachuted into Serbia and was supposed to infiltrate Hungary to sabotage the deportation of Hungarian Jews to Auschwitz. She was captured as she tried to cross the Hungarian border with a radio transmitter. She was repeatedly tortured by the Hungarian fascists who wanted to know the code for her transmitter so they could find out who the other parachutists were. She did not tell them, even when they brought her mother into the cell and threatened to torture her too. Eventually she was tried and executed by firing squad in November 1944. Her remains were brought to Israel from Hungary in 1950 and buried in the cemetery on Mount Herzl, Jerusalem. Her tombstone was brought to Israel from Hungary in November 2007 and placed in kibbutz Sdot Yam. In Israel Hannah Szenes is one of the nation's heroins symbolizing armed resistance against the Nazis. In 1988 a very successful and moving motion picture was made about her life, "Hanna's War" by director Menahem Golan.

2 | The Róna (Rothmüller) Branch

2.1. From Pécs to Budapest

My great-grandfather on my mother's side, Salamon (Sámuel) Rothmüller was born in December 1845 in the small town of Bonyhád (Tolna Province). Bonyhád is about 25 miles northeast of the regional center, Pécs. There were about 1500 Jews living in this town of about 8,000, constituting approximately 20% of the town's population.

Sámuel, who grew up using the name Salamon even though he never officially changed his name, was the son of Lipót Rothmüller and Netti (Anna) Freud. Unfortunately, beyond their names, nothing is known about Salamon's parents or the family. Sometime in the 1860s Salamon moved to the city of Pécs, the largest city in Southern Hungary west of the Danube.

Sámuel was a peddler traveling from village to village selling mirrors, paintings, clocks, mechanical music players and similar items. I found his peddler's license for the year 1899 and it is a goldmine of information. On page one we find his personal data: Born in Bonyhád in 1845, permanent residence in the city of Pécs, married. It is interesting that the peddler's license specifically lists the religion of the holder, in this case, Jew. Page two contains the description of Salamon's appearance: medium height, longish face, brown eyes, hooked nose, normal mouth and thin brown hair. His particular feature is "projecting ears." The peddler's license also shows the villages he was peddling in that year: Magyarszék, Abaliget, Egerág, Pellérd, Kővágószőlős, Ódombovár, Szászvár, Mágócs, Bátaszék, Nagyatád and Igal. Most of these places are within about 20 miles of Pécs, within a day's travel for a horse drawn carriage. A few of the villages are about twice as far, implying

Map of Hungary and the places of origin of the Róna (Rothmüller) family. The insert shows the villages where Salamon Rothmüller peddled in 1899.

Pages from Salamon Rothmüller's peddler's license for the second half of 1899.

that they must have presented business opportunity sufficient to make the longer travel worthwhile.

In the summer of 1871 the 26 year old Sámuel married 17 year old Jozefin Jónap who had been born in 1854 in the town of Hódmezővásárhely. Her parents were Mór and Rozália Jónap. It is interesting to note that Jozefin's birth certificate is for Jozefin Kohn. However, I found an official certificate from the 1920s stating that Jozefin Kohn and Jozefin Jónap were the same person. This implies that the Kohn family "Hungarianized" their name sometime between 1854 and 1871. Jozefin's parents were local merchants in Hódmezővásárhely at a time when many Hungarian Jews changed their German sounding names to Hungarian ones (see Appendix A.9).

These maternal great-grandparents, Sámuel and Jozefin had six children. Their first child, Ottilia was the only girl. Born in November 1873, her birth certificate lists her name as Ottilia, but the family called her Etel. She was followed by Móric Lipót (1876), Lajos (1882), Adolf (1884), Miksa (1888), and Jenő (1890).

For the Rothmüller children learning a trade provided an opportunity for upward social mobility. Sending the children to high school was financially impractical, but they were encouraged to study and learn. Lajos and Jenő were the most ambitious of the Rothmüller children and they had a very close relationship. Unfortunately not much is known today about the childhoods of the children with the exception of my maternal grandfather, Lajos.

Born on January 18, 1882 in Pécs, Lajos finished six years of elementary education and in 1894 started a typographer[1] apprenticeship at the local newspaper, the *Pécsi Napló*. He was a good and ambitious worker and a quick study. He finished his apprenticeship in the fall of 1898 and at age of 16 was immediately employed by the newspaper as an assistant typographer.

Lajos's brother, Adolf Rothmüller, died of pneumonia sometime the next year, at the age of 15. This tragedy shocked the Rothmüller family. In the wake of it, Lajos, not even 18, decided that life was too short and he needed to conquer the world. On December 16, 1899 he left his job at the *Pécsi Napló* and started the new century by traveling. He was young, had some savings and, as one would say in modern America, was trying to discover himself. He traveled around Hungary during the first half of 1900. According to his employment records, he took two temporary jobs in Budapest in the summer, both at printing companies. Apparently they paid well enough to support travel as between September 1900 and September 1901 he had no job and was discovering Hungary and Austria.

From September 1901 through February 1903 he worked as a typesetter in Apatin,[2] about 75 miles southeast of Pécs. In March 1903 he returned to Pécs, where he worked at the famous Taizs Printing Company and again at the *Pécsi Napló*. In January of 1905 he worked a month in Kaposvár before once again returning to Pécs. From February 1905 to October 1907 he worked for the *Pécsi Napló*, the Wessely Printing Company and for the Minerva Printing Company.

Of the other children of Sámuel and Jozefin I know only that Etel died in 1940, Móric survived the Holocaust and died in 1954, Miksa lived until the mid-1960s, and Jenő committed suicide in 1935. It is interesting that none of the Rothmüller children perished in the Holocaust: three died earlier and three survived. Móric, Lajos and Miksa all lived in Budapest where the survival rate of Hungarian Jews during World War II was higher than in the countryside (see Appendix A.12). The relevant family trees are shown in Fig. C.1 and in Fig. C.2.

✂ ✂

Egerszeg is a tiny village southeast of Pécs. In 1877 it had approximately 300 inhabitants, including 3 Jews. One of these Jews, Mór Singer, was a peddler. He worked pretty much in the same general area in which Sámuel Rothmüller sold his wares. It is quite likely that they knew each other, and I suspect they were friends. In 1878 Mór married Amália Mülhoffer who was 26 years old at that time, four years older than he. These people were to become my maternal grandmother's parents.

Amália and Mór had five children. The similarity to the Rothmüllers is quite striking. Their oldest child, József was born 1881. He was followed by Karolin (1883), the only girl in the family. Later the Singers had three more sons: Jenő (1884), Sámuel (1886) and Emánuel (1888). József was just a little older than Lajos Rothmüller and they both

---

[1] A typographer arranges type for books and newspapers including the selection of typefaces, point size, line length, and leading. Using small letters made usually of lead, the typographer arranged them in a hand held case, quickly adjusting the spaces between groups of letters and between pairs of letters so that sentences fit properly into the column inches of a publication.

[2] Today Apatin is part of Serbia.

Singer couples in 1907 shortly before the family moved to Budapest. From left to right: Margit Rozenbaum and Jenő Singer, József Singer and his bride Lujza Schlesinger, Mór Singer and the matriarch of the family, Amália Mülhoffer, and my maternal grandparents, Lajos Rothmüller and Karolin Singer. Two of the Singer children are missing from the picture: Sámuel and Emánuel (the family called him Manó). I never heard anyone in the family mention Sámuel and my suspicion is that he died as a child. Manó's absence is more of a mystery. He was 19 and one would expect him to be present at major family events. I guess we will never know the full story.

were typographer apprentices at the same time. It is thus very likely that the Singer and Rothmüller boys were acquainted with each other and I think that József Singer and Lajos Rothmüller were friends. It is also very plausible that Lajos met Karolin through József.

Margit and Jenő Singer in 1908.

It is not known when Lajos Rothmüller started to court Karolin Singer. Actually, if I were cynical, I could guess that Karolin was chasing Lajos and this was one of the reasons for his absence for several years from Pécs. We will never know. Lajos was tall (about six feet) and handsome, a commanding figure with strength and authority radiating from his appearance. He returned to Pécs in 1905 and he and Karolin Singer married in August 1907, by which time the Singers had moved to Pécs and were living on the outskirts of the city.

Less than a year later, in May 1908, Karolin's brother József Singer married Lujza

Schlesinger in Pécs. At this time József worked as a typesetter in Dombovár, a city not far from Pécs. Lujza's family was also from Pécs and it is very likely that they met during his apprentice years.

A few months after their wedding Lajos and Karolin moved to Budapest and in November 1907 Lajos started to work at the Kellner Printing Company. Six weeks later he joined the daily newspaper *Magyar Hirlap* where he worked until the end of World War I. They lived in an apartment at 13 Ede Horn Street (today Leo Weiner Street) in the heavily Jewish Terézváros district of Budapest. The rest of the Rothmüller and Singer families soon followed them to the capital.

Karolin Singer and Lajos Rothmüller shortly after their wedding. Pécs 1907.

2.2. From Rothmüller to Róna

My grandmother, Karolin, was the glue that kept her birth family together. She was very family centric, and as the only girl, used to looking after her brothers. The age difference between her and her youngest brother was only 5 years, and they were a very closely knit group. As I have noted, her brother József married about the same time she did. Her brother Jenő was not far behind and these three young couples formed the nucleus of the extended family.

During 1909-10 the first children were born to all three couples. In March 1909 József and Lujza had their first son, Imre. He was soon followed by Olga, the only child of Jenő and Margit, and finally by Miklós (Nicholas), the first son of Karolin and Lajos. There was less than a year between these three children and they grew up as very close friends.

The first three children of the extended Singer family were soon followed by four more: László (1911) and György (1914) Singer were born to József and Lujza. Between László and György, Karolin delivered their only daughter, my mother, Magda (1912). And, a year after his cousin György was born, Magda and Miklós were joined by their little brother, László Rothmüller (1915).

✂ ✂

World War I broke out in August 1914. Karolin was pregnant with her third child and things were going very well for the young couple. Lajos, 32 years old, was called up for military service. A born leader, he was soon promoted to master sergeant in the Austro-Hungarian infantry.

A very interesting tidbit of Lajos' World War I service is that in 1917 he was entangled with the military justice system. Charged in a court-martial with "slander and bodily harm" of a fellow soldier, he was sentenced to 8 days in military prison. It is interesting to see that

Left: Sergeant Lajos Rothmüller's discharge certificate (written in German) from the Austro-Hungarian Army after World War I. Right: Photograph of Master Sergeant Lajos Róna at the of World War I.

when, in the 1920s and 1930s, he was issued "certificates of good standing" they always mention the court-martial but do not consider it as a disqualifying factor. Though I am not certain where he was stationed or where he saw action, Lajos received a medal for bravery and leadership. He served until the end of World War I and was honorably discharged in August 1918.

It is very likely that military service made his commanding personality even stronger. Later in life he ruled his family like a master sergeant: he gave commands and "took no prisoners" when someone was not quick enough to follow his orders. He was, however, a benevolent dictator who loved his family though he did not take no for an answer.

By the middle of the 1910s Amália and Mór had seven grandchildren. At this time, however, Amália's health was declining and she died in June 1917.[3]

The other Rothmüller boys were also drafted. Móric was seriously wounded in the war and for the rest of his life used a prosthetic leg. After recovering he was discharged from the army and returned to Budapest where he soon married Eugenia Rosenspitz. Their daughter, Aliz, was born in September 1919. Shortly afterwards, Eugenia abandoned her family and was never heard of again. Móric took care of his daughter and tried to make a living. I am sure he also had what we call today post-traumatic stress disorder (PTSD). Sometime in the

---

[3]Her genes were quite dominant even generations later. This became evident during an interesting encounter some 75 years later. In the summer of 1994, I was at the events commemorating the 50th anniversary of the deportation of Jews of Pécs to Auschwitz. During a reception an older lady, who at that time lived in Australia, asked me "Are you a Mülhoffer?" Needless to say that I was extremely surprised. She was far too young to know Amália, so she must have identified the "Mülhoffer-look" by some resemblance to someone else. I was so surprised that I forgot to ask her about the Mülhoffers she knew. What a lost opportunity.

early 1920s he also abandoned his daughter and disappeared for many years. It was Etel and Jenő, the unmarried members of the Rothmüller family, who took in Aliz and raised her. In practice Etel became Aliz's mother and Jenő, her father.

Móric reappeared in the 1940s and for a while lived with Grandfather Lajos and his family. My sister, Éva, remembers that after the death of our great-grandma Jozefin in 1941, Móric lived in the Izabella Street apartment for a while. Once, he left his prosthetic leg in the long hallway and that scared Éva so much that even today she vividly remembers the incident. Móric survived the Holocaust, but had no contact with the rest of the family. He died in 1954.

Not much is known about the adventures of Miksa Rothmüller during World War I. He served in the Austro-Hungarian army, but no details are known today. He remained a bachelor and never changed his name. He was not interested in Hungarianizing, since he had no family and he did not worry about his descendants. In the 1950s he used to visit Lajos and his family on a fairly regular basis. In the late 1960s he was moved to a retirement home where he died in 1969.

✂ ✂

In February 1908 Jenő Rothmüller officially changed his name to the Hungarian sounding "Róna." The name refers to the Hungarian plains, sometimes also called "puszta." Tradition was that when people changed their names they usually kept the initials (so that they did not have to change the monograms). Looking at the available documents, I think that Jenő Róna was the most entrepreneurial in the younger generation. Shortly after his arrival in Budapest, he entered the coffee business. The name and the location of this café is not known. It is, however, known that Jenő became such a successful café operator that

The Abbázia and Japán cafés around 1900. The photo shows the famous Octogon at the intersection of Andrássy Street and Teréz Ring. In the background is Jókai square.

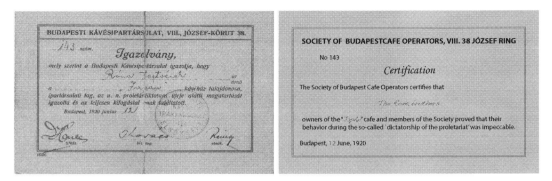

The document and its translation that certified that the Róna brothers did not participate in the activities of the Tanácsköztársaság.

in the early 1910s he bought his own café.

Coffee culture was thriving in Budapest from around the early 1910s until the beginning of the 1930s. In this era around 500 cafés were scattered around the city. Many served as meeting places of talented writers, poets and artists. Some of them spent most of the day in their favorite place, musing or writing at their regular tables. Ink and paper were free for them and they could eat the "writer's menu" (bread, cheese and cold cuts) at a discount price. Many of the most famous and best cafés were owned and operated by Jews.

Newspaper culture throve together with the popularity of coffee houses. By this time typesetting machines were replacing manual typesetting. Lajos quickly mastered this new technology and became a highly valued (and well paid) member of the *Magyar Hirlap* production team. He was so well compensated, that by the early 1910s he was able to save some money which he invested in Jenő's coffee house. Eventually, they became partners in the café business.

After World War I, Lajos worked full time with Jenő in the café business. In December 1918 he also changed his name to "Róna" so that it was obvious that Jenő and Lajos were brothers. In 1920 they owned the famous "Japán Kávéház" (Café Japan) located one block from one of the most famous cafés of Budapest, Café Abbázia. The Japán Kávéház was at the corner of Andrássy Street and Jókai Square, a prime location in Budapest. Today, it is the location of a bookstore called "Írók Boltja" (Authors' Bookstore).

After the defeat of the Tanácsköztársaság (Communist Revolution of 1919) the reign of terror followed (see Appendix A.11). Jews were particularly singled out, partly because, as noted in the Section 1.2 and in Appendix A.11, most of the leadership of the failed dictatorship of the proletariat was Jewish. If you were in any kind of business you had to prove that you did not participate in the Tanácsköztársaság.

This "proof of innocence" requirement is a recurring element of recent Hungarian history. After the Tanácsköztársaság, after the fascist Nyilaskeresztes regime of Szálasi, after the 1956 Hungarian uprising, after the fall of Communism, and even after the takeover of the present FIDESZ government (see Appendix A.14) people had to prove that they had not actively supported the previous regime. Needless to say, these certifications did not mean much. Many previous supporters of the fallen regime became prominent in the new one.

In the early 1920s, the Japán Kávéház was at its zenith. It was a popular place and provided a nice income for Lajos and Jenő. A few years later Lajos opened a deli at 27

Szondi Street. These delis sold a variety of cheeses, processed meat products and all kinds of other grocery items. However, they were not licensed to sell fresh meat, fish, fruits and vegetables. Officially, the deli was Karolin's business and I do not know what financial (tax) advantage this gave to the family.

Toward the end of the 1920s the world-wide economic decline was having an impact on the cafés in Budapest. Japán Kávéház became unprofitable and the deli was not doing well either. In 1928 Lajos and Jenő had to sell the café and Lajos closed the deli. I do not know what Jenő Róna was doing, but Lajos returned to his original profession and was hired by Légrády Press as a typesetter. As usual, he was also looking around for a better job and a year later he joined Hungária Press where he stayed until 1942. At Hungária Press he became a very popular union leader and this was the time when his colleagues started to call him by his last name, "Róna." Referring to Lajos as "Róna" became so common that even his family started to use this name. When I was growing up I did not even know my grandfather's first name for a long time, we just called him "Róna."

Lajos Róna at his deli shop in 1927.

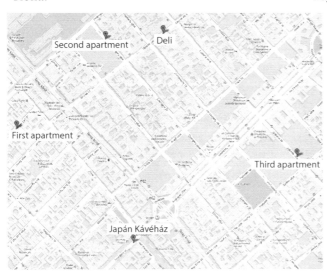

Róna residences and businesses in Budapest.

The Great Depression left his brother Jenő financially devastated and emotionally drained. He was supporting his sister and niece and his income became very uncertain. Most likely he also had some mental health issues, but I cannot be sure. Just like many other people during the Great Depression, he committed suicide in May 1935. He was only 45 years old. After his death, Etel and Aliz Rothmüller were supported by the other Rothmüller brothers, mainly Róna. Etel died in 1940, but by that time Aliz was already 21 years old and could survive on her own. Soon after Etel's death Aliz married Róbert Vermes and after the Holocaust they had one daughter, Viktoria (everyone called her Viki). Aliz stayed in regular contact with her cousins until her death in 2007. I remember occasional visits to our Budapest apartment by Aunt Aliz and cousin Viki when I was growing up, though we very seldom met Róbert (everyone called him Robi) who kept his distance from our side of the family.

After World War I, the youngest of the Singer brothers, Manó, married Aliz (Alice) Schönberger and in 1920 they had a son, Tamás (Thomas) Singer. The marriage, however, did not last long and Aliz left Manó and her son sometime around 1930.

Manó had a fine leather shop that was going quite well. In the 1930s he married his secretary of many years, Rózsi, (unfortunately nobody seems to remember her maiden name). She was very pretty and Manó, probably because of his previous experience, pampered her, but at the same time jealously guarded her. Family legend says that while she was wearing valuable fur coats and had a large diamond ring, she never had enough cash on herself to buy an ice cream.

Manó's ex-wife, Aliz Schönberger Singer, remarried and in 1937 she immigrated to the U.S. with her new husband. She arrived in

Tamás and Manó Singer in 1930.

New York under the name Alice Seboek Shybekay. While I cannot be sure of the etymology of this name, I can guess. Seboek most likely comes from the Hungarian name "Sebők" that was a commonly used Hungarianization of Jewish names and "Shybekay" probably comes from the English mispronunciation of "Schönberger." This name implies that the last name of her second husband was Sebők and that she also used her (distorted) maiden name.

Manó and Alice's son, Tamás Singer graduated from high school in 1938. As a graduation present he was allowed to visit his mother who at the time lived in Chicago. It is not known if it was foresight or selfishness, but Alice did not allow her son to return to Hungary, where he may well have been swallowed in the Holocaust. Instead, Tamás stayed with his mother and enrolled in the University of Chicago where he earned a Ph.D. in chemistry. He became a Professor of Chemistry at Stanford University and went on to be a well-known scientist.

After the Holocaust, Manó and his new wife followed his son and immigrated to the U.S. Eventually they settled in New York where he opened a shoe store in lower Manhattan on John Street (Financial District).

Tamás also married twice. He has one son from his first marriage and a son and a daughter from the second. Sometime in the late 1970s my sister, Éva, had a conference in San Francisco and contacted Tamás to re-establish the family ties. Tamás, however, did not want anything to do with this "fresh from the boat" relative and the family has not had any contacts with him or his children ever since. Public records show that Tamás died in 1999, but this is all I know about this branch of the family.

2.3. The Róna Children

The children of my grandfather Lajos had a sheltered life. The family was well to do and their social status was quite high among the Jewish middle class. Lajos and Jenő were successful businessmen, even though they lacked more advanced education. The social stratification at the time was very interesting. People with university degrees were in very high esteem, even though many of them were in tight financial situations. They typically did not socialize with the less educated masses. For instance, I am not aware of any friends (let alone family members) of my parents or grandparents who had university degrees. These were distinct social circles. The entrepreneurial, but not highly educated, middle class usually kept to itself, just as the educated class did.

There was, however, a very important aspect of the family value system: they pushed their children to study and to attain higher education and, consequently, higher social status than their parents had. There is a clear progression on both the Róna and Gombosi sides from only elementary education for all four of my great-grandfathers to learning a marketable trade by my grandfathers to the high school education of my father to advanced postgraduate degrees earned by my sister and I. The desire to learn and study was there for generations.

Left: The Rothmüller children in 1914. Miklós was 4 and Magda was 2 years old. Center: Magda in 1915. Right: The Róna children in 1920. Laci(left), Miki (center) and Magda (right).

In 1920 Lajos and his family moved to a bigger apartment in Terézváros. As a matter of fact they never left this heavily Jewish district. The new apartment was on the third level (second floor) of a middle-class apartment building at 84 Csengery Street. At the time there were no elevators in these buildings (only luxury apartment buildings had elevators) and climbing two floors was not easy for grandma Jozefin who lived with Lajos and his family.

The three Róna children had very different personalities. Miklós was a good student, always eager to learn. Magda, my mother, was the delicate flower of the family. Laci was never interested in school.

Miklós attended Kölcsey Gimnázium (high school) located near the north-west corner of Terézváros. He was a good student and graduated in 1928 at the age of 18. Just as János Gombosi, he was unable to attend a university because of "numerus clausus." The Róna family was well to do by middle class standards, but they were unable to send Miklós

Karolin with her three children in 1925. At this time Miklós was 15, Magda 13 and Laci 10. The photo is unfortunately quite damaged and this is one of the few pictures I have of my grandmother. At this time she was 42 years old and had dark hair. In the only other set of pictures I have of her (made in 1937) her hair is already gray. From left to right: Laci, Miki, Karolin and Magda.

abroad to study. Instead, he started to work in an office and remained an administrator for the rest of his life.

Magda is said to have cried easily and to have been very sensitive. Family legend says that she easily fainted and had to be treated with great care. Knowing my mother in her later years, this is hard to believe. She was also a very obedient daughter, following her parents' wishes. She was very close to her mother and somewhat afraid of her father, who, I think, was the only one she ever feared in her life. She attended a civic school run by

Left: Magda (left) and Klára Friedman. Right: Magda is sitting on the shoulders of Imre Singer. Laci is at Imre's feet. At this time Laci was 17, just coming of age.

nuns, something quite common at the time even for Jewish girls. Catholic schools offered very high quality educations, and as I have noted education seems always to have been important to our family. Magda was a slight girl, typically the smallest in her class. She was, however, a good gymnast and quite athletic. She graduated in 1926 having learned typing and stenography, and at the age of 14, joined the workforce as an office girl.

Her younger brother, my uncle Laci, was barely able to finish six years of school and could hardly wait to get out into real life. Family legend asserts that when he was unprepared to face the teacher he simply pulled his hat over his eyes assuming that if he could not see the teacher, the teacher would not see him either. Unfortunately, this ostrich strategy did not work well. As is often the case with men like Laci though, while not good at school, he was the most street-smart of all Róna and Karolin's children.

2.4.   The Singers

Olga: Jenő Singer's daughter, Olga was a few years older than my mother, Magda, but they were the only two girls in the extended Singer family. I do not know much about Olga's life. She married István Hillinger and died during the Holocaust. Her husband survived the war and died sometime in the 1950s. They had no children.

Imre: My mother, Magda, and her maternal cousin, Imre Singer, were particularly close. In the early 1930s Imre courted Klára Friedmann, who – I think – was one of my mother's friends. Imre was an accountant and made a good living. They rented an apartment on Dohány Street not far from the main synagogue. In 1935 Klára had a son, Péter. Three years later she delivered their second son, András. After the Holocaust, Imre changed his name to the Hungarian sounding Rudnai. I do not know why he deviated from the custom of keeping the initials unchanged.

After the Hungarian uprising in 1956 Imre and his family immigrated to Canada where he settled in Toronto. (They received quite a bit of help from his younger brother László, who as we will see, emigrated shortly after the war.) They had a small drapery business in Toronto that provided a reasonable living for the family. Imre died of diabetes sometime in the mid-1970s and Klára about a year later.

Imre and Klára's older son, Péter, became a taxi driver and married a woman named Gladys around 1960. They had a son who died at the age of 8 from bacterial meningitis. This tragedy completely devastated Péter and Gladys. A few years after the death of their son, they had a daughter, Cindy. We visited them in Toronto sometime in the 1980s. They lived in a small house and he was making a decent living, but, like his father suffered from diabetes and had serious health problems. He died of diabetes related complications in 2004.

Imre and Klára's younger son, András, tried several professions. I am not sure about the specifics,

Wedding picture of Klára Friedmann and Imre Singer.

Péter (right) and András (left) Singer in 1941.   *Lujza and József Singer in 1950.*

because he was alienated from his mother and brother, but at some point he was a car sales-man in a dealership. Sometime in the 1990s he moved to California and we lost all contact with him.

László: Sometime in the late 1930s László Singer married Irén Weisz. Shortly after the wedding they left Hungary and moved to Barcelona, Spain. In 1941 Irén gave birth to their son, Tomas. Suffering from severe post-partum depression, shortly after giving birth she jumped out of a window and died on the spot. László was left with an infant son and had to hire a nurse to take care of the baby. This nurse was Marina Casado, whom he married in 1943.

In April 1944 László and his family immigrated to Canada where he settled in Toronto and had two children, Charles and Mark. Marina was a very good mother for all of László's children. Tomas tragically died in a motorcycle accident in 1962 at the age of 21, never knowing that Marina was not his biological mother.

In the late 1940s Lujza and József Singer immigrated to Canada to joint their son, László. They, however, could not get along with their daughter-in-law, Marina, and a few years later returned to Hungary. In addition to personality differences, the fact that they did not speak English (or Spanish) and had difficulty communicating with their grandchildren also contributed to their frustration and isolation. József died a few years after their return, but Lujza lived until the mid-1960s. I remember occasionally visiting Aunt Lujza who was always invited to our house for Passover dinners.

György: The third son of Lujza and József Singer also had a tragic life. In the late 1930s when Lujza had a linen shop specializing in making custom shirts for men, she employed several seamstresses. One of them, the 20 year old Irma Miklós attracted the attention of the young György and they fell in love. This created a major crisis in the entire Singer family because Irma was not Jewish. At the time intermarriage was very uncommon, especially since there were restrictive anti-Jewish laws in effect in Hungary. It took unusual courage to marry a Jew. Christian society usually shunned those who had sexual relations with Jews and later there were laws forbidding such relations. At the same time, a Jewish man who married a "shiksa" was commonly disowned and considered dead. Nevertheless, Irma and

György married sometime in 1941. Shortly afterwards, György was conscripted to MUSZ[4] and shipped to the Eastern front where he died sometime in 1942. Their daughter, Zsuzsa, was born in October 1942, after her father's death.

After the war, Irma opened her own linen shop and raised her daughter alone. She stayed in close contact with the Singer family and she was a frequent visitor in our home. The shop was at the corner of Lenin Ring and Szófia Street, about 10 minutes walk from the Izabella Street apartment. Róna regularly visited Irma in the shop and I suspect that occasionally he also helped them financially.

Zsuzsa became a very attractive young woman. She was a trained pastry chef and worked in upscale restaurants. Like many single parents, Irma tried to fulfill her dreams through her daughter. She worked hard to bring Zsuzsa together with a young man who could provide a good life. Like many great intentions, her constant interference resulted in mixed results. In 1963 Zsuzsa married Albin Kästner, a distant relative of the famous writer Erich Kästner.[5]

Zsuzsa's marriage was not successful and ended in divorce, just a month after she gave birth to their daughter, Monika. A decade later Zsuzsa entered into an arranged marriage with György Dános, a Hungarian-Canadian who took Zsuzsa and Monika to Toronto. The marriage was arranged by Irma and László Singer, who was trying to help his niece to leave Communist Hungary. The arranged marriage, however, soon dissolved. Zsuzsa found herself in a foreign country raising her daughter alone. She found work with the Johnson and Johnson cosmetics company and she also ran a small beauty salon on the side. Later, she met Peter Almagor, a Hungarian-Israeli-Canadian architect and they married in 1994. Since Zsuzsa and Peter met without outside "help," it is not surprising that they have been happily married ever since. After Zsuzsa and Monika left Hungary, Irma remained alone. She regularly visited her daughter until her death in 1999.

Monika grew up in Canada and earned a Ph.D. in electronic health service research from the University of Toronto. She is married to Ernesto Avilla, and they live in the Toronto area.

---

[4]Munkaszolgálat (in English Military Forced Laborer Service), for more details see Appendix A.12.

[5]Author of such famous books as "Emil und die Detektive" (Emil and the Detectives), "Der 35. Mai" (The 35th of May), "Das doppelte Lottchen" (Lottie and Lisa, adapted into film as The Parent Trap).

Magda and János

3

3.1. Marriage

Multigenerational households were typical in Hungary in the 20th century. There were several reasons for this: tradition, financial necessity and practical arrangements. Tradition was that people were responsible for their parents and immediate blood relatives unable to make an independent living, like sisters. Financial necessity arouse from the fact that, with few exceptions, a single income was not adequate to support a middle-class lifestyle. The practical side of the arrangement was that shops were typically only open during working hours and a family needed someone who could do shopping and take care of daily errands as well as housework. In addition, apartment rents were very high and it was advantageous to share the costs. A typical household spent a very large fraction of their income on food, rent and other basic necessities. As a result it was quite common for young people to live with their parents. Young couples usually lived with the bride's family.

My father, János Gombosi, was 22 years old when he returned from Paris. By the social standards of the 1930s he was among the *petit-bourgeois*, the lower middle social class of small entrepreneurs who worked alongside their own employees. In Budapest at the time it was a social class dominated by Jews, and upon his return from Paris, János became an active member of it.

János Gombosi in 1931.   *Magda Róna around 1930.*

According to family legend, he was already courting Magda Róna before he left for Paris. Though very young, Magda was quite receptive, but her mother was vehemently against the relationship because, "his father already buried three wives, and what can you expect from such a family?" Eventually it was decided, "we will see if the relationship survives" János's time in Paris.

Both the Gombosi and Róna families were quite assimilated at this time. For instance, I found several letters, book inscriptions, and other documents where János spelled his name as "Gombossy." The "ssy" ending implied Hungarian nobility and gentile roots as opposed to the "si" which was indicative of "Hungarianization" and made the person suspect of being Jewish).

The 18 year old Magda was smart, a spoiled beauty, and came from a very respectable Jewish middle-class family. She had many suitors. Family legend has it that she broke up with one of them when for some occasion he gave her an expensive bar of fragrant soap. She accused him of implying that she was "unwashed."

Upon his return, János and Magda renewed their relationship. But, serious courtship between the two created tension not only in the Róna family but also among the Gombosis. Social norms and expectations were rapidly changing in the first half of the 20th century. While most professions were not available to women, and traditionally, unmarried women lived with their parents, brothers, or other male relatives, by the 1930s, dramatic changes were taking place in the workforce creating more economic opportunities and independence for women. At the same time, the young generation of men did not want to be responsible for their sisters any more. The old and new expectations were the root cause of the emerging (and lifelong) animosity between János's sister, Juci, and Magda.

In the early 1930s Juci was working as an "office girl" for a well-known lawyer. "Office girls" were quite poorly paid and these jobs were generally considered to be stepping stones toward marriage. While her sister Rózsi appears already to have de-

Wedding picture of Magda Róna and János Gombosi.

veloped TB by this time and stopped working, between János' salary, income from the Műhely, and Juci's office job, the family was able to afford a decent middle-class lifestyle. Juci however, was very concerned about her future. She was approaching 20 and did not have any suitors. She was old fashioned and expected her family to take care of her. She had been spoiled by Rózsi who loved her "baby" sister. At some point when she was quite sick, Rózsi made János promise that he would take care of Juci as long as she needed help. Decades later (in the 1960s and 1970s) Juci still bitterly remarked that "János promised Rózsi that he would take care of me and instead he married Magda." The relationship between Magda and Juci was stormy from the beginning. At some point, according to family legend, Juci publicly called Magda names and the firebrand Magda slapped her cheek.

Magda and János married on August 6, 1933. Magda worked in an office (and was paid pennies) and János's income was not enough to rent a suitable apartment. Like most young people of the time, they could not afford to start their life together independent of their parents. (Actually, this situation did not change in Hungary for the rest of the century –

Magda's wedding party in front of the Dohány synagogue. The father of the bride is in the very back of the picture, while the father of the groom is standing behind his younger daughter, Juci. The bridesmaids are (from left to right) Rózsi Gombosi, Olga Singer, Juci Gombosi and Aliz Rothmüller. I am pretty much guessing about the identity of the leftmost bridesmaid, but I think that she is Rózsi. It is interesting to note that Aliz was only 14 years old at this time and probably this is the reason she does not have a long gown. I only recognize two of the groomsmen: Magda's brothers Laci and Miklós. Unfortunately we cannot identify others in the party.

only the very lucky could afford a place of their own – eventually.) The newlyweds moved in with Magda's parents and two brothers who lived in an apartment on Csengery Street.

3.2. Éva

On March 23, 1935 Magda and János had their first child, my sister Éva. The birth of a girl was a surprise, since they were both convinced that they would have a son. They already had a name selected, Tamás. Éva was the first child in the extended family and was adored by her grandparents and uncles. The apartment in Csengery Street soon turned out to be too small for the family and in the fall of 1935 they moved to a larger one at 45 Izabella Street.[1]

The apartment was located in the heart of Terézváros (or VI. district), a heavily Jewish neighborhood. It was certainly more "upscale" than the petit-bourgeois commercial center of town where the Műhely was located and where the Gombosi family lived. I included an aerial view that shows part of Terézváros near the new home on Izabella Street. Several

---

[1] All the apartments I mentioned so far in this book were rental apartments. Condominiums started to be available only in the 1960s

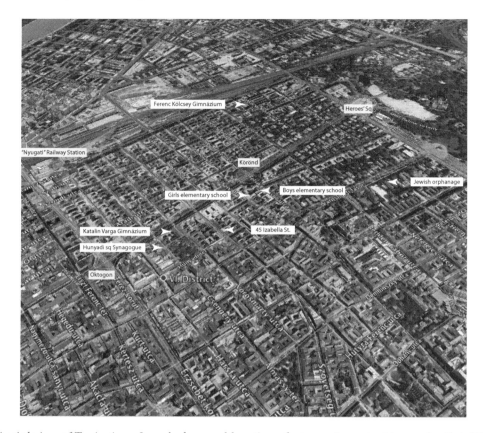

Aerial view of Terézváros. I marked several locations that were important in our family's life.

locations are marked. These locations will be mentioned later in this book, since they are related to the life of our family. Here I only note that all these locations are within a 15 minute walk from the Izabella Street apartment.

The new apartment was on the second level of a four story apartment building. It was about 120m² (∼1250 sqft) and had three rooms of living space, a large kitchen, a bathroom, a separate toilet, a pantry and a maid's room. This apartment housed four generations: Magda's paternal grandmother, Jozefin Jónap, lived in the maid's room; Magda's parents, Lajos and Karolin, slept in the smallest room overlooking an internal courtyard; her two brothers, Miklós and Laci, slept in the larger room overlooking the street; and Magda, János and Éva lived in the third room. The advantage of this arrangement was that the young family's room had a direct door to the bathroom. The maid (most middle-class families had maids at this time) slept in the kitchen. Nine people living in a ∼1250 sqft apartment sounds very crammed today, but by the standards of the times it was considered a very comfortable lifestyle.

Except for the short interruption when all Jews were moved to the Ghetto late in 1944, the family stayed in this apartment for over 70 years, until Magda's death in 2006. Sometime around 1958, two years after Éva married and moved out of the apartment, it was divided into two independent units and the smaller of these (created from the kitchen, the maid's room and the pantry), was "sold." At that time there was no legal market for apartments, but a very active black market existed during Communism when there was a serious shortage of apartments.

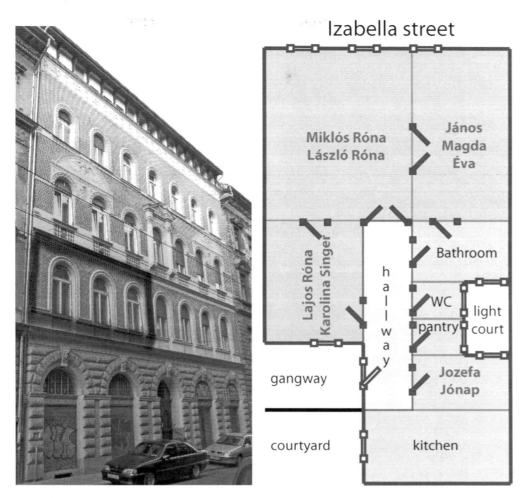

Izabella street

Miklós Róna
László Róna

János
Magda
Éva

Lajos Róna
Karolina Singer

hallway

Bathroom

WC

pantry

light court

gangway

Jozefa
Jónap

courtyard

kitchen

45 Izabella Street in 2011. The red box marks the family apartment. A 5th level was added in 2007.   *The layout and sleeping arrangements of the Izabella Street apartment in 1935.*

Four generations living together had some advantages and many drawbacks. On the one hand, the young Gombosis had considerable financial assistance from the Róna grandparents. On the other hand, privacy was extremely limited. Magda's father, Lajos Róna, was a very strong personality and János Gombosi found himself in a situation in which his family's life was pretty much run by his father-in-law. This never changed as long as Lajos Róna was alive. I vividly remember that in the 1950s and 60s, when my grandfather "Róna" (as everybody called Lajos) was long retired, and János was the primary breadwinner of the family, it was still my grandfather who dominated all decisions.

The family dynamics of the Róna family were extremely traditional. The men brought home the money and the women took care of everything in the home. Jozefin Jónap, the Róna great-grandmother, was in her eighties when Éva was born and the grandmother, Karolin Singer, became seriously ill about the same time. Suddenly Magda was taking care of her elderly grandmother, her ailing mother, her little daughter, her husband, her father, and even her two unmarried brothers. Shepherding a large family made Magda even more

Éva Gombosi's early childhood pictures from 1935, 1937 and 1940.

Éva Gombosi with her Róna grandparents, Karolin and Lajos, in the summer of 1937 just before Karolin's health seriously deteriorates.

assertive. She learned how to stand up to men, and became a real "Jiddische Mame."

Éva was cute and smart and her grandparents adored her, as did her uncle, Laci Róna, who treated her as a younger sister. Her Uncle Miklós was a bit more distant, but family legend has a funny story about his adventures with Éva. One day he took the two-year old Éva for a stroll on Andrássy Street. At some point Éva announced that she needed "to go." Miklós had no idea how to handle the situation. He pointed to a tree and told his niece to do her business there. Éva dutifully followed the instructions and was in the process of relieving herself when a gentleman turned to Miklós and said, "You should at least pull down her panties."

3.3.   War Years

Sometime around 1937 Karolin Singer's health started to deteriorate (see Section 3.4). At the same time she was concerned about her two sons. Miklós was in his late twenties; it was time for him to choose a bride and settle down. Laci was in his early twenties, good looking and a ladies' man. Family legend says that one evening he saw a young woman home to the outskirts of Budapest. On the way back he was caught by a heavy downpour and became seriously ill afterwards. Eventually he was diagnosed with nephritis (bacterial inflammation of the kidneys). He recovered, but the incident resulted in the slow degradation of his kidneys. He eventually died of kidney failure at the age of 60.

In the late 1930s Miklós started to court Éva Schwarz, nine years younger than himself. Tall and pretty, she was the only child of a well to-do Jewish family that lived in a nice apartment at 11 Miksa Street (today Osvát Street) near the intersection of Erzsébet Ring and Rákóczi Avenue. The apartment was on the third floor (fourth level) in a building that had an elevator.

✂ ✂

Meanwhile, the political situation was rapidly deteriorating (see Appendix A.12 and Section 3.4). After the Anschluss (the Nazi occupation of Austria in March 1938) Adolf Hitler promised to return to Hungary territories lost after World War I if Hungary allied herself with Germany. In addition, threats of military intervention and economic pressure "encouraged" the Hungarian Government to support the policies and goals of Nazi Germany. On November 2, 1938, the First Vienna Award transferred parts of Southern Slovakia and Carpathian Ruthenia back to Hungary. Between November 5 and 10, Hungarian armed forces occupied the newly transferred territories without resistance.

Hungary began to adopt anti-Jewish legislation. First, the country passed a law that restricted to 20% the ratio of Jews in intellectual professions, commercial, financial and industrial companies. Second, in May 1939, Hungary further limited Jews in the economic realm and distinguished Jews as a "racial," rather than religious group.

In the wake of all of this, in early 1940, Éva and Miklós became engaged and picked September 1 for their wedding date. But, in the summer of 1940, tension flared up between Hungary and Romania about Transylvania which had been transferred to Romania by the Trianon Peace Treaty. Troops massed on both sides of the Hungarian-Romanian border and war seemed imminent. The crisis was averted by the Second Vienna Award which transferred the northern half of Transylvania back to Hungary.

However, during the standoff at the southern border the Hungarian army was mobilized and reserve units activated. Reservist Master Sergeant Lajos Róna was mobilized and, being Jewish, was assigned to a MUSZ unit stationed in the northern town of Szentendre. He was called up in early August and was on active duty until the end of September.

He tried to convince the Schwarczes to postpone the wedding of his oldest son, but since all arrangements had been made, the Schwarczes were not willing to do so. Éva and Miklós married in Budapest's Dohány synagogue on September 1, 1940.

After the wedding Miklós left the Izabella Street apartment and moved in with the Schwarczes. The distance between the two locations was less than a mile, easy walking distance. But as a result of the refusal to postpone the wedding, tension between the parents remained. Róna resented missing his son's wedding for a very long time.

Wedding picture of Éva Schwarcz and Miklós Róna. (September 1, 1941)

In November 1940 Hungary entered World War II on Germany's side. In April 1941 Germany, with the participation of Hungarian troops, invaded Yugoslavia. Hungarian troops retook Vajdaság (Vojvodina) and some other areas with majority Hungarian populations. In June 1941 Hungary declared war on the Soviet Union and a few months later the Hungarian Second Army joined German troops on the Eastern Front. This was the same year that the Hungarian government passed a racial law similar to the Nuremberg Laws officially defining wh wa to be considered Jewish.

In December 1941, Éva Schwarcz gave birth to a daughter, Judit Róna. She was lucky to have her parents around, because Miklós could not be with his wife and newborn daughter. These were very difficult times. The men of the family were conscripted to forced labor units. Miklós was taken to the Russian front and later to one of the most horrible labor camps – in the copper mines of Bor (Serbia). His unit was immortalized by the poems of Miklós Radnóti, one of the greatest poets of Hungarian literature, who was also there.

✄ ✄

My father, János Gombosi, was conscripted to MUSZ[2] sometime in September of 1940 at the age of 32. At first he was taken for only three months to Vác and in December he was allowed to return to his family. After Hungary joined World War II on the side of Nazi Germany he was taken again in September 1942 when he was in Szentendre and later

---

[2]The forced labor service system (munkaszolgálat or MUSZ) was introduced in Hungary in 1939. This affected primarily the Jewish population, even though some people belonging to minorities, sectarians, leftists and Roma were also inducted. Conscripts in MUSZ were stripped of their former military rank, were forced to wear yellow armbands, and were not allowed to carry arms. MUSZ units were guarded by a special type of military police recruited from the most brutal elements of the Hungarian armed forces (these units were called "cadres" or "keretlegények"). MUSZ units were used for the most difficult and dangerous tasks, like digging trenches, clearing mine fields, and working under horrible circumstances. Tens of thousands of Jews served in MUSZ units attached to the Hungarian Second Army which was fighting in the Soviet Union. 80% of them never returned; they either died on the battlefield or in captivity. Other MUSZ units served in the Vajdaság where they worked in copper mines, cleaned up after the Hungarian troops massacred local hostages, or were assigned similar tasks. Overall, less than half of those conscripted into MUSZ units survived.

János was a talented artist and during his MUSZ service regularly made drawings about his life. I found two drawings which were made sometime in 1943 while he served on the Eastern Front. The title on the left cartoon is "Somewhere in Russia..." The verse is : "My profession is joiner; My wage is three marks; But my stomach is not empty; Because I supplement it; With moonlighting." The verse on the right cartoon is: "I am changing my profession; As often as I change my underwear when home; I was shoemaker, taylor and carpenter; Joiner and Ukrainian translator; If it helps me; Today I will be a bricklayer."

was quarantined in the city of Mohács (probably because of some infectious disease due to poor living conditions). From here his unit was moved to the Eastern Front where he survived hard labor near Kiev, Konotop (today these cities are in the Ukraine) and Minsk (today the capital of Belarus). His unit, however, was not on the frontline but was attached to support services, so their survival rate was "high." I do not have reliable numbers since my father never liked to talk about his experiences either with me or with my sister, Éva. My estimate is that about two-thirds of his unit survived. He never told us anything specific about his experiences, but I gather that among the "keretlegények" there were some pretty brutal individuals who enjoyed torturing, and even killing, my father's comrades. János, however, also mentioned that there were some "nicer" cadres who did not go beyond the call of duty to make the conscripts' life more miserable.

After the retreat of the Hungarian Second Army from the Soviet Union, János's unit was moved to southern and western Hungary: Pécs, Szombathely, Kőszeg, Vác and eventually to Budapest where he was liberated by the Red Army in January 1945.

✂ ✂

When János was taken to forced labor service my mother, Magda, and my sister, Éva, were left behind without any stable income. Magda made a little money by making custom clothes for children, but this irregular income was far from adequate to support the two of them. In effect, Magda was almost fully supported by her parents. Occasionally she visited

Dezső – who always gave her some money – at the Műhely. This created additional tensions with my paternal Aunt Juci, who resented that "their" little income was shortchanged to support "that woman."

János Gombosi in 1944 while serving in a MUSZ unit.

This resentment was probably exacerbated when Éva started elementary school in September 1941 a few months after Hungary joined the war. She attended the school associated with the Jewish orphanage which also accepted tuition paying students from the larger Jewish community. Even though sending Éva to a private school added to the financial challenges of the family, it was decided that they did not want to expose her to the rampant anti-semitism in public schools. I think that the Róna grandparents insisted on sending Éva to private school and they paid for it.

From Magda's point of view 1941 and 1942 must have been extremely difficult. Jozefin Jónap, the maternal grandmother she'd been nursing, died at age 87. Her husband was in forced labor. Her mother, Karolin, was hospitalized several times and Magda took care of her mother until she died much too young, at age 59, in February 1942.

There is an interesting story about the ailing Karolin that I heard from my sister. Sometime in the fall of 1941 when Karolin was already very sick they went for a stroll on Andrássy Street, a main thoroughfare connecting the Bazilika to Heroes' Square. Near Izabella Street the thoroughfare is an alley formed by two parallel pedestrian islands with benches under old chestnut trees. Karolin was sick and could not go far without taking some rest. She needed to sit down to collect her strength. There were, however, no empty benches. One of the nearby benches was occupied by a young girl and her governess. Magda politely asked the girl if she would give up her seat to the ailing Karolin. The girl obliged, but the governess intervened saying, "Do not give up your seat for that Jew."

Éva Gombosi in 1942.

After Karolin's death Éva, Magda and Róna remained in the Izabella Street apartment which suddenly seemed far too large for the three of them. They lived in constant fear for their men somewhere in harm's way. At the same time everyday life became more and more difficult. Food shortages became common and it was increasingly difficult to provide for the family.

Yet, before 1944 the Róna family's life went on with some resemblance of normalcy. Miklós and János were in forced labor, but those in Budapest did not have to worry about their personal safety, yet. I found a photograph that demonstrates this point. It was taken in the summer of 1943 and shows Róna with his daughter, daughter-in-law and his two granddaughters at the time.

Karolin Singer's grave in Budapest. Lajos Róna and the ashes of Laci Róna are also buried here.

The last "peaceful" summer, 1943. Left to right: Judit Róna, Éva Gombosi, Magda Róna, Éva Schwarcz and Róna.

3.4. Genocide

The war was not going well for Hungary. In 1942 the Second Hungarian Army suffered an 84% casualty rate in the battle of Stalingrad losing over 150,000 men. This was devastating for the morale of the country. At the same time extreme right wing and fascist elements became louder and louder. Demagoguery, chauvinism, xenophobia, and increasing anti-semitism became mainstream.

On March 19, 1944, German troops invaded and it took less than a day for the German troops to occupy Hungary. The next day Adolf Eichmann arrived to oversee "The Final Solution." On April 5, 1944 Jews were ordered to wear a yellow star (sárga csillag) on their clothing, marking them for humiliation and dehumanization. On 3 May orders were issued to register apartments and houses in Budapest belonging to Jews. These were called "yellow star houses" (sárga csillagos házak). Following an eight-day deadline no Budapest Jew could live outside a yellow star house (non-Jews, however, were allowed to live in yellow star houses thus reducing the number of apartments available for Jews). Each Jewish family was allocated only one room. Up to 200,000 Jews moved into fewer than 2,000 houses. The Izabella Street apartment building became a "yellow star house," so Róna, Magda and Éva were not forced to move. My grandfather and aunt, Dezső and Juci Gombosi, on the other hand, lived in a non-yellow star building and were forced to leave their apartment.

It is well established that the fascist regime could be called the reign of terror of janitors

(házmester) and janitors' helpers. These people usually belonged to "lumpenproletariat[3]."
It was their responsibility to supervise execution of decrees concerning the Jews, and indeed, in some cases to carry out these orders. These janitors happily spied and reported
on the Jews to the Nyilas authorities, and often were rewarded with some stolen Jewish
property.

One example of the corruption of the lumpenproletariat, as well as the anti-semitism of
the surrounding neighborhoods came when Laci Róna's Catholic girlfriend, Gizella (Gizi)
Duda, wanted to provide 9 year old Éva Gombosi a break from the tension of being confined
all day in a "yellow star house." Inhabitants were allowed to leave the building only between
10:00 a.m. and noon. At other times the front doors were locked by the házmester. One
evening, Gizi bribed the janitor to let Éva out after hours. They went to the nearby Royal
Theater to see a movie. Unfortunately, a woman with a large cross on her necklace, as
Éva remembers it, recognized her and made a huge commotion calling for Éva's arrest.
Fortunately, in the ensuing chaos Gizi and Éva managed to slip away.

In mid-May 1944, the Hungarian authorities, in coordination with the German Security Police (Gestapo), began to systematically deport Hungarian Jews. SS Colonel Adolf
Eichmann was chief of the team of "deportation experts" that worked with the Hungarian
authorities. The Hungarian police carried out the roundups and forced the Jews onto the
deportation trains. In less than two months, nearly 440,000 Jews were deported from Hungary in more than 145 trains. Most were deported to Auschwitz, but thousands were also
sent to the border with Austria to be deployed in digging fortification trenches.

By the end of July 1944, the only Jewish community left in Hungary was in Budapest.
Most of the Singer and Róna (Rothmüller) family members were in Budapest, but almost
everyone in the Gombosi (Glauber) family lived in Bihar province. The entire extended
Glauber family was deported from Bojt, Váncsód, Berettyóujfalu and Nagyvárad (Oradea).
To the best of my knowledge only one of them survived the Holocaust. Gizi (Gizella)
Glauber, Dezső Gombosi's 23 year old niece on his father's side, survived the concentration
camps and was liberated by British troops in Bergen-Belsen. She returned to Hungary and
settled in Budapest. She eventually immigrated to Israel in 1957, married and had two
children (see family trees in Fig. C.3 and Fig. C.4).

After the deadly summer of 1944 there was a relatively low key and mildly effective
international effort to protect the Jews of Budapest. The Swedish, Swiss, Portuguese and
Vatican diplomatic missions began to hand out papers which offered a degree of personal
protection with the vague promise of post-war immigration to their country or to Palestine.
The best known of these efforts was the one led by the Swedish diplomat Raoul Wallenberg. With authorization from the Swedish government, Wallenberg began distributing
certificates of protection issued by the Swedish Legation to Jews in Budapest shortly after
his arrival on July 9, 1944. By this time all Jewish communities outside of Budapest were
deported, so Wallenberg focused his efforts on protecting the Jews of Budapest. He used
established hospitals, nurseries, and a soup kitchen, and designated more than 30 "safe"
houses that together formed the core of the "international ghetto" in Budapest. The interna-

---

[3]This term was first defined by Karl Marx and Friedrich Engels in "The German Ideology" (1845) and later
elaborated on in other works by Marx. Marx refers to the lumpenproletariat as the "refuse of all classes," including "swindlers, confidence tricksters, brothel-keepers, rag-and-bone merchants, beggars, and other flotsam
of society."

tional ghetto was reserved for those Jews and their families holding certificates of protection from a neutral country.

Even though the "protection papers" were free, it took either money or great effort to obtain them. Since Magda had no money, she spent a lot of effort to obtain protection papers from the Swiss embassy. Magda had a copy made and somehow (probably by bribing an honest soldier returning to the front from a furlough, who could have kept the money and thrown away the paper but did not) sent the copy to János. With the copy János managed to get into a less lethal MUSZ unit. But when Magda presented the original after she was taken to the deportation staging area (see below), the Arrow Cross thug tore it up laughing.

✂ ✂ ✂ ✂

Ferenc Szálasi was the leader of the Hungarian Nyilaskeresztes (Arrow Cross) movement that, with the armed assistance of the occupying German forces, carried

Letter from the Swiss Embassy for János Gombosi and his family certifying that they are part of a Swiss group passport.

out a successful putsch on October 15, 1944 and formed a new Hungarian government. Szálasi seriously believed in the theory of a worldwide Jewish conspiracy. In June 1943, he declared that Jews ruled the world: "Plutocracy, freemasonry, the liberal democracies, parliamentarianism, the gold standard and Marxism are all but instruments in the hands of the Jews so that they can hang onto their power and control over the world."

During the Szálasi regime, Nyilaskeresztes gangs perpetrated a reign of arbitrary terror against the Jews of Budapest. Jewish men between sixteen and sixty, and Jewish women between sixteen and forty, were "requisitioned" for military forced labor service by the Nyilas regime. They went from house to house, gave people 10 minutes to put together a light backpack with a change of clothing, and drove the victims to staging areas where they were registered, and then sent at once to fortification works. Later, they were "loaned" to Germany and were marched on foot under Hungarian guard toward the Austrian border in November and December 1944. Many, too weak to continue marching in the bitter cold, were shot along the way.

Of our immediate family members living in Budapest, Dezső and Róna were over sixty, and Éva was only nine, so only my mother, Magda, Aunt Juci and Uncle Laci were in danger of being taken away.

Sometime in October a Nyilas gang was driving a truck on Izabella Street stopping at each yellow star house and rounding up Jews. Everyone knew what to expect: the thugs would drive the truck to the Danube and shoot the Jews into the river, a favorite pastime. Magda was terrified, especially about the survival of nine year old Éva. Finally, in total despair, they hid Éva under a wooden tub in the light-court.[4] She was told to be very quiet when the shouting men came, and after they left she was supposed to climb back into the apartment – somehow. Miraculously, the truck filled up before they reached our building, and Éva was lifted back into the relative "safety" of the apartment.

✂ ✂ ✂ ✂ ✂ ✂ ✂ ✂ ✂ ✂ ✂ ✂ ✂ ✂ ✂ ✂ ✂ ✂ ✂ ✂

Laci was the most colorful member of the Róna family. He loved women and they loved him. He was street-smart, kind and brave, but, as I mentioned before, he was not good at studying. After finishing school he worked in several shops, learned how to drive a car, which was unusual at that time, and started several business ventures. Sometime around 1940 he started dating Gizella (Gizi) Duda. Gizi was a kind and very tolerant woman and she helped the entire family a lot. She was Catholic and this fact caused tensions in the Róna family, though the initial unease evaporated when the family got to know her better. My sister, Éva, is forever grateful to Gizi for all the help and kindness she demonstrated during the times of suffering and horror.

Gizi helped Laci to obtain false papers – papers that had belonged to one of her relatives who escaped from the Romanian part of Transylvania. With the help of these papers Laci managed to avoid conscription into MUSZ units, which probably prolonged his life since he had been prone to illnesses since childhood and would not have survived the cruel life in force labor units. With these false papers, Laci hid in Gizi's sublet on Bajza Street.

Laci had owned a small fabric store on Csengery Street. When anti-Jewish laws forbade Jews to own a store, Laci turned it over to Gizi. The store was horizontally divided by a thin floor; surplus inventory was kept upstairs. There was a small opening in the main floor ceiling, and a ladder could be positioned under it. If one climbed up, closed the opening, and allowed another person to put the ladder away, it was not obvious that there was a space above. In late fall the Nyilaskeresztes government started to round up working age men and women to use for forced labor. Magda was of prime working age and Gizi offered to hide her upstairs in the store. Magda only spent one day there, where even the smallest movement was clearly heard down in the store. For my mother, Magda, it was excruciatingly difficult to stay absolutely motionless. She felt it unlikely that she would not be found out, imperiling both herself and Gizi, and so they abandoned the idea.

✂ ✂ ✂ ✂ ✂ ✂ ✂ ✂ ✂ ✂ ✂ ✂ ✂ ✂ ✂ ✂ ✂ ✂ ✂ ✂

In the meantime 63 year old Dezső's health was rapidly declining. His heart condition, somewhat stabilized with medications, which, however, were ever more challenging to obtain, made it more and more difficult to continue physical work. His only employee, Mr. Ferenc Széles, a Christian, was doing most of the work and he also helped Dezső to circumvent some of the anti-Jewish restrictions.

---

[4]The light court was a small empty space between adjacent buildings. There was a small window in the bathroom that opened to a ~10 square feet area lower than the apartment.

His daughter, my aunt, Juci Gombosi, was rounded up by Nyilaskeresztes gangs and taken to a holding place to be deported to Germany, but she managed to escape and returned to the Műhely. When the gangs came to search the Műhely, Juci tried to hide behind a big cabinet. Unfortunately she was a bit clumsy, and the edge of her skirt was visible. She was taken to an abandoned brick factory (Téglagyár) on the outskirts of Budapest, was processed and sent marching toward Austria and Germany. Juci had lingering suspicions that Mr. Széles might have been the one who reported that she was hiding in the Műhely, but to the best of my knowledge this was never more than a suspicion. On the other hand, after the war, her brother, my father, János Gombosi, had a long and friendly professional relationship with Mr. Széles. I guess, we will never know the truth.

Magda was not hiding, and soon enough, fell victim to the Nyilas regime. In late October 1944 a few Nyilas came into the courtyard of 45 Izabella Street and gave the now customary 10 minutes for the women between sixteen and forty to get down to the courtyard with clothing and supplies. They were taken to the same abandoned brick factory to which Juci had been moved.

Magda was marched from the brick factory to the Austrian border and transported by cattle cars through Austria to Germany. On the way they had short stops at the Mauthausen and Dachau labor camps, but those camps were filled to capacity and the Hungarian women were forced to march hundreds of kilometers north from Dachau. The conditions were horrible. There was little food, water and other essentials. In the evenings when the convoy stopped for the night the wells were often poisoned and those who were first to drink, died. Her march ended in Bergen-Belsen.

✂ ✂

By the end of October Éva and our grandfather Róna were the only ones of the family still in the yellow star building on Izabella Street. They took in another Jewish family, but at least they had most of the apartment for themselves.

Róna took the restrictions on Jews badly, especially the Yellow Star badge that he had to wear. He considered himself a true and enlightened Hungarian who had served the country well, both in peace and in war. After Magda was taken away he kept a very close eye on Éva. Whenever they left the apartment, he sent her ahead while he walked a few steps behind, his hands clasped behind his back, his coat opened and turned back so that the Yellow Star was not visible. One day, Éva passed a street-sweeper and his grandson, who was about her age, on the street. The boy spit in Éva's face. This was quite normal in fascist Hungary. Róna picked up the boy by his collar and shook him hard. As he put the boy back on the ground, his coat unfolded. A hostile crowd started to form, egged on by the street-sweeper. A Nyilaskeresztes militia member came by and took Róna to the gateway just behind the nearest building leaving Éva in the middle of the crowd. She started to wail loudly, shouting to no one in particular, "They took away my mother and my father. I only have my grandfather, and now they are taking him. I have nobody but my grandfather..." A uniformed Hungarian officer who was in the crowd went in after Róna and brought him out. Éva and Róna were lucky that an honest officer was willing to intervene.

Sometime in early November 1944 the Nyilas regime ordered the remaining Jews of Budapest into a ghetto which, covering an area of 0.1 square miles, became temporary residence to nearly 70,000 people. Having been given 10 minutes to get down to the inner

Dezső Gombosi's leaf on the Tree of Life.   *Graves in the courtyard of Dohány Synagogue.*

courtyard with whatever they could carry, Éva and Róna ended up in an apartment at 32 Akacfa Street. They were among the first to be taken to this apartment and Róna took over a double bed for the two of them in one of the rooms. Later, more people slept in the room on straw mattresses on the floor. Soon there were people on straw mattresses all over the apartment.

By sheer accident Éva and Róna were put next door to three year old Judit Róna, Éva Schwarcz and her parents who had been forced to move from their nice apartment. A few days before they had been moved to a yellow star house near Szent István Park, next to the Danube river. Then, when the Nyilaskeresztes gangs rounded up Jews to move them to the Ghetto, they gathered a group in Szent István Park. They separated the children and the elderly from the working age population. The older Schwarcz's were sent to one group, and Éva Schwarcz and Judit were sent to the other group. At some point a young Nyilas member approached Éva and surreptitiously asked: "You do not have anyone to leave this child with, do you?" Éva took the hint and said she did not have anyone. The man took her and Judit and put them in the other group, where Éva's parents were. They were escorted to the Ghetto. The other group took a short trip to the bank of the river and was never seen again.

Despite the luck of finding themselves living near relatives, here was not much inter-action between the two families. Róna clung to his grudge against the Schwarcz family who had refused to delay his son's marriage to their daughter until he could attend. The Scwarczes, on the other hand, were not eager to take care of another child. It is really sad that even the gravest danger could not unite the family.

After Róna and Éva were taken to the Ghetto, Laci Róna, with his false papers, visited them wearing an Arrow Cross armband. The gates to the Ghetto were guarded by Nyi-laskeresztes gangs and they checked all identity papers. When Laci visited the Ghetto the second time he was probably recognized by a gang member, because Róna saw him being led away by one of the guards. Róna and Éva were in despair, sure that Laci would be tortured and executed by the Nyilaskeresztes gangs. Being walked from the Ghetto to the Nyilaskeresztes Party headquarters, Laci asked the guard if he could buy one last cigarette. He bribed the guard, offering to buy him a whole pack of smokes. The guard stood on the Street in front of the store entrance waiting for Laci and his cigarettes, apparently not even thinking about the fact that the store had a back door. That was the last time Laci tried to visit his father and niece.

Dezső Gombosi was also taken to the Ghetto with no access to any medication to control his heart condition. He was in a nearby building and when Róna and Éva visited, he was very sick on a straw-mattress on the floor. Shortly after this visit, on December 31, 1944, he passed away.

Dezső was buried in the temporary cemetery of the Ghetto, located in the courtyard of the main synagogue on Dohány Street. There were over ten thousand people buried in the tiny courtyard and even today about five thousand remains are unidentified. Unfortunately, Dezső Gombosi is one of them. His name is on the Holocaust memorial "Tree of Life" standing in the courtyard of the Dohány Synagogue.

✄ ✄

During the dark period of German occupation and Nyilaskeresztes terror, survival sometimes required unorthodox approaches. As I mentioned, the Róna family survived by determination and luck. Karolin's niece, Olga Singer perished in concentration camps. Róna's niece, Aliz Rothmüller survived with the help of her beauty. Twenty-five years old and her husband in forced labor she did not have many choices. According to her own account she seduced a high ranking German officer and had an affair with him, thus avoiding the yellow star houses and the Ghetto.

3.5. Life Starts Again

As the Hungarian Army retreated (fled?) from the Eastern front the MUSZ units were forced to march back thousands of kilometers. János was among the lucky ones; he managed to get back to Budapest alive. His unit was stationed at the Albrecht barracks.[5] After the liberation of Budapest János went to Gizi's apartment on Bajza Street where Laci was hiding. The Budapest Ghetto was liberated by Soviet troops on January 18, 1945. János, Miklós and Laci found Éva and Róna the same day.

The next day tragedy struck the family. Karolin's brother, Jenő Singer, left the Ghetto and his wife Margit to check on their apartment. However, sporadic fighting was still going on, so called "mop-up operations." On the way back he was struck by a stray bullet and died on the spot. His only daughter, Olga, had been deported sometime in November 1944 and never returned. The loss of her daughter and her husband devastated Margit who could not comprehend how such things could happen after they had survived so much.

✄ ✄

Magda's march had ended in Bergen-Belsen. Even as Nazi Germany was crumbling, its well-oiled bureaucracy of death was still operating efficiently. Finally, Bergen-Belsen was liberated on April 15, 1945, by the British 11th Armored Division. The liberators discov-

---

[5]The Albrecht Military Baracks are still in use. The building is located at the corner of Dózsa György Street and Lehel Avenue, less than two miles from the Ghetto.

Jewish women after the liberation of Bergen-Belsen.

ered around 60,000 prisoners inside, most of them half-starved and seriously ill, and another 13,000 corpses lying around the camp unburied. Shortly, the horrified British looked at the list of survivors and tried to unite people who might be related. Since Magda Gombosi and Juci Gombosi had the same last name the authorities united them. As far as they knew, the two sisters-in-law with a history of acrimony were the only survivors from the family.

Like survivors of all the Nazi concentration camps, the inmates of Bergen-Belsen were in very poor condition. Even after liberation many died during the first few weeks – from illnesses contracted while in captivity as well as from the lasting effects of malnourishment and mistreatment. Bergen-Belsen was so filthy and infested with diseases, especially typhus, which like the plague is spread by rats, that the British burned down the entire complex.

I found a photograph taken of Hungarian women just after the liberation of Bergen-Belsen. The photo is just a glimpse at the terrible conditions in which these women were found. Burning the camp was probably the right decision at that time, but it erased the proofs of the horrific conditions people were living under. Many of the liberated inmates were scarred for life. It was only after many years later that we learned that Magda lost a kidney while marching through Austria and Germany in the winter. Juci never regained her full health and always struggled with some kind of ailment.

In July, three months after liberation, 6,000 former inmates were taken by the Red Cross to Sweden for convalescence; Magda and Juci were among them. They never became close friends, but they worked out a "cold peace" that lasted for the rest of their lives.

✂ ✂

For János and Éva Gombosi life slowly started again. Soon after the liberation of the

Ghetto the family reclaimed the Izabella Street apartment from the family who had occupied it. They moved back in, together with Róna and Laci. János decided to reopen the Műhely and continue the family business. Ten year old Éva helped her father to deal with government bureaucracy and became an indispensable part of the family business.

Éva had begun 4th grade in September of 1943. Interrupted by the war, she finished it in the summer of 1945. After Róna's intervention Laci finally married Gizi (more about this in the next chapter) and she moved into the Izabella Street apartment. There was still no news about Magda. Éva recalls hearing tidbits of adult conversations implying that János was dating another woman. This relationship, however, stopped after Magda was located with the help of the Red Cross.

The Red-Cross regularly published lists of concentration camp survivors. These lists provided information about present location and how to contact them. Sometime late in the summer or early fall of 1945 a neighbor came to Éva with one of the lists. Her mother and Aunt Juci were on it; they were in a rehabilitation center in Sweden.

✂ ✂

After arriving in Sweden, Magda and Juci spent some time in a rehabilitation center (or sanatorium). After they regained their health, they were moved to the city of Jönköping about 200 miles southwest of Stockholm. They were together with a group of other Hungarians (mainly women). Magda and Juci started to work in a local clothing factory sometime in the fall of 1945.

Sometime in the fall of 1945 Magda got word from Budapest that János and Éva were alive. From this moment her only goal was to save enough money to return to Hungary. János and the family were unable to send her money for the trip because at this time Hungary was undergoing the worst hyperinflation in the history of the world. The currency was so worthless that people got paid twice a day and the economy almost completely reverted to a barter system.

It took Magda nearly half a year to save money for the trip and arrange all necessary documents. During this time she worked overtime and tried to spend as little as possible. Not long before her departure the liberated Hungarian Jews celebrated their first free Passover. This was an emotionally important event, since Passover itself is a celebration of the liberation of Jews from captivity and slavery in Egypt. The symbolism of the event did not escape the group of Hungarian Jews who had been detained in Bergen-Belsen.

Among those survivors was Miklós Farkas. I think that he was a descendent of the extended Farkas family of Berettyóujfalu and a distant relative of Matild Farkas, Juci's mother. This, however, is just a guess, and Juci always insisted that Miklós was not related to our family at all. In any case, Miklós was evacuated to Sweden with Magda and Juci. Shortly after their arrival to Sweden he started to court Magda. After Magda learned that her family was alive in Budapest, she suggested to Miklós that he court Juci. Miklós took Magda's advise and he and Juci eventually married. Since neither of them had any immediate family left after the Holocaust (and Juci still resented János' treachery in chosing Magda over his own sister) they decided to settle in Sweden. A few years later they moved to Stockholm where they lived the rest of their lives. They never had children. Miklós died in 1966. Juci is still alive as I am writing this book in 2013. She is now 100 years old and suffers from advanced dementia. She lives in a nursing home and is taken very good care of.

First free Seder in Jönköping on April 15, 1946. Magda, Miklós and Juci are marked on the photo. It is interesting to note that Miklós and Juci are sitting next to each other, while Magda is sitting separately.

By the middle of April 1946 Magda was ready to move back to Hungary. She had almost enough money for a train ticket and all the documents necessary for the trip. With her usual courage she approached the owner of the clothing factory and asked him if she could borrow money to return to Budapest. She promised that she would pay back the loan as soon as possible. The owner was moved by Magda's story and donated the necessary money. At the end of April, Magda arrived in Budapest where Éva, János and the rest of the family were eagerly awaiting her. At this time the relation between Hungary and neighboring Czechoslovakia was less than friendly due to the forced population exchanges.[6] When Magda crossed the Czechoslovak-Hungarian border the Czechoslovak authorities took her off the train and confiscated everything she was taking back from Sweden. She never forgave the Czechoslovaks for this cruelty.

✂ ✂

The Róna and Singer families survived the Holocaust relatively intact compared to less fortunate families. There were horrific losses, but the core of both families bounced back after the Holocaust. As we will see, our ancestors who lived outside of Budapest, were not so lucky.

---

[6]Immediately at the end of World War II, some 30,000 Hungarians left the formerly Hungarian re-annexed territories of southern Slovakia. In addition, there was a forced population exchange between Czechoslovakia and Hungary. About 70,000 ethnic Hungarians from Slovakia were exchanged for a similar number of Slovaks from Hungary. Slovaks left Hungary voluntarily, but Czechoslovakia forced Hungarians out of their nation.

Nine month after Magda's return, on January 19, 1947, Magda and János had a son, Tamás. For the Gombosi family Tamás' birth represented the end of the Holocaust, the beginning of revival. The Phoenix was reborn.

4 The Bíró (Strauszer) Branch

4.1. The First Diploma

My wife's great-great-grandfather, Jozef Strauszer, was born in 1786. The place of his birth is not known, and we do not know anything about his parents. Because written documents were not very reliable at this time his name is spelled somewhat differently in different sources: Strauszer, Strausser, Strauzer, Strosser are the most frequent variants. By the late 19th century the name is consistently spelled "Strauszer," so that is the version I use in this book.

In the 1818 Hungarian Jewish Property Census, carried out by the government for taxing purposes, he is listed as a property owner in the city of Beczkó, Trencsén Province. Thirty years later, according to the 1848 Jewish Census, he was a merchant and had a large family.

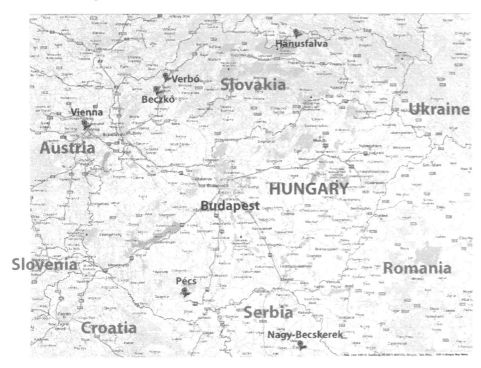

Map of present day Hungary and neighboring countries and the places of origin of the extended Bíró family.

Júlia Goldberger and Henrik Strauszer in 1906.

He was married to Regina Fischhof and they had seven children: a daughter, Hani (1824) followed by four sons, (Mózes (1826), Jakab (1828), Bernát (1830), Wolf (1834), a second daughter, Anna (1837) and a final son, Henrik(1839). Several of the children were born in nearby Verbó, so the Strauszers probably moved to Beczkó sometime in the second half of the 1840s. We do not know what happened to the children with the exception of my wife's great-grandfather, Henrik. It is, however, known that there was an extended Strauszer clan in the Beczkó area even in the early 1900s. In order to make it easier to understand family relations we show family trees in the Appendix. The relevant family trees are shown in Fig. C.7 and in Fig. C.8.

Henrik Strauszer was the first in our combined extended families to attend an institution of higher learning. He became a teacher and moved to the city of Pécs where he taught in various Jewish schools. He was married to Júlia Goldberger (1846) and they had a total of thirteen children. Four of the thirteen children died in childhood: Riza (1869-71), Vilmos (1876-77) and twins Aladár and Imre (1881-82). Three girls and six boys reached adulthood: Gyula (1868-1912), József (1871-1954), Etel (1872-1944), Móric (1873), Béla (1875-1944), Nepomuk János (1876-1916), Jenő (1878-1944), Zelma (1879-1944), and Flóra (1883-1964).

While Henrik was beginning his family, in 1868, Baron József Eötvös, the Minister of Religious Affairs and General Education submitted to the National Assembly a new National Education Act, which, after a stormy debate, was passed by both the Chamber of Representatives and the Upper House. This revolutionized the Hungarian education system by creating a state funded national school system and 30 teacher colleges, giving the state control of the curriculum, and specifying the subjects every school must teach. The list of subjects was the following:

- speech and comprehension exercises;
- reading/writing;
- religious knowledge;
- arithmetic/geometry;
- geography/history/civics;
- natural history/physics;
- singing/drawing/physical culture;
- practical farming and gardening experience.

In 1868, as a direct consequence of the National Education Act the Jewish community of Pécs began a new school that was finished in 1872. Four teachers were invited to teach in it: Ábrahám Vessel, Izsák Grünwald, Jakab Klingenberg and Henrik Strauszer. He worked in this school until his death in 1907, eventually becoming the superintendent of the Jewish school system in the city of Pécs.

A document dated February 20, 1893 lists the entire Strauszer family based on official Jewish records. At this time Gyula, the oldest son of Henrik and Júlia, was an apprentice salesman in a shop, József was in the armed forces, while Móric, Béla, Nepomuk János and Jenő were listed as students. No occupation was listed for the girls, even though Etel was 21, Zelma 14 and Flóra 11 at this time. It is quite possible that Etel was already married, but Zelma and especially Flóra were most likely still in school.

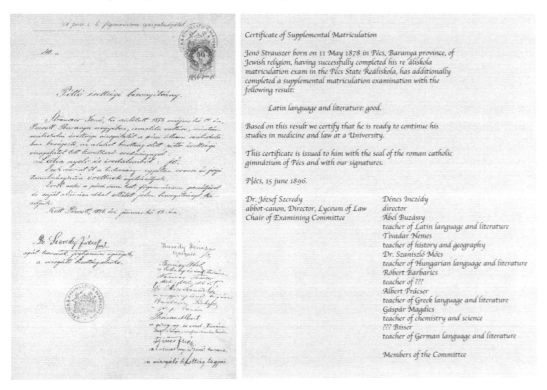

Certificate of Supplemental Matriculation

Jenő Strauszer born on 11 May 1878 in Pécs, Baranya province, of Jewish religion, having successfully completed his re áliskola matriculation exam in the Pécs State Reáliskola, has additionally completed a supplemental matriculation examination with the following result:

Latin language and literature: good.

Based on this result we certify that he is ready to continue his studies in medicine and law at a University.

This certificate is issued to him with the seal of the roman catholic gimnázium of Pécs and with our signatures.

Pécs, 15 June 1896.

Dr. József Szeredy
abbot-canon, Director, Lyceum of Law
Chair of Examining Committee

Dénes Inczédy
director
Ábel Buzássy
teacher of Latin language and literature
Tivadar Nemes
teacher of history and geography
Dr. Szaniszló Mócs
teacher of Hungarian language and literature
Róbert Barbarics
teacher of ???
Albert Prácser
teacher of Greek language and literature
Gáspár Magdics
teacher of chemistry and science
??? Bisser
teacher of German language and literature

Members of the Committee

Jenő Bíró's supplemental examination certificate enabling him to enroll in law school.

Jenő Bíró (sitting) and a colleague as law clerks in Jenő Bíró in Budapest in a photograph taken in Budapest. This photograph was taken on July 18, July 1903. See text for more details. 1903.

My wife's grandfather, Jenő, graduated from Reáliskola in 1896. He wanted to enter the university and study law. For law and medical studies, a Latin language examination was required. However, studying Latin was not a requirement in Reáliskola which focused on physical sciences (see page 15). To be able to enter law school, Jenő Strauszer had to take a supplemental Latin language exam.

Jenő was smart, ambitious and a bit cocky. One example is the story behind the Hungarianization of his name. He was just about to finish law school when he made a wager with one of his friends. At this time practitioners of law had two separate career paths: judgeships or private practice. Just as today, private practice was more financially rewarding, but being a judge granted very high social status. Young law students were somewhat idealistic and most of them were dreaming about becoming judges. Young Jenő Strauszer was no exception. He was jokingly arguing with a friend about becoming a judge. At the end they made a wager about who would become a judge first. Family legend does not remember the name of the friend or what the winner was supposed to get, but does claim that Jenő, being smart and a bit irreverent, the next day filed papers to change his name from "Strauszer" to "Bíró," which in Hungarian means "judge". He not only won the wager, but also got a new family name. Soon afterwards all the sons of Henrik Strauszer changed their last names to Bíró. The girls, however, did not. I do not know the reason behind this difference. I can only guess that at that time women had secondary social status and it was not important for them to have Hungarian sounding family names, since they were expected to eventually take on their husband's name.

In 1900 Jenő graduated from law school receiving the title "juris doctor" which entitled him to be called "doctor." He was the first one in all of our extended families to earn this title.

Jenő started to work as a law clerk at one of the most prestigious law firms in Budapest. Unfortunately, we do not know the name of the firm. There is, however, a photograph dated July 1903 showing Jenő and another young lawyer in shirt sleeves working in the office. The title of the photo is "when the boss is on vacation." I assume that they were not supposed to be in the office without a jacket.

Another photograph, taken in Budapest on July 18, 1903 shows the 25 year old Jenő Bíró standing on "15th Március" (the date of the 1848 uprising, see Appendix A.8) square in central Budapest. The more interesting thing about the picture is the dedication on the back. It reads: "For your birthday, I think, I cannot give You anything more valuable than ... myself. Pécs, September 2, 1903. Dr. Bíró." Based on this dedication I assume that Jenő gave this photograph to the young woman he was courting at this time. From the fact that this picture stayed in the possession of the family, this young woman was probably his future bride, 17 year old Rózsika Hirtenstein.

At first glance it is surprising that Jenő and Rózsika knew each other. As we will see in Section 4.2 the Hirtenstein family is from Nagy-Becskerek, quite far from Pécs or Budapest. Yet, two of the Hirtenstein sisters, Rózsika and Felice, married two Bíró brothers, Jenő and József. This implies a strong relationship between the two families. The most likely answer is that both families had strong and extended family ties to the Beczkó – Verbó area. At the time the population of these cities was about 30% Jewish and a number of Strauszer and Hirtenstein family members lived there. It is very likely that the two families had been acquainted for a long time and that the younger members of the families had known each other since early childhood.

Coming back to Jenő's photograph, the dedication on the back suggests an already close relationship with the recipient of the photograph, and, using a modern expression, a pretty big ego. Based on family lore it is obvious that Jenő Bíró was self-confident and had a well-developed sense of self importance. The dedication on this photograph fits the overall picture. My guess is that by the time this photo was given as a birthday gift to Rózsika they were already engaged, or just

Rózsika Hirtenstein in 1905.

about to be engaged – century ago morals were different and offering himself as a present was clearly sort of a marriage proposal. This interpretation is supported by a photograph of Rózsika Hirtenstein taken around 1905 with a dedication on the back "to my Jenő."

4.2. The Hirtenstein Family

The Hirtenstein family tree can be traced back to 1850 when Márkus Hirtenstein was born in Verbó (Nyitra province). Family legend says that during the 1848 Hungarian revolution his father served in the revolutionary army, but I was unable to find any record to confirm this. Sometime around 1880 he married Karolin Friedman of Hanusfalva (today it is near the border between Slovakia and Poland) and they moved to Nagy-Becskerek (today it is part of Serbia).

Márkus was a very successful businessman who amassed a significant fortune. According to family lore he was given nobility by Emperor Franz Joseph I, but I was unable to confirm this. Other family legend says that one of Márkus' siblings married a countess who was afterward disowned by her family. Again, today it is impossible to confirm or repudiate

Márkus Hirtenstein around 1890 (left), Márkus Hirtenstein in 1907 (center) and Karolin Friedman in 1907 (right).

these stories.

Karolin and Márkus had six children, five girls followed by a boy. The girls were Hilda (1882), Felice (1884), Rózsika (1886), Janka (1889) and Frida (1890). The only boy, Andor, was born around 1895, the exact date is not known.

There is also some confusion about the birth date of Janka. Family records indicate that she was born in 1889, but I found her social security death record showing a birth date of September 14, 1886, two days ahead of Rózsika's birth date (September 16, 1886). It is very likely that the social security record is incorrect, since I found a photograph from 1891 showing the four older Hirtenstein girls. It is clear that Janka is much younger than Rózsika, so it is most likely that Janka was really born in 1889.

What we know about Karolin and Márkus's children is spotty. We mainly have materials related to the lives of Janka and Felice and know very little about the fates of Hilda, Frida and Andor. Here is what we know: Hilda married Márton Kohn

The four oldest Hirtenstein girls in 1891. From left to right: Felice, Janka (sitting), Rózsika and Hilda.

in 1900 and in 1901 their daughter, Lola, was born. It is very likely that both Hilda and Márton perished in the Holocaust. Their daughter, Lola Kohn, died in 1942. We do not

Left: Hilda Hirtenstein and her husband, Márton Kohn in 1900. Right: Frida Hirtenstein and her husband, Lajos Borsodi in 1909.

know the cause of her death, but I suspect she died of natural causes.

Around 1906 Felice married an older brother of Jenő Bíró, József. József was a dental technologist. At the time of the wedding József was about 35 and Felice about 22 years old. They never had any children. Soon after the marriage they emigrated to New York City where they lived the rest of their lives. In New York, József owned a dental laboratory and was quite successful.

In 1907 Rózsika married my wife's grandfather, Jenő Bíró. Their life will be discussed below.

Probably Janka was the most beautiful of the Hirtenstein girls. In 1906 or 1907 she married a wealthy industrialist from Vienna, Leo Langfelder who owned several factories

Left: Janka Hirtenstein in 1905. Right: Janka Hirtenstein dressed as gypsy girl in 1906.

in Austria and in England. After the wedding Janka moved to Vienna. She eventually gave birth to two daughters: Willy (1908) and Annie (1911).

Janka and her family lived in a small mansion in Vienna and had significant business investments in England. After Hitler's rise the situation became increasingly dangerous for Austrian Jews and the Langfelder family debated what to do. Eventually they decided to stay – and paid dearly for this decision.

After the Anschluss[1] the Langfelders were held hostage by the Nazis until they gave up all their properties in Austria. At that point they were allowed to move to England. Unfortunately, Leo died shortly after their arrival leaving his family behind. Willy married a Hungarian noble, Zoltán Gyérey. He took over the day-to-day management of the business and gradually alienated Janka.

Andor Hirtenstein in 1910.   Felice Hirtenstein in 1916.

Just around the time World War II broke out Janka's younger daughter Annie moved to New York City with the help of her uncle, József Bíró. In the beginning she had very little money and lived with József and Felice. However, she was able to find work quickly and was able to help József and Felice who were having financial difficulties at the time. Later she worked in the fashion business and was quite successful. Eventually she married Alfred Hamber; they had no children.

By the mid-1950s Janka's relationship with her son-in-law Zoltán Gyérey became so strained that she too moved to New York City and joined Annie. Nearly thirty years later, in 1978 when Willy and Janka both died, Zoltán kept all the family assets excluding Annie from the fortune her father had established. She lived in New York City until her death in 2007. While she was not poor, she had very little money. It is really sad how this big fortune was stolen first by the Nazis and finally by a less than honest son-in-law. Another sad fact is that neither Willy nor Annie had any children, so this branch of the family died out with them.

Annie and Willy's aunt Frida, Janka's sister, married Lajos Borsodi in 1909 and their son, Ferenc, was born in 1911. It is likely that Frida and Lajos perished in the Holocaust. Frida's son, Ferenc Borsodi was taken to MUSZ (see Appendix A.12) and died in forced labor.

Andor Hirtenstein married a Christian woman (causing serious heartaches for the family) sometime during the 1920s and had two sons: László and Károly. Andor perished in the Holocaust, but his wife and sons survived and emigrated to Israel. It is quite ironic that

---

[1]German for "link-up," it refers to the occupation and annexation of Austria into Nazi Germany in 1938.

the non-Jewish branch of the family ended up in the Jewish state.[2] Sometime in the 1970s, my mother-in-law, Juci Bíró, told us the story of Andor's sons. She mentioned that because they were not considered Jews, they could not serve in sensitive military units. We have no additional information about Andor's family.

4.3. Rózsika and Jenő

In the early 1900s Jenő's brothers and sisters reached marrying age. His oldest brother, Gyula, was the first to marry around 1900. He was soon followed by Móric (∼1902), Béla (∼1902), Zelma (∼1903), Etel (∼1904), József (∼1905) and finally Flóra (∼1907). It is interesting to note that Flóra's wedding was a week after Jenő's. I have no idea how the family could deal with a wedding in Nagy-Becskerek followed immediately by a wedding in Pécs.

Consequent to their marriages, Etel moved to Nyíregyháza, Zelma to Barcs, and Flóra to Nágocs. József married Rózsika's older sister, Felice, and they emigrated to New York around the time Rózsika and Jenő married.

Béla and his wife, Teréz Roth, had two children, Olga (1904) and József (1905). Shortly after the children were born, Teréz died at the age of 30. Béla soon remarried. His second wife was Helén Kunstädter,

Jenő and Rózsika Bíró shortly after their wedding in 1907.

who gave birth to a son in 1910. According to family legend, Helén was the embodiment of the wicked stepmother. She tortured Olga and József any way she could and pampered her own son, Lajos. Sometime during the 1910s Béla and his family moved to Budapest and there was little interaction between them and the rest of the family.

Jenő Bíró returned to Pécs after passing the bar exam and started his own law practice. He was now established and had the financial resources to start a family. In January 1907 he married his bride, Rózsika Hirtenstein, 20 years old at the time. Since Rózsika came from a well to do family she had a considerable dowry. A prenuptial agreement was signed on the day of the wedding spelling out the dowry and the division of assets in case of divorce or death. This prenuptial agreement survived all the turmoil of history and provides a glimpse into the life of well-to-do Jews in the early 1900s. Here we briefly summarize the content of the prenuptial agreement. The language is so archaic and legalistic that it would be very difficult to translate, but one can easily capture the essence of the agreement between my wife's maternal grandparents.

---

[2]According to Jewish law, Jewishness is inherited from the mother.

Nagy-Becskerek, January 7, 1907

We, Dr. Jenő Bíró and Rózsika Hirtenstein, married today and we agree to the following about our assets and rights of inheritance:

1. Mrs. Rózsika Bíró (neé Hirtenstein) brings 15,000 Kr³ cash to the household of her husband and hands over this sum to him. This cash dowry remains her exclusive asset and she is free to use it any way she sees fit. She can request the repayment of this sum at any time and she can put a lien on all of her husband's assets to assure the repayment.

2. In addition to the cash dowry described above Mrs. Rózsika Bíró (neé Hirtenstein) also brings a completely equipped household to her husband's home. These items are listed in the attached household items inventory. These household items are the property of Mrs. Rózsika Bíró (neé Hirtenstein) and she has exclusive rights to these items.

3. Dr. Jenő Bíró obligates 5,000 Kr as collateral to his wife.

4. If the couple separates for whatever reason, Dr. Jenő Bíró is obligated to pay to Mrs. Rózsika Bíró (neé Hirtenstein) monthly alimony of 200 Kr at the beginning of each month. In addition he must return all household items that were part of the dowry and any other jointly acquired item(s) primarily for the use of women.

5. In case one of the parties dies and there is no offspring mutual inheritance is determined by the following way:

   (a) If the wife dies within two years following the marriage all dowry (cash and household assets) is inherited by the wife's parents (or their descendants) and the surviving husband must return these items.

   (b) If the wife dies beyond two, but within five years following the marriage half of the dowry (cash and household assets) is inherited by the wife's parents (or their descendants) and the other half is inherited by the surviving husband.

   (c) If the wife dies beyond five, but within ten years following the marriage $\frac{1}{4}$ part of the dowry (cash and household assets) is inherited by the wife's parents (or their descendants) and $\frac{3}{4}$ part is inherited by the surviving husband.

   (d) If the wife dies beyond ten years following the marriage all dowry (cash and household assets) is inherited by the surviving husband.

   (e) If the wife dies at any time during the marriage, all items acquired during the marriage are inherited by the surviving husband.

   (f) If the husband dies before his wife does, all his estate is inherited by his wife, independent of when he dies.

   Both parties agree to abide by this agreement. All disputes will be resolved by the district court selected by the plaintiff according to family law 1874/XXXV/X.

---

³In 1907 the Hungarian currency was the "Korona" (Kr). In 1907 the exchange rate was about 5 Kr = $1. In 2013 dollars 15,000 Kr would be approximately $75,000. However, in investment value it is probably worth around $300,000.

The investment value of Rózsika's total dowry was about half a million in 2013 dollars. Considering that the Hirtensteins had five daughters they had to be pretty wealthy to be able to afford this kind of dowry for their children. It is, therefore, not surprising that the prenuptial agreement primarily protected her interests. In the early part of the 20th century, most women did not work outside the home, therefore their long term financial stability had to be protected.

Inventory of Rózsika Hirtenstein's dowry

pc	description	value, Kr
36	women's shirt	480
	petticoats:	
6	silk	250
12	white	
12	dressing gown	240
3	hairdressing gown	30
6	house coat	200
47	handkerchief	90
36 pairs	stocking	80
12	apron	24
4	silk dress	660
6	textile dress	600
2	spring overcoat	160
2	winter coat	180
2	wool coat	100
1	boa and muff	175
12	various blouses	160
6	various textile skirts	100
1	gold chain with watch	200
1 pair	diamond earrings	500
2 pairs	other earrings	200
1	dining room that consists of:	
1	credenza	800
1	cupboard	
1	table	
6	chair	
1	tea table	
1	curtain and cornice	600
1	carpets,	
1	tablecloth	
1	mahagony piano	1000
	serving sets:	
1	dinner set	
3	tea set	300
2	coffee set	

Continued on next page

Table 4.1 – *Continued from previous page*

pc	description	value, Kr
1	mocca set	
1	complete glassware set	100
1	complete silver silverware set for 12 persons	500
5	silver tray	
1	coffee, tea, milk pot	200
1	sugar bowl	
	various silver plates	
3	bread basket	
4	vase	150
2	silver cake serving tray	
6	various trays	
1	bedroom that consists of:	
2	bed	
2	night stand	
1	wash basin cabinet	
1	reclining chair	1000
2	throw rug	
2	curtain with cornice and drapery	
3	complete bed with horsehair mattress	
2	wardrobe cabinet, all in English style	
1	budoir that consists of:	
2	large armchair	
1	table with mirror (English style)	
1	Sirma carpet	600
1	desk	
2	painting	
60	various knick-knacks	
60	pillow case	600
14	duvet sheet	400
24	bed sheet	96
10	feather pillow and feather bed	200
3	cotton quilt	90
2	summer quilt	48
18	various tablecloths	350
180	various napkins	300
48	towels	96
2	duster	60
100	dish towel	50
60	various embroidery	160
1	Fully equipped kitchen with racks and pots	300
1	Full pantry with large lard-can	100

Continued on next page

Table 4.1 – *Continued from previous page*

pc	description	value, Kr
1	Fully equipped laundry with kettle, mangle, iron, washing tub and water tubs	200
	total value	**12,729**

The inventory of Rózsika's dowry gives us an interesting glimpse into the life of the Hungarian upper middle class a century ago. It describes the wardrobe of a young woman at a time when people were washing their clothes by hand (actually, they hired laundresses to do this very demanding work). I cannot imagine any modern woman owning 50 blouses, 10 dresses, 18 petticoats, 36 pairs of stockings and, most of all, 12 aprons!

It is interesting to note that Rózsika's dowry includes a complete 24 person Rosenthal dining set valued at 300 Kr ($1,500 to $6,000 in 2013 dollars). Parts of this dining set survived the storms of the 20th century and we still have about a third of it. We use it only on special occasions.

It is also interesting to note that the dowry provided furniture for a dining room, a bedroom and a boudoir only. Typical upper middle class Hungarian families lived in three or four room houses (or apartments) and the center of life was a room that combined the functions of dining, family and living rooms. In some respect it was like the "great room" in contemporary American designs favoring large open spaces. Most houses (apartments) were between 1,000 and 2,000 square feet, with three or four rooms for the family, plus kitchen, bathroom and a room for the maid and other servants. The boudoir was the realm of women, male family members seldom went there. Customarily women retired to the boudoir after dinner, while the men had a cigar with cognac in the big room. Intellectual families also had a study for the husband, but the study furniture was bought by the husband and was typically not part of the dowry.

✂ ✂

Jenő Bíró became a very successful lawyer in the city of Pécs and even nationally. He was smart, confident, and a dominating personality. While he was establishing his law career the world around them underwent dramatic changes. World War I broke out in the summer of 1914 and Jenő, just like all Hungarian men of military age, had to submit draft registration forms. I do not know why, but he was never actually drafted. He was luckier

Pieces from the Rosenthal dining set included in Rózsika Hirtenstein's dowry.

than some of his brothers who were drafted to the Austro-Hungarian armed forces. One of them, János, died in action sometime in 1916. He was 40 years old and had no children.

János' death was not the first tragedy in the family. Henrik Strauszer died in 1907, shortly after Jenő and Rózsika married. He was fortunate enough to see his children mature and succeed in life. Móric Bíró died sometime around 1910 at the age of 36. He was unmarried and had no children. 1912 was a particularly trying year for the family. First Jenő's mother died, then in June he lost his oldest brother, Gyula, who left behind an 8 year old son, Pál.

By the end of the 1910s Jenő and Rózsika had no immediate family left in Pécs. Jenő's parents were dead and their brothers and sisters lived quite far from them. Moreover, following the Trianon Peace Treaty (see Appendix A.11), some family members now lived in foreign (and sometimes hostile) countries: Nagy-Becskerek was in Serbia, Beczkó and Verbó were in Czechoslovakia. It was not even easy to visit most of the relatives, with the exception of Rózsika's sister, Janka, who lived in Vienna with her husband and two daughters. There was a very close relationship between Rózsika and Janka, and the two families often visited each other until the Anschluss forced Janka and her family to move to England.

4.4. Julianna

Jenő and Rózsika waited more than nine years for a child. Finally, in June 1916 their daughter, Julianna, my wife's mother, was born. Everyone called her Juci. The parents were overwhelmed with joy and adored their daughter.

Picture of the two-year-old Juci Bíró in 1918.

Juci was smart and eager to learn. As I am writing this book I realize that many of her characteristics developed as a direct consequence of growing up with such a dominant father. In elementary school she was already an outstanding student. Since the family spent a lot of time in Vienna she was practically bilingual, easily switching between Hungarian and German. I found a photograph taken during one of these visits. It shows Jenő and Juci with the Langfelder girls, Willy and Annie.

During summers they often traveled around Europe spending a month or so at famous vacation spots. Later in life Juci always fondly remembered her childhood family trips to Germany, Italy, France, Switzerland and other popular tourist destinations. Very often the Bírós traveled with Janka and her family. We have a photo showing Janka and her daughters together with the Bírós in Venice in the summer of 1926 when Juci was 10 years old.

One story that she told us several times concerned her father who evidently was a bit challenged in foreign languages: one summer they spent several weeks in Evian on the French side of Lake Geneva. Once they went to a restaurant to have dinner and Jenő ordered a bottle of wine to go with the food. The waiter brought the wine to the table, but forgot to

Jenő Bíró in 1926 with his daughter and nieces. From left to right: Annie Langfelder, Jenő Bíró, Willy Langfelder and Juci Bíró.

The Langfelders and the Bírós at the St. Mark square in Venice in the summer of 1926. From left to right: Rózsika, Willy, Jenő, Juci, Annie and Janka.

open the bottle (I guess waiters never change). Jenő became annoyed that he could not get his wine and called back the waiter, saying: "Garçon!" When the waiter came back, Jenő could not remember the French word for "cork." He wanted the waiter to uncork the bottle, so he pointed to the bottle and said, mixing the Hungarian noun with a French definite article: "le dugo" (dugo is cork in Hungarian). Needless to say, the bottle was opened immediately.

Jenő Bíró's law career was at its peak in the late 1920s and 1930s. He was very successful and highly respected in the community. He was in his fifties and his biggest joy was to watch his daughter grow.

Jenő was also active in the civic life of Pécs. He was a member of the Freemasons, a fraternal organization that arose from obscure origins in the late 16th to early 17th century.

Left: This photo of Jenő Bíró was probably taken for his 50th birthday. I remember this picture, hanging on the wall of my future wife's family home in Pécs when I first visited them. It shows her grandfather at his peak: strong, confident and proud. Right: Another photo shows Rózsika and Jenő in 1931. I recently discovered this 1931 photo in a collection of old pictures we have not seen before.

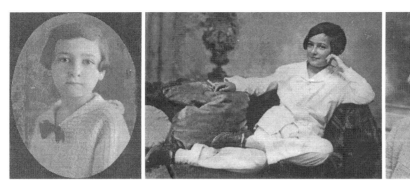

Juci Bíró in 1928 (left), 1932 (center) and 1934 (right).

Freemasonry explicitly and openly states that it is neither a religion nor a substitute for one. Freemasonry's central focus is charitable work within a local or wider community, moral uprightness, as well as the development and maintenance of fraternal friendship. Nazi Germany persecuted Freemasonry along with Jews and Gypsies. It is estimated that between 80,000 and 200,000 Freemasons were killed under the Nazi regime. Masonic concentration camp inmates were graded as political prisoners and wore an inverted red triangle. The fact that Jenő was both Jewish and a Freemason most likely contributed to his arrest immediately after German troops occupied Hungary on March 19, 1944.

✂ ✂

Juci finished elementary school in 1924 and entered the only high school (gimnázium) available for girls in Pécs. It was the St. Elizabeth (Szent Erzsébet) Catholic high school run by nuns. She was an outstanding student, hardworking and ambitious. She was also driven by her overachieving father who would not accept that his daughter was not the best in everything.

In my favorite picture of the young Juci she is 16 years old and she looks as relaxed and confident as I ever saw her. The most interesting aspect of this picture is the striking resemblance to her daughter, Eszter, when Eszter was about the same age. Maybe it is because I am married to Eszter that I like this photo so much. Another interesting aspect of the photo is that it shows Juci with a cigarette in her hand. We know that she started to smoke at age 16, so this is consistent with family legend. Later in life she was a very heavy smoker and smoking considerably contributed to her ill health and untimely death. Smoking was socially much more acceptable in the 1930s than it is today. Knowing Juci, she would not have taken on a socially unacceptable habit.

Juci told us several funny stories about her school years. Two are about her adventures with the German language. She was a fluent German speaker, but most of her classmates had a difficult time learning all the intricacies of the language. In class they were taught to read the "classical" German typography, popularly referred to as "gothic." As part of the class they read gothic German texts aloud. One girl had difficulty with the strange characters and misread the word "kind" (child) pronouncing it as "rind" (beef). For adolescent girls this was such a hilarious event that Juci kept telling about it for the rest of her life. A second story relating to German class involved homework in which they had to translate the word "kerités" (fence) to German. The dictionary listed all possible meanings of the word, including an obscure legal expression in which "kerités" means human trafficking for prostitution, or pimping. The German word for this is "Kupplerei" and also means "brothel." One can imagine the shock on the face of the nun teaching them German when she heard a girl explaining that they just had a new brothel built around their house. One can also imagine the giggling of teenage girls when this incident happened. Juci proudly told and retold this story as one of the highlights of her high school years.

Juci graduated from high school in 1934. Her graduation certificate is very boring, since she was the perfect student. She aced all her classes and exams, and her overall grade is "outstanding." Instead of translating the certificate let me just list the subjects she aced: behavior and aptitude, Hungarian language and literature, Latin language and literature, German language and literature, history, mathematics, science, religious studies, French language and literature, philosophy, geography, botany, zoology, geology, chemistry, health science and drawing.

In spite of *numerus clausus*, Juci was admitted to the University at Pécs. For her, however, the biggest problem was not government sanctioned anti-semitism, but the limited opportunities available for women. She told us on several occasions that she was very interested in physical sciences and had wanted to study chemistry. However, this was not possible for women at the University of Pécs in the 1930s, so she enrolled in the Teachers College and studied French and German language and literature to become a language teacher.

It is needless to say that Juci was an outstanding student at the university too. She spoke fluent Viennese German. During their summer travels the Bírós spent considerable time in French speaking countries, so her French was also very good. In addition, during her university studies she spent a year at the Sorbonne in Paris studying French literature and improving her French. During this year she also traveled to London to learn English. Even though she was a very talented linguist her English was far from perfect as we can see from her speech to the liberating American troops (see Section 6.2). Her English vocabulary was excellent, but she made some grammatical errors typical of Hungarians. (I am a much less

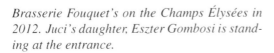
Brasserie Fouquet's on the Champs Élysées in 2012. Juci's daughter, Eszter Gombosi is standing at the entrance.

Juci Bíró with her parents in 1938.

Juci Bíró's high school graduation certificate.

Juci Bíró's Ph.D. certificate.

talented linguist and I am still making similar errors after having lived in the U.S.A. for more than 30 years.)

Juci spent the 1937-38 academic year in Paris where she took classes at the Sorbonne. She was way ahead of her time, because U.S. universities are just now discovering the value of the "study abroad" programs. In Paris, Juci shared a small apartment with another young woman (unfortunately we do not know her name). They loved to explore Paris and visited all museums and exhibits that Paris could offer. Many years later, when Juci and her husband, Pista, visited relatives in Paris, Juci went back to the places she loved as a young woman. She "forced" the group to visit many museums giving detailed lectures about French art, history and literature.

She also visited the famous Brasserie Fouquet's on the Champs Élysées where she had a memorable adventure during her year in Paris, one she told again and again over the years. In the 1930s the Brasserie Fouquet's was probably the most elegant and expensive brasserie on the Champs Élysées. It was many times more expensive than nearby restaurants. One day Juci and her girlfriend were window shopping on the Champs Élysées and decided to have dinner at this nice looking restaurant. Little did they know about the prices before they sat down and they were shocked when they looked at the menu. They could not decide what to do: they were too embarrassed to get up and leave, but did not have enough money to order more than one appetizer. When the waiter came to take their order they had to tell him that they were out of their league and could not order. The waiter felt sorry for the two young women and said that he could split an appetizer between them. He brought two plates with half an appetizer on each to help them save face. In the summer of 2012 my wife and I finally visited Brasserie Fouquet's and had coffee and dessert while recalling the memory of Juci. It was a very heartwarming experience for us.

I found a photo showing Juci with her parents sometime in 1938. This was after the Anschluss. At this time Jenő and his brother-in-law Leo Langfelder were debating what action, if any, they should take to protect their families. Jenő suggested that the Langfelders should leave Nazi occupied Vienna and come to Pécs which seemed safer at that time. He also considered moving his family out of Hungary and emigrating to Western Europe. In the end, inertia won and the Langfelders stayed in Vienna and the Bírós remained in Pécs.

Historians are still debating whether Austria was a victim or a willing partner, but as far as the Jews were concerned this does not make a difference. As I mentioned earlier, the Langfelders were persecuted and held hostage until they transferred all their assets to the Nazi government. It is also a fact that the invasion of Austria was a "Blumenkrieg" (when the invading German troops were greeted with flowers). When the Austrians talk about being the first victims of Nazi Germany I always tell one of my irreverent jokes: "Question: Where was the modern political spin machine invented? Answer: In Austria; they convinced the world that Beethoven was Austrian and Hitler was German."

Juci earned her doctorate in French and German language and literature in September 1939. In spite of her top qualification, however, she could not find a job because of the anti-Jewish laws and discrimination. Instead, she gave private German and French lessons and was quite frustrated with the situation.

5 The Gárdos (Günsberger) Branch

5.1. Origin

The Constitution of the United States of America went into effect when, on June 21, 1788, New Hampshire become the ninth state to ratify it. This happened a year before the Bastille was stormed and dramatic changes started in Europe. My wife's ancestor, József Günsberger was born at this historic time in 1788. Nothing is known about his parents, or the location of his birth. Around 1820 he married Judit Sratler who was three years younger than he and they settled in a small Hungarian town, Inke. Inke is located in Somogy Province about 70 miles northeast of the city of Pécs. They were both around 30 years old when they married, a fact that implies József had humble origins and had to work hard to have enough financial stability to start a family. The fact that Judit was not married at the ripe age of 30 also implies that her family could not afford a dowry large enough to attract many suitors. In order to make it easier to understand family relations we show family trees in the Appendix. The relevant family trees are shown in Figures C.5 and C.6.

From what I can gather, József ran a general store in the village of Inke. These villages

Map of present day Hungary and the places of origin of the Günsberger family.

usually had a general store, a few taverns and very few other businesses. His social status and financial resources were certainly higher than the peddlers who were the ancestors of the Glauber and Rothmüller branches of our family.

According to an 1848 comprehensive census of all Jews in Hungary, the Günsberger family lived in the village of Rajk (Zala Province) near the present-day border between Austria and Hungary. They had 10 sons and a daughter living in their household. The children were all born in Inke between 1824 and 1844. It is interesting to note that in 1844 Judit was 53 years old. It is quite unusual, even today, for a 53 year old woman to be still fertile. It is also likely that the Günsbergers moved to Rajk sometime between 1844 and 1848, since the youngest child was still born in Inke.

The ten Günsberger boys were Lőrincz (1824), Dávid (1826), Bencze (1828), Herman (1830), Salamon (1832), Muki (1834), Sándor (1835), Boldizsár (1836), Károly (1839) and László (1840). The eleventh child, Mari (1844), was the only girl in the family.

The fact that in 1848 the adult children lived with their parents implies that they were not married, and, most likely, they worked in the store with their father. We have no further information about most of the Günsberger children with the exception of Boldizsár. The fate of the rest of the Günsberger family is unfortunately lost.

✂ ✂

My wife's great-grandfather, Boldizsár Günsberger lived in Nagykanizsa, a town of 50,000 inhabitants about 15 miles west of Inke. He was a shopkeeper and ran his own business. Sometime in the late 1850s he married Erzsébet Kasztl who was four years younger than he. They had six sons and two daughters: Bernát ($\sim$ 1860), Lipót ($\sim$ 1865), Gyula (1871), Gusztáv, Lajos, Zsigmond, Hermina and Karolina.

Not much is known about Bernát, Zsigmond and Karolina. Lajos was a paper merchant and lived with his sister, Hermina. They both perished in the Holocaust. Gusztáv became a sugar merchant and married Gizella Krausz. They had four sons and two daughters. Most of the family perished in the Holocaust, but two sons and a daughter survived (see Fig. C.5). They lived until the 1980s, but our family lost contact with them.

Lipót married Blanka Krausz, five years younger than he and probably a sister of Gizella Krausz. They had four children: László (1901), Béla (1904), Imre (1907) and Erzsébet (1912). László and Imre perished in the Holocaust. Béla married and had a daughter. He survived the Holocaust, but his family perished. He died in 1963 at the age of 59.

Erzsébet (or as the family called her, Erzsi) had a sad life. She married Béla Kellner who later became a famous cancer researcher and was elected to the Hungarian Academy of Sciences. After World War II he was director of the Department of Pathology of the University of Debrecen (1947-1954), and later director of the Hungarian National Onco-pathological Research Institute (1954-1974) in Budapest. In 1946 they had a son, János who died of leukemia at the age of 23. It was heartbreaking for Erzsi and Béla to watch their only child die of the disease his father was researching. After János' death they became emotionally broken and refused to meet young people of János' age. I remember that Eszter and I were not allowed to meet them, because they could not bear the presence of healthy young relatives.

Gyula was educated as an accountant, but later followed his brothers' example and became a merchant. They were known in Pécs as the merchant Günsberger brothers: Gyula traded in salt, Lajos in paper products and Gusztáv in sugar. Around 1900 Gyula married Izabella Handlei. She was born in 1881 in the village of Farád (Sopron Province), located in northeast Hungary near the Austrian border. Her parents were Adolf Handlei and Mária Arnstein.

The Handlei family has a very interesting story. Their ancestors lived in Great Britain for centuries, where they were very established in commerce and even in engineering and technology. The original family name was spelled with a "y" at the end: Handley. Probably the most famous member of the Handley family was Sir Frederick Handley-Page (1885-1962), a pioneer in the design and manufacture of aircraft. His company Handley-Page Limited produced a series of military aircraft, including the Halifax bomber in World War II, of which around 7,000 were produced. They also produced civilian aircraft, including the H.P.42, flagships of the Imperial Airways fleet – remarkable at the time for no passenger deaths. He was the son of Theodore Page, a furniture maker, and Eliza Ann Handley. There is strong indication that Eliza Handley and Adolf Handlei were cousins, however, we do not have direct proof. The Handleys were salt merchants and around the middle of the 19th century were expanding their business from England to Germany, Austria and Hungary. This is how Adolf's parents moved to the continent and eventually to Central Europe.

The change from Handley to Handlei is a revealing story in itself. In Hungarian replacing the "i" with the letter "y" at the end of family names indicated nobility and common folks (especially Jews) were not supposed to have names ending with "y" unless it was part of a so called "double letter." Examples are "gy," (pronounced in English like "**d**uke"), "ly," (pronounced in English like "da**y**"), "ny," (pronounced in English like "**n**ew") and "ty," (pronounced in English like "s**t**ew").[1] According to this linguistic rule "Handley" implied nobility, but "Handlei" did not, even though both names were pronounced the same way.

When the Handleys moved to Hungary they kept using the original (English) spelling of their name. Part of the family ended up in the city of Szombathely, located in western Hungary near the Austrian border. For some reason, they were able to keep their original name and there is still a branch of the Handley family living in the Szombathely area (even though many of them perished in the Holocaust). Adolf Handlei, however, was not so lucky. Judging from his first name it is quite likely that he was born in Austria (Adolf was a very popular name in Austria, very seldom given to Hungarian children) and moved to western Hungary sometime after the Austro-Hungarian "Compromise" (see Appendix A.9). The local magistrate was not willing to allow a Jew to "pretend" nobility and unilaterally changed the name from "Handley" to "Handlei."

✂ ✂

The Handlei family had five children. The first four, Emil (1872), Regina (1875), Izabella (1881) and Irén (1884) were born in Farád. Sometime in the second half of the 1880s the Handlei family moved to Pécs and Adolf also moved his salt mill and trading business. It was in Pécs that Mária delivered the late baby of the family, Rezső (1893), nineteen years younger than his older brother, and nine years younger than his nearest sibling. Mária was 41 years old when she gave birth to her fifth child. Unfortunately the delivery was difficult and she died of complications a few days later.

---

[1] Other double letters are "cs" (pronounced in English like the "ch" in "**church**"), "sz," (pronounced in English like "e**s**timate") and "zs," (pronounced in English like "plea**s**ure").

After the death of his wife, Adolf Handlei was in a difficult situation. He was about 45 years old, still had children at home and was very busy running his salt mill and trading business. His oldest child, Emil, was 21 years old and already had his own life. Regina was 18, Izabella (everyone called her Iza) 12 and Irén 9 when their mother died. Adolf juggled family and work until his two older daughters married.

We do not have precise dates, but Iza and Regina married sometime around 1900 (probably a little earlier). Regina's husband, Andor Nyitrai, had a successful animal feed business and was not interested in becoming a salt merchant. On the other hand, Iza's husband, Gyula Günsberger, was an accountant, quite willing to join the salt business. He moved in with the Handlei family and a few years later completely took over the salt business from Adolf.

After her mother's death Iza became the de facto mother to Rezső. She raised her younger brother first with the help of their father and later with significant help from her husband. By the early 1900s Gyula was running the salt business and Iza was running the family. Gyula was not a good merchant, he was often grumpy and did not treat his customers well. These were, however, good economic times and the business was still successful and quite profitable. They were able to purchase a nice house surrounded by their own private park, a large and valuable lot which provided them an economic lifeline later during the Great Depression.

Iza had her hands full with her younger brother. Rezső was a charming but undisciplined child who could not (or would not) accept the strict discipline of the school system. He was expelled from several schools and the family eventually gave up on his education.

When Rezső was about 20 the family decided that it was time for him to start his own business. They loaned him enough money to start a small moving company. Rezső had a very charming personality and he turned out to be a good businessman. His company quickly grew and throve. He paid back his family loans and was able to afford a comfortable lifestyle.

✂ ✂

The Handlei family shared the tragedy of most Hungarian Jewish families who lived outside of Budapest. The oldest child, Emil, changed his last name to the Hungarian sounding Horváth and moved away from Pécs (Horváth literally means ethnic Croat). Later, Emil and his wife were murdered in Auschwitz, but their only child, Ede, survived the Holocaust. We know that he lived in Mohács (Baranya Province) and died in 1982, but we know nothing about his life or family.

Irén married, had a daughter, Lili, and they all perished in Auschwitz. Unfortunately we do not know much about her family.

Regina married Andor Nyitrai and they were both killed in Auschwitz. The Nyitrais had three sons: Ferenc (1901), László (1906) and Sándor (1909). Ferenc and Sándor died in Auschwitz, but László miraculously survived the Holocaust, even though his family was exterminated. After the liberation László remarried. His second wife, Judit Spitzer was 19 years his junior. They had two sons: István (1946) and Pál (1950). I remember that we met Judit and her sons sometime in the early 1970s, but after our emigration to the U.S.A. we completely lost touch with the Nyitrai family.

✂ ✂ ✂ ✂ ✂ ✂ ✂ ✂ ✂ ✂ ✂ ✂ ✂ ✂ ✂ ✂ ✂ ✂ ✂ ✂

Sometime in the early 1920s Rezső married Erzsébet Schulhof and in 1925 they had a daughter, Veronika (the family called her Vera). Vera is my wife's first cousin once removed – the first cousin of my wife's father. The Schulhof family also had an interesting history.

At the end of World War I they were a well-to-do industrialist family in Pozsony (today Bratislava). During the short lived Communist regime (Tanácsköztársaság, see Appendix A.11) in 1919 the government nationalized all major industries. The Schulhofs were told to hand over the keys to their factory and home and get on the first train. That train happened to be headed for Pécs. After the defeat of the Tanácsköztársaság, the Horthy regime was not eager to restore the property rights of Jews and the Schulhofs lived the rest of their lives in Pécs with very modest financial resources.

Since Rezső was quite a bit younger than his siblings, Vera was also much younger than her cousins. She was particularly close to Iza's son, Pista, whom she considered to be her older brother. We have a photo of Vera taken by Pista in 1938 with his brand new camera in the garden of the Günsberger home.

Vera Handlei in 1935.

When Vera was 16, Rezső became ill. As a result, Vera ran the family business for an extended period while still attending high school. She had a quick mind and was a talented businesswoman. During this time an incident happened that strained the relations between Vera and her first cousin, László Nyitrai. Rezső's moving company used horses (as heavy trucks were not available at that time) and purchased their animal feed from Andor Nyitrai's company. Under normal conditions this was a mutually beneficial arrangement. However, when Rezső became ill in 1941 and needed surgery, László Nyitrai, who was running his father's business at the time, was unwilling to postpone the settling of current accounts between the two businesses until Rezső's recovery. Vera had to scramble to raise enough capital to settle the account. This incident was never forgiven and even in the 1970s I noticed the cool relations between the two branches of the family.

When Vera was 17, she started to date a medical student, János Heinrich. This was her first love, and as with everything else in life, she was head over heels. Among the family photos I found Vera's high school graduation picture and János Heinrich's medical school graduation picture, both were taken in 1943. After graduation János became an obstetrics and gynecology specialist in the city of Zalaegerszeg (Zala Province).

On July 4, 1944, Rezső, Erzsébet and their daughter Vera were deported to Auschwitz together with the rest of Pécs's Jewry. Rezső and Erzsébet were immediately murdered in the gas chambers, but 19 year old Vera survived. She returned to Pécs where she found strangers living in their house and their company's assets in the hands of the occupying Soviet forces who needed them for transporting goods. Rather than fight more unreasonable

Vera Handlei and János Heinrich in 1943.

authorities, she walked away from everything. A couple of months later she moved to Zalaegerszeg where she married her long-term sweetheart, János, who had also survived the Holocaust.

Vera's marriage ended in tragedy. She believes that during a difficult delivery János was infected with tuberculosis. He died in 1947. At the age of 22 Vera became a widow. For a short time she moved back to Pécs where she lived with her cousin, Pista, and his wife, Juci. A few months later Vera moved to Budapest where she finished the Hungarian School of Economics and started to work at the Ministry of Heavy Industry (Nehézipari Minisztérium).

Vera enjoyed life in Budapest. She was single and was well compensated by the standards of the day. In 1956 she found a boyfriend, Andor Földes, a charming and bohemian Hungarian. When, in the fall of 1956 the iron curtain was temporarily raised during the Hungarian revolution (see Appendix A.13), Andor left Hungary leaving Vera behind. Being head over heels in love, and in spite of the fact that she had met Andor only a couple months earlier, Vera followed him leaving behind everything. They settled down in Paris where they married. Unfortunately Andor turned out to be an undeserving partner and after some calamities Vera divorced him in 1961. So far Vera had not had much luck in her personal life.

She had a difficult time adjusting to the life in Western Europe. Her university degree in socialist economic planning was not useful in the capitalist West and she had to start all over again with no support system or financial resources. She became a waitress in Paris working in a 24 hour restaurant near the Pigalle. There she met Claude Jubiniaux who was managing the restaurant. Much younger than she, and good natured, Claude is a warm man who deeply appreciates Vera's many talents and accepts her weaknesses with a smile. They are a great fit together.

The La Fringale in 1993. Vera and Tamás Gombosi are standing in front of the restaurant.   *Vera Handlei and Claude Jubiniaux in 2003.*

Eventually they opened their own restaurant,"La Fringale" (urge to eat). It was in an upper middle class area on Rue de Curcelles. Open for lunch during weekdays, catering to the professionals working in nearby law and medical offices, it gave them a comfortable living. They married in 1995 and still live in the neighborhood. Finally, Vera had found happiness. She and Claude are the only relatives on the Günsberger/Handlei side we keep regular contact with.

5.2. From Günsberger to Gárdos

Very few photographs or documents of the Günsberger family survived the turmoil of history. An entire generation of Günsbergers and Handleis – the children of Erzsébet and Boldizsár Günsberger and Mária and Adolf Handlei – were murdered in the Holocaust. The only photo we have shows Gyula and Iza around 1910, three years after their only child, István (everyone called him Pista), was born on July 22, 1907.

My father-in-law, Pista grew up in a middle-class environment that valued education. As I mentioned earlier, in Hungary there was a clear class difference between the "university elite" (as we would call it today in the U.S.) and the skilled workers and merchants. Since none of the Günsbergers or Handleis had university degrees, their social circle consisted of people with similar backgrounds: Jewish merchants and skilled workers.

Just like his maternal uncle, Rezső, Pista was a wild and undisciplined child. This might have been a consequence of Iza's loving and forgiving parenting style, but we will never know. There are quite a few stories about his misadventures, mostly told by both Pista and his cousin, Vera.

Pista was about five or six years old when he and his parents were about to go for a Sunday walk. Pista was dressed in white pants, white socks and a white shirt. Just before leaving the house he decided to hide. The best hiding place he could find was the empty coal container. One can only imagine the expression on his parents' faces when he climbed out.

When Pista was about 10 years old, the family wanted to spend a vacation in Fiume (today Rijeka) on the Mediterranean. The vacation, however, was cut quite short. On the first day after their arrival Pista was so excited to be at the sea, that he ran into the water fully clothed in his best Sunday outfit. He was eventually taken back to the hotel and grounded for the day. The next day they were walking in town when a tram passed by. Pista has never seen a tram before, and he picked up a small rock and threw it toward the tram. This was before tempered glass that does not shatter had been invented, and even a small boy's stone shattered a window. Gyula had to take care of the damage and they were told that it would be best if they cut their vacation short. The third day of the vacation they packed their suitcases and returned to Pécs. That was the last Günsberger family vacation for a long time.

Gyula Günsberger and Izabella Handlei around 1910.

After finishing elementary school Pista attended Reáliskola (science focused high school, see page 15) in Pécs. He was not an outstanding student, but his grades were good enough to gain admittance to a university. He graduated from high school in 1925 but, just like my father János Gombosi, and my maternal uncle Miklós Róna, and many other Jews, due to numerus clausus (see Appendix A.11) was unable to enter the university at Pécs. Instead, he attended business school (Handelsakademie) in Vienna for a year. Finally, in 1926, he was admitted to the University of Pécs where he earned his law degree in 1931.[2]

By the year he graduated there was already a strong wave of government sanctioned antisemitism in Hungary and there were rumors in town that extreme right wing students were planning a violent protest against Jews at the university's graduation ceremony. Since university administrators were (and still are) always eager to avoid negative publicity, Pista was asked not to attend the ceremony. He received his law degree a few days later in the office of the Rector (President) of the University. Needless to say he was less than pleased with the fact that the university backed down to the threat and ruined the celebration of his academic accomplishment. To protest the situation he attended his personal graduation ceremony in a gray suit rather than dark suit and white gloves expected at a time when graduation ceremonies were very formal – the faculty wore academic attire and the graduating students were expected to wear dark suites and white gloves. I am not sure how

---

[2]In the modern Hungarian educational system university undergraduate education provides a 3 or 4 year Bachelor degree and a 5 year Masters degree. Graduate degrees (Ph.D.) require additional studies and the defense of a dissertation. The exceptions are law schools and medical schools, where students automatically receive the degree "doctor" after finishing their undergraduate degree. These professions, however, require an additional national exam (the bar exam or medical speciality certification exam) as a precondition for legal representation, judgeships or practicing a medical specialty. In the 1930s, however, students automatically received a doctorate after 5 years of university education.

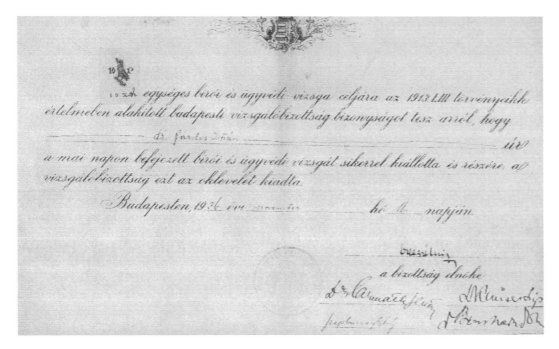

Bar exam certificate of István Gárdos.

much impact this protest had on the university administration, but later in life Pista told, (and many times retold) this story. Obviously, he was quite pleased with his "standing up to the Rector."

After receiving his law degree, Pista worked as a law clerk in the law offices of Mózes Kelemen, one of the most prominent law firms in Pécs. In May 1936 he changed his name from the typical Jewish Günsberger to the Hungarian sounding Gárdos. Shortly afterward he passed the national bar exam and became eligible to open his own law office.

✂ ✂

Gyula Günsberger was not a good merchant and during the Great Depression his business faltered. By the late 1930s he lost so much money that the family was having serious financial difficulties. It was the street-smart Vera who suggested a way to generate more cash – selling a parcel of the large park that belonged to the Günsberger family home. As the hard times continued Gyula sold several lots, until he finally ran out of cash in 1940. At this point he had to file for bankruptcy and in 1940 he closed the salt business. From this point on Pista supported his parents.

After the Anschluss (see page 66) – at Vera's urging – Pista contacted the Handley relatives in England and inquired about the possibility of their going there. It is not quite clear whom he contacted, but "come here and we will help you" was the essence of the reply. By the time they were ready to move, however, it was too late and they never left.

6   Juci and Pista

6.1. Newlyweds

Pista was a handsome and charming young man. He was very musical and a good piano player. Family legend says that at parties he often entertained the younger crowd by playing popular songs on the piano. He was a good example of a young man ready for upward social mobility. With his newly minted law degree Pista was admitted to the Jewish "high society" of Pécs, (though needless to say there was very little social contact between the Jewish elite and the "keresztény" [Christian, meaning non-Jewish] intelligentsia).

Sometime in the early 1930s he started to court Julianna (Juci) Bíró, the only child of Jenő Bíró and Rózsika Hirtenstein (see Section 4.4). As Pista's cousin, Vera Handlei, told me several times, the fact that a Günsberger was marrying into the Bíró family was an incredible event. Clearly, there was a huge social divide between the two families.

Merging announcement of the Bíró and Gárdos law practices.

Juci was smart, talented and ambitious. She was not a beauty, but was usually at the center of conversation and very popular among the upper class Jewish youth of Pécs. According to family lore, she had several suitors, but she (or her parents) decided that Pista would be the most appropriate husband. Sometime in late 1938 or early 1939 they were engaged. They married on 24 December 1939; Juci was 23 and Pista 32 years old. Unfortunately no wedding picture survived.

Shortly after the wedding Pista joined Jenő Bíró's very prestigious law firm which then became *Bíró and Gárdos*, a huge step for Pista, who after all was a freshly minted lawyer.

6.2. Devastation

World War II started in September 1939, but tensions were high even before. In 1937 Pista served 3 months in the Hungarian infantry and was discharged as a lance corporal. In 1939 he was called up for six weeks of active duty. He was mobilized again in 1940 and served in the infantry from 26 April to 10 October. This was the time when the Second Vienna Award returned part of Transylvania to Hungary and military tensions were high between Hungary and Romania (see Section 3.3). Anti-Jewish discrimination was growing almost by the day and on 15 October, (less than a week after he was honorably discharged from the Hungarian Army), he was sent to a MUSZ (military forced laborer) unit where he was kept until December 1, 1940. During one of his periods at home between military services, Juci became pregnant, but they decided that these were not the times to have a child and she had an abortion which was legal in Hungary at the time.

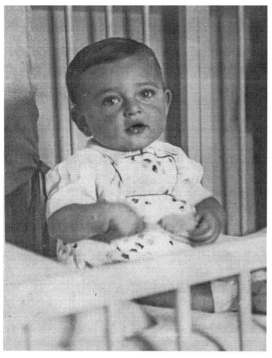

Miklós Gárdos in 1943.

1941 was a somewhat calmer year and Pista was able to stay in Pécs and care for his family. In spite of her stellar academic performance and outstanding credentials, Juci was unable to find permanent work and was giving private German and French lessons to students who needed extra help. She became pregnant again in early 1942 and this time they decided to keep the child. On October 3, 1942 their son Miklós – my wife's brother – was born. The only photograph we have of Miklós was taken sometime in the summer of 1943.

Pista saw his son only for two months. He was again taken to MUSZ on April 26, 1942 and could return only for a short period between March 1 and May 1 of 1943. He left again for MUSZ service on May 1, 1943 and was in forced military labor service for the next eighteen months, until November 1, 1944. If MUSZ was not bad enough, things became much worse after the fascist putsch in October 1944 (see Appendix A.12).

German troops had invaded Hungary on March 19, 1944. Days afterwards, the Gestapo arrested all prominent Jews and immediately deported them to various concentration camps. Juci's father, Jenő Bíró, 66 years old and suffering from advanced diabetes was amongst them. He passed away four months later on July 19, 1944 in the Mauthausen concentration camp. I was able to find the date of his death by searching the Holocaust database at the Yad Vashem web site.

✂ ✂

On May 10, 1944 all the Jews of Pécs were ordered to move into the local Ghetto, among them most of the Günsberger and Bíró families. About two months later, on July 4, 1944 the entire Jewish population (everyone who was still alive) was put in cattle cars and transported to Auschwitz. Among the 4,000 Jews deported from Pécs, were Gyula and Izabella Günsberger, Juci Bíró, her twenty-two month old son, Miklós Gárdos and her mother, Rózsika Bíró. After three days of horrible journey the train arrived at Auschwitz-Birkenau where Miklós (21 months), Rózsika (57), Gyula (72) and Izabella (62) were immediately taken to the gas chambers. Juci was not aware of their fate until much later.

Juci (28 years old) was a working age woman and her life was spared so that she could do slave labor. After the Holocaust only 200 out of the 4,000 Jews who were deported from Pécs survived. Most survivors had lost their entire families: parents, spouses, children. According to family lore, only two couples in Pécs both survived the Holocaust, and Juci and Pista was one of them.

While Juci was in Auschwitz, on November 1, 1944 Pista and his entire MUSZ unit was deported to the infamous concentration camp in Dachau. He was kept for six months, until the camp was liberated by US troops on April 29, 1944. During this period he did not have any information about the fate of his family, nor they about him. We do not know much about his life and survival in Dachau. As many survivors did, he tried to block out his experiences and was never willing to talk to us about life in the concentration camp.

✄ ✄

Shortly after she was liberated by U.S. troops in the Kaunitz concentration camp in early April, Juci gave a talk to the U.S. troops. Her notes survived and I am including her speech. It is hard to read, but this is the only first-hand account of what happened to our family. In later years none of our parents were able (or willing) to tell us much about the daily horrors of the Holocaust. Juci's English was good, but not error free. I only corrected those misspellings that could interfere with the understanding of the speech. Aside of these minor corrections, here is her entire speech:

> *The 19 March 1944 German troops occupied Hungary. This day was the beginning of our sad story and this story is not finished until today because each one of us does not know its end.*
>
> *War is finished in Europe, but not finished for us. We are far from home, the most of us alone, what happened to our family, nobody can tell.*
>
> *We already tried to travel in other camps, to ask for lists of names there was a very few result. Between 700 women only tree found till this time their husbands, perhaps two our four saw the names of their children written on a list, but still not met them.*
>
> *The news we got of the kind of treatment Germans behaved with prisoner of concentration camps, with working slaves and things we know by ourselves, which happened to us, and could as well happen to every other, are not very comforting.*
>
> *Still we have the hope to go home as soon as possible, and we try till this time to harden ourselves to be able to bear every shock which is waiting for us there.*
>
> *The same day Germans entered to Hungary they began their work. It seems the most important occupation was to make people suffer. One hour after they arrived through the frontier, the wireless[1] already spoke propaganda, propaganda against the Allied Nation, propaganda against the Jews, propaganda*

---

[1] radio broadcast

against everybody, who was not able to accept the ideas of Hitler. The next day Gestapo arrived and the arrests and deportations began. Germany's spies worked already a long time before in Hungary and Gestapo had lists prepared from the people who were against them and knew all the names of the most intelligent and important Jewish persons. Going from one lodging to the other they arrested hundred of persons, first only them, whom they mistrusted, after it everybody, who was denounced by some Hungarian or German Nazi.

Weeks of fear began. Nobody could be sure to remain in liberty, old enmities forgotten for years found their vengeance now. It was enough to write an anonymous letter and Gestapo came to arrest.

Where they entered the fear entered with them. They came, looked through the house, took what they found pleasant, as money, jewels, carpets, sometimes they rung up by telephone a furniture remover, called a truck and took the mobiliar[2] of the whole lodging and sent it to their place. They took the wirelesses[3], the photographs, the bicycles.

The arrested people did not stay long time in Hungary. After some weeks or some days of prison, without listening to them, without searching for a sin they committed, they were taken to Germany. They went off without the permission to see their family again, without saying goodbye to their dears. They could take two days food with them, but as we heard afterwards, it happened that with the two days food they traveled a week or more till they arrived on the very crowded German railways on the place of destination.

After the travel, this arrested people, Jews and non Jews, disappeared. We could not get any news of them.

Some weeks after Germans occupied Hungary the order came by the German influenced government: Jews may be concentrated in ghettos. (Ghetto word coming from the middle age means a place surrounded with gates in one town, where Jews had to live in the hardest years of anti-Semitism.) This ghettos were chosen by the Bürgermeister[4] of each town and reviewed by some delegate of the government, because they had to be after the law out of the center of the town and if possible near the railway or near a munitions factory or any other place dangerous because the air raids. This part of the town was surrounded by fence and the doors of the fence were guarded by Hungarian policeman. It was not allowed to have mail or newspapers in the ghetto, people could not leave it without extra permission and then only in groups guarded by policemen and it was not allowed to speak to anybody in the Street or to enter in a shop. So we were already shut up off the world, we did not know any news.

It was not allowed to non Jewish people to enter in the ghetto, so our only visitors were the German and Hungarian police and the only cause to work for them, either to be arrested. The work they did do us from the first moment were

---

[2]furniture
[3]radios
[4]Mayor

to clean rooms where soldiers have had their amusement, to wash, to cook for them, to clean the Street and so on. The work was not hard but degrading.

Now I am sure, the Germans (as they did it already in other countries like Yugoslavia) had from the first moment the idea to transport all the Jews to Germany, but they never warned us and even if somebody tried to inform himself they denied it completely. Some weeks already we lived in the ghetto in the constant fear of deportation, we heard that some of the other ghettos moved away, but we did not know were they went and did not know the conditions.

Before going to the ghetto they robbed us everything we had and this by a legal way. Order of government was given to make lists of all mobile and immobile[5] we had and to hand out the lists with our fortune to government officers. A very little some of money was allowed to take with us and the most important things to life: a bed, a chest table, a chair some dresses, cutlery and so on. Now they robbed us again. I remember, it is just a year now, it was a brilliant morning of summer, when at six o clock we all were called together, and Hungarian policemen gave us the order to leave behind everything we possessed to make a poor bag with three changes of clothing, plate, a knife, a spoon. No money, no things of any worth, no food and no papers or photographs could be taken.

Before leaving the ghetto, detectives inspected our bags nurses made personal search after making us strip.

Never in my life can I forget the pictures of our sad way from the ghetto to the stables of the great barracks, where we were placed. We walked sad and tired through the well known Streets of our town in groups of fifty guarded by policemen on horses. The bags on our backs. My mother, weak and old, could not bear the power of her bag, I helped her to walk and on my other arm I carried my little son, only eighteen month old. The sun was burning, the bag was heavy, the child was heavy to held, but the heaviest were our hearts. People were standing around in the Streets and at the windows, some cried, other laughed and pointed to us with their fingers. People who were our best friends only some weeks before.

At the stables we lived a whole week, lying and sitting on straw, crowded that it was impossible to stretch out our limbs, the whole day inside, only once a day our guards allowed the mothers to take the children on the open air. Machine guns were turned in the direction of the doors. To go out without permission was the death. The nights were awful. Sick people grouned, children cried for fear, policeman entered time to time and shouted. All the food we had there was given once a day, some bread, bad sausages, and a little jam every second day for children. There already we began to starve.

It was told us, that we shall go somewhere in Hungary, families shall remain together, the old one will keep the house and take care of the children, the young will work. Germans even wished that families remain together, when the 4th July we went to the train.

---

[5]assets

In the cattle trucks we went in 75 persons with their bags. Sick, old, children, young one together. Everybody had only the place to sit on his bag, without moving, the heat and the air were terrible, doors of the wagon closed. There was no water, very little food and hot to be sick of it. In the morning guards only opened the door and asked: "How many dead?" The small windows were covered with barbed wire, we stared at them and tried to find out the way we are going. Till the last minute the German guards told us, we will not be taken out of the country. And all of them lied.

At the end of the forth day we arrived on the station of Auschwitz. We had to wait till the night. That the whole spectacle may be as it had to be, they needed darkness. When light was gone the guards opened the doors and we climbed out, half crazy from hunger, thirst, tiredness and fear and blinded by the shine of reflectors directly shining in our eyes. The picture was one of the grand-guignols[6]. Handsome young men in blue-white striped costumes jumped in and out of the wagons, threw down our packages. We did not know who they were, only after days we acknowledged the men prisoners of the camp, working at the transport division. The sick from the hospital and the insane, because they were deported in separate wagons, were undressed by them at the place, and we saw from the far as they dropped them, one on the other, packed in trucks, like pieces of wood. They cried and shouted, it was horrible.

We had to form two lines then, man and women separated. It was difficult to form this lines. We felt already, that it was a separation perhaps forever. In line already, people, people again and again left their place, women were running to their husbands, daughters kissed their fathers for the last time, they could not separate until SS Guards arrived with their dogs and beaten us for the first time. They whipped with the sticks here and there in the foot, the dogs bite our legs and immediately the noise ceased, and we were standing like frightened sheep, holding the hand of the next one.

Then we began to march. In our excitement and again blinded by the shine of the reflectors we did not see, till it was our time, what happened.

In front of the reflector a tall and good-looking German officer stand and suddenly I felt, he took my shoulder and throw me to the left almost causing me to fall. My mother and my son remain on the right and disappeared. I tried to return to them and felt only a shock on my head and was slung back.

From this moment things arrived suddenly and like in a factory. We went to a building, we had to undress, let everything we had on the floor. Passing on a gangway some girls shaved our hairs, we arrived in a shop and after it we got some clothes, wrong and faulty, and going in the painted a red stripe in our back. We could not recognize each other when we met again. Then we came on the air, were led on a place, had to stand there in lines as soldiers, without speaking or moving, for hours. We saw the sun rise, we felt the coolness of the morning and the heat of the sun. It could be perhaps five o'clock in the

---

[6]Big puppet show

afternoon, when we got for the first time to eat, a little piece of bread, with margarine.

Three weeks followed then, what I can hardly remember. All of we were almost crazy. We slept in barracks, where it was raining in, on the naked earth, without blankets, crowded about a 120 women in one room. At 3 o'clock in the morning we were awakened and had to go out immediately. It was a hard climate on his place, in the morning everything like frozen, by day hot to suffer. In the morning was the first Zehl-Appel[7], we were standing in lines for 3 or 4 hours and were counted over and over again. After we got sometimes some drops of coffee or vegetable tea. At ten o'clock we had to stand again, and got our only meal. I cannot describe what it was. Some vegetables cool in water, cold, little, and with a bad taste. The first days we could not eat it at all. As we heard it afterwards, the bad taste came from medicine as bromide, arsenic, and so on. It was to quiet us, and we had always the feeling to be half in dream. When we had not to stand we were lying on the earth, in the dust, just lying, without speaking or thinking.

sometimes a whole day we had no water to drink, and it was all impossible to have the things necessary to wash ourselves.

In the afternoon we stand again Zehl-Appel for the third time. This one was the longest. It happened that we stand in the hottest sun without permission to cover our heads, from 12 o'clock till 5 o'clock in the evening. Then we got our supper: a piece of bread and margarine and after it we stand again till about nine o'clock. When it was over we all were running in to the barrack, shouting and hurrying, everyone to get a place where we could stretch out our limbs only to the half of the night, if possible.

Once a week, we went in troupe to the bath, the same proceedings as the first time. Once we got dresses without underclothing, once blankets instead of dresses. The way to the bath was long, because Auschwitz is like a big town of barracks. We passed near the electrified gates of other camps, from the far we saw people in. We looked around exited expecting to see one of the members of our family. We have known already that the nice tale, we should be together again in some weeks, was a lie as all the other stories of Germans. We lived there half unconscious feeling day and night the smell of burning bodies of the crematorium, knowing but not courageous enough to pronounce it, what kind of hospital it was where they took day after day thrown naked in trucks, our sick comrades.

Beaten and mishandled we were every day and hour, with or without reason: as we tried to bring some water from the lake, as we hold our bowls for food, as we were lying in the sun or going in to the barrack by day. The worst of our guards were not the men, but the SS women, and the dogs, which were jumping on us, as they heard only the name: Jew.

One day again the tall and good-looking officer appeared in the camp. The

---

[7]Roll call

hated name of dr. Mengele was whispered in fear. We have known already that the chief dr. of the camp was the devil in person. Thousands and thousands of deaths were on his conscience, thousand and thousands again went to the gas chambers, when he found them too weak to work.

We had to undress in the middle of the Street and S.S. soldiers were staring on us and laughing. The feared doctor went through our lines and choose the people, one was sent on one side, the other on the other, separated again those, who were together, without mercy.

What happened to the others, I do not know. We were sent again to a bath, same proceedings. This time we got for first underclothing and our dresses were a little bit better than other times.

We slept one night on the stony floor of the bath and the next day we were put in wagons. We traveled again fifty in a truck with one armed soldier in each of them, with tree days food five days long. When we arrived to Lippstadt we were so weak from hunger, that our knees true-bled, and we hold one another on the arms as we climbed out of the train.

Now a new period of our life begun, the longest but the shortest to tell. 8 month of constant work in bad conditions, one day after another one like the others, without holiday, without exception, work 12 hours a day and next week 12 hours a night. The only exception were the weekends, when we worked 18 hours instead of 12.

We lived in wooden barracks, slept on straw sacks without sheet or pillow, with only one, very thin blanket. There was a central heating always wrong. When they heated it intoxicating fumes came out of the pipes and it happened that in the morning by standing up one after another was fallen unconscious at the earth. Naturally it was not enough to stay in the barrack. Our nurse came and brought us round again, and with dizzy had and upset inside, we had to work the whole 12 hours again. Mostly because they would not loose their workers, they did not heat at all. In January when the walls of the barracks were wet from snow we slept tree weeks without heating and could not warm ourselves even in the factory and felt more cold because of the hunger.

The possibilities to clean ourselves very bad. Other hygienic circumstances as bad as to imagine. One of the barracks was the hospital. The same beds the same heating as in the others. Nearly no drugs, the same poor food, without any diet. It was not allowed to stay in the hospital, whose only work was to through out everybody , whom she did not find ill enough. It happened that in cases of diphtheria naturally there was no serum stall, the sick had to leave the hospital immediately as the fever was gone. The danger of infection did not frighten them. Naturally our clothing were wrong in a very short time, because, we had no change, worked ate, and slept in the same, but they did not give us others. Same happened to the shoes. In snow time people who had not at all shoes, got some wooden ones in which it was hard to work and to walk.

When the alarm of air-raid was to be heard we had to leave the factory and run to our barracks which were immediately at the entrance of the factory separated only by a gate. At the door of the gates SS soldiers were standing as sentries and in case of alarms, when in our wooden shoes we could not run quickly enough they beaten us with their belts.

The food at the beginning was not good, not sufficient but just enough to live on it. Later another transport with again 400 women arrived and from this time our rations became from day to day less. When the Russian Army approached to the German frontier we got only once a day an eighth part of a loaf, with about a 20 grams of margarine, once day about a half a liter of water soup, with some slices of turnip in it. And even the whole time we did not get the whole rations due to us, because of the commandant of our camp, an SS sergeant bought cigarettes with the sugar of our kitchen, and the SS women guards paid with margarine and jam for the French powder and eau de Cologne they used.

In the last week we hungry always, even after the meals, we always felt the hunger biting our inside. We could not sleep for hunger, we could hardly walk, that we continued to bear the work, even standing work, it was only possible because we were used to it. We could not think, we could remember. The names of our nearest relations we could not tell and this only by weakness. Hours and hours we spent in the factory by standing or sitting at our machines and having only one thought a pancake or feeling the taste of a fruit.

The work itself was of different kinds. The most of us were from the first moment initiated to handle machines, big and heavy machines which were served till this time only by men. Others carried heavy iron sticks from one part of the factory to the other. Again others cleaned the machines, work difficult and dangerous, because the burning iron splitters, the had to take out of the machines with their hands.

If we did not do our work as they wished it, they beat us and punished us with overwork. After 12 hours we had to stay longer if our work was not good or not enough.

When we arrived late in the factory, which was not our fault, because we were led there by our guards in closed lines, we got the punishment to lay for half an hour in the snow, or we were beaten that the traces of it remained for days and days.

Even in this conditions we had enough self control not to let us go. We learned our work in one day, but we learned the sabotage in two hours. Soon we remarked the weak points of our machines, and tried to spoil them, that the reparations lasted trough a whole workday. The munitions, we fabricated we tried to spoil to, they were a little bit to long, or to short, the holes on it were not on the right place. It was not too obvious rendered ammunitions useless. In control Russian, Polish, and Italian worked and cheated for our sake.

When the American troops came near to the town we worked, our guards led us away. We think they had in mind to lead us in a big concentrations camp perhaps to Bergen-Belsen. And they had the order to kill us on the way in event of us being overtaken by the Americans. We found the hand grenades later in the car, which were there to kill us. But thank God, their program did not result.

Juci was liberated at Kaunitz, a concentration camp about 20 miles northeast of Lippstadt. Pista was liberated at Dachau and taken to the Feldafing Displaced Persons (DP) Camp about 30 miles away.

6.3.   Starting Over

The Feldafing Displaced Persons (DP) camp was operated by the United Nations Relief and Rehabilitation Administration (UNRRA). An international relief agency, it was largely dominated by the United States but represented 44 nations.[8]

Certificate issued by the United Nations Relief and Rehabilitation Administration to István Gárdos that enabled him to visit his wife in the Kaunitz Displaced Persons Camp.

With the help of UNRRA Pista was able to locate Juci in Kaunitz, about 400 miles away. They also helped him visit her and provided him with appropriate documentation. They were reunited sometime in August, nearly three months after their liberations.

In September they returned to Pécs in the hope of finding more surviving members of their families. They did not. From their parents' generation nobody survived the deportations. Of the 23 members of Pista's generation of the Handlei and Günsberger families

---

[8]UNRRA's purpose was to "plan, co-ordinate, administer or arrange for the administration of measures for the relief of victims of war in any area under the control of any of the United Nations through the provision of food, fuel, clothing, shelter and other basic necessities, medical and other essential services."

only six of his cousins survived, several physically and emotionally devastated. The entire generation of Pista's parents, as well as all the children, were murdered.

Three of Pista's maternal cousins survived: László Nyitrai, Vera Handlei and Ede Horváth. As was mentioned earlier, László lost his first wife in the Holocaust. He returned to Budapest, eventually remarried and had two sons. He lived his remaining life in Budapest and died around 1970. His sons – my wife's second cousins – were about our age, but as far as I remember we met them only once.

Vera's life after the Holocaust has been discussed above (see Section 5.1). We do not know much about Ede Horvát's life except the fact that he died in Hungary in the early 1980s.

Three of Pista's first cousins on his father's side also survived the Holocaust: Rudolf, Irma and László Günzberger. I do not know anything about the fate of Rudolf and Irma, but I know that László Günzberger Hungarianized his name to Gáti and later emigrated to the U.S. He lived in California and had a daughter, Zsuzsa. We met Zsuzsa once in California, but I do not know much about her life.

The devastation of the Bíró family was also extensive. Juci's paternal aunt Zelma and her entire family were murdered, so were Etel, her husband and their four children. Juci's paternal uncle, Béla starved to death in the Budapest Ghetto, while his wife and two children were murdered. His third child, József Bíró (everyone called him Józsi to distinguish him from his uncle), survived the Mauthausen concentration camp. When Juci and Pista returned to Pécs from deportation in September 1945 they only found two relatives alive on the Bíró-Hirtenstein side of the family: Juci's paternal cousin, the younger József Bíró (Józsi) and Juci's paternal aunt Flóra. Józsi's wife, Márta Reiner, and their little daughter Zsuzsa had survived by hiding in Budapest. We will hear about them in later chapters of this book.

By the 1930s, Flóra and her family had moved to Budapest. She and her husband, Ármin Gyulai, survived the horrors in the Ghetto. He was blind from the wounds he suffered during World War I and he was in poor health. Their 34 year old son, József Gyulai, died in forced military labor (MUSZ). Except those who survived abroad, everyone else perished.

In 1949 Flóra's husband suddenly died and Juci and Pista invited Flóra to move in with them. She accepted and she became the "grandmother" of Eszter.

That same year, 1949, the Iron Curtain cut off those who lived abroad from those who had survived the Holocaust and it was only in 1968 that Juci again met her "Western" relatives.

✂ ✂

There have been many studies discussing how Holocaust survivors reacted to the unspeakable horrors they went through. Some became deeply religious, some had survivors' guilt and never forgave themselves for getting through alive. Some became Zionists and the creators of the state of Israel pledging that Jews should never again depend on anybody else for defending themselves. Some decided that being a Jew caused so much tragedy for themselves and their loved ones that the only practical solution was rapid and full assimilation to the general population. Juci, Pista and Vera belonged to this latter category.

When Juci and Pista returned to Pécs they found strangers living in their apartment.

They were ethnic Hungarian refugees who had had to leave their homes in Serbia or Romania. They felt that being "real" Hungarians they had every right to "inherit" Jewish property. They felt so comfortable in the house that they preserved (and used) all household items, including furniture, dishes, linens, everything. In one respect this was fortunate, because this way Juci and Pista regained most of their belongings. But, it took Pista quite a bit of effort to repossess their own apartment.

Juci was the intellectual leader of the family. Smart and persuasive, she had great influence on Pista. After all the horrors of World War II and the Holocaust she came to the conclusion that the only "good guys" on the political scene were the Communists. She was also very impressed by the determination of the Soviet Union to defeat fascism, and highly appreciated the sacrifices the Soviets had made in the war. She had come from a very well to do family but she did not care about wealth any more. She never wore expensive jewelry, neither did she want to own any. She knew that all money and wealth could be taken away any minute, and that only the knowledge one had was his/her own. She decided that they were not Jews, but Communists, and tried to live according to these principles. As we will see later, she only partially succeeded.

After their return to Pécs, Juci and Pista lived according to these principles. They almost immediately joined the Hungarian Communist Party and remained members until the collapse of the Communist regime. They never talked openly about their Jewish roots, even though everyone in Pécs knew about them. This reaction was fairly typical among Hungarian Jews. Unfortunately, as recent Hungarian history shows, assimilation did not work because the "real" Hungarians dislike and mistrust Jews. Their attitude is reflected by the old saying: "A Yid is always a Yid." In other words, most people believe that Jews will always be loyal to the Jewish people before they consider the interests of their country. This was the intellectual tragedy of Juci and Pista: the incompatibility of their beliefs and Hungarian reality.

✄ ✄

Juci was a sophisticated modern woman who had deep contempt for housework. She particularly despised cooking and avoided the kitchen at all cost. The first few years after the Holocaust she did not have any household help and was forced to do some cooking. There are several often repeated stories about her misadventures in the kitchen, but one is particularly funny (or sad if you wish). After the death of Vera's husband she returned to Pécs and lived with Pista and Juci for a few months. These were still difficult economic times with food shortages. Pista was already practicing law focusing on individual litigations. Sometime in 1947 he successfully represented a farmer who was very grateful for the service and gave Pista a live goose to express his appreciation. This was a huge gift at the time and the three intellectuals, Pista, Juci and Vera, decided to join forces to turn the goose into meals. Pista managed to kill the goose and remove its feathers. At this point the goose was turned over to Juci and Vera who decided to roast it. They found a huge pan, placed the goose in it and into the oven it went. Since they had never spent any time in the kitchen they had no idea that the internal parts needed to be removed first. Finally, after several hours the goose was ready. It was nice, brown and crispy. It was also inedible, because the gall had ruptured and its contents penetrated every bit of the bird. They had to discard the entire goose.

✂ ✂

On June 14, 1946 the second son of Juci and Pista was born. They named him György. The birth of a "Phoenix Child" brought them great pleasure. The joy, however, soon turned into tragedy. When György was 4 months old he had a bad attack of hiccups. They called their pediatrician who gave a tranquilizer injection to the child. György fell asleep and never woke up. He was buried in the Jewish cemetery of Pécs. Juci and Pista used this tragic occasion to erect a small memorial to their murdered family.

Juci and Pista did not give up. Just like many other Holocaust survivor couples they were determined to have a child to renew life. Their second Phoenix Child was born on August 24, 1948. They named her Eszter, a very appropriate name for a post-Holocaust girl: Eszter (or Esther) is one of the most important figures in Jewish history – a woman who saved the Jewish people from extermination.[9] Eszter was also a brilliantly chosen name because it was popular among both Jews and Christians. When Eszter was growing up she was always told that she had an old Persian name. While this was literally true, it kept her ignorant of her Jewish roots.

György Gárdos' grave in the Jewish cemetery of Pécs commemorating the murdered members of the Bíró and Günsberger families.

Like most post-Holocaust Phoenix children Eszter was cherished beyond belief. Her parents were always afraid of losing her. Subsequently she was raised in a most protective environment. We will talk about her upbringing in the next part of this book.

---

[9]According to the Bible, Esther was the Jewish wife of the Persian king Ahasuerus. Ahasuerus is traditionally identified with Xerxes I during the time of the Achaemenid empire. The Book of Esther is a book in the Ketuvim ("writings"), the third section of the Jewish Tanakh (the Hebrew Bible) and is part of the Christian Old Testament. It tells the story of a Jewish girl named Esther (her Hebrew name was Hadassah), who became queen of Persia and thwarted a plan to commit genocide against her people. The Book of Esther (or the Megillah) is the basis and an integral part of the Jewish celebration of Purim.

Part II

The Phoenix Generation

7

Tamás

7.1. Early Years

I, Tamas István Gombosi, was born on January 19, 1947, almost exactly nine months after my mother, Magda Róna, returned to Budapest from Sweden where she had been taken after her liberation from the Bergen-Belsen concentration camp (see Section 3.5).

Hope was abundant, even though the winds of the Cold War were already blowing through Europe. On the Glauber side of the family the devastation was almost complete. My grandfather, Dezső Gombosi, perished in the Ghetto, my aunt, Juci Gombosi, stayed behind in Sweden and my father's older sister, Rózsi Gombosi had died before the war. On the Róna side, however, the immediate family remained mostly intact. Both of my mother's brothers survived, so did their families. My Uncle Laci was now married to Gizi Duda and they lived in the Izabella Street apartment together with Róna, Magda, my father, János and my sister, Éva.

Az én testvérem.	My Brother
Megjöttél, megjöttél Nem hiába vártam Elhoztad szemedben Az ég kék ragyogását.	You arrived, you arrived I did not wait in vain You brought in your eyes The blue shine of the sky.
Elhoztad szájadban Angyaloknak csókját Két kis kezed meg a lábad Mindig kapálódzik	You brought in your mouth The kiss of angels Your two little hands and feet Are constantly jiggling.
Szájacskád meg, ha Valami nem tetszik Félre, félre csússzik Fogsz te még sírni megríni,	If you do not like something Your little mouth Slides, slides aside You will cry and cry.
De én azt se bánom Hogy is haragudnék Én rád ezen a világon.	But I do not mind that How could I be angry With you in this world.

Éva Gombosi's poem to Tamás written in 1947.

Three children were born in the extended Róna family in rapid succession. Since Miklós found his wife and daughter the day the Ghetto was liberated, they were the first to have a Phoenix Child, my maternal cousin, Ágnes (Ági), who was born in December 1945. She was followed by two cousins on her father's side: myself (January 1947) and two months later, Laci's daughter, Mariann (March 1947). Mariann (everyone called her Mari) and I lived in the same apartment, and consequently became "twins." The only boy among the Róna grandchildren, I was particularly pampered and spoiled. My grandfather Róna adored me, even though he always tried to bring some discipline to the family.

My sister, Éva, was elated to have a little brother, even though I was not a beautiful newborn (very few are). When she first saw me in the hospital she started to cry. Later however, I gained weight and started to look like a typical, well fed baby and Éva soon made peace with her little brother. Indeed, during the 1945-47 time pe-

Éva and Tamás Gombosi's in 1947.

riod she had regularly been writing poetry. Most of her early poems were expressions of yearning after her missing mother. Yet, after my birth she wrote a moving poem to her baby brother.

As the poem shows she became very fond of her brother, and loved to push me in my stroller and take me along. Éva still has a little booklet of her poems from this time. They are very moving and show much more maturity than one would expect from a 10 year old.

Once, Éva was babysitting for me and tried to feed me some fruit. I was sitting in my high chair, and, as usual, was restless and wiggled until I managed to free myself and leaned over until I fell out, head first, to the floor. Needless to say, I started to scream my head off. Éva got so scared that she picked me up and ran directly to the doctor's office. On the way she met our mother, who listened to her son's screaming and decided that he was just fine. Ever since, Éva has teased me that in that fall I managed to knock a screw loose in my head. In return, I retort that Éva intentionally dropped me on my head to make her brother a bit crazy.

Another family legend demonstrates the unconditional love and adoration my mother, Magda, had for her son. Since several families lived together in the Izabella Street apartment (Róna, Laci and his family, and Magda and our family) they made it a custom to have Sunday lunch together. According to custom (at least at that time) lunch ("ebéd" in Hungarian) was the main meal of the day. Sunday lunch was always a big family event when everyone gathered around the large oval dinner table. Once the soup was served and after the family started to eat, Magda moved to change my diaper on a sofa near the dinner table. The moment I had no diapers, I immediately released a fountain and had a direct hit in Laci's soup. Family lore says that Magda was genuinely offended when Laci refused to

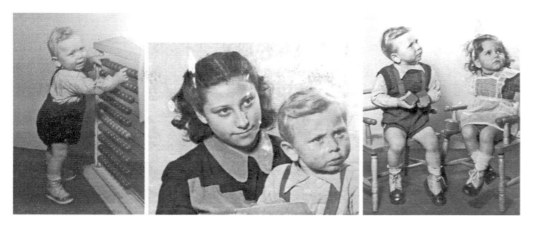

A set of pictures taken in 1948. From left to right: Tamás expresses early interest in scientific computing, Éva and Tamás, Tamás and Mari.

finish his somewhat diluted soup.

These were very happy times for the Róna-Gombosi family. The babies brought joy and chaos to the life of everyone. Éva blossomed into a young woman and Mari and I adored her. In effect, we had two mothers, since Éva was happy to help out with the babies. I became a pretty chubby baby (I am still not exactly underweight) and was dubbed "Hercules." I found three pictures taken around the time when Mari and I were a year old. The picture on the left shows me playing with an abacus.[1] I personally love this picture because it foretells my future life; even at this early age I loved playing with "computational" devices. As a matter of fact, I still do. The middle picture shows Éva and me. Love is radiating from Éva's face and I am looking very seriously into the camera. The picture on the right shows the "twins." At this age Mari and I were inseparable. We remained very close for the rest of our lives until Mari's untimely death of a very aggressive form of breast cancer in 1992.

✂ ✂

In the late 1940s Hungarian culture was quite biased towards boys – it still is. Even in the middle of the 20th century, in rural Hungary, the word "child" only referred to male children. A Hungarian farmer would have said "I have two children and a daughter." Sons represented income and economic stability. Men supported their female relatives until they married. Being the only boy in the Róna-Gombosi family, among five grandchildren, endowed me with a special status hard to comprehend in present day America. This status is well represented by a family photo taken sometime in 1949. It shows the entire Róna family. The patriarch, Róna, stands in the middle of the adult generation. The five grandchildren sit in front of the adults. Note who is in the middle. It is not Éva, the oldest grandchild, but myself, the only grandson.

Today I sort of understand the psychology of the family, but it still amazes me how spoiled these children – and especially myself – were. We were supposed to make up for all the tragedies, horrors, and suffering our parents and grandparents had gone through. As

---

[1] The abacus, also called a counting frame, is a calculating tool used primarily in Russia and parts of Asia for performing arithmetic processes.

The extended Róna family in 1949. Standing (from left to right): János Gombosi, Magda Róna, Éva Schwarcz, Róna, Laci Róna, Gizi Duda and Miklós Róna. Sitting (from left to right): Éva Gombosi, Ágnes Róna, Tamás Gombosi, Mari Róna and Judit Róna.

a result, I was raised as a "fetish," or "sacred taper" (szentelt gyertya) as Róna called me. This upbringing had some very positive and some negative impacts on my life. I became very self-confident (sometimes overconfident) which served me well later in life. I was fortunate to be talented enough to justify my confidence most of the time, but sometimes I did get into trouble when I overplayed my hand. We will see plenty of examples of both later in this book.

✂ ✂

After World War II ended Róna returned to work. He was 63 years old, way beyond retirement age, but he was a good typesetter and there was great demand for his services. He joined the Független Nyomda (Independent Press) and became very active in the Social Democratic Party (SDP) and in the Trade Union movement. Soon he was elected to be the union representative for all union workers at Független Nyomda. When in 1948 the SDP was forced to merge with the Hungarian Communist Party (at that time it was called the Hungarian Working Peoples Party), Róna refused to join the new party. In spite of (or because of) his principled action he remained extremely popular with his colleagues. In 1950 he was awarded the highest civilian medal of the country, the Gold Medal of the Order of Merit of the Peoples Republic of Hungary (Magyar Népköztársasági Érdemérem Arany Fokozata).

The early 1950s were the darkest years of Hungarian Communism. There were shortages of food and of all consumer goods. It was difficult to buy the most basic necessities and the political atmosphere was very repressive. Independent small businesses were tolerated, but regularly harassed by the authorities. My father, János, was working alone in the Műhely and business was quite good. He was a good and honest craftsman and his customers liked his work very much. Among the customers were a number of artists and, somewhat surprisingly, churches. During the war many of the churches had been damaged or vandalized and there were a lot of large picture frames to be restored.

Lajos Róna's Gold Medal of the Order of Merit of the Peoples Republic of Hungary (Magyar Népköztársasági Érdemérem Arany Fokozata) certificate.

Sometime around 1950 Magda went back to work. I think the main reason was that Éva was getting close to high school graduation and Magda and János were worried about her future. Small business owners were labeled "x-class" (see Appendix A.13) and their children were practically excluded from higher education. Thus, Magda wanted to work in an office, so that she could claim to belong to a politically acceptable class. She found work as a typist in the Budapest offices of "Sztálin Vasmű" (Stalin Ironworks), a huge, politically motivated government investment. The Communist government created an entire new city called "Sztálinváros[2]" named after Joseph Stalin to host this new heavy industry. Since all core ingredients had to be imported (Hungary had only low quality iron and coal) the Sztálin Vasmű always operated with huge losses.

Just about this time Magda became pregnant again. I am sure that this was a very difficult decision for my parents, but they eventually decided to terminate the pregnancy. Many years later my mother told me that she would have had a second son. For the rest of her life she deeply resented the fact that she could not bring all of her children to this world.

Róna retired at the end of 1952 at the age of 70. After his retirement he became the chief food purchaser for the family. Food was difficult to come by; most shops were either empty or had very limited stocks. The Hunyadi tér market was only a couple of short blocks from the Izabella Street apartment and Róna very quickly established himself as an insider at the market. The costermongers, who were selling everything from fruits and vegetables to goose and any other farm products, loved him. He flirted with the women and drank wine in the neighborhood bar with the men.

Shopping took up the mornings, but in the afternoon Róna went to the Abbázia café

---

[2]Today the city is renamed to Dunaujvaros.

and spent a couple of hours talking politics with his fellow retirees. They had a regular table with a core group of about six people. He kept this habit until the late 1960s and only stopped going to Abbázia when he became too ill.

Magda and János had a small circle of friends, all with children of similar age. Their closest friends were Mária (Marcsa) and László (Laci) Koltai (they Hungarianized their name from Küchler after the war). The Koltais had two children, Vera and István (Pista) who were the same ages as Éva and I and had been close family friends dating back to the time when Éva was born. Laci Koltai was a tailor who made coats for children. Just like János, he ran his own small business. A born salesman, he could talk up his merchandise and sell almost anything. He was also a charming name-dropper who could make himself look very important. In spite of his weaknesses, Magda and János were really fond of him. Marcsa was much quieter, since

Magda Gombosi in her office at Sztálin Vasmű around 1952. At the time there were practically no electric typewriters in Hungary, and certainly none that allowed back-spacing to correct errors, so the office work was quite demanding.

not much room was left for her around Laci. Unfortunately, she died in 1962 of breast cancer and I only have some very vague memories of her.

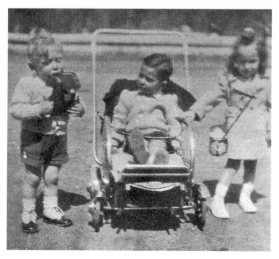

Childhood friends in 1949. From left to right: Tamás Gombosi, István Koltai and Ágnes Rózsási.

There were several other couples in the inner circle of Magda and János, the Áldor, Gyimes and Rózsási families. György Áldor had a fine leather shop that was quite profitable. His wife, Erzsébet (Bözsi) was a stunning redhead. In the circle of friends she was referred to as Vörös (Red) Bözsi. They had two children, Judit and Péter. Péter was my age, Judit a little bit older (if I am not mistaken). During the 1956 Hungarian uprising (see Appendix A.13), the Iron Curtain was briefly lifted and about 200,000 people left Hungary. The Áldors were among those who left, leaving practically everything behind. They eventually moved to Canada. We pretty much lost contact with the Áldors, even though my sister once met them in Toronto sometime in the early 1970s.

I do not remember much about the Gyimes family except that they had a son and a daughter, Ágnes and Gábor. Ágnes was my age and Gábor was a few years younger. Unfortunately, I do not know what happened to them.

László (Laci) Rózsási worked for the Hungarian Airlines (MALÉV) as a bus driver. Later, he became the head of the ground transportation department. They had a daughter, Ágnes (Ági). Smart and pretty, she first became a flight attendant for MALÉV and a few years later finished college and worked as the representative of IATA (International Air Transport Association) in Hungary.

Until the 1970s the workweek in Hungary was 48 hours long; Saturday was a regular weekday. This left Sunday as the only day families and friends could get together and relax. So, Sundays the Gombosis met with their friends. When the weather was nice they liked to go for short hikes in the hills on the Buda side of town. I still remember these hikes with a large group of adults and children. One of my most vivid childhood memories is when my parents, Magda and János, got together with their friends and we children were playing around. The adults thought that we did not hear anything, but we were all ears. On these occasions they talked about their horrors. I remember hearing words like "lager" (concentration camp), "kapo[3]," "SS," and other Holocaust related expressions. Needless to say, we had no idea what these words meant, but we were able to understand that they had very bad meanings. Even today I deeply dislike Sunday afternoons because in my mind they are associated with these whispered words.

✂ ✂

On page 112 I included a map showing the main locations of my daily life before high school graduation. Note that all these locations were within about a square mile, making my childhood very localized. During this time I had very little contact with the outside world.

Because my mother was working full time, I needed daycare. Fortunately for the family, there was a Jewish daycare facility very close to the famous Fasor Gimnázium (see Appendix A.10).

My first days at daycare were disastrous. I've been told that I just sat in a corner crying. After nearly a week, when my mother was ready to give up, I finally started to warm up and joined some games. Later I loved daycare and very much enjoyed the company of other children.

The daycare was for children between the ages 3 to 6. It was organized to three classes: "little," "intermediate" and "big" groups. These three groups had separate tables at lunch and separate areas for afternoon naps. Most children (including myself) spent a full day at the daycare, usually from about 8 a.m. to 5 p.m. It also provided three meals

Tamás Gombosi in 1951.

---

[3]A kapo was a prisoner in a Nazi concentration camp who was assigned by the SS guards to supervise forced labor or carry out administrative tasks in the camp. The system was designed to turn victim against victim, as the kapos were pitted against their fellow prisoners in order to maintain the favor of their SS guards. Many kapos were recruited from the ranks of violent criminal gangs rather than from the more numerous political, religious and racial prisoners; those were known for their brutality toward other prisoners. This brutality was tolerated by the SS and was an integral part of the concentration camp system.

The main places of Tamás' life before the age of 18. ① – Izabella Street apartment, ② – Jewish daycare, ③ – elementary school, ④ – Hunyadi tér synagoge, ⑤ – József Mandl's apartment, ⑥ – Ferenc Kölcsey high school, ⑦ – practical mechanics class, ⑧ – location of daily soccer games, ⑨ – Ervin Szabó library branch, ⑩ – former Fasor Gimnázium.

for every child: a midmorning snack, lunch and a mid-afternoon snack. I have no idea who paid for all of this, but I am quite sure it was heavily subsidized by the Hungarian Jewish community (government subsidies were not given to faith-based organizations).

There are three events I still remember from daycare. The first was a horrifying experience and I am still amazed how lucky I was. One day Róna picked me and we were walking home in the Fasor (literally Esplanade, a major street in the heart of Jewish Budapest). Suddenly I noticed Mari on the other side of the street as she was taken home from her daycare. Within a fraction of a second I freed my hand from Róna's grip and ran across the street to greet Mari. The driver of a trolley approaching at full speed was able to stop the vehicle a few inches from me. There was a huge commotion. The driver shouted at Róna, speechless from the scare. I vividly remember him taking me home and locking me into the WC (toilet) for at least an hour until my mother returned home. I think this was one of the very few occasions that my grandfather punished me.

The second event happened at the beginning of my second year in daycare. I was a boy with strong loyalties and habits. In the first year I had an assigned seat at lunch at the table of "little" kids. In September 1951 I started my second year and was now in the middle group with different teachers and a different lunch table. I was, however, so used to my old teachers and old assigned seat that I refused to move to the new table, even though it represented a higher "social status" among kids. The teachers finally allowed me to stay in my old place, allowing me gradually to warm to the idea of change.

My third memory is of March 6, 1953. As I was walking with my mother to daycare, I noticed that all buildings had huge black flags hanging from the walls and flagpoles. It was as if the entire city had been covered with black. I asked my mother about the flags and she said that Stalin had died. I had no clue who Stalin was (lucky me), but the sight of the city covered with black stays in my memory.

7.2. Éva and Gyuri

My sister Éva played a major role in my life. When I was little Éva was a substitute mother. Later, when I was big enough to show some independence, a strange type of sibling rivalry developed between us. I instinctively learned how to push her to her limits while I could always count on our mother to intervene and rescue me when Éva lost her patience.

She attended an all-girls high school, the Katalin Varga high school, only a couple of blocks from the Iz-abella Street apartment. The principal of the school was Mrs. István Otta, the wife of Major General István Otta, the all powerful commander of the Hungarian Military Academy during the Rákosi regime (see Appendix A.13). Mrs. Otta ran a very tight ship and Communist indoctrination was at the center of most after-school activities. There was a strict dress code (as unfashionable as possible) and frivolous activities (like dancing with boys) were

Éva Gombosi in 1953.

strictly forbidden. Over the years I met with several graduates of the Varga Katalin high school, and without exception, they uniformly hated Mrs. Otta.

My sister was an outstanding student: hard working, smart and ambitious. Her grades were uniformly excellent and she dreamed of a career in mathematics or physics. At first this looked somewhat questionable because of her "x-class" background (see Appendix A.13), but in her senior year she placed first or second (she does not remember) in the national science competition for high-school students. This gave her an almost automatic admission to the School of Natural Sciences of the Loránd Eötvös University (ELTE TTK), the premier science university in Hungary.

Our parents were delighted to have such a talented, driven daughter. Éva was the first in the entire Gombosi-Róna family to be admitted to a university and the fact that she won a national recognition made her parents even prouder. They bragged about their daughter to anyone who would listen, including the regular costumers of the Műhely. In a strange way, this bragging turned out to be critical for the future of not only Éva, but myself as well.

In the 1950s, one of the regular customers of the Műhely was Mrs. Gertrude Lukács, the wife of György (George) Lukács, a famous and highly controversial Marxist philosopher, oscillating between communist movement discipline and sovereign philosophical thought and causing a lot of headaches for the party leadership both in Hungary and in the Soviet Union. But it was *Mrs.* Lukács who had a lasting influence on Éva's life.

Gertrude Borstrieber was the daughter of a rabbi and by training, a mathematician belonging to the first generation of Hungarian women with university degrees. Around 1910 she married the Hungarian astronomer/mathematician Imre Jánossy and they had two sons:

Lajos (1912) and Ferenc (1914). They lived in Vienna where Imre died in 1920 leaving Gertrude with two small sons. After the death of her first husband she married György (George) Lukács, who was wanted by the Hungarian authorities as one the leaders of the Hungarian Communist Revolution of 1919.

György Lukács had been born György Löwinger in 1885 in Budapest to the investment banker József Löwinger and his wife Adele Wertheimer, a wealthy Jewish family. His father Hungarianized the family name to Lukács in 1890. In 1901 the family obtained nobility and György officially became "Georg Bernhard Lukács von Szegedin."

After the Russian Revolution of 1917, Lukács became a committed Marxist and joined the fledgling Communist Party of Hungary in 1918. As part of the government of the short-lived Hungarian Soviet Republic (see Appendix A.11), Lukács was made People's Commissar for Education and Culture. After the collapse of the short-lived regime Lukács faced a certain death sentence in Hungary. He hid with friends and eventually was smuggled out of Hungary by a high ranking military officer for an enormous amount of money. This sum was provided by his father whom he had previously renounced.

He hid in Vienna with false papers. But, was eventually recognized by an acquaintance and arrested. The Hungarian government demanded that Austria extradite all the Commissars, including George Lukács. In the end Austria did not give in – due to the combined pressure of western intellectuals and the Soviet government which threatened to harm all high ranking Austrian officers it was holding as prisoners of war if the Commissars were extradited to Hungary. Eventually the Commissars were given political asylum and were able to stay in Austria.

George Lukács and Gertrude Borstrieber knew each other from pre-war Budapest (Lukács was Gertrud's wedding witness) and they got together in Vienna after Imre Jánossy's death. Eventually they married and thus George Lukács became the stepfather of the two Jánossy boys. In 1930 George and Gertrude Lukács moved to Moscow, but the Jánossy boys, sixteen and eighteen at the time, stayed behind and moved to Berlin. Lukács survived Stalin's purges which claimed as many as 80% of the Hungarian émigrés to the Soviet Union. After the war Lukács returned to Hungary with Rákosi and became a respected but controversial intellectual leader of Hungarian communist ideology. He remained very influential until his death in 1971.

Lajos Jánossy attended high school in Vienna and university in Vienna and Berlin. In 1936 he moved to London where he worked at Birbeck College. In 1938 he joined the cosmic ray[4] research group at the University of Manchester. The leader of this group was Patrick Blackett who later received the Nobel Prize in physics for his work on cosmic rays. In 1947 he joined Erwin Schrödinger at the Dublin Institute for Advanced Studies in Ireland. By 1950 Lajos Jánossy was a promising scientist with a worldwide reputation, but he certainly was in the second tier, well behind the young stars of the day, like Richard Feynman[5] (1918-1988) or Lev Landau[6] (1908-1968).

---

[4]Cosmic rays are very high-energy particles, mainly originating outside the Solar System.

[5]Richard Phillips Feynman was an American theoretical physicist. For his contributions to the development of quantum electrodynamics, he received the Nobel Prize in Physics in 1965. He assisted in the development of the atomic bomb during World War II and became known to a wide public in the 1980s as a member of the Rogers Commission, the panel that investigated the Space Shuttle Challenger disaster.

[6]Lev Davidovich Landau was a prominent Soviet physicist who made fundamental contributions to many

After her return from Moscow, Gertrude Lukács was very eager to have her sons back in Hungary. Her younger son, Ferenc, had already returned from exile, but Lajos was in Ireland. She used her influence and the Hungarian government made an unprecedented offer to Lajos Jánossy. He was offered regular membership in the Hungarian Academy of Sciences (a nearly unprecedented step, since he was not even a Corresponding Member), a full Professorship at the most prestigious Hungarian science university, the Loránd Eötvös University (ELTE), and a large research group at the newly founded Central Research Institute for Physics of the Hungarian Academy of Sciences (the Hungarian abbreviation is KFKI[7]). Lajos Jánossy accepted this irresistible offer and in 1950 returned to Hungary.

When Lajos Jánossy returned to Budapest the Hungarian physics community was pretty much "Judenrein" (cleansed of Jews). The "Martians" (see Appendix A.10), including Szilárd, Teller, Wiegner and others, were in the U.S.A. and many lesser known Jewish scientists had either perished in the Holocaust or left Hungary. Those who remained in Hungary were solid scientists, but far from world class. They mainly belonged to the Christian intelligentsia that had a moderately nationalistic and anti-semitic world view (see Appendix A.15). Even though they themselves did not participate in cleansing Hungarian physics of Jews, they did like the end result of the "Judenfrei" (free of Jews) physics community.

Jánossy's return upset this community for two reasons. First, they resented that someone was brought back from abroad and given recognition and resources they did not have. Second, they did not like the fact that Jánossy was not only a highly connected Communist, but also a Jew. Clearly, there was noticeable friction between Jánossy and the rest of the physics community from day one.

Soon after his return, Jánossy started to assemble his team of scientists. In the 1950s cosmic ray research encompassed what today we call quantum mechanics,[8] astrophysics,[9] elementary particle physics[10] and space physics.[11] Jánossy founded the Department of Cosmic Rays at KFKI and started hiring his associates.

By 1953 Jánossy had hired most of his key personnel. Among the new hires were several Jews who later played a major role in KFKI and in the Hungarian physics community. From the perspective of the Gombosi family the important early hires were Ervin Fenyves and Antal Somogyi. Fenyves was the leader as he had the most actual experience with cosmic ray research, while Somogyi was his deputy. These hires were typical of Jánossy's group in the sense that Fenyves was Jewish and Somogyi was a typical member of the Hungarian Christian intelligentsia. Intentionally or unintentionally, about half of Jánossy's hires were Jewish, in stark contrast with ELTE, which was pretty much kept Judenfrei with very few exceptions.

---

areas of theoretical physics. He received the 1962 Nobel Prize in Physics for his development of a mathematical theory of superfluidity.

[7]Központi Fizikai Kutató Intézet.

[8]Quantum physics deals with atomic and subatomic length scales. It provides a mathematical description of much of the dual particle-like and wave-like behavior and interactions of energy and matter.

[9]Astrophysics is the study of the physics of the universe, including the physical properties of celestial objects, as well as their interactions and behavior.

[10]Particle physics studies the existence and interactions of subatomic particles.

[11]Space physics is the study of solar system plasmas.

From left to right: Lajos Jánossy in the 1950s, Ervin Fenyves in 1960s and Antal Somogyi in the 1970s.

✄ ✄

When Éva graduated from high school in 1953 she was brought to Gertrude Lukács' attention by our father János Gombosi. Gertrude was an active patron of talented young people, and particularly eager to help young women. Gertrude suggested that Éva should apply for a summer internship in her son's research group at KFKI. Éva applied, and needless to say, received a highly coveted internship right away. Ah, the power of Jewish mothers; Éva was not even a university student at the time and I am sure that her sudden appearance at KFKI raised curiosity among the young research staff.

During her summer internship Éva met György Bozóki (everyone called him Gyuri). Gyuri was a physics student about to start his fifth (senior) year at ELTE and planning to write his senior thesis concerning cosmic ray research. They were attracted to each other and when later that summer Gyuri was called up for reserve military duty he kept in contact with Éva. Later that year Gyuri was introduced to the Gombosi family, and as they say, the rest is history. I adored Gyuri, and I took him as my older brother. It is due largely to Gyuri's influence that I decided to become a physicist.

Gyuri was born in 1930, the only son of Gyula Braun and Erzsébet Kronstein. Gyula was a Jewish merchant in Kunhegyes (Jász-Nagykun-Szolnok Province). He owned a general store in this city of about 8,000 people. The entire Braun family had miraculously survived the Holocaust. When they were deported from Kunhegyes the Jews were crammed onto two trains. One went directly to Auschwitz, the other to Austria where the deported families were kept together and "loaned" to local farmers to work on the fields. The Brauns were on this second train. Practically nobody returned alive from the first train. Even though the Brauns had to live under deplorable conditions in Austria, their lives were not in constant danger. Luck was on their side this time.

After the Holocaust, the Brauns returned to Kunhegyes. Gyuri finished high school and as soon as he turned eighteen, changed his name from Braun to the Hungarian sounding Bozóki. In 1949 he was admitted to ELTE where he studied physics. Shortly after the formation of the cosmic ray group, Gyuri started to work with Ervin Fenyves who was one of Jánossy's deputies.

Ervin came from a well-to-do Jewish family (they owned a pharmacy, so they belonged to the "x-class," see Appendix A.13), but he masterfully adapted to the new regime. He was a good politician and able to earn Jánossy's trust. He was a good enough scientist, but not so good as to threaten Jánossy's supremacy. It is interesting to note – with the hindsight of history – that Jánossy was very careful not to allow any of his disciples to be good enough to challenge him. This is fairly typical among mediocre scientists. By mediocre I mean compared to the best in the world. Jánossy and his associates were as good as anyone in Hungary, but one has to realize the isolation and lack of resources impacting Hungarian scientists due to travel restrictions and the lack of access to advanced technol-

Gyögy Bozóki with the electronics unit of a cosmic ray experiment in 1956. The roomful of controllers today could be replaced several times over by an iPhone.

ogy. It was not until years later that scientists as talented and ambitious as Jánossy himself were hired to the Cosmic Ray Division.

Gyuri officially joined the Cosmic Ray Division of KFKI in 1953 when he started his senior year at ELTE (today you need to have your M.Sc degree completed before you can do this). It was customary at this time for students to write their senior thesis while already working. Gyuri obtained his M.Sc. degree in the summer of 1954 and at this point officially became a member of Jánossy's research empire.

Gyuri was a very talented physicist with extremely broad interests from high energy particles, to astrophysics, to quantum physics. I know very few scientists with such broad interests. Gyuri, however, was not a good politician and, as we say today in the U.S., he was too nice to succeed. He was constantly outmaneuvered by Fenyves and the other politically astute scientists. Worse than that, Fenyves and company regularly took Gyuri's ideas and ran with them. In the KFKI, Gyuri was destined to be a valued but exploited second fiddle.

✂ ✂

Éva and Gyuri decided to get married sometime in 1955 and scheduled a wedding date for late October of 1956. However, fate did not allow Éva to have her dream wedding. On October 23, 1956 the Hungarian Revolution broke out (see Appendix A.13) and the country quickly descended into total chaos. There was fighting and it was quite unsafe to be on the streets of Budapest.

During a brief lull in the fighting Éva and Gyuri married on November 2, 1956 just before Soviet troops providing "brotherly help" killed nearly 3,000 people. Years later Gyuri joked that their wedding was celebrated by thousands of gun salutes. During the uprising 200,000 people, about 2% of the entire population, left Hungary. Unfortunately only the immediate family was able to attend the wedding held at a major wedding hall just a few blocks from the Izabella Street apartment. It was a simple affair; they stood in front of a government clerk who gave some brief remarks before asking them to sign the wedding registry. They were also scheduled to have a Jewish wedding, but it was impossible during the fighting and later they just never got to it. I am teasing them until this day that, by Jewish law, they are not married, but only domestic partners (by the way, so are my wife and I).

Wedding picture of Éva and Gyuri.

My sister graduated from ELTE in 1958 and she too was hired by the Cosmic Ray Division of KFKI. As a student she had worked for Antal Somogyi (everyone called him Tóni), but after graduation she joined the particle physics group in the Cosmic Ray Division. This is an interesting twist of history, since years later it was Somogyi who hired me when I graduated from ELTE. Éva was a combative woman with a temper and no patience for fools. She could not tolerate pontification and was quick to tell people what she had in mind. She was extremely smart, but a bad politician who always managed to dig a big hole for herself. This style was not well suited to get ahead in the politically charged world of Hungarian Socialism. It is funny to note that her male colleagues, even those who were much senior to her, were afraid to pick a fight with her. Her quick wit and sharp tongue generated both appreciation and contempt.

There is a family legend that even Jánossy was afraid of Éva. The story goes that once Éva was telling Jánossy why he was wrong and the only way Jánossy was able to stop her was by saying: "stop and take a breath." Éva is still being teased (by you can guess who) to shut up and take a breath.

7.3.   School Years

I started elementary school in the fall of 1953. At this time there were separate schools for boys and girls and I attended the boys' school a few short blocks from the Izabella Street apartment (see ③ on page 112). The school was in the heavily Jewish Terézváros district of Budapest and about 20% of my classmates were Jewish. Considering that after the Holocaust only about 1% of the Hungarian population was Jewish, this was a very high concentration of the "Phoenix generation."

There are several interesting stories about my elementary school adventures. In first grade kids were taught basic arithmetic, like addition and subtraction. These concepts came very naturally to me and soon I could do more basic arithmetic than was expected at the first grade level. Towards the end of the school year the fourth grade teachers "borrowed" me and made me demonstrate my skills in front of the fourth grade classes. The aim of this show was to shame the fourth graders that even a first grader could do better arithmetic than they were able to do. You can imagine how popular I was with the older kids after this "road show." I cannot imagine anything like this happening in an American school where the "self-esteem" of students is more important than actual learning.

In fourth grade I got into an argument with the teacher about basic arithmetic. The class was discussing how to check that you did not make a mistake in addition or subtraction. The teacher explained that one can check the result of addition by subtracting one of the terms from the result and getting the other term as the result. Next the class started to discuss how to check the result of subtraction. The teacher said that there was no simple way to do this. I responded that you can check the result of subtraction by adding the term we just subtracted to the result: this should result in the other term. The teacher said that I was wrong and I should not interrupt her. I insisted that I was right and I went to the blackboard and gave several examples. In the end the angry teacher sent me to the School Principal for disrespectful behavior.

While good in arithmetic and reading, I had a difficult time with writing neatly. I never learned to properly hold a pencil or pen (even today I hold them in a strange and uncomfortable way) and my homework typically looked horrible. At this time in Hungarian elementary schools students were also graded on "penmanship" (in Hungarian "külalak") and I often received low marks for the neatness of my work. Éva and Gyuri are still telling the story of me sitting with my mother doing homework while crying with frustration. Needless to say, tears made the homework even more messy, so my mother sometimes forced me to start over again. This, of course, caused even more crying, and the end result was that Magda lost her temper and the torture ended.

I also had serious problems with my behavior in school. In retrospect I probably suffered from ADHD (attention deficit hyperactivity disorder), but such problems were not diagnosed at that time. A very active child, teachers (and my parents) had difficulty focusing my attention. I easily grew bored in class and I showed it. On the other hand, when something really interested me I jumped on the problem immediately and did not rest until I solved it. I was respected by the other students, but I was not a popular kid.

In school I was always there when some mischief was committed. When I was in third or fourth grade the boys took advantage of the fact that most teachers were women and they could not go to the boys' bathroom to supervise. The urinals in the bathroom were quite old fashioned: there was a narrow trough running along the bottom of the wall and the wall above was covered with black tar up to about six feet high. During the breaks my friends and I held real pissing contests. We drew a line about six feet from the wall, lined up along the line and tried to pee as high on the tar covered wall as we could. Needless to say there were some accidents during these contests and sometimes the boys did have a particular odor around them.

I had a particularly difficult time with music classes. I was tone-deaf and could not sing even the simplest tunes. On the other hand, I was quite interested in the history of music and in the stories of famous operas. At this time I was not yet familiar with the famous quote from Jenő Rejtő, "when a story is so silly that one cannot tell it without being ashamed, they sing it." My lack of musical talent was unfortunate because the famous Hungarian composer, Zoltán Kodály, lived just around the corner from the Felsőerdősor elementary school and on several occasions visited the school. On these occasions I was relegated to the back of the classroom and told to remain silent.

When I was in 6th or 7th grade the Felsőerdősor elementary school changed its name to "Karikás Frigyes Elementary School." Frigyes Karikás was a Commissar during the short lived Hungarian Communist revolution of 1919 (see Appendix A.13) and escaped to the

Tamás Gombosi in 1957 (left); Róna, Magda, Tamás and János at the Műhely in 1958 (right).

Soviet Union after the fall of the revolution. On the occasion of changing the name of the school Mr. Karikás' widow and son visited. We were told that we could talk to them about anything, but under no circumstances should we ask how Mr. Karikás died. Needless to say this question became the talk of the school. Eventually most of us figured out what had happened to Mr. Karikás: he fell victim to Stalin's purges and had been murdered.

The most memorable event of my childhood was the Hungarian uprising of 1956. I was just 9 years old at this time, but the events left a very deep impression. It started on October 23 when government forces opened fire on demonstrators protesting against government restrictions. Fighting quickly escalated and eventually the Hungarian government asked the occupying Soviet troops to leave the country. There were a few days of quiet at the end of October before a provisional government was formed by János Kádár who asked the Soviets to return and help to defeat the revolution. The Soviet troops turned around and the uprising was quickly defeated.

From my perspective the uprising was fun. School was closed, the shops and factories were closed, so my parents were at home all the time. Since the stores were closed there was no bread and my mother baked pastry. I loved this pastry and had a great time playing with other children who lived in the Izabella Street apartment building. When the Soviet troops returned to Budapest there was Street fighting for a few days. This was the best part of the entire uprising. There was a technical high school just across from the apartment building where our family lived. This high school became a local headquarters of the revolutionaries. At some point three Soviet tanks moved in and started to shell the high school from close range. Their targeting was less than perfect, and the apartment building next to the high school also suffered several direct hits. In the end the revolutionaries escaped from the high school and the fighting ended.

During the fighting all residents of the apartment building moved to the bomb shelter of the building that also served as an underground storage area. It was large, poorly lit (when there was electricity) and a perfect place for hide and seek. The kids had a great time playing while the adults were very worried. When the fighting was over and the residents emerged from the bomb shelter, I found a handgun on the street. I immediately picked up the new toy and took it home. Little did I know that the Kádár government had declared martial law and anyone caught with any weapon was summarily sentenced to jail. When my mother noticed the gun she got really scared. She threw it out and slapped me for the first time in my life. I could not understand why she was so upset.

There were several scary moments during the uprising. As in any uprising, there were mob atrocities. Mobs regularly searched for members of the hated internal security forces, the ÁVH (AÁllamvédelmi Hivatal). When an ÁVH officer was found, the mob lynched him. This was pretty ugly, but there was so much hatred against the secret police that it was impossible to control the mobs. It was my maternal uncle, Laci Róna, who got in trouble with the mob. Laci liked to wear a coat that looked similar to the ones worn by the secret police (one can imagine how secret those police were when everyone could recognize them from their civilian clothing). Sure enough, a mob mistook Laci for an ÁVH officer and started to chase him. Finally Laci managed to escape, but this was a close call. I think he never wore that coat again.

As I have noted, Éva was supposed to marry during the weekend that the uprising began. The wedding had to be postponed because of the ongoing street fighting, but eventually took place. Because of the street fighting, Magda insisted that they spend their wedding night in the Izabella Street apartment – with Éva sleeping in her own bed in the room she shared with me, and Gyuri sleeping on a cot in the kitchen. With such arrangements it is no wonder it took them nine years to have a child...

At the same time, Éva and Gyuri already had a one room apartment in the Zuglo district of Budapest a few miles from the Izabella Street apartment. (According to the moral standards of times, they could not be there alone before the wedding.) The story behind this apartment is long and complicated, since there was a serious apartment shortage in Budapest. It took quite a bit of money and manipulation (Magda was great in this) to secure it. Éva and Gyuri were worried that someone might move into their empty apartment, so the day after their wedding they went to the Zugló apartment planning to spend a day or two there. When the fighting intensified they got stuck in the Zugló apartment and Magda was very worried about them. Eventually the war veteran Róna walked the few miles to Zugló and escorted the young couple back to the relative safety of the Izabella Street apartment.

Between November 1956 and January 1957 the western border of Hungary was open and about 200,000 Hungarians left the country. This was a huge brain drain; many of those who left were young, the best and brightest of the country. The loss of 2% of the population had a lasting impact on many aspects of life. My family was also debating the big question:

Tamás Gombosi's certificate of outstanding achievements at elementary school graduation. Translation: "To Tamás Gombosi for outstanding academic achievements ~~and exemplary behavior~~."

to go or to stay. Magda and Éva were ready to leave, János was ambivalent but ready to do whatever Magda decided. In the end it was Gyuri who refused to leave. Éva said that she was not going to leave without Gyuri, and Magda said that she was not leaving without Éva. Time ran out and the iron curtain closed again. It is ironic that 15 years later it was Éva and Gyuri who left Hungary and at that time the rest of the family could not go with them.

School started again in January 1957 and life slowly returned to normal. For a while there were shortages of everything: food, fuel, electricity, many everyday necessities. Occasionally school was closed due to the shortage of coal and I was very sorry when spring came and the heating season was over. Several relatives and close friends of our family left Hungary. The Áldors and the Rudnais moved to Canada and many others moved to the U.S. For a while we stayed in touch with those who left, but eventually we lost contact with them. The exception is my father's much younger paternal cousin, Gizi Glauber, with whom Éva and I still have regular contact.

I finished elementary school in the spring of 1961. On this occasion the school gave certificates of achievement to the best students. I received a pre-printed certificate that said "to Tamás Gombosi for his outstanding academic achievements and exemplary behavior." Unfortunately, the "exemplary behavior" was crossed out. I was somewhat ashamed about this insult, but my mother carefully saved the document. Many years later, when my daughter, Judit (Judy) had her most difficult teenage years my mother proudly presented her with this certificate with the comment, "You know, your father was not an angel either." I think this was my mother's revenge for all the grey hair she got because of my adventures.

✂ ✂

I had many adventures outside of school, some funny, others embarrassing. When I was 7 years old I got into an argument with two aggressive four years olds. They beat me up! When Róna heard what had happened he was furious that his grandson was such a wimp. To calm my grandfather I explained that since 2 times 4 was eight, two 4-year-olds were more than a 7 year old, so I was outnumbered. While I was mathematically correct Róna never let me forget that I was beaten up by two little kids.

I was in first grade when Éva started her university studies. There were very few women in physics at that time (unfortunately, even today their numbers are small) and Éva was particularly friendly with two of her fellow female students, Gabi (Gabriella) Pálla and Lonci (Ilona) Lovass. The three young women often studied together for exams. Once they were sitting around the big oval dinner table at our home working on their homework assignment. I was bored and crawled under the table and started to grope their legs. The girls were too well behaved to scream, but they did not enjoy the harassment. I got my punishment many years later when I started work at KFKI and met Gabi Pálla, who by that time was a senior scientist at the institute. "Tamás, I am so glad to see you!" cried out Gabi, "I have not seen you since you were groping my legs!" At this public humiliation I turned red, orange and purple at the same time and wished I could just disappear from the face of the Earth. Gabi got her revenge.

My closest friend in elementary school was József (Jóska) Mandl, the son of Holocaust survivors who had lost their first families in the Shoah, married after World War II, and had a late child. Thus, Jóska was as much a Phoenix Child as I, and we became close friends. Jóska lived just a few short blocks from our apartment (see ⑤ on page 112). We shared a desk for 8 years in elementary school. We started Hebrew school (Talmud Torah) at the Hunyadi tér Synagogue together in second grade. Jóska and I were the only Jewish children in our class who openly practiced Judaism. The other families either did not want or did not dare to show their

Typical shared schooldesk used in Hungary.

religion openly during a time when all religions were publicly denounced by the government and religious practice was a big negative for advancement.

After we graduated from elementary school Jóska and I parted company. I attended the Ferenc Kölcsey high school, while Jóska went to the Imre Madács high school. However, we kept in touch over the years. Jóska attended medical school and became Professor and Chair of the Department of Biological Chemistry at the Semmelweis Medical University at Budapest.

I loved to play soccer and spent many afternoons in the Városliget (City Park) where I played with school friends. The location of these soccer games is marked with ⑧ on page 112. This was a little bare corner in the Városliget, but it was only a ten minute walk from the Izabella Street apartment. We used our clothing to mark the goalposts and there

Rabbi István Dér

Tamas Gombosi

József Mandl

István Koltai

Talmud Torah class at the Hunyadi tér Synagogue in 1960.

was no referee. Free kicks, penalties, and even scores were decided by negotiation. Regular shoes were expensive and we usually changed to our gym shoes for the games. One day the game took a bit longer to finish and I was in a rush to get home. I had used my regular shoes to mark goalposts and I forgot to change back into them after the game. When I arrived home in gym shoes my mother got really upset. We went back to the Városliget, but by the time we got there, the shoes were gone. I was grounded for a while, and my parents had no choice but to buy a new pair of shoes for me. This was such a memorable event in my life that I never lost my shoes again.

I had my Bar Mitzvah at the Hunyadi tér synagogue in 1960. I worked with Rabbi Dér who later became the chief rabbi of Hungary. This was such an important event in the life of our family that my mother ordered printed invitations. Unfortunately she forgot to include the starting time of the service, so I had to add the time by hand. To have a Bar Mitzvah was an open act of opposition to Hungary's political regime. I did not really understand the significance of this aspect of the event, but my parents were certainly

Gombosi Tamás

szeretettel meghívja Ont és b. családját

1960 január 23-án 9h

Hunyadi tér 3. sz. alatti imaházban tartandó

„Bar Micvoh"

ünnepére

Tamás Gombosi's Bar Mitzvah invitation.

more than aware of it. My Bar Mitzvah was also a symbolic event for the entire family. By Jewish tradition the Phoenix had risen, reaching adulthood.

✂ ✂

While I excelled in math and science and really loved history, there were several subjects I did not like. I did not like Hungarian language and literature, even though I loved to read. The problem was Hungarian grammar and the books students were supposed to read. Many of these books were political propaganda and I instinctively rebelled against them. I was not good in learning languages. Starting from second grade my mother forced me to take private German lessons at a significant expense. I hated everything German and "resisted" learning anything. Starting with the fifth grade, all Hungarian students had to study Russian language and literature in school. Most teachers, however, were not very qualified and my classmates and I did not learn much Russian in school. My parents were not used to this kind of erratic performance since Éva had been uniformly an excellent and well-disciplined student. When they got frustrated with me they always brought up Éva as the positive example. "Oh but Éva never got a '3'[12] in anything" became a legendary exclamation in the family. After a while I started to call my older sister "Oh but Éva."

My parents were not sure what my future could be. In the 1960s the Hungarian educational system was highly stratified. One pretty much had only one chance to get into an elite university; there were no second chances. When I reached 7th grade the family had to decide where I should continue my studies after finishing elementary school. The choice, still made by European children at about age 13, determined the rest of my future – trade school or preparation for university – a choice most American kids don't face until they are nearly 18. My grades were mixed and my parents were unsure whether I would eventually be admitted to a university. To help with the decision, I was taken to career counseling.

The counseling started with a long test where students had to answer many questions. To prevent the publication of "illicit" leaflets and uncensored literature, mimeograph machines were highly restricted in Hungary (and of course there were no computer printers.) Rather than having a sheet of questions each to themselves, the questions were placed on an easel in the front of a large room. My eyes were very bad (even with glasses) and I could only guess what the questions were. I did very poorly. The test was followed by an individual interview where I did well, but not spectacularly. The result of the evaluation was very bad: I was not suited for any intellectual career.

My parents had a dilemma. If I went to a regular gimnázium (high-school) and I failed to get into the university, I would be left with no profession. Learning a trade after high school was not a good option either since I had little aptitude for anything that involved handcraft. (When I was little and visited my father in the Műhely, I exhibited a complete lack of talent. I could not even drive a nail into a piece of wood without bending it.) Finally my parents came up with a solution.

In the 1960s the Hungarian educational system had a special kind of high school, called technikum (technical high school). Technikums combined a somewhat watered down high school curriculum with teaching a skilled trade. After finishing technikum, students obtained a certificate of graduation and a technician certificate in the profession in which the technikum specialized. My parents decided that I should apply to the Hiradástechnikai és Műszeripari (communication and instrument technology) Technikum. After finishing this technikum I would have the choice of applying to the university or starting work as an

---

[12]The mark 3 was something like a C in the American grading system

Left: Eszter and Zoltán Gombosi in front of the Nagyenyed Street apartment building. The Bozoki (and later Gombosi) apartment is marked with red. Right: Éva Gombosi with the first Trabant of the family (sometime in early 1960s).

instrument technician.

The plan failed miserably. As I have noted, I was not good with my hands, so I was sent to private lessons to learn how to draw. I was good in math and physics, but made no effort to learn anything about instruments and technology. These were all subjects for the entrance exam which had to be passed before one could even be admitted to the Technikum. In the end I got mediocre grades at the exam and was rejected. My parents were quite disappointed, but I was relieved, since I did not really want to go to technikum. I wanted to go to gimnázium and eventually become a physicist, like my adored brother-in-law, Gyuri.

✄ ✄

In 1961, with significant help from their parents, Éva and Gyuri were able to purchase a condominium. In a new apartment building at the intersection of Nagyenyed Street, Kékgolyó Street, Böszörményi Street and Istenhegyi Street, the apartment was large by the standards of the day: three rooms plus a kitchen, a bathroom, a balcony and a WC (toilet). It was 66 m^2 (720 sq ft) plus a 12 m^2 (130 sq ft) balcony. By Hungarian standards this apartment was the embodiment of luxury, especially for a young childless couple.

Soon afterwards Éva and Gyuri were given the opportunity to buy a car. At this time it was not enough to have money to buy a car, because there was a great shortage. The government strictly controlled the waiting list, and certain people, like young scientists, were given preference. The typical waiting list was several years long, but Éva and Gyuri were able to pick up their brand new Trabant[13] after only a few months of waiting. This was the first car in the extended family and everyone was eager to get a ride in the new "status symbol" as it was often referred to.

---

[13]The Trabant was produced by former East Germany. With its poor performance, outdated and inefficient two-stroke engine (which returned poor fuel economy for the car's size and produced smoky exhaust), and production shortages, the Trabant is often cited as an example of the disadvantages of centralized planning. In 2008, *Time Magazine* rated the Trabant as one of the 50 worst cars ever made.

I was excited about my sister's car. Éva was the primary driver, since she was the "alpha" person in the Bozoki family. Éva had an assertive personality (reinforced by her mother) and Gyuri was what we would call today "passive agressive." They argued all the time, but actually they got along very well.

I was very impressed by my sister and brother-in-law and spent considerable time with them. This was highly encouraged by Magda, who mistakenly thought that Éva could have a positive influence on her rebellious brother. However, I was at the age when I knew everything better than anybody else and was convinced that everyone in the family, with the exception of Gyuri, was retarded.

When I reached puberty and started to be interested in girls I used Gyuri as my sounding board. Once I surprised him by asking what he and Éva did when they were alone. Gyuri did not know how to answer this delicate question. He became red and quickly changed the subject.

✄ ✄

After I was denied admission to a technikum, I continued my studies at the Ferenc Kölcsey gimnázium (high school) (see ⑥ on page 112). At this time there were no individual electives in Hungarian schools. Students were assigned to a group with a permanent "home" classroom and the teachers rotated from room to room. Each freshman group had a permanent classroom and a home teacher[14] who was responsible for the group. Different groups had different electives. All the boys who came from the Felsőerdősor elementary school were put into group "a" that had advanced Russian and Latin as electives.

Our freshman class at Kölcsey Gimnázium had a significant distinction. This was the first time in the school's history that girls were admitted! Until the spring of 1961 Kölcsey was an all-boys high school. The freshman class in the fall of 1961 had seven groups four of which were co-ed. The other three groups had only boys.

My high school group had a high concentration of Jewish children: there were 15 Jews out of the approximately 40 students. Most of them came from families of Jewish professionals (doctors, engineers and others) and many of them from the post-Holocaust second marriages of survivors who had lost their first families. They were prime examples of the Phoenix generation. An interesting social structure developed among the students and I was quick to recognize it. I created quite a stir when, at one of the regular classes with the home teacher, I explained the "caste" system in the group. According to my observations there were three castes which seldom interacted with each other. The "elite" caste members came from high-income Jewish families. This caste also included some other students who had special talents admired by everyone. The "lower caste" came mainly from low income non-Jewish families. Finally, the "mixed caste" included the children of non-intellectual Jewish families as well as kids from middle-class gentile families.

Everyone felt uncomfortable with my caste system. Socialism was all about "equality" and acknowledging a stratified social structure was disconcerting. This entire episode alienated many classmates and the anchor teacher, Mr. Dénes Kövendi. Kövendi was a

---

[14]In some schools in the U.S.A. there is a period each week that is set aside in which students meet with their "home teacher," during an informal discussion session. Not every school has this policy, therefore it's not commonly known.

bad match for this heavily Jewish group. He was a typical Christian intellectual with high moral standards. He intrinsically did not like Jews, but tried to be fair with them. He was teaching three subjects to the group: Russian, Latin and history. I disliked Russian (and did not perform well in that class) but liked Latin and loved history. Kövendi and I had a mutual dislike for each other. Kövendi was irritated by my brashness and I disliked his sanctimonious style.

Kövendi's teaching career ended with an anti-semitic incident. One of the prominent Jewish students was Péter Hercz. Sometime in the second year of high school one of the other students, Gyula Futó, was chatting with Péter and somehow they started talking about their future plans. During this discussion Gyula said something like, "We will not get into the university because these Jews take up all the places." It was obvious that he was parroting something he had heard somewhere, though hard to understand how he could say it so unwittingly to Péter – who looked like the prototypical Jew. Péter and his parents made a big fuss about this incident and the school principal was ready to expel Futó from the school. Kövendi vigorously defended Gyula arguing that he was not a hard core anti-semite just an immature kid who repeated things he did not understand. In the end the scandal grew, attracting the attention of higher authorities. Eventually Kövendi was fired and Gyula Futó was allowed to stay.

✂ ✂

In high school I had two great teachers who had a major impact on my life. Not surprisingly they were mathematics and physics teachers. My math teacher, Antal Lovas, was a former priest who had taught math in Catholic schools before the war. He was a very good teacher with a great sense of humor. He was able to challenge me to the point that I got frustrated with my own inability to perform at the level I expected of myself. Mr. Lovas always gave me top grades while making me feel inadequate. The other teacher of great influence was my physics teacher, Miss Erzsébet Bartók (no relation to the famous composer). She was a former nun who had to return to civilian life after the government disbanded most religious orders.[15] She recognized my talent and inspired me by public humiliation. On one occasion she told me that my solution of a problem was overly complicated. "If you have to cross the street, why do you go to the Moon and back, landing on the other side of the street?" she asked. I was furious that my solution was criticized and worked hard to prove myself.

One other teacher who had an impact on my life was István Käfer, a young teacher of Hungarian language and literature and the home teacher of a group in the class one year behind me. In that year all groups had co-ed classes, and Käfer actively promoted joint activities between the groups. 1964 was the time when the Kádár regime started to ease travel restrictions and people could get passports to travel to neighboring Communist countries. One of Käfer's specialities was Slovak language and literature and during the spring break of '64 he organized a week-long bus tour to Czechoslovakia.

After much preparation the two groups of students with about five or six chaperones (both male and female) got on two buses and visited historical Hungarian places in Slovakia.

---

[15]Following World War II the Catholic Church lost 3,300 schools, numerous hospitals and newspapers. 11,500 Hungarian priests and nuns were asked to leave their convents and monasteries and return to civilian life.

The buses were in poor shape and broke down with predictable regularity. For us kids this just added to the fun as we tried to restart the buses. The trip ended in Prague, a city that makes a big impression on everyone and made a huge impression on Hungarian high school kids. The trip was a huge success and became a formative event in my life.

Trying to start the broken down tour bus during the 1964 spring break trip to Czechoslovakia.

My most hated subject was politechnika (practical education). Supposed to give some real work experience to students, my group was assigned to the train depot at the Nyugati Pályaudvar (western railway station) where we learned how to work with metals. Still without aptitude for anything that required handiwork, I was always frustrated with the results. Fortunately politechnika was not considered to be a "major subject," so the poor grades did not hurt my overall school performance.

The train depot is marked with ⑦ on page 112. The main entrance was through the railway station, a good half a mile from the depot. The depot itself was located right where Izabella Street ended, so to take the "official" route to the depot meant a good mile detour for most of the students. There was an eight foot stone fence around the railway station that protected the depot and other infrastructure buildings. This fence, however, was no obstacle to 16 year old boys who regularly climbed over the fence to get to and from the depot, shortening our commute by about a mile.

I loved to read. I was a frequent visitor at the local branch of the Ervin Szabó Library system (see ⑨ on page 112).

Photo taken by a professional press photographer sometime in 1962. It shows me and two of my friends, Péter Kardos and András Markos, in action during politechnika. I am using a file to make an equipment part. This was, however, staged, since I never succeeded in making any useful part during my adventures in politechnika.

My photos over my high school years.

Sometimes I finished a book a day. I usually came home from school around 2 p.m., had lunch and headed to the library. I spent a couple of hours in the library and went home around 5 p.m. Homework usually took about 30 to 45 minutes (I certainly did not overdo it) and my parents came home between 6 and 7 p.m. (my father ran his own business and mother worked full time). After dinner I read until I was forced to go to bed. In the 1960s television did not represent a major distraction in Hungary: while my family was among the first to own a TV set, there was only one channel and it broadcast two or three times a week from 5 p.m. to 10 p.m. So, after dinner I read until I was forced to go to bed.

I read just about everything, but my favorite books were historical novels, adventures and some of the classics. I read Alexandre Dumas, Stevenson, Walter Scott, Jane Austin, G.B. Shaw and many others. My favorite, however, was Jenő Rejtő (his pen name was P. Howard). Jenő Rejtő (born as Jenő Reich in 1905) was a Hungarian journalist, pulp fiction writer and playwright, who died in 1943 as a forced laborer during the Holocaust. Despite the "pulp" nature of his writings, he is not only widely read in Hungary, but is also much appreciated by literary critics. It is a prevalent opinion that he lifted the genre to the level of serious art and his works will long outlive him. I read and reread his most famous books to the point that I was able to quote entire passages. Some of Rejtő's books are translated to English, *The 14-Carat Roadster* and *The Blonde Hurricane* among them. But, his special humor and play of words are very difficult to translate.

✂ ✂

I never experienced co-education in elementary or high school. But an old tradition brought adolescent boys and girls together, the tánciskola (ballroom dancing class). Middle class children in the 14 to 18 year old age group took ballroom dancing classes in special studios. The studios also taught social etiquette and were fertile ground for first dates. I was not a particularly talented dancer, but I liked these classes. We learned old fashioned dances like the minuet, the polka, the Viennese waltz, the English waltz and the tango, as well as more modern dances such as samba, rumba, rock and roll and finally the twist.

Hungarian high schools traditionally organized annual balls. These were major social events. Students brought dates and there was relatively free mixing of the sexes. These formal balls usually opened with a formal dance with 16 couples performing a series of

My high school group. About half the group has advanced degrees.

classical ballroom dances. When I was 16, I reached the peak of my dancing career and was selected to be in the group that performed the opening dances. There were many practice sessions in the ballroom dancing studio and the performance went flawlessly. I was very proud of myself.

The high school years were the most formative years of my life. During these years I changed from a boy to a young man. This was also the time when I formed long-term friendships. My closest friends were Aladár Ackerman, András Markos and Daniel Tóth. Interestingly, only András Markos was Jewish, both Aladár and Daniel came from working class non-Jewish families. In addition I was also close to Péter Hercz and Péter Kardos. Page 131 shows the graduation roster of my high school group. There were about 40 students in the graduating group and 15 of them were Jewish. 17 of them (40%) received advanced degrees or became very famous in their professions. It is interesting to note that 11 of these are Jewish, making the percentage of advanced degrees among the Phoenix kids about 75%. On page 131 I marked the advanced degrees achieved by individual students and I also noted with an asterisk those who were Jewish.

✂ ✂

During the 1960s The Iron Curtain kept Hungary a pretty isolated country. The authorities seldom granted exit visas and it was difficult to travel. I was lucky, in addition to the school trip that ended in Prague, two foreign trips had major impact on my world view.

The first trip took place in the summer of 1963 when I spent nearly three months in Stockholm with my paternal aunt, Juci. In some respect the trip was a disaster; Juci had no children and no idea how to deal with a rebellious 16 year old. On the other hand, it was the first time I was away from the protective cocoon of the Izabella Street apartment and I had a chance to see for myself "rotting capitalism" as Communist propaganda described it. I visited nearly all museums and monuments in Stockholm and started to pick up a little bit of Swedish. I was very receptive to the culture and attitude of the Swedes. The downside was that Juci did not enroll me in a summer camp and so I spent too much time with the Hungarian immigrant community. These were first generation immigrants with a lot of struggles, disappointment and self-justification. I was not mature enough to understand the nuances and psychology of immigrant communities, but I was certainly put off by some of Juci's friends. Still, Juci was extremely generous with me. She bought me a new wardrobe (I was growing rapidly) and even an 8-mm movie camera. After this trip I became an amateur moviemaker and I very much enjoyed this activity.

The second memorable trip was in the winter of 1964, just before graduation from high school. At the time Éva and Gyuri were spending a year in Dubna, Russia, the Mecca of high energy physics of Eastern Europe in the 1960s. Dubna is a small town about 60 miles from Moscow and Éva and Gyuri rolled out the red carpet for me. The train ride from Budapest to Moscow took two days including a several hour-long stop at the border between Hungary and the Soviet Union. At the time it was forbidden to take any fruits or vegetables to the Soviet Union, but there was a shortage of fruit in Dubna. Our mother had hidden a large bag of apples in my suitcase, but Soviet customs officers found and confiscated it. Even today Éva bitterly recalls this incident and will never forgive the Soviet system for confiscating her desperately craved apples.

I had two very memorable events on this trip. The first was a visit to Moscow where we went to see *Swan Lake* in the Congress Hall with Galina Ulanova in the lead role. I always liked classical ballet and to see the legendary Ulanova was a very special event in my life. The second memorable event was that somehow at the time when foreigners had to get special permission to travel anywhere in the Soviet Union, Éva arranged for me to go to Leningrad (present day St. Petersburg). It was the most impressive, beautiful city I had ever seen in my short life. I spent an entire day in the Hermitage museum, one of the best

Andrea Bozóki in 1967 (left), 1968 (center) and with Tamás in 1969 (right).

art collections in the world. The city made a huge impression on this 18-year old.

7.4. Andrea

After eight years of marriage, Éva became pregnant while she and Gyuri were working in Dubna, creating huge excitement in the entire extended family. On October 31, 1965, shortly after her parents' return to Hungary, the first grandchild of Magda and János and the first great-grandchild in the extended Róna family was born, shortly after her parents' return to Hungary. Éva and Gyuri named their daughter Andrea. Everyone called her Andi.

The new baby became the center of family attention. Gyuri was the proud father who explained to anyone who would listen (and even to those who would not) everything about children. Éva was always exhausted (like all new mothers) and worried about her daughter. Magda was in heaven and János quietly enjoyed his new role as grandfather. I was extremely proud to have a niece, especially since everyone said that the baby looked just like me.

Andi was a few months old when on a Saturday afternoon, Magda and Éva went shopping leaving her with the men of the family, Gyuri, János and myself. After a short while a strong – and unmistakeable – odor came from the direction of the baby. As a good Jewish grandpa, János immediately left the room. Gyuri felt nauseated and withdrew to the bathroom. I, on the verge of throwing up, realized that I could not count on my father and brother-in-law. As a physics student, I knew that warm air rises. I made the assumption that the smell was entrapped in warm air emanating from Andrea's diaper. I concluded that close to the floor the air would be colder and therefore less filled with the penetrating aroma of the baby's output. I got on the floor, crawled to the couch, reached up and with great effort changed the baby. When Magda and Éva returned, János and Gyuri proudly announced that Andi had had a poop but "we changed her."

Andrea was a very bad eater and this caused great concern to Éva and Magda. Behind her age both in size and weight, Éva tried to force feed her. This created a negative feedback loop, and the baby was just not interested in eating. The more desperate Éva became, the more resistant Andrea grew. This vicious cycle did not break until Andrea entered adolescence.

As Andi was growing up she grew very close to her uncle. This is not surprising, since I was the youngest member of the family and I still had the energy to keep up with the small girl. Andrea called me "Tamásom" (my Tamás) and she was right. She could wrap me around her finger.

As did most Hungarian children at that time, Andrea started daycare when she was about six months old. She was dropped off in the morning when Éva and Gyuri went to work and they picked her up after work. Sometimes they were unable to get there in time and they asked Magda to pick up the baby. Needless to say, Grandma was more than happy to do so.

Once when Andrea was about three or four years old and Éva was travelling for work, Magda and Gyuri were in charge of Andi. They usually agreed in the morning who would pick her up from daycare. One day they miscommunicated. Both got home in the evening shocked to realize that Andi was still at daycare. They immediately panicked and rushed to the closed daycare center. When they looked around they found Andrea peacefully playing on the playground just outside the daycare. The teachers had also forgotten about her. This was a very scary experience and the entire family was shocked. Needless to say it never happened again.

In January 1970 Éva and Gyuri left for year-long visiting appointments in France. Éva had a visiting appointment at the Linear Accelerator Laboratory in Orsay (a southwestern suburb of Paris), and Gyuri was working at the University of Paris. At the time they were already dissatisfied with their opportunities in Hungary and were mature enough to recognize how backward Hungarian physics was compared to the best institutions. In addition, some of their closest colleagues (Ervin Fenyves, Péter Surányi and Péter Domokos) had already left Hungary and found good jobs in the United States. After the Six Day War in the Middle East, they also felt the increasing anti-semitism in Hungary. They were ready to defect and wanted to use this year to make all the preparations. Because Éva and Gyuri had no background or support system in France, they left Andi with Grandma Magda for a couple of weeks until they could rent an apartment. Then, the four and a half year old Andrea flew to France with her own passport – a big adventure for the entire family.

7.5.   Follow Your Dreams

In the summer of 1965 I graduated from high school with a perfect record. My graduation exam was rated "outstanding" and the transcripts showed a perfect score in physics and mathematics. There were only three research physicist programs in Hungary at the time: one at the School of Natural Sciences of the Loránd Eötvös University (ELTE TTK) in Budapest, the second at the University of Szeged and the third at the University of Debrecen. ELTE TTK was the most prestigious of the three, and it was located in my home town, so it was natural that I applied to the masters program in physics at ELTE.[16] I had taken the university entry exam in the spring of 1965 and done well enough to be admitted. At the time students were admitted into specific programs and it was unheard of to choose (or switch) a major later; at 18 we had to make career decisions. But I was ready for the next stage of my life – as a physics major.

---

[16]At the time Hungarian universities only had five-year masters programs; there were no Bachelor of Science programs available.

I came from a high school where physics and mathematics education was not very strong and some of my classmates came from schools that specialized in math and physics. I quickly realized that I was well behind of the best students in my class and worked very hard to catch up. At the end of the first semester, my grade point average (GPA) was C` and I was very disappointed. Hard work eventually paid off though and by the end of the first year I was the best in the class with a perfect GPA.

The freshman physics class had about 50 students, only 6 of whom were Jewish. However, in the top 10% of the class there were four Jews: György Ferenczi, Gábor Juvancz, András Patkós and myself. The 10% or so ratio of Jewish students was fairly typical at elite Hungarian universities and a factor of ten higher than the percentage of Jews in the general population.

It is interesting to note what happened to these four men later in life. In 1973 Gábor Juvancz had a freshly minted Ph.D. and took a trip to Northern Europe. During a ride in a small plane with three friends, the plane crashed and Gábor died. György Ferenczi became a talented and entrepreneurial solid-state physicist who invented a new technology to create solar cells. He was well ahead of his time with this invention. He created a small company and hired several of our classmates to work for him. He was also a chain smoker and suffered a fatal heart attack in his early forties. András Patkós became a particle physicist, stayed at ELTE after graduation and rapidly rose through the ranks of the faculty. He became Chair of the Department of Atomic Physics at ELTE TTK and was elected to the Hungarian Academy of Sciences. Recently he stepped down as department chair but he is still active as a faculty member. I became a space scientist and this book extensively deals with my life.

8   Eszter

8.1. The Rákosi Years

After Eszter's parents Juci and Pista Gárdos returned to Pécs from the displaced persons' camp in Germany in the fall of 1945 (see Section 6.3) it took them a while to recover most of their possessions and to start life again. Fortunately (or unfortunately) a refugee family who considered all the belongings of deported Jews to be their own had moved into their house. It took some effort by Pista to get their home back, but when he did they discovered almost all of their furniture and china intact. Most of the family photographs were found because the new inhabitants had not bothered to dispose of them. However, most of the true valuables had disappeared.

As I mentioned in Section 6.3, shortly after their return, Pista started practicing law again, Juci became pregnant and Pista's cousin, Vera Handlei, married János Heinrich and left Pécs (see Section 5.1). Juci and Pista had high hopes for their "Phoenix" child, who, like the rest of the generation, represented the future after all the horrors of the Holocaust.

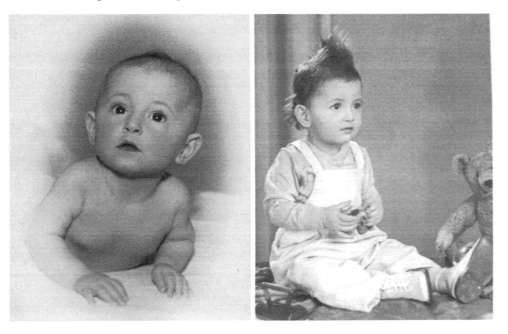

Left: Eszter Gárdos in February, 1949. Right: Eszter Gárdos in the summer of 1949.

The baby, however, tragically died at the age of four months due to medical malpractice. After this loss Juci was in no shape to look for work and it took her a while to be ready to enter the workforce.

A year after the loss of their son Juci became pregnant again. In August 1948 she gave birth to a daughter, Eszter. A sickish child, Eszter was about a year old when she came down with nephritis (inflammation of the kidney). Juci and Pista were in a panic that they would lose their third child as well. Fortunately, Eszter fully recovered and life returned to normal. As she grew older her resilience greatly improved and she became a pretty healthy girl. Yet, another health scare occurred when Eszter was about five years old. A polio epidemic swept through Hungary. One afternoon Eszter played with a neighborhood girl. The next day the girl came down with polio. The Gárdos family lived in fear until the incubation period was over. Fortunately Eszter was not infected with this deadly disease.

Eszter was ten months old when the Gárdos family moved to a larger apartment at 16 Anna Street in Pécs. They remained in this apartment until the mid-1970s when Juci and Pista moved to Budapest to be close to their daughter and grandchildren.

Shortly after the family moved to the new apartment, Juci's Aunt Flóra lost her husband, Ármin Gyulai. This came just four years after her son, József Gyulai, died in forced military labor (MUSZ) (see Section 6.3). A few months after the death of Flóra's husband Juci and Pista convinced her to move to Pécs and become a de facto grandmother to Eszter. They created a

The Gárdos apartment at 16 Anna Street in Pécs.

small but separate apartment for her in the same building where they lived and sometime in early 1950 Flóra moved to Pécs.

Because of anti-Jewish laws Juci Bíró never had a "real" job before the Holocaust. She had given private lessons in German and French, but after World War II these languages were not in high demand in Hungary. After Aunt Flora moved to Pécs, and Juci and Pista had built-in childcare, Juci was able to look for regular employment. She was very eager to enter the workforce.

In October 1950 she secured work as a librarian in the foreign language collection of a national bookstore chain. Six months later she was transferred to the library of the Hungarian-Soviet Friendship Society (Magyar-Szovjet Baráti Társaság) where she led the foreign language branch of the library. Later, this library was taken over by the local government of Pécs and renamed "Gorkij library" (Gorkij kőnyvtár), after the Soviet writer Maxim Gorkiy. She stayed in this job until 1962 when she joined the faculty of the Teachers College of Pécs.

Juci took her job very seriously. In the fall of 1952 she entered the Library Science program at the Teachers College of Budapest as a correspondence student. Though she would have preferred to be in a classroom with other students, at the time the only library science program in Hungary was located in Budapest. Needless to say, even completing course material by mail, during the three years she was in the program she never received any grade below an 'A.' She earned her library science degree in 1955, during the darkest times of the Rákosi regime.

By 1955 the Hungarian economy was reorganized according to the Soviet model. The regime forced most farmers to join collective farms and required them to make deliveries to the government at prices lower than the cost of production. Banking, trade, and industry were nationalized and nearly 99% of the country's workers had become state employees. The government introduced Soviet-style central planning. Planners neglected the production of consumer goods to focus on investment in heavy industry, especially steel production, and economic self-sufficiency. At the same time, the country was terrorized by political show trials that targeted "enemy spies." The atmosphere was filled with fear, people were afraid to say anything, and large fractions of the population were impoverished. (For more details see Appendix A.13).

While her parents worked, Eszter attended daycare where she had her first encounter with anti-semitism, such a traumatic event that she vividly remembers it sixty years later. Most of Pécs' Jewry had been exterminated in Auschwitz, so there were not many Jewish children her age in the city. As a reaction to the Holocaust, as noted earlier, Juci and Pista became Communists and tried to raise their

Vera Handlei and Eszter Gárdos sometime in 1952 when, recovering from the death of her husband, János Heinrich, she was a frequent visitor in Pécs.

daughter according to Communist ideas, completely abandoning their religious and ethnic backgrounds. When Eszter started daycare she had never heard the word Jew, neither did she know about ethnic and religious stereotypes. The Hungarian lumpenproletariat (see page 48) habitually used (and still uses) the derogative expression "stinky Jew" when they talked about anyone Jewish. One day, Eszter came home from preschool and asked her parents: "Why am I stinky when I take a bath every night?" Obviously, some kids had heard their parents referring to their classmate as "that stinky Jew" and taking it literally, called Eszter stinky in school.

During Communism lawyers were not allowed to practice privately in Hungary. They were forced to form "lawyers cooperatives" where several lawyers shared offices, staff, expenses and incomes. There were government imposed rates for all legal services and the cooperative made sure that nobody could make more money than the government saw

Eszter Gárdos's early childhood pictures from 1952 and 1953.

fit. It was one of the ways the Communist government controlled wages and redistributed incomes.

Pista became a member of "Lawyers Cooperative No. II" in the city of Pécs. He was a scrupulously honest lawyer who never accepted more than he was supposed to (many lawyers accepted – even expected – "gratitude payments"). There were four Jewish lawyers in Pista's cooperative, and about another dozen or so non-Jewish ones. We do not know the details, but sometime in the summer of 1955 Zoltán Telfel and several of his non-Jewish colleagues filed a criminal complaint against the four Jewish lawyers at the cooperative. I went through all the documentation that Pista kept over his lifetime, but could not find the charges against the four. Family lore says that one of the complaints was that Pista regularly put two cubes of sugar into his espresso, but I cannot believe that this was all they could come up with against such prominent lawyers.

On July 2, 1955 the law licenses of Pista and his three colleagues were suspended. They were arrested three weeks later, on July 21 and taken to a detention center. Their families were not informed about their whereabouts. Needless to say, Juci tried desperately to find her husband. Eventually, it was the Pista's street-smart cousin, Vera, who found Pista. She used her government connections (at this time she was a rising star in the Hungarian government administration) to locate Pista who finally managed to send a message to Juci that he was fine.

During the Rákosi regime truth did not matter and only high level political intervention could save Pista and his colleagues. This intervention came from Gyula Hajdú, a high profile Communist leader with roots in Pécs. He had participated in the Hungarian Communist revolution of 1919, had lived in exile in Italy and France, had been a member of the French resistance and returned to Hungary after World War II. In the Communist regime he had held various high level jobs including the presidency of the Hungarian Bar Association. When he learned about the charges against the four Jewish lawyers in Pécs he intervened. In November 1955, four months after their detention, Pista and his colleagues were acquitted of all charges and their law licenses were reinstated. However, as far as we know nothing happened to those who filed false charges against the four Jewish lawyers. Pista had to endure their presence in his law cooperative for many years to come.

✂ ✂

The Gárdos family had very few close friends. In spite of the fact that they were Communists and repudiated religion, all their friends were Jewish. They were very close to Ferenc (Feri) and Sarolta (Sári) Wolf and their daughter Ágnes (Ági). Feri Wolf was a lawyer who had survived the Holocaust, but lost his first family. After he returned to Pécs he married Sarolta Schiffer who was in her twenties at that time. Their daughter, Ági was born in the same year as Eszter, and the families were very close. Feri Wolf also worked in Lawyers Cooperative No. II and was among the falsely accused, so he and Pista went through the ordeal together.

The other couple Juci and Pista were friendly with was Ferenc (Feri) and Klára (Klári) Kertész. Klári, who was not Jewish, had hidden Feri during the Holocaust. They married after the liberation of Hungary and they also had a daughter, Anna (everyone called her Annuska) a couple of years younger than Eszter.

The third couple Juci and Pista were friendly with were their next door neighbors, Kató and György Révész. Both had lost their first families in the Holocaust and married after the liberation of Hungary. Unfortunately they never had a child together.

Eszter and Ági Wolf had an interesting relationship. Ági's mother, Sári, was a real "Jewish tigress" and ran her daughter's life with iron hands. Ági was a very talented pianist and Sári was always raving about her daughter's talent and accomplishments. This made Eszter feel inadequate (and also made her mother mad). Later Ági was admitted to a special "music high school" where she was trained as a classical pianist. However, when she graduated from high school it was decided that the life of a professional pianist was far too uncertain and instead of applying to the School of Music (Zeneakadémia) she applied to medical school. After graduating from medical school she married one of her professors and they had two daughters. A few years later, Ági divorced her husband and worked at the city of Pécs as a public health official. She became quite disillusioned and somewhat depressed. Rumors floated around about her alcohol abuse. Ági's life should be a warning about the pitfalls of overly dominating mothers. In her youth Ági did what her mother wanted her to do. She got depressed when she felt that she fell short of expectations. It is unfortunate that Sári never let Ági be Ági.

While Eszter lived in Hungary she kept regular contact with Ági, but she met only occasionally with her other childhood friend, Annuska Kertész. Annuska became a teacher and lived all her life in Pécs. I think I only met her once when we visited Pécs.

✂ ✂

Two of Juci's closest friendships started while they were attending high school. We know that these friendships are very strong and tend to last a lifetime, as these did. One of these close girlfriends was Gertrud Schwartz, or as everyone called her, Trude. She was the daughter of the Bíró family doctor, Dr. Vilmos Schwartz, with whom the family also socialized. Before the Holocaust, Trude started dating Viktor Kiss (pronounced as Kish), a Catholic priest. He also had a medical degree and practiced medicine within the Catholic

Church. It is not clear why, but Viktor left the priesthood sometime during World War II and started his own medical practice. My hunch is that this had something to do with Trude. At the same time, Trude was hiding outside of Pécs. She was hidden by a farming family who created a walled-in compartment in their house for her. She survived the Holocaust there, but her parents perished in Auschwitz. After the Holocaust, Trude and Viktor married and had a son, Iván, a couple of years older than Eszter. In the 1950s, Viktor was the family doctor of the Gárdos family.

There are several interesting stories involving Trude. In the 1950s Viktor's private medical practice was very successful and they were very well-to-do by the standards of the times.[1] Trude did not work outside the home and they had a live-in maid which was very unusual in Hungary during these dark times. Trude liked to sleep late and usually had her breakfast in bed brought by the maid. This habit made a huge impression on the young Eszter who once declared: "When I grow up I want to be a doctor, not a regular doctor, but a doctor like aunt Trude." In order to understand this comment one needs to know that in Hungarian female medical doctors are called "doktornő" (female doctor), while the wife of a medical doctor is called "doktorné" (Mrs. Doctor). This remark became a family legend and even many years later we are joking about "aunt doctors."

Another funny story about Trude involves Vera. At the time Vera lived in Budapest in an apartment building on Akácfa Street. A young woman living in the same building worked in the best and most expensive designer studio in Budapest and was friends with Vera. One day this young friend told Vera that they had just designed a fantastic dress for a woman from the boonies (i.e. outside Budapest) and that she was willing to make a copy of that dress for Vera. Vera accepted the offer (she claims reluctantly, but I cannot believe it) and her dress was ready just before she left to spend the Christmas holidays with the Gárdos family. Once Vera arrived in Pécs she was told by Juci that they were all invited to a Christmas party at Trude's house. Vera proudly put on her new dress and off they went. One can only imagine the shock of hostess and guest when they faced each other wearing the same dress. They quickly figured out the connection and had a great laugh about the story.

Juci's other close high school girlfriend was Erzsébet Kálmán (everyone called her Zsozso). She moved away from Pécs and attended medical school in Budapest. She became an oncologist and after the Holocaust married Viktor Fáber who eventually became a professor of pathology at the Medical School in Budapest. They had a son, András, who was a year or so older than Eszter. Even though they lived in different cities Juci and Zsozso were quite close and regularly visited each other over the years. Sometime in the 1980s Zsozso was diagnosed with cancer. As an oncologist she had no illusions and took her own life soon after the diagnosis.

✂ ✂

Eszter started school in 1954. She attended a school affiliated with a Teachers College, where future teachers gained their guided classroom experience. It was supposed to be the best elementary school in Pécs. At this time in Hungary, teachers colleges were gender segregated and the Teachers College Eszter's school was affiliated with admitted only women.

---

[1] Medical doctors had to have a "day job" in a government controlled medical facility, but they were allowed to have an after-hours private practice.

Eszter Gárdos showing off her ballet skills in 1953 (left) and in 1964 (right).

(There was a separate Teachers College for men.)

Eszter really liked school, fortunately, because Juci set very high expectations for her daughter. Eszter vividly remembers that the only time her semester grade point average fell below the A level, her mother sternly commented: "We do not get B's." As a matter of fact, Eszter very seldom got anything other than A's. In addition to school, Eszter also had many extracurricular activities. She took piano lessons. She took ballet classes for nearly twelve years. She loved ballet, and her figure was well suited for dancing. But, ballet classes began late in the afternoon and they did not end before 9 p.m. Since they lived in a very safe small town, children were usually allowed to walk to and from extracurricular activities alone. Eszter, however, was required to be home by 8 p.m. She truly resented the fact that while all other girls could stay for the entire ballet class, she had to leave early every single time. In fact, more than fifty years later, she still resents it.

Another extracurricular activity was learning Russian. Eszter had not yet started school when Juci decided that it was time for her daughter to start to learn a foreign language. In Juci's mind the most important foreign language was Russian, so she hired native Russian speakers to teach her daughter the language. At the time there were a number of Russian women in Pécs who had married Hungarian men while they attended universities in

Russia. Most of these women had difficulty finding employment, partly because they did not speak Hungarian sufficiently well (a difficult language to begin with), and partly because of the resentment against Russian domination of Hungary and Eastern Europe. These Russian women were delighted to teach Eszter their native language and by the age of ten she was quite fluent. She regularly met with visiting Soviet delegations and gave welcoming speeches to visiting Soviet orchestras, dance and theater companies and other artistic groups.

✂ ✂

Juci never liked housework which she considered a waste of her time. She never learned to cook well. Raised in an environment that valued education and accomplishment and looked down upon homekeeping, when she started full time work she decided nevertheless that the family needed a "housewife." After a short search she followed the recommendation of her friend, Trude, and sometime between 1953 and 1955 hired Anna Strattman (everyone called her Annus) as full time housekeeper. Annus worked 48 hour weeks (the normal workweek in Hungary at the time), but she did not live with the Gárdos family. Annus did not live far. She came early every morning and left after 5p.m. She took care of all cooking (Juci never set foot in the kitchen), cleaning, laundry, shopping and household chores. On Sundays the family usually ate cold meals prepared by Annus ahead of time.

It is an interesting contradiction that Juci had a full time maid. Having servants was considered a defining characteristic of the capitalist ruling class which was actively oppressed during the Rákosi regime. It is my suspicion, without any evidence, that having a maid contributed to the resentment that eventually resulted in the false charges against Pista and his colleagues. I find it interesting that Juci could so easily reconcile her Communist ideology with paying someone to do her housework. As an aside, when I was growing up in Budapest I did not know any family with full time maids or other employees.

Annus was the undisputed queen of the kitchen. When Eszter was about four or five years old she wanted to help in the kitchen, even though she was highly discouraged by her mother. "You need to focus on your studies and not waste your time in the kitchen" – was the message. Nevertheless, Eszter was interested in helping Annus. Once Annus was making dough and the little girl was trying to be helpful. She used her hair brush to mix the dough. In spite of her best intentions this was not really appreciated either by Juci or by Annus. Eventually, Eszter was expelled from the kitchen and she did not return to cooking until her own children were born.

It was also Annus' job to make sure that Eszter received a healthy, balanced diet. The problem was that Eszter hated to eat (today she wishes to return to this state, but cannot) and used all her tricks to avoid food. She used to climb the huge chestnut tree in the backyard to hide from Annus when she tried to force her to eat her afternoon snack. During the Rákosi regime cocoa powder was hard to get (it was imported for hard currency which was in short supply). Juci and Pista somehow managed to get some cocoa for Eszter, but the little girl regularly spilled her hot chocolate into the drain when nobody watched her. It was hand-to-hand combat to feed Eszter.

8.2. The Good Girl

The 1956 Hungarian Revolution (see Appendix A.13) had a traumatic impact on Eszter. While there was relatively little fighting in Pécs, she vividly remembers guards chasing inmates who had escaped from a nearby prison randomly shooting at everything that moved. Pista barely escaped being shot by the panicked guards while coming home from his office. There were also anti-semitic incidents in Pécs and while Eszter did not understand the issues she could sense her parents' tense reactions. She was so scared that for months after the revolution she slept in her parents' bed.

Shortly after the uprising Juci was diagnosed with Bazedov syndrome (or Graves' disease). This is an autoimmune disease in which an overactive thyroid produces excessive amounts of thyroid hormone. Caused by thyroid growth and resulting in a diffusely enlarged goiter, Graves' disease usually presents itself during midlife, affects up to 2% of the female population, and is between five and ten times as common in females as in males. About half of the people with Graves' disease will also suffer from Graves' ophthalmopathy (a protrusion of one or both eyes),

Juci Bíró and Pista Gárdos in 1962. Juci was 46 and Pista was 55 years old at this time.

caused by inflammation of the eye muscles by attacking autoantibodies. Patients can experience a wide range of symptoms and suffer major impairment in most areas of health-related quality of life. An interesting aspect of this disease is that it can be triggered by psychological trauma. Juci, of course, had more than her fair share of psychological trauma, and as such may have been primed for this disease. Juci developed a serious form of Graves' disease which resulted both in ophthalmopathy and heart disease. Finally, she had surgery in 1960 to remove her thyroid, but by that time she had suffered irreversible heart damage.

Eszter was about ten years old when her mother became ill and was twelve when Juci had her surgery. In the 1960s, thyroid surgery was quite complicated and people were hospitalized for a long time afterwards. Eszter was sent to summer camp while Juci recuperated in the hospital. Eszter hated camps and was worried about her mother, so there was quite a family struggle to convince her to go.

Eszter was growing up fast. A very happy girl, she was adored by her parents and gave lots of pleasure to everyone around her, even grumpy Aunt Flóra who could not resist Eszter's charms in spite of the fact that as a typical child Eszter could not keep any information she picked up to herself and created some friction between Aunt Flóra and her friends by repeating sharp tongued Flóra's comments. Once Eszter repeated an off-hand comment about the mental state of one of Flóra's closest friends, after which the adults did not talk to each other for months.

Aunt Flóra, who was seriously diabetic, was supposed to keep a very strict diet. She, however, was not very good at keeping to these restrictions and her blood sugar levels

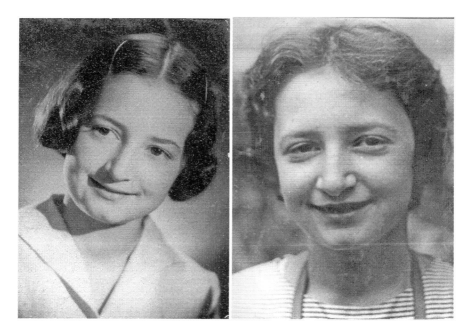

Eszter Gárdos in 1956 (left) and 1958 (right).

fluctuated highly. In 1964, at the age of 80, she suddenly passed away while vacationing near the town of Eger.

✂ ✂

One of the few relatives who survived the Holocaust, Juci's cousin Józsi Bíró, and his family lived in Budapest. Józsi was a very talented mechanical engineer with an iron will. According to family legend, he invented a copy machine (similar to Xerox machines) but his invention was not appreciated and was never developed into a commercial product. Józsi and his wife, Márta Reiner, had two daughters: Zsuzsa and Ágnes (everyone called her Ági).

Ági was just a few months older than Eszter but the two did not meet until then were 8 years old. They lived in different cities and travel was limited in the early 1950s. Still, Aunt Flóra occasionally visited her nephew, Józsi Bíró, in Budapest and during these visits, apparently, she often raved about Eszter. "Esztike" (as the family called Eszter) "is excellent in ballet," Flóra bragged, "and she speaks Russian and plays the piano." The accolades usually ended with, "And why can't you be like Esztike?" Needless to say, Ági instinctively disliked this "oh but Esztike." However, when they actually met in the summer of 1956, they instantly bonded. It turned out that "oh but Esztike" was a normal girl and not the ideal Aunt Flóra depicted.

A memorable event involving Eszter and Ági was their polio vaccination. Preceding World War II, polio epidemics appeared usually every four years in Hungary, but as in many parts of the globe, outbreaks became more frequent and more deadly from 1952 onwards and were perceived as a constant threat. In the midst of the '50s epidemic, there was new hope: an inactivated vaccine, developed by Jonas Salk in the U.S. in 1955, became available. The vaccine contained dead viruses that helped the immune system of the body to develop defense against the poliomyelitis virus. By 1957 the Salk vaccine was widely available in the U.S.A. and in Western Europe, but Hungary only had a very limited supply and that was primarily given to the children of higher level government and Communist Party officials. Neither the Bíró nor the Gárdos families were able to get their children vaccinated. The parents were quite distressed and Juci and Józsi approached their uncle, József Bíró, who lived in New York, about the shortage. At the time, domestic commercial airplane flights still existed in Hungary. József bought three doses of the Salk vaccine in New York for his three Hungarian nieces (Zsuzsa, Ági and Eszter) and managed to send the vaccine to Budapest. Shortly after it arrived, Józsi put his daughters on an airplane to Pécs where all three girls were vaccinated. (Later domestic flights were discontinued because they were not economical in such a small country.)

While Ági and Eszter were very close, there was considerable tension between cousins Juci and Józsi. Both extremely bright individuals with strong world views, they represented two extreme reactions to the horrors of the Holocaust. Juci became a true believer in Communism and believed that assimilating all Jews would end anti-semitism. She was also a strong supporter of the current regime, while Józsi despised it. However, for the sake of their daughters, they were able to set aside differences and the two families stayed in regular contact. The girls visited each other a couple of times a year and the adults managed to avoid sensitive subjects during their meetings. Eszter and Ági's very close relationship has survived time and distance. Even today they spend hours on the internet chatting with each other.

Both Eszter and Ági were in awe of Ági's older sister, Zsuzsa. Eight years older than the two younger girls, very smart and an outstanding student, she was their role model. She attended a special school that immersed students in Russian language (Gorkij school). Zsuzsa was an outstanding student and when the Gorkij school was created the authorities selected the best students from all over Budapest for the new school. It was a great honor to be selected for this school that was supposed to be the breeding ground for the next generation of Communist leaders. IHowever, the Gorkij school was dissolved after the

Left: Ági Bíró (left) and Eszter Gárdos (right) in 1957. Right: Eszter and Ági on a pony ride in the Budapest Zoo in 1957.

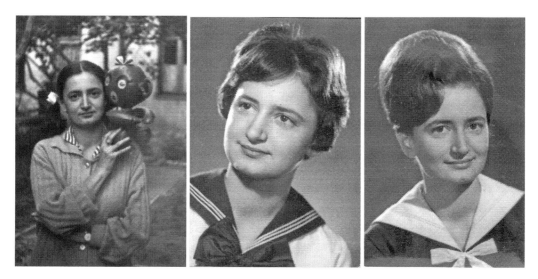

Eszter Gárdos in 1963 (left), 1964 (center) and 1966 (right).

1956 uprising and Zsuzsa was transferred to a regular school.

✂ ✂

Eszter started high school in the fall of 1962, at the age of 14. She attended the girls-only Janus Pannonius high school in Pécs. Her high school classmates were mainly from farming or working class families and most of them were not very ambitious. Eszter's best friend in high school was the only other Jewish girl in the class, Zsuzsa Ábrahám. Zsuzsa's parents were Holocaust survivors who married after they returned from deportation, thus Zsuzsa was another of the "Phoenix Chidlren." But Zsuzsa's life made rising difficult. An only child, when she lost her mother at the age of 8 her life changed dramatically. Her father, László Ábrahám had no idea how to raise a girl and eventually Zsuzsa ended up running the entire household while attending school. The combination of household obligations and lack of a supporting family environment undercut her motivation in school and she was a mediocre student at best. In spite of their big differences in academic achievements and family backgrounds Eszter and Zsuzsa became very close friends. This friendship is still strong today, fifty years later.

Zsuzsa's early life was not a happy one. Just around the time she finished high school her father developed Alzheimer's disease. He passed away when Zsuzsa was 23 years old. Longing for family life, shortly after her father's death she married a young army lieutenant, Tamás Bodori. They had two children, Ágnes and András. A few years later, however, Tamás left his family for another woman. Zsuzsa remarried, but her second husband was quite sick and died of kidney failure a few years later. Zsuzsa eventually found a new partner with whom she now lives. Her joys in life are five grandchildren. When we visit Hungary, Eszter always meets Zsuzsa and they keep in touch via the internet.

Eszter was not only an excellent student, she was also busy with extracurricular activities. She continued ballet through her high school years, took piano lessons and was very active in the Communist youth movement, KISZ (Kommunista Ifjusági Szövetség). About 90% of all high school students were members of KISZ because if one was not a member of this organization it was very difficult to be admitted to a university or to get a good job. The only exceptions were religious schools, where students were not expected to join KISZ. KISZ was a combination of Communist indoctrination and fun activities. In some respects the organization combined the boy/girl scouts with a communist ideology. KISZ was such a broad-based organization because of the Kádár doctrine that declared that "those who are not against us, are with us." This was a huge change from the mantra of the Rákosi regime that followed the "those who are not with us are against us" approach.

✂ ✂

Meanwhile, Juci was not satisfied with her job in the library. Her dream was to join academia and teach college students. Her doctorate was a teaching degree in German and French, but there were no German or French departments in Pécs. The only foreign language the Teachers College of Pécs offered was Russian. Already quite fluent in Russian by the mid-1950s, and convinced that Russian was the most important foreign language for modern Hungarians, she was quite motivated to earn a degree in Russian language. Finally, in the summer of 1962 she was offered a teaching position in the Department of Russian Language and Literature in the Teachers College of Pécs. This offer was contingent on Juci earning a Russian language teacher certificate from an accredited university. In the fall of 1963 she started her studies in the liberal arts college of the Loránd Eötvös University (ELTE) in Budapest. She got credit for the courses she had already taken and finished this five-year degree in two years. Needless to say, all her grades were A's. She was 49 years old when she earned her third, and final, university degree.

A very conscientious and popular teacher, she also got along well with her colleagues in the department, some of whom were native Russians. Sometime in the late 1960s she was appointed to lead the Russian Department and a few years later was promoted to serve as Vice President of the College. She retired from the Teachers College in 1975 when she and Pista moved to Budapest to be close to their grandchildren.

✂ ✂

Eszter was 16 years old when Juci was awarded a month-long scholarship to attend a continuing education workshop for teachers of Russian language. The workshop was held in Moscow and Juci decided to take her daughter along. This gave Eszter a great opportunity to perfect her Russian. She stayed with a Jewish family whom Juci had met while they were visiting Pécs a few years earlier. Alexander and Rebecca Zilberkvit were a highly accomplished couple. Alexander, an architect, was the chief designer of Lenin stadium, the main sports stadium in Moscow. Rebecca was a piano teacher. They had an extremely talented son, 21 year old Mark, a student in the school of architecture. He was also a very talented musician. In fact, he wanted to be a pianist, but his parents pushed him to get a "real" profession. After finishing his degree in architecture Mark was admitted to the Moscow Conservatory, the most prestigious music school in the Soviet Union. He graduated with a degree in piano and tried to make a living as a performing artist, and later as a music critic. Unfortunately, he only had limited success in this highly competitive field. Later he and his family emigrated to the U.S.A. and settled in the New York area.

Eszter had a great time in Moscow. Rebecca and Juci did not want to let a 16 year old girl roam alone in a foreign city, but the independent minded Eszter sometimes managed to explore Moscow alone. She vividly remembers visiting the Lenin Mausoleum. The Kaaba of Communism, every true Communist must visit the Lenin Mausoleum at least once during his or her lifetime. In those days and for many years before the fall of the Berlin Wall, the crowd queued around the block to catch a quick glimpse of the great leader. Visitors were kept moving, so one only spent a few minutes inside the mausoleum before being hurried out by the guards. The waiting time was sometimes five or six hours, but foreigners were allowed to go to the head of the queue. Eszter told the guards that she came from a foreign country and was taken inside almost immediately. Needless to say the crowd was not pleased.

Most of the time, however, Eszter had to explore Moscow with chaperones. Among Rebecca's students was a young woman who volunteered to accompany Eszter to various places, including museums and swimming pools. Mark was an insider among the young classical music crowd and managed to smuggle Eszter into Tchaikovsky Hall, the most famous concert hall in Moscow. Tickets were impossible to buy, but Mark managed to get them inside to listen to the world famous International Tchaikovsky Competition.

Eszter also visited the other main attractions in Moscow: she explored the Museum in the Kremlin, the Palace of Congresses where she enjoyed a performance of the Moscow Ballet, the Tretyakov State Gallery of Russian paintings. She visited the largest department store in the Soviet Union, GUM, and spent considerable time at the suburban dacha of the Zilberkvit family. The month in Moscow was one of the brightest points in Eszter's young life. It opened her eyes to the world beyond her small home town, Pécs.

8.3. Leaving Town

Eszter graduated from high school in the summer of 1966. Her final exam was excellent and her future bright. In high school she excelled in mathematics and physics and won second place in the physics competition of Baranya Province beating boys who attended elite high schools. There was a debate, however, in the family about where she should continue her education. Juci and Pista would have preferred their daughter to stay in Pécs. However, at that time there was no university level education there in mathematics and physics. The Teachers College only offered a program for elementary school teachers and Eszter was too ambitious to settle for such a program. There was an opportunity to apply for a physics or mathematics program at Moscow State University, one of the leading institutions of higher learning in the Soviet Union. The idea of letting Eszter go abroad to study really frightened Juci and Pista and they vehemently argued against it.

The eventual compromise was that Eszter would apply to the Loránd Eötvös University (ELTE) in Budapest. ELTE had three programs involving mathematics and physics: a five-year master of physics program that trained physicists for research and industry, a five-year master of mathematics program that trained both applied and pure mathematicians, and a five-year mathematics and physics teachers' master's program that trained high school physics and mathematics teachers. Eszter was not really interested in doing research, and was under the influence of a mother heavily involved in teaching. After some discussion, she applied to the mathematics and physics teachers program at ELTE and was admitted.

The next question was, where would she live in Budapest? She did not want to live in the over-crowded, uncomfortable dormitories. Students who stayed in dorms usually had lower grades and fell behind those living under better circumstances. Eventually, Juci and

Pista approached Józsi Bíró who agreed to give Eszter a home. Juci and Pista covered room and board, and Eszter had a family environment on the Buda side of Budapest, on Ulászló Street, only a fifteen minute bus ride away from ELTE. Here, Eszter was under the supervision of Józsi's wife, Márta, which gave great comfort to Juci and Pista.

Eszter Gárdos studying for an exam in 1968.

The Bíró family lived on the second floor of a two-story villa. The apartment had three large rooms plus several smaller ones that served as work areas. But, in addition to the four members of the Bíró family (Józsi, Márta, Zsuzsa and Ági) it also was home to Márta's elderly aunt and a friend of Ági's, also paying for room and board. Eszter moved into this crowded apartment, but it was still much better than a dorm.

However, it was also difficult to find a corner to study in for exams. Semester grades were primarily determined by individual oral exams in which the professor asked penetrating questions and the student answered on the spot. An exam could take anywhere between 15 and 30 minutes and were very challenging. During examination periods Eszter usually went home to Pécs to study, returning to Budapest only to take the exams.

✂ ✂

Eszter's cousin Ági was admitted to medical school and started her studies at the same time Eszter started hers. Ági however, was not very motivated and thus was a mediocre student. She was smart enough to pass her exams and steadily progressed through her medical degree. During these years Eszter and Ági grew very close; they bonded like sisters. As a matter of fact, Ági was closer to Eszter than to her own sister, Zsuzsa. This is not surprising, since Zsuzsa was some 8 years older than Ági, and she was the perfect child: smart, motivated with a world view very close to her father's.

Zsuzsa obtained a master's degree in Chemical Engineering from the Budapest Technical University. I think this was her father's wish. She, however, had no interest in working as a chemical engineer and instead worked as a tour guide leading groups in Russian and German. (She was also fluent in English, but usually did not guide English speaking groups.) Austria is close to Hungary, and Zsuzsa guided Austrian groups quite frequently. Through her work she met a manager of one of the Austrian tourist agencies, Christian Gloskowsky. This work connection eventually evolved into a close personal relationship and Zsuzsa married Christian sometime around 1967 while Eszter was living with the Bíró family. After the wedding Zsuzsa obtained a Hungarian exit visa and moved to Vienna. It is a bit ironic that in Vienna she returned to her original profession and worked as a chemical engineer. She was employed by the Austrian Customs Service and her job was to make sure that important chemical products met Austrian standards.

Life with the Bírós was anything but boring. After Zsuzsa moved to Vienna there were three young women living in the apartment: Ági, Eszter and Ági's friend, Szilvia. All three young women started dating about the same time. Ági's boyfriend was Gyula Nagy, a car mechanic who came from a working class family. This created a major crisis in the Bíró family. Józsi was vehemently against his daughter's mésalliance,[2] forbidding her to date Gyula. Ági disobeyed her father's explicit order. Things reached crisis level when Ági became pregnant in 1970. Józsi disowned his daughter and Ági moved out of the Ulászló Street apartment. For a while she lived with Gyula's grandmother in a tiny apartment with no indoor plumbing. Eventually, Márta and Zsuzsa convinced Józsi that he was making a mistake and Ági was reluctantly readmitted to the family. She married Gyula and gave birth to a beautiful baby girl which she named after her older sister Zsuzsa.

After the birth of Zsuzsa, Ági and Gyula were allowed to move back to the Ulászló Street apartment. Things were a bit frosty at the beginning, but the baby created strong bonds between the generations. There is nothing better to butter-up a reluctant father than giving him an adorable grandchild. Later, Ági had two more daughters, Ágnes (everyone called her "little Ági") and Gabriella (Gabi).

Willy Langfelder (left) and Eszter Gárdos (right) in 1967.

Eszter was not well traveled when she started her undergraduate studies. Except for her month in Moscow, her travels had mainly been restricted to Budapest and Lake Balaton, where the Gárdos family vacationed almost every year. It was, therefore, with great excitement that in the summer of 1967 she was getting ready for her first trip beyond "The Iron Curtain," to nearby Vienna. At the time Juci's Aunt Janka was splitting her time between London and Vienna and invited Juci and Eszter to visit her in Austria. Janka lived with her older daughter, Willy, and Willy's husband, Zoltán. (Janka's younger daughter, Annie, had moved to New York some 30 years earlier).

Eszter was 19 years old and had grown up in a sheltered environment. Everything she knew about the "rotting" West came from Communist propaganda or the opinions of her domineering mother. The visit to Austria was very short and Eszter had no time to understand the lies behind the Communist propaganda. Juci and Eszter spent a week with Janka, Willy and Zoltán. They visited the usual tourist places, including the Hofburg Palace, the Kunsthistorisches Museum (Art Museum) and the summer residence of the Emperor, the Schönbrunn Palace. They also took a day-trip to the Austrian Alps and window shopped on the elegant Kärntnerstrasse.

Eszter was too young to recognize the awkwardness of the situation. At this time the Hungarian currency (Forint) was not convertible and tourists traveling abroad were only allowed to buy a trivial amount of western currency ($70 per person). Thus, Juci and Eszter

---

[2]Mmésalliance is a marriage with a person of inferior social position.

were completely reliant on Janka's hospitality and generosity. They could not afford to pay for their restaurant meals or admission fees. This greatly bothered Juci, a proud Communist who had only very reluctantly accepted the invitation to Vienna. I think that the main reason she eventually decided to go was that she wanted to show her daughter to Janka. Since neither of Janka's two daughters had any children, Eszter was the only child in the extended family. Both Janka and Willy died in 1978 and this was the only time Eszter met them in her life.

9 Eszter and Tamás

9.1. University Years

Eszter and I first met sometime in 1967. I was a sophomore and Eszter a freshman so our classes did not overlap. We were both active in KISZ (the Communist youth movement) and served on the committee dealing with international student programs.

Eszter remembers an interesting incident when we were just superficial acquaintances. Her mother was in Budapest on some business and took Eszter shopping in the downtown area, as it turned out, not far from the Műhely. I was a frequent visitor at the Műhely and we ran into one another. After exchanging a few words I left and actually don't remember this event at all. Juci turned to Eszter and asked, "Did you know that boy is Jewish?" Eszter probably remembers the moment because she was very surprised. Her Communist mother had never brought up Jewishness before, especially not about someone she'd just met for a few minutes. Perhaps Juci had a sixth sense of what was coming.

Every year there was a university competition for students majoring in physics and in the teaching of physics. The winners were taken for a field trip to the astronomical observatory in the Mátra mountains (the highest peak is 1016 meters, so not much of a mountain). The largest instrument at the observatory was (and still is) a 50 cm Schmidt telescope. In 1968, we were among the winners and sometime in the early spring a group of about 15 students and young faculty hiked to the observatory from the nearby town.

After dinner one evening the group decided not to return to town but to stay at the observatory and play murder mystery games all night. The rules were very simple. Everyone drew a card from a standard deck. Everybody kept their cards secret, except the detective – the person who had drawn the ace of hearts. The ace of spades was the murderer. The lights were turned off and people mingled in the dark. At some point the murderer put his or her hands on the neck of the victim, who screamed. The lights were turned on and the detective came in. The detective asked questions trying to figure out what had happened. Everybody was supposed to tell the truth with the exception of the murderer who could lie. At the end, the detective had one chance to identify the murderer by asking for his or her card. If the detective was correct, he or she won. If the detective missed, the murderer won. When everyone was playing well, a game lasted a couple of hours, or even more.

That evening, the first game lasted a very long time. There was a very skilled murderer lying extremely well and misleading everybody. Well after midnight the detective made a guess, and missed. At this point everybody showed their cards. It turned out that Eszter was the murderer. She was so innocent looking and so expertly evasive that nobody really

Left: The portal of the Gourmand café. Right: Eszter and Tamás in the Gourmand café in 2013.

suspected her. The group had great fun, and I was very impressed. On the way back to Budapest I asked Eszter out.

On our first date, we met in the Gourmand café located only a few short blocks from ELTE, at the corner of Lajos Kossuth and Semmelweiss Streets. I did not drink coffee at all, but also ordered an espresso when Eszter asked the waitress for one. I had a difficult time drinking the bitter coffee, but was too embarrassed to admit it. We stayed an hour or so. When the bill came I was not sure how to handle the situation. Tradition was that when women were in the company of men they were not supposed to pay in public places. On the other hand, many younger women considered this custom insulting and insisted on paying their own bills. I erred on the side of modern attitudes. Even today, some 45 years later, I still hear, "And you let me pay for my coffee on our first date." I guess a man can never win... Still, the fiasco with the bill did not deter Eszter from seeing me more and more frequently. By early summer we were a couple very much in love.

Sometime in the fall of 1968 we introduced one another to our respective families. Just like in most families, these introductions were full of memorable and embarrassing moments. Eszter was very much concerned about the reactions of Magda and Éva and pleasantly surprised when she received a warm reception. Magda and Éva were very much impressed that I'd finally brought home a nice, smart and ambitious Jewish girl. My father, János, was also pleased, but, as usual, he kept his opinion to himself.

Eszter was also concerned about the reaction of her mother. Juci had extremely high standards and was a confusing mixture of Communist and elitist. My humble origins and low social status were certainly not what Juci imagined for her daughter. In addition, my family was not Communist; if anything, they belonged to the remnants of capitalistic society. To everyone's surprise, however, Juci was quite impressed with me. As an experienced educator she recognized, I think, a kid with potential. I was well informed, smart, ambitious and very familiar with history and literature. And last, but not least, I was Jewish. As Juci explained it to her daughter, "At least he will not call you a stinky Jew." Actually, Juci was wrong. Today, after more than four decades of marriage, I jokingly call Eszter "stinky" and usually add, "and your mother was wrong."

While each of us was enthusiastically embraced by the other's family, the relationship between our mothers, Magda and Juci, was rocky from the first moment they met. They were polar opposites. Juci was highly educated, disliked and did not appreciate homemaking, was elitist, looked down upon uneducated people, and had a natural aura of aristocracy around her. In addition, she was a hard line communist who defended the Communist government and the Soviet Union even when they were obviously wrong. Magda was uneducated, down to earth, very practical, ran the household alone, worked full time and was a street-smart businesswoman. Juci felt contempt for Magda and Magda deeply resented Juci's mixture of communism and aristocracy. Juci called the Gombosis "Jews from Dob Street"[1] and Magda considered Juci a hypocrite.

✂ ✂

I was not a born adventurer. I liked the comfort of city life and did not particularly enjoy camping or similar adventures. However, in the summer of 1968, with five other young people, I skippered one of three inflatable motorboats along the Danube from the city of Győr to the Danube delta in Bulgaria. The trip covered about a thousand kilometers through Hungary, Romania, Yugoslavia and Bulgaria and took over a month.

I have a photo showing me as I was preparing for the trip. At this time Eszter and I were already seriously dating. When I returned from the trip, Eszter greeted me at the airport.

I adored my niece, Andrea, and she immediately liked Eszter. Eszter and I very much enjoyed taking Andrea to the amusement park, the Budapest Zoo and to other child-friendly places. At the time Andrea still very much resembled me and people often remarked about the nice young couple with a cute child. Eszter and I proudly accepted these compliments, never admitting that Andrea was not ours.

Tamás Gombosi preparing for his month-long Danube trip in 1968.

By the end of 1968 we were already talking about getting married after graduation. There was no "popping the question," no big moment; we just knew we wanted to marry. This situation created several hilarious and awkward moments.

In the late 1960s young couples were expected to behave quite properly in public places. What today are called "public displays of affection" were considered improper behavior; holding hands, even for married couples, was riské. Living together without being married was taboo; couples doing this were usually social outcasts. Needless to say, human nature always found ways to carry on affairs, but these affairs were supposed to be very private. Once, Eszter and her father were going home to Pécs. I accompanied them to the train station. When the train was about to depart Eszter gave me a kiss on the cheek and I left. Less than a minute later, Pista lectured Eszter about her improper behavior, demanding that she never do this again. Eszter ignored her father's warning, but was afterwards very careful

---

[1]This expression refers to the main street of Jewish Budapest before World War II. Dob Street was the center of Jewish life and home to the Jewish petit-bourgeois class.

Left: Eszter and Tamás with Andrea in 1968. Right: Eszter and Tamás in 1968.

in the presence of her parents.

Hungarian universities have a semester system. The first semester starts in the second half of September and ends just before Christmas. Examinations typically are held in January and the second semester starts early in February running through the end of May with the examination period in June. Eszter invited me to visit her family in Pécs at the end of December 1968. Juci and Pista decided, however, that it was improper to host a young man in the home of an unmarried young woman. They rented a room for me a couple of hundred meters from their apartment.

The visit went reasonably well (as these first visits go) with countless introductions to the many acquaintances of the Gárdos family. Everyone was curious to see Eszter's suitor and I just could not keep up with the names and faces. Still, under Eszter's watchful eyes I was on my best behavior and things moved along smoothly.

For me, the most awkward moment of the visit came toward the end when one evening Juci and Eszter mysteriously disappeared and I suddenly found myself alone with Pista. After a brief period of neutral conversation Pista suddenly asked what my plans with Eszter were. I was, perhaps naively, unprepared for this question and did not know how to answer. After all, we'd been dating for less than a year and even though we spoke privately about marriage, nothing specific had ever been discussed. Recovering from my surprise, I told Pista we were planning eventually to marry but had no specific plans. This reply satisfied Pista. From this point we were treated as an engaged couple by the Gárdos family.

By the middle of 1969, everyone treated us as a stable couple. My sister and brother-in-law, Éva and Gyuri, were planning a month-long road tour to discover Transylvania and the rest of Romania. They invited us to come along. We had no car and now Éva and Gyuri had a Russian made Moskvitch sedan with a 1.3 liter engine that gave it a hopping 50 horse powers. The car was small, underpowered and unreliable. However, at the time owning a car was a big luxury in Hungary. Éva and Gyuri were only able to buy it because they worked in Dubna where foreigners got special treatment.

The trip to Romania was interesting but full of misfortunes. We visited some of the historical Hungarian places and enjoyed the beauty of the countryside. Sanitary conditions, however, were substandard and Eszter ended up with food poisoning that ruined the second half of the trip. Due to poor sanitary conditions Gyuri developed hemorrhoids (because he had problems using the filthy facilities) that eventually required surgery. In spite of these complications, we enjoyed the trip.

Éva Gombosi in her Mokvitch in 1965.

✂ ✂

As noted earlier, sometime during the second half of 1969, Éva and Gyuri received visiting positions in Paris (see Section 7.4). They had pretty much decided that at the end of their visiting positions they would defect to the U.S.A., if they could line up jobs there. A big question was what to do with their condo. They wanted to make sure that it was still available if their defection plans failed, but they knew that the government would confiscate it if they defected. There was a huge housing shortage in Budapest and their condominium not only represented a large financial asset, but had an even bigger practical value for a young couple – privacy.

While the government *could* confiscate the apartment of defectors, evictions was almost never used. Anyone who lived in the apartment at the time the Bozokis defected would have the inside track for eventually owning the condo. The dilemma was how to ensure that Éva and Gyuri could keep it in the family. Finally, they came up with a solution: let us move in. If they returned, we certainly would give the apartment back. If they didn't, the condo stayed in the family.

There was only one problem with the plan: as noted earlier, in the late 1960s cohabitation was socially unacceptable. If we wanted to move in together, we had to get married. Magda and even Juci were quite receptive to the idea. After all, Eszter was not much younger than they had been when each of them married. János and Pista on the other hand, had misgivings. We were still students at the time, unable to support ourselves. If we married, the two families had to support us for at least a few years. Both János and Pista expressed their misgivings, but in the end the women won (as usual).

Sometime in the fall of 1969 there was an "official" engagement party and we went out to purchase wedding rings. We could only afford the cheapest rings. They were so flimsy that they wore out in a few years. We bought a new set of wedding rings for our tenth anniversary.

The wedding took place on January 3, 1970. It was a relatively small, inexpensive affair without a fancy dinner or reception. In the afternoon, Magda invited the immediate family to the Izabella Street apartment where she served small party sandwiches and finger food. There was wine and champagne, but no fancy drinks. The "reception" was over by 5 p.m. We changed to regular clothing and left for our "honeymoon," a three-day long trip to

Eszter and Tamás in the fall of 1969.

nearby Eger.

It was, however, more a study trip than a honeymoon. January was examination period at the university. I was a fifth-year student already working on my master's thesis, so did not have any exams. Eszter, on the other hand, was only a fourth-year student. She took along her books and studied most of the time. It was a real fun honeymoon.

✂ ✂

Shortly after the wedding Éva and Gyuri left for France and Andrea followed them a couple of weeks later. We moved in to the Nagyenyed Street condo, from our perspectives, a most luxurious place. After all, we were just starting our lives together and suddenly had our own place without need to live with our parents. It was a rare luxury in Hungary at the time.

Eszter had no cooking experience. Unlike her mother, she wanted to be both an intellectual and to run her own household. She was very protective of "her kitchen" and did not want anyone else to interfere with her housework. She made a great effort to learn how to cook. At the beginning there were a few misfires, but eventually she became a good cook. Some of the initial challenges were really funny.

I loved bony meat. My mother often made breaded pork chop, leaving the bones inside. One weekend, Eszter wanted to make me something that I really liked and decided to make breaded pork chop bones. She carefully cut all meat off the bones and with heroic effort prepared the breaded bare bones. I was delighted that my bride made such an effort for me. I was, however, quite surprised to discover there was no meat on the bones. We had a good laugh at the misadventure and I tease Eszter even today that I was treated like a spoiled dog with breaded bare bones.

Wedding pictures of Eszter Gárdos and Tamás Gombosi.

Another cooking adventure involved making my favorite shredded zucchini dish (tökfőzelék). Eszter used a cookbook to make it, but she somehow forgot to put all ingredients into the dish. The result was so underwhelming that we decided to send the completely flavorless shredded zucchini down the toilet. In spite of the initial failures, Eszter eventually became a good cook who enjoys making nice dishes. Today I, her children and her grandchildren, very much like her cooking.

9.2.   The Young Couple

In June 1970 I received my Master's Degree in physics. My thesis was in theoretical high-energy (or elementary particle) physics, a very popular subject at that time. Éva and Gyuri were experimental high-energy physicists and I was hoping to be able to work with them at some point. Life, however, turned out very differently. My dream was to join the Department of Theoretical Physics at ELTE. This department, however, was dominated by Christian intelligentsia not very eager to admit a Jew into their circle. Instead of me, they hired my classmate, András Patkós, who was only half Jewish. An interesting aside is that György Ferenczi (who was also Jewish) managed to get an extra position given to the Theoretical Physics department targeted to him (he used some family connections at the Ministry of Education). The department, however, rejected this slot so that they did not end up with too many Jews. After rejecting the extra position, they blamed me saying that I had vehemently lobbied against giving someone a preferred job without proper competition. It was a lie; while not pleased to see my classmate get preferential treatment, I never publicly objected. Besides, we all know how much the opinion of a job candidate matters in hiring decisions. This entire incident just demonstrates the deeply rooted anti-semitism in the Hungarian physics community at the time.

Job hunting was a difficult task. There were very few available positions at highly coveted institutions. The top opportunities were in the various physics departments at ELTE: the Department of Nuclear Physics, the Department of Theoretical Physics, or the Department of Solid State Physics, and at the Central Research Institute for Physics (KFKI). Only the top students got jobs at these places, the majority of the graduating class ended up in non-research type jobs.

I was hired by Antal Somogyi who at the time was the head of the Cosmic Ray Division at KFKI. He was one of the lieutenants of Lajos Jánossy and was leading the particle astrophysics effort. Somogyi was a Christian gentleman in the best sense of the word. He was religious (a bit pious), but he was very fair and willing to stand up for his people. He never particularly liked me but he very much appreciated my talent, drive and accomplishments. I always had high respect for Tóni (as everyone called Somogyi) but we never became close to each other.

Interkosmos was a Soviet space program, designed to give nations on friendly terms with the Soviet Union access to space missions. The organization was created in 1967, but it took Hungary a few years to create an organizational structure ready to participate in the scientific program. As part of the Hungarian Intercosmos program, the Cosmic Ray Division of KFKI was given two positions to start *in situ* (satellite based) observations of outer space. For one of these positions Somogyi hired me.

The Cosmic Ray Division of KFKI was an interesting mixture of misfits. When Jánossy started cosmic ray research at KFKI there were no powerful particle accelerators and the only way to study elementary particles was by studying the interaction of very high energy cosmic rays with matter. By 1970, however, there were powerful accelerators built in the U.S., Europe, the Soviet Union and Japan. Particle physics (or high energy physics) became a completely separate discipline from cosmic ray studies. Elementary particle physics was considered the frontier. Those who switched from cosmic rays to high-energy physics looked down on their "uninspired" colleagues who stayed in the "old" discipline. In KFKI the original cosmic ray research group was split into several new discipline groups, including nuclear physics, elementary particle physics and cosmic ray astrophysics. Most people (including Éva and Gyuri) moved on to the new groups and only Tóni Somogyi remained in the cosmic ray astrophysics group. Somogyi was a true gentleman but a bad politician and manager. Most talented people left his group and, exploiting his compassion, a number of "losers" were transferred to his group.

In addition to Antal Somogyi and me the division included György Benkó, József Kóta, György Válas and András Varga. They were all misfits in their own ways. Benkó and Varga were graduates of Moscow State University (MGU) and were less than mediocre scientists. Benkó was a very nice guy and tried very hard to do a good job, however, because he was not good at office politics he usually ended up with the most unpleasant and unrewarding tasks. Varga was very different. Semi-openly gay and quite paranoid about it, to compensate for his internalized homophobia, he was overly political and played the Communist party card. He was part of KFKI's party leadership and used his influence to his maximum advantage. He was also viciously anti-semitic. He passionately hated Válas (who was Jewish) and badmouthed him at every opportunity. He was jealous of me from day one, and over the years tried to undercut me at every possible opportunity. György Válas was a mediocre scientist and a very unpleasant personality. He was an embodiment of negative Jewish stereotypes: rude, inconsiderate and opinionated. It was not easy to get along with him, and he was universally disliked at KFKI. József Kóta was completely different. A brilliant mathematician and a very good physicist, he was unfortunately, also communication challenged. One needed to know him quite well to recognize his talents. I seemed instantly to recognize them and actively worked on finding joint projects with him. This eventually benefited us both.

✂ ✂

During her studies at ELTE, Eszter realized that being a high school math and physics teacher is less interesting than doing research. An outstanding student, in her senior year she won the prestigious Scholarship of the People's Republic – the same scholarship I had won two years earlier.[2] This scholarship came with a stipend of 1,000 Forints a month (roughly $80 at the official exchange rate). Today this sounds like nothing, but at that time 1,000 Forints was the average monthly salary in Hungary. Eszter became interested in astrophysics and for her master's thesis worked with Judit Németh, a professor of theoretical physics.

Judit Németh was the daughter of a very famous Hungarian writer, László Németh[3] and a well known socialite. She was married to József Dörnyei, who was leading the mathematical research and development department at the Central Statistical Office of Hungary. Eszter was working at KFKI as an undergraduate research assistant and hoping to join KFKI

---

[2]During the 1968-69 academic year, when we were not yet even engaged, I was awarded the Scholarship of the People's Republic. Since I was living with my parents at the time, I could not spend it all and was left with considerable amounts at the end of each month. After a few months, Eszter and I decided that we would open a joint savings account. This idea created some friction with Pista who, as a lawyer, understood the potential downsides of such a move in the case Eszter and I broke up. We, however, considered Pista's concerns unjustified since we could not imagine ever breaking up. In the end we opened our first joint savings account.

[3]László Németh wrote a very successful book about his three daughters with the title *Lányaim* (my daughters). It did not paint a pretty picture of Judit.

after graduation. However, in early 1971 everything changed.

Gyuri, while in France, was able to get a visiting appointment in the U.S. and he and Éva decided to defect. Their official leave from KFKI ended at the end of January 1971. From France they requested an extension for a second year. After KFKI replied that they could only request another leave of absence while in Hungary, requiring a return to behind The Iron Curtain, they informed the institute that instead of returning to Hungary they would move to the U.S.

This announcement made life difficult for Eszter and me. In order to make people think twice about defection, it was customary that Hungarian authorities confiscated all their left-behind belongings and punished the relatives who stayed behind. It was not unusual for a close relative to be fired from his or her job. Even those who were not fired were banned from foreign travel for a long time.

The backlash started shortly after the defection letter was received at KFKI. I was in a weak position, because – as a new hire – I was still in my 12 month probation period and easy to fire. However, Antal Somogyi stood up for me and in the end I was not terminated. Eszter, however, was not so lucky. She was only a student assistant, so officially she was not an employee of KFKI. We were summoned by the head of the personnel office who told us that there was no way that KFKI would hire another member of the Bozóki-Gombosi family. "We've had enough of your family" was the statement. This stern message devastated Eszter who very much lost interest in a research career at this point.

Éva and Gyuri were sentenced in absentia to several years in prison. Magda was summoned by the Hungarian security services who lectured her about raising such traitors. I was told that I could not travel abroad for several years, even on official business.

The retaliation did not end with my grounding and denying Eszter her dream job. The Nagyenyed Street apartment was confiscated and we lived in limbo for a while. Eventually we were given the opportunity to purchase the apartment for about five years' worth of our combined incomes. While this amount was well below market value, we didn't have enough money even for the down payment. Juci and Pista came up with the money, but Pista, as a lawyer, wanted to ensure that Eszter was protected if anything went wrong. He insisted that I sign a legal agreement acknowledging that the downpayment for the condo came from Eszter's private funds and it was not joint property. This event greatly offended me, but in the end I had no choice but to agree.

Eszter still needed a job and her advisor came to her rescue. Judit Németh recommended Eszter to her husband who was looking for a young mathematician to work with sophisticated statistical packages. After graduation Eszter joined the Central Statistical Office of Hungary and started to work with advanced statistical analysis tools. Over time she became an expert in this field and was very successful.

9.3. Life Goes On

Éva and Gyuri started their new life in the U.S. with great expectations. Gyuri had a visiting professorship at the University of Pennsylvania. Friends who had left Hungary in 1968 had all ended up with good academic positions at leading American universities: Ervin Fenyves was a Professor of Environmental Science at the University of Texas at Dallas, Gábor Domokos was Professor of Physics at Johns Hopkins University in Baltimore, and

Péter Surányi landed a job as Professor of Physics at the University of Cincinnati. Gyuri was convinced that he too would immediately be offered a professorship at a good university and Éva was willing to take any job in related fields.

But, the timing of the Bozokis arrival in the U.S. science scene was very unfortunate. Federal research and development (R&D) funding peaked in 1967 at around $17 billion (about $120 billion in 2013 dollars) and by 1975 would decline by about 30%. This precipitous decline hit hardest the academic research communities in high-energy physics, space research, and many other areas of science and engineering. When Gyuri started his position at the University of Pennsylvania he was told that the federal grant supporting his salary was ending soon. Instead of working on new projects he had to start looking for a job. Across the U.S. the mid-70's was a difficult time in academic budgets, not only in the sciences. There were very few academic positions available, so in the end both Gyuri and Éva had to look outside of academia. This was particularly hard on Gyuri who never could completely come to terms with the collapse of his dreams.

Still, in a few years the Bozoki family adjusted to life in America. After working as a programmer for various companies, Éva ended up at Brookhaven National Laboratory (BNL), where she worked on control programs for the National Synchrotron Light Source project. Gyuri tried to stay in various temporary positions in academia, but by the late 1970s accepted a job at the BNL where he first worked on superconducting magnets and later transferred to BNL's nuclear safety group (which worked in collaboration with the Nuclear Regulatory Commission). His office was also located at BNL, so they ended up commuting together from their home in Stony Brook, NY. Andrea grew up to be a smart, hard-working – but spoiled – only child.

✄ ✄

In the spring of 1972 Eszter became pregnant and she did not need a test to know it. She started throwing up after a Sunday lunch at Magda's house and did not stop for more than four months. She did not have morning sickness, she had all-day sickness. The situation became so bad that she was hospitalized for several weeks and lost a lot of weight. She was about 45 kg (99 lb) when she became pregnant and 42 kg (92.5 lb) when she was three months pregnant. The second half of the pregnancy was normal and the entire family eagerly awaited the baby.

In the morning of January 14, 1973 Eszter started to have frequent contractions. It was a cold Sunday morning and we debated whether it was a smart thing to go to the hospital on a Sunday. By the afternoon, however, it was obvious that the baby did not care about Sundays and we took a taxi to the Rókus Hospital where Eszter's obstetrician worked. Needless to say, the doctor was not in the hospital on a Sunday afternoon. By the evening the contractions were quite frequent and finally the doctor arrived around 7 p.m. He examined Eszter and determined that the baby was not in a final position and it might be necessary to perform a Caesarian section. At this point I almost fainted. For a couple of minutes the doctor worked on me. Everybody felt sorry for me and neglected Eszter. After all, she was just giving birth, while her husband underwent a trauma. Sounds like a normal Jewish family.

At the time, husbands were not allowed into the delivery room (at least not in Hungary). I was sent home and the doctor promised that he would call as soon as the baby was delivered. Judit Gombosi was born in the early morning hours of January 15, 1973. She was a healthy baby of 3,000 g (6.6 lb). She arrived with natural birth, so the C-section possibility was only a false alarm.

Juci Gombosi, Tamás and Eszter at the Műhely in December 1972.

The standard procedure in Hungarian hospitals was that babies were kept in the nursery and given to their mothers only at feeding times. Judit's first feeding became a minor trauma. The nurses handed out the babies to their respective mothers, but Eszter did not get a baby. When she asked about her child, the nurses frantically searched for Judit and finally found her. She had been accidentally given to another woman who was an experienced mother and who had delivered a baby by Caesarian section. At the time in Hungary women were not allowed to feed their babies for 24 hours after a Caesarian. The lady was surprised to get a baby to feed, but she did not complain. Judit had a great first meal and was soundly asleep when the nurses found her. She did not even wake up when she finally was reunited with her mother.

Mothers were kept in the hospital for a week. This was medically not absolutely necessary, but it provided a little rest to new mothers while they learned how to feed their babies. Eventually I was allowed to take my wife and daughter home. The two excited grandmothers were eagerly waiting in the Nagyenyed Street apartment. When we arrived home, the grandmothers pushed the young mother aside and took over. Eszter and I stood, just looking at each other, but had no chance with the two dominating grandmothers. Fortunately, Judit solved the problem. Her grandmothers immediately tried to change her together. This started by opening the diaper and trying to put a clean one on the baby. Uncovered, Judit released a huge and quite liquid poop that flew out like scattershot. Both grandmothers were equally covered and had to retire to the bathroom to clean themselves. Eszter used this opportunity to regain control of her daughter and chased away the grandmothers when they returned. From this point on Eszter stayed in firm control of her baby and did not let the grandmothers take over again.

✄ ✄

Eszter was working full time and Judit started daycare in September 1973. Daycare in Hungary was quite good and, being heavily subsidized, very cheap. Overall, Judit liked daycare and we were quite happy with it as well. Judit was a very healthy baby and developed very nicely, despite the ways that children in daycare are very often sick since they trade all kinds of infections with each other. She was the center of the extended family.

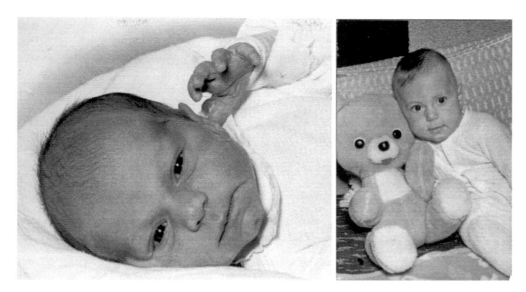

Left: Judit Gombosi shortly after her birth. Right: Judit Gombosi at six months.

With Andrea far away in the U.S., Judit was the only grandchild on both the Gárdos and the Gombosi sides and her grandparents could not get enough of her. There was a not so covert competition between the two grandmothers, but Eszter tried to keep this rivalry under control – as long as she was able.

In the summer of 1974 Eszter again knew that she was pregnant without any tests. She again had constant nausea, and was unable to keep anything down. She was hospitalized again, but this time in a different hospital, since she had a new obstetrician. Her nausea was a little bit better controlled the second time, but she still spent weeks in the hospital and was quite weak when released. During this time I was the primary caregiver for Judit. I took her to daycare in the morning, and picked her up in the afternoon. I fed and bathed her. In the meantime, Eszter was so weak that sometimes she had to sit down on a sidewalk curb to prevent fainting. The Nagyenyed Street condo building had only a single elevator and that was often broken. When this happened I carried Judit on one arm and Eszter on the other up seven floors to our apartment. Fortunately I was young and strong, and could manage the physical challenge.

Zoltán Gombosi was born on March 31, 1975, as it turned out, an Easter Monday, a national holiday in Hungary. We went to the hospital in the early morning (around 6 a.m.) and Zoltán was born by 10am. The doctor arrived too late to help with the birth, so Eszter was helped by the delivery room nurses.

The birth of a boy was a surprise for both of us. We'd convinced ourselves that we would have a second daughter and thus did not prepare much for a boy. Fortunately though, we had selected both a girl's and a boy's name, so we did not have to argue over the name after the birth. Zoltán (everyone called him Zoli) was a healthy boy, somewhat smaller than Judit (6.2 lb).

The arrival of a sibling traumatized Judit. She was a little bit more than two years older and it was hard to understand that this thing was not only going to stay with the family, but also get a lot of attention from everyone. The first encounter between Judit and Zoli was

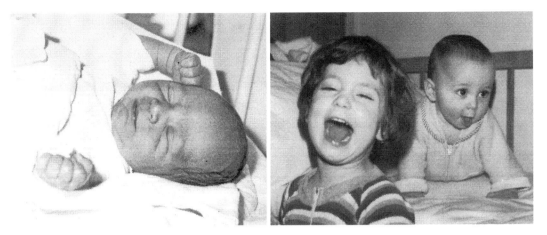

Left: Zoltán Gombosi shortly after his birth. Right: Judit and Zoltán Gombosi in the summer of 1975.

very interesting. In the daycare, Judit had learned that at the end of the day children put away all toys. There were life-sized dolls in the daycare kept in large paper boxes. When Zoli was taken home from the hospital Judit observed him for a few minutes then she turned to me and asked: "Dad, where is his box?" She was in for a rude awakening.

It took a long time for Judit to overcome the trauma of Zoli's birth. While she was a seemingly happy child at home, her teachers at the daycare observed that she withdrew and sometimes sat alone, crying. This lasted quite a few months and we became quite concerned about our daughter. When Zoli was about six months old, Judit took a pair of scissors and tried to check what was inside her brother. Fortunately, I noticed what she was trying to do and stopped her. I was, however, so frightened and shocked that I spanked Judit who still remembers this incident. Afterwards, we kept a very close eye on her whenever she was near her younger brother.

The irony of the situation was that Zoli adored his sister. Whenever she was in the room Zoli watched only Judit and he tried to imitate whatever she was doing. At the time they shared a room in the Nagyenyed Street apartment and Judit started to make peace with the idea of having to share all the attention with her brother.

✂ ✂

In the summer of 1975 Juci and Pista both retired and decided to move to Budapest to be close to their daughter and grandchildren. At the time there was no legal housing market in Hungary, so they had to find an "exchange" of apartments. Budapest was a much more desirable place than the city of Pécs, so they ended up with a pretty bad deal. They gave up their nice, large apartment in Pécs for a tiny studio apartment in the XIIIth district of Budapest (not far from downtown). They moved sometime in the late summer of 1975. The studio apartment was about half an hour by public transportation from the Nagyenyed Street apartment.

Having the Gárdos grandparents in town was a mixed blessing for us. On the one hand, Juci and Pista were a lot of help with the children. We both were working full time and Pista arrived every morning with fresh bakery products for the children; Juci was available

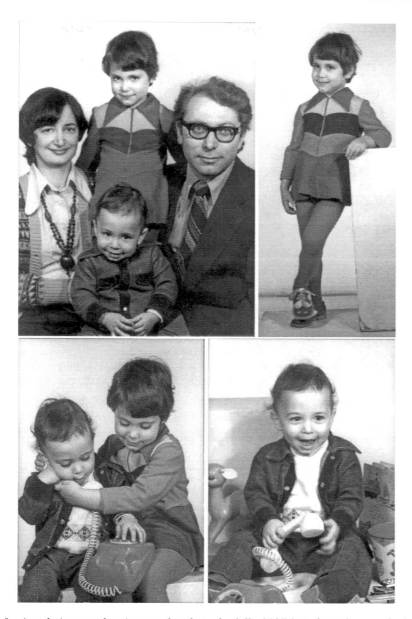

A set of professional pictures showing our family in the fall of 1976. Judit is three and a half and Zoli about 18 months old. Zoli is still attending daycare, but Judit is already in preschool. By this time they both showed signs of their future personalities. Judit had strong convictions and was willing to stand up against anybody (including parents and teachers). Zoli disliked confrontation and was more willing to compromise. Judit was a daredevil and Zoli was much less adventurous. They were the centers of the world for their grandparents and parents.

to babysit whenever the children got sick and could not go to daycare. On the other hand, we had no privacy. Juci and Pista had a key to the apartment and they came unannounced. They never rang the bell, they just opened the door as if they were at home (and in some respect they were). To a large extent it felt as if Eszter's parents had moved in with us.

This arrangement was not unusual in Hungary at that time. Most young families lived with their parents and grandparents played a very important role in family life. Multigenerational households were the standard, both because of a severe housing shortage and because it was the tradition. Another practical reason for the important role grandparents played in the life of young families was low, compressed salaries. The salary of a leading scientist or university professor was only two or three times higher than the salaries of manufacturing workers with only elementary school educations. The end result was that the combined salaries of young couples were inadequate to support an independent life. We were heavily subsidized by the Gárdos_and Gombosi grandparents all the time we lived in Hungary. I do not have exact figures, but my guess is that about a third of all expenses were covered by our parents.

9.4. Moscow

My scientific career had a slow start. Hired with a Master's degree in physics, I was tasked to start a brand new scientific field in Hungary. Several groups were somewhat involved in research that fell under the broader umbrella of space research, but all these investigations were carried out with Earth-based observations. Nobody in Hungary could help me to understand how to use spacecraft measurements to understand the environment beyond the dense atmosphere, an environment that today is called *geospace*.

My first task was to work on the data analysis of the Intercosmos-3 spacecraft built by Soviet and Czechoslovak scientists to study the Earth's radiation belts (Van Allen belts). Since Hungary did not participate in the design and manufacturing of the instruments, it got the unenviable task of converting telemetry signals to useful instrument measurements. My task was to do this conversion. It was technically challenging and required long hours of repetitive work. Eventually, I found a very elegant solution to the problem which impressed my Soviet colleagues. It, however, involved extensive use of digitizing equipment that was available at KFKI but required technicians to operate it. I recommended Eszter for the technician job and thus she was employed as a part time research assistant during her fifth year as a master's student.

I had learned computer programming during my university years. This was quite unusual in the late 1960s when computers were bulky and their computing power very limited. After starting work at KFKI, I became one of the most active users of its "mainframe" computer, a British made ICL-1905. This computer had 32 kbytes memory, used 7-track magnetic tapes as "mass storage" and the computer codes were stored on paper punch tapes. The computer consisted of several cabinet-size racks and occupied a large air-conditioned room, at the time the only air conditioned room in the entire institute. For comparison, note that the first MacIntosh desktop computers in the 1980s had 32 kbytes of memory and more powerful processors. Today's desktop computers have about a million times more memory and computing power than the ICL machine had.

Most of my work was carried out on the ICL. This was a big step forward for the Intercosmos collaboration, since most participants did not have access to computers at all. My knowledge of computer programming gave me a competitive edge over peers in Hungary and Eastern Europe. Mainframe computers were kept in controlled environments and specially trained operators ran them. Computer operators worked in three shifts and – at least in principle – the computer was run on a 24/7 schedule (except for the frequent hardware failures). User programs were run in two shifts: short runs during the day and longer runs during the night. Most of the time, however, there were not enough programs to fill up the night shifts and the "idle" time was given to anyone willing to come in at night and operate the machine. Learning how to operate the ICL computer allowed me to increase my productivity. The price was countless nights away from my family and living in a state of near constant sleep deprivation. The upside: I made very good progress with my work and was able to defend my Ph.D. dissertation in the fall of 1974.

✂ ✂

That first project, as it turned out, was the key to my later scientific career because it caught the eye of a very influential Soviet scientist, Pavel Efimovich Elyasberg. During World War II Elyasberg had been a Soviet artillery officer and had participated in the liberation of Hungary. He was a brilliant mathematician and quickly rose through the ranks of the officer corps; by the mid-1950s he had become a colonel in the Red Army. He survived the Jewish purges after Stalin's death, and in the late 1950s became a leader in the Soviet ballistic missile program. Eventually he became responsible for the trajectory determination of ballistic missiles. When the Soviet space program started in the late 1950s he also became responsible for the orbit calculations of Earth orbiting and deep space satellites.

Elyasberg's military career suddenly ended when the first Soviet mission to the Moon (Lunik-1) missed its target (due to an incorrectly timed upper stage burn) and flew by the Moon. Since he was in charge of the spacecraft's orbit, Elyasberg was immediately discharged from the army and assigned to the civilian space program where he was put

Tamás Gombosi's Ph.D. diploma in Hungarian and Latin.

Pavel Efimovich Elyasberg in the 1950s (left) and the 1970s (right).

in charge of spacecraft communications, orbit determinations and scientific computing. Though a very powerful job in civilian space exploration, it was a huge step down from his former military position.

After I presented my satellite data reconstruction method at a data processing meeting, Elyasberg took me under his wing. I was introduced to members of Elyasberg's own research group at the Space Research Institute (in Russian it is called Institut Kosmicheskich Issledovaniy or IKI) and Elyasberg started to spread the word at IKI that he had discovered a talented Hungarian. Elyasberg's mentorship gave me the opening I needed to break into the international scene.

As one can imagine, Elyasberg was a strong personality with quick (and usually correct) judgement and firm opinions. Being a Jew and a World War II veteran he was very sensitive to anti-semitism and historical revisionism. He could not stand fools and mediocre people. He ruthlessly humiliated those he considered unworthy of being in space research. At IKI everyone showed great respect and deference to Elyasberg and his opinions were not dismissed easily.

There is one incident involving Elyasberg that will stick in my mind forever. It occurred at a small Intercosmos project meeting in Warsaw, Poland with about a dozen participants from the Soviet Union, Czechoslovakia and Hungary. As was customary, one afternoon the hosts organized a sightseeing tour of Warsaw. We were put on a small tour bus with a guide and spent a couple of hours visiting historic sites. After World War II not much was left from old Warsaw, most of it had been completely destroyed. The tour took us to the usual places, including the Jewish Ghetto that was leveled after the heroic uprising in 1943. We visited the memorial where the loading ramp to Treblinka once stood as well as the memorial to the Ghetto uprising. The tour guide was a young Polish woman in her thirties. As the tour went on her comments and remarks became increasingly anti-semitic. She was talking about the exploitation of the Poles by Jews, about Jews who thought they could buy everything including their freedom, and so on. Finally, Elyasberg exploded and using the authority that came with having been a member of the Red Army that actually liberated Eastern Europe, gave a lecture to the woman about history and Polish anti-semitism. I wanted to hug Elyasberg after his lecture, but I just stood there, speechless.

✂ ✂

Sometime around 1974 Elyasberg convinced the leadership of IKI to involve me in the data analysis of the Prognoz satellites. Ten Prognoz satellites were launched between 1972 and 1985 to highly elliptic orbits. The satellites were primarily used for solar and magnetospheric research and were on par with the best NASA satellites of the times. I became involved in the third Prognoz satellite, launched in 1973. As part of the collaboration, satellite data on two magnetic tapes were sent to KFKI through diplomatic channels. The security services at KFKI panicked. Never before had KFKI received satellite information, much less through diplomatic channels. After a short period of uncertainty the Hungarian security people did what any bureaucrat would do: classified the tapes as secret and locked them up in a safe. Fortunately, I had been able to make copies of the tapes before they were locked up, and so was able to complete the work and return the processed data to IKI.

✂ ✂

As I have noted earlier, Antal (Tóni) Somogyi was a bad politician. One of the original Jánossy lieutenants, he was left behind by the politically much more savvy ones. When I started work at KFKI, Tóni had the rank of Division Head, while his peers were one or two levels above him. This greatly bothered Tóni who felt unappreciated by the institute. His unhappiness culminated around the mid-1970s when, after a leadership shakeup, two management levels above him were filled with scientists about half his age. Tóni's reaction to this "insult" was typical: he would show to KFKI how indispensable he was by going abroad for a year and also sending two of his best people away for an extended period. It did not occur to him that nobody would notice their absence at KFKI, since cosmic ray and space research was only of marginal interest for the institute. He secured a year-long fellowship for himself to visit Leningrad State University (today Saint Petersburg State University) and strongly encouraged me and József Kóta to apply for extended fellowships to the Soviet Union. Kóta applied to the Lebedev Physical Institute in Moscow (FIAN) and I to IKI. By late 1975 all three fellowships were approved and Somogyi left for Leningrad. He was soon followed by József Kóta who was accepted to work in the group of Nobel Laureate Vitaliy Ginzburg.

Elyasberg decided that during my extended stay I needed to work with a space science group and not with his applied mathematics group. At that time I didn't understand the difference, but in retrospect it is very clear that Elyasberg was right (as usual). He recommended me to Konstantin Iosifovich Gringauz, the head of a space plasma instrumentation group at IKI. Gringauz accepted me and sometime in late November of 1975 I boarded the train to Moscow. At the railway station I was seen off by Eszter, the almost three-year-old Judit and eight-month-old Zoli. Eszter and I parted with very heavy hearts, but we both realized that this was a unique opportunity to work with some of the world's best space scientists.

✂ ✂

Konstantin Gringauz in the mid 1970s.

Konstantin Iosifovich Gringauz was born in 1918 in Tula, Russia. In 1941 he started to study frequency modulation of radio waves, then a brand new topic. During World War II he worked on the design of small, rugged, sensitive radio transmitters and receivers for tanks. After the end of World War II he started to study radio-wave propagation in the ionosphere. In 1947 Gringauz moved to a laboratory for radio-wave propagation in Sergei Korolev's new Bureau for Rocket Development. In 1948 he participated in the launching of a V-2 rocket which carried a radio sounder to study the ionosphere. In 1949 he was put in charge of a laboratory for radio technology.

In 1956 he began designing instruments for measuring ions in the Earth's atmosphere from a satellite that became Sputnik-3, and was assigned to design the transmitter-antenna system for what became Sputnik-1. His idea that this satellite should use a decameter transmitter was intensely debated and Korolev decided in favor of Gringauz's position, partly because he wished Sputnik-1 to be heard around the globe.

During 1957 Gringauz continued his ionospheric studies, and had radio and Langmuir probe experiments on two geophysical rockets. On October 3 he climbed the rocket at Tyuratam to check out the Sputnik-1 antennae and transmitter. He was the last person to touch the satellite. Following the launch of the world's first artificial satellite, Sputnik-1, on October 4, 1957 the 'beep, beep' of the transmitter which was produced in his laboratory was heard by politicians as well as by amateurs and scientists around the globe.

From 1958 onward his research concentrated on *in situ* measurements of ionized gases surrounding the Earth and the planets Venus and Mars, where he is credited with numerous scientific discoveries and "firsts." He received the Lenin Prize (the highest civilian award in the Soviet Union) in 1960 in recognition of his pioneering work in these fields. In 1959 he moved with his group to the Radio-technical Institute of the Soviet Academy of Sciences and became head of the space research department, which was transformed in 1971 to the laboratory for interplanetary and near-planetary plasma studies of the newly organized Space Research Institute of the Soviet Academy of Sciences (IKI).

Gringauz was a very strong personality, a true fighter. His nickname was "bulldozer" because he plowed ahead with his ideas no matter the opposition. He was highly respected but not liked by his peers and managers. At the same time he always treated his people fairly and was willing to fight for them at any time. His group was very loyal to him and he very loyal to his group.

✂ ✂

The Venera-9 and Venera-10 spacecraft were launched in June 1975. In late October they successfully landed on Venus and operated in the extremely hostile environment for about an hour. The main spacecraft were captured by the gravitational field of the planet and

Top row from left to right: Valentin Etkin, Pavel Elyasberg, Yan Ziman, Yakov Zeldovich, Georgiy Petrov and Iosif Shklovskiy. Second row from left to right: Georgiy Narimanov, Konstantin Gringauz, Yuriy Galperin, Semyon Moiseyev and Vasiliy Moroz. I knew them with the exception of Etkin.

they operated for two months providing a goldmine of information about our sister planet. These were the first orbiters around a planet other than Earth and they revolutionized our knowledge of Venus. When I arrived in IKI the Venera orbiters were at the center of space research not only in the Soviet Union but in the U.S.A. as well.

I reported for work the day after my arrival. I was expecting to be assigned to a project investigating the Earth' space environment, since this was the area in which I had some experience. I was shocked when Gringauz asked if I wanted to work on the analysis of the Venus orbiter results. For an aspiring space scientist from Hungary, with no space program of its own, the opportunity to work on the hottest project of the times was like winning the lottery. I was a scientific adventurer and pretty self-confident (should I say cocky?). The fact that I knew nothing about Venus or planetary space environments did not even make me pause for a second. I immediately agreed, and jumped into a new adventure.

I have a photo which demonstrates how highly regarded Elyasberg and Gringauz are in the Soviet-Russian space program even today (2013). The photograph shows the "Wall of Space Pioneers" at IKI. This exhibit is at a prime location in the institute (next to the Director's office). It shows a spare unit of the first Sputnik and eleven of the pioneers who created Soviet space science. Both Elyasberg and Gringauz are among the pioneers. Of the others Petrov was the first director of IKI, Narimanov was the chief engineer of IKI, Etkin

The Space Research Institute (IKI) in Moscow.

was the head of applied space science (he lead the early Earth observations program), while the others were leading scientists.

In the winter of 1976 life was not easy in Moscow. It was a particularly cold winter with food and fuel shortages. The only thing never in short supply was vodka. The temperature at IKI was kept at 12°C (54F); people worked in heavy coats and gloves. It was cold, but not so bad as outside where temperatures sometimes dipped to -40°C (-40F) and it was next to impossible to walk on the wide open, very windy streets. I lived in a bug infested room in the Hotel Akademicheskaya (Academy Hotel) that was at least well heated. József Kóta lived in the same hotel and we spent most of our free time together.

Eating was a challenge. The hotel had a restaurant, but it was very difficult to get in (there were few restaurants in Moscow then and they were almost always full). Besides, restaurant dining was a ritual with a dinner usually taking three to four hours. We just did not have the time during the week to go out to restaurants. The hotel also had two fast food type places, but they had very limited menus and very long lines. Cooking in the room was impossible (besides it was extremely difficult to buy ingredients), so we lived on a fast and feast diet, eating very little during the week and binging in restaurants during the weekend. Once we got into a restaurant, food was good and cheap. We particularly liked Russian-style appetizers. Sometimes dinner consisted of two large portions of salmon caviar, two large portions of Beluga caviar and a bottle of champagne. Such a dinner would cost over a thousand dollars in the West, but at this time caviar was cheap in Moscow, cheap enough that we could easily afford it almost every week. Needless to say, life was not all champagne and caviar, but these dinners made life bearable.

The daily routine at IKI was complicated. I took the direct Metro line from Oktyabrskaya to Kaluzhskaya stations and from there walked to the 400 meter long building that housed IKI. At the entrance I was met by one of my "mentors" who took me through security and accompanied me to the office with my assigned desk. There were six or seven desks in the large office, most occupied by young scientists working on various projects. My "mentors" were Tamara Breus, Anatoliy (Tolya) Remizov and Mikhail (Misha) Verigin, all just beyond their Ph.D. degrees and actively working on the Venera missions. Tolya was an instrument developer leading the development of the instrument operating around Venus. Tamara and Misha were data analysts. Their main job was to interpret the data and create models of the space environment of Venus. Needless to say, all three of them were among the best of the best young Soviet space scientists.

Tamara, Misha and Tolya were tasked by the IKI internal security office to keep an eye on me at all times, including when I went to the bathroom. Needless to say, poor Tamara had difficulties fulfilling this task. She usually just waited outside the men's room. I did not care much about what the IKI security people thought, often escaping to the library, the computing center or just to chat with colleagues. I was as undisciplined at IKI as I was all my life. The situation was best characterized by Tamara who in 1997 wrote an article about Gringauz' career. In the article she devoted a paragraph to my adventures at IKI:[4]

In 1975 we obtained results from the first near-Venus orbiters, Venera 9 and 10, during minimum solar activity. Tamas Gombosi, now a professor at the University of Michigan, came to Moscow to join Gringauz's team in processing and interpreting data from these missions. It was the time when Sagdeev had just started his perestroika in space research and Gombosi was practically the first foreign visitor-scientist in the history of the Institute. The charming young scientist from Hungary did not entirely care for the strong rules pervading our Institute. According to these rules, foreigners were obliged to be accompanied by a member of the Institute staff to any place they wanted to visit. I was responsible for accompanying Tamas to begin with but got into a lot of trouble because of his independent behavior. He very often appeared alone at another floor of the Institute, where the Computer Center was located, escaping somehow from my vigilant eyes. As a result Misha Verigin was ordered to take on this duty and Gombosi's care was in more suitable hands.

Tamás and his "mentors" in 1976. From left to right: Mikhail Verigin, Tamás Gombosi, Anatoliy Remizov, Tamara Breus and Valeriy Afonin.

During my stay at IKI, I automated the data analysis of the Gringauz instrument. At this time computing facilities were quite limited at IKI and much of the data analysis was done by tedious manual work that took a long time. Taking advantage of my access to Elyasberg and my knowledge of computers, I quickly wrote a data analysis program that saved months of work for the group. I spent a few nights at the IKI computer center (accompanied by poor Misha Verigin) operating the computer myself and making fast progress in producing useable data products for Gringauz's group. In the end, the data analysis program even produced some simple plots visualizing the observations. Gringauz was so impressed that he took the computer output and went around the Institute's leadership to brag about it. While this part of my work was the least scientific, it was undoubtedly the most visible. Soviet scientists were used to smart young people making new scientific insights, but a space scientist with computer skills was something new.

---

[4]Tamara Breus: An unforgottable personality. *J. Geophys. Res.*, *102*, 2027, 1997.

✂ ✂

Three other people at IKI played an important role in my life: Roald Sagdeev, Albert Galeev and Vitaliy Shapiro.

Roald Sagdeev is an ethnic Tatar. He had attended the Moscow State University (MGU) and was one of a few of Lev Landau's students, and the only space physicist, who passed the so called "Landau minimum," the most challenging qualifying examination in the world. In the university dormitory he lived next to Mikhail Gorbachev, a law student, (later to become General Secretary of the Communist Party and Head of State from 1988 until the dissolution of the USSR in 1991) and Raisa Gorbacheva, a sociology student. In 1955 he joined the Kurchatov Institute of Atomic Energy as a member of the controlled fusion team. From 1961 he worked at the Institute of Nuclear Physics in Novosibirsk. At the age of 35, he was one of the youngest people ever elected as a full academician of the Academy of Sciences of the USSR. His work on the behavior of hot plasma and controlled thermonuclear fusion won international recognition. While working at the Kurchatov Institute he married Tema Frank-Kamenetskii, daughter of the famous nuclear physicist David Frank-Kamenetskii. In 1973 he was appointed director of IKI where he modernized and opened Soviet space science. After my time there, in the 1980s, he became science advisor to Soviet leader Mikhail Gorbachev and played an important role in Gorbachev's perestroika. In 1988 he divorced his wife Tema and married the granddaughter of U.S. President Dwight D. Eisenhower, Susan Eisenhower. Following his second marriage he moved to the U.S.A. where he became a Professor at the University of Maryland.

Albert Galeev was born in the city of Ufa, and like Sagdeev, to an ethnic Tatar family. From 1961 to 1970 he worked at the Institute of Nuclear Physics in Novosibirsk which was leading the nuclear fusion work in the Soviet Union. He worked with Roald Sagdeev on theoretical problems concerning magnetically confined plasmas. When Sagdeev became Director of IKI he invited Galeev to join him as the head of the Space Plasma Physics Department. After Sagdeev moved to the U.S.A. in 1988, Galeev became the director of IKI and stayed in this position until his health forced him to retire in 2002. Galeev was an excellent space plasma theorist with major international impact.

Vitaliy Shapiro received his D.Sc. from the Institute for Nuclear Physics in Novosibirsk

Left to right: Roald Sagdeev, Albert Galeev and Vitaliy Shapiro.

in 1967. He also worked with Roald Sagdeev on theoretical plasma physics and became the leading theorist of the institute. In 1976, Shapiro joined IKI, where he became head of the Laboratory for Fundamental Plasma Studies. He was also Professor of Space Physics at the Moscow Institute of Physics and Technology (FizTech), the "Soviet MIT." Shapiro followed Sagdeev to the U.S.A. and in 1992 he joined the faculty of the University of California at San Diego (UCSD).

Gringauz, Sagdeev, Galeev and Shapiro all played different roles in my life. Galeev was the head of the Space Plasma Physics Department at IKI that included several experimental Laboratories (Gringauz was head of one of these laboratories) and a powerful theoretical division (headed by Shapiro). Gringauz was my immediate supervisor and took me under his wing. He was not trained in space physics, but he had a great talent to recognize new ideas with potential. He had an instinct for science. Sagdeev was the "big boss," but he had a special talent for recognizing the potential of young people and helping them with their careers. He gave me opportunities very few people had at that time. Galeev was a more distant figure, but he was great in pointing me in the right direction. Shapiro was a complex personality. He was very paranoid about his Jewish background, but probably he was the best plasma physicist in this group. He was always ready to share his ideas and was very patient with me when I did not immediately understand what he had in mind.

During my extended stay at IKI, I worked closest with Misha Verigin, a very well trained and talented space scientist who had a solid background both in theory and instrumentation. We made good progress with the analysis of Venera-9 and -10 data and used the observations to explain the origin of the mysterious night-time ionosphere of Venus. This work was very enjoyable and productive. By the time I returned to Hungary, I was considered an expert in the space environment of Venus and had started to gain international recognition as an up-and-coming scientist.

✂ ✂

While I was working in Moscow my family had a challenging time in Budapest. Eszter was working full time at the Central Statistical Office and gaining recognition for her pioneering work with advanced statistical data analysis software packages. She was very good in understanding the state-of-the-art and applying it to the particular problems faced by the Office. She also ran training courses which were very successful and popular. Her teacher's training paid off in these courses and she became quite well known in her institution.

At the same time, running our home with two little kids was challenging. She got a lot of help from her parents as well as from my mother, Magda. Eszter's parents spent most of the day at our apartment caring for the children, shopping, doing daily chores and many other day-to-day activities. Eszter mainly focused on cooking (she did not trust her mother) and organizing the daily schedule. At the same time she very much missed her husband, who regularly called but could not be there to participate in the life of the family. This was before the internet and other modern ways of communication, so staying in regular contact with the family was quite a challenge.

9.5. From Moscow to Michigan

When I returned from Moscow I continued close collaboration with Konstantin Gringauz and his group. I visited IKI at least every other month and Gringauz, Verigin and Remizov paid extended visits to me at KFKI. For the Soviet scientists, Hungary was part of the "West" and they very much liked to spend time in Budapest. Gringauz particularly enjoyed these trips and befriended Eszter's mother, Juci, who spoke a near perfect Russian (with a heavy Hungarian accent), was practically Gringauz' age, and held very similar political views.

My success in Moscow did not go unnoticed in KFKI. The leadership of the institute was very pleased to have a young, rising star able to impress the leading Soviet space scientists and who was publishing high visibility results in leading scientific journals.   My close colleagues, however, had very mixed reactions. András Varga just could not stomach my success and tried to undercut me in

Konstantin Gringauz and Juci Bíró in the Nagyenyed Street apartment.

any way he could. Antal Somogyi reacted differently. On the one hand he was impressed by my success, on the other hand he felt that as the leader of the group he should at least share the credit with his younger colleague. In all fairness, I didn't care about either Varga or Somogyi, but just kept pushing my work with the Soviet scientists. In retrospect, I think I should have been more considerate with Somogyi, who had given me an opportunity and stood up for me early on.

Gringauz, with his international recognition and Lenin Prize was treated as royalty at KFKI and was not shy about using his fame to advance his research and people. He was really fond of me and decided to expose me to prime time. In the fall of 1976, Gringauz visited and asked for a meeting with the Director General of KFKI, Lénárd Pál.

In order to understand the significance of this meeting I need to make a brief detour and talk about NASA's Venus orbiter, Pioneer Venus. The Pioneer Venus Orbiter (or PVO) was launched in May 1978 and arrived at Venus in December 1978. It was one of the most successful planetary missions NASA ever had, orbiting Venus for nearly 14 years before it entered the atmosphere and burned up. From the beginning of the space age, NASA regularly announced its future missions, so it was well known to everyone in 1976 that NASA would launch its Venus orbiter in a couple of years. At this time, however, the Venera-9 and -10 observations were the only data available about Venus's space environment. This made the Soviet Venus observations particularly valuable to U.S. scientists; access to them could provide their last opportunity to make changes in the instruments and mission profile of PVO. In short, Venera-9 and -10 results were of great interest for the world's planetary research community and any presentation at major international meetings about these results was certain to attract a lot of attention.

When Gringauz met Lénárd Pál he made a simple proposition: if KFKI would cover my plane ticket to the upcoming meeting of the International Association of Geomagnetism and Aeronomy (IAGA), I could give the high profile invited presentation about the Venera-9 and -10 observations of Venus' space environment. Gringauz, as an official of IAGA, would also offer a stipend for me, so that my living expenses would be covered while at the meeting. The catch: the next IAGA conference was to be in Seattle, Washington. The plane ticket to the U.S.A. would be expensive and it had to be purchased for hard currency which was in very short supply in Communist countries. Even so, this was an irresistible offer, and Lénárd Pál accepted it.

✂ ✂

I arrived in Seattle at the end of August, 1977. I had a round-trip plane ticket: BudapestCopenhagenSeattleNew YorkCopenhagenBudapest, and $50. I stayed at the dorms of the University of Washington where continental breakfast was included in the heavily discounted price. I received an additional $200 from IAGA and that was all the money I had for a two-week long stay. I ate breakfast every morning and practically nothing else, since the money was barely enough to cover the dorm expenses. I still felt like the king of the world, at a major international conference in the U.S.A. and about to give a high profile invited presentation.

The presentation went very well. I managed to stay within my allocated time and was able to answer all questions. This was not trivial; at this time I had difficulty understanding American English (and British English as well). But, Gringauz looked like a proud father, so I was pretty certain that things had gone well.

During the break following my presentation, several American scientists approached asking follow-up questions. They were very curious about the Hungarian kid (I was just 30 years old) giving one of the major Soviet talks. This was very, very unusual. Among these Americans was a bearded guy in his forties. To my great surprise, he started to speak in Hungarian. It turned out that his name was Andrew Nagy (everyone called him Andy). He was a professor at the University of Michigan and an Interdisciplinary Scientist of the Pioneer Venus Orbiter program. This meeting changed the life of the entire Gombosi family forever.

Later that day, Andy asked me if I wanted to join him and a group of colleagues for dinner. I was in a bind. I had no money, and was about to decline the invitation when Andy – sensing the real reason behind my hesitance – added that he actually wanted to invite me to dinner. I readily agreed and that evening had a real dinner in Trader Vic's, a Polynesian style restaurant, my first hot meal in over a week.

During the rest of the conference Andy and I had several more discussions and at the end Andy asked me if I was interested in joining his Pioneer Venus research group at the University of Michigan. I responded that yes, I would be very interested, but it was not easy to get permission in Hungary to work in a Western country for an extended period of time. In the end, we agreed to stay in touch.

After the meeting in Seattle I flew to New York where I was able to spend a few days with Éva, Gyuri and Andrea who lived in a high-rise condominium building on the New Jersey side of the George Washington bridge in a town called Cliffside Park. This was my first trip to New York and I was fascinated. I just could not have enough of the city. Éva took me to some of the most famous places, but I also wanted to explore on my own. One day, I visited the statue of Liberty and then walked from the southern tip of Manhattan up to Columbus Circle and back to the bus terminal. I was so exhausted after this outing that I laid down for a few minutes after my return to Éva's condo and did not wake up until the next morning.

✂ ✂

My successes in Seattle made the situation in KFKI even more complicated. My relationship with Somogyi was correct but frigid, and András Varga was boiling with hatred. He used all his influence in the Communist Party to undermine me. Fortunately the upper management of KFKI was quite supportive; there were not many thirty-year-olds with international reputation and visibility. IKI's leadership was also standing behind me from Gringauz to Elyasberg to Sagdeev, so there was not much Varga could do (except bad-mouthing).

During Socialism, the Hungarian postgraduate degrees combined the German and Soviet sys- tems. The "doctor of philosophy" or Ph.D. degree was awarded by universities and for full-time Ph.D. students it typically took two or three years to finish a Ph.D. program. (I was working full time, so it took four years to complete my Ph.D. degree.) There were two additional degrees beyond the Ph.D. modeled on the Soviet system. The Candidate of Science and Doctor of Science (D.Sc.) degrees were awarded by the Academy of Sciences and these represented advanced research credentials. Leading scientists typically completed their Candidate degree in their late thirties and their D.Sc. degree around the age of fifty. Most scientists never completed the D.Sc. degree.

Tamás Gombosi's post-Ph.D. diplomas: Candidate of Physics (top) and Doctor of Physics (bottom).

Somogyi was very sensitive to seniority (mainly because he was overlooked quite often) and expected that the most senior members of his group would complete their advanced degrees first. However, András Varga and György Benkó were not good scientists and it was obvious that they would never finish any postgraduate degree. József Kóta certainly had the talent, but he lacked the motivation to start writing a postgraduate thesis. I was in a bind. I had the drive and the scientific accomplishments to write a Candidate and even a D.Sc. thesis, but this would break the mold and create even more tension inside the group. In the end, I decided to go ahead and submitted my thesis for the degree of Candidate of Science. The process took a long time and I eventually defended my thesis in January 1979. Less than five years later I defended my D.Sc. degree – at the age of 36, becoming one of the youngest Hungarian physicists earning the degree of Doctor of Science. Needless to say "jumping the line" did not go well with Somogyi, Varga and many others and the resentment and jealousy increased to even higher levels.

✂ ✂

I received the invitation to join Andy Nagy's group at the University of Michigan in the spring of 1978. I was offered a one year postdoc position with a salary of $14,500 ($43,500 in 2013 dollars). I would be working on the data analysis of NASA's Pioneer Venus spacecraft under the supervision of Andrew Nagy. This position was a big demotion – in Hungary I was already a full Research Scientist with a growing international reputation. On the other hand, this invitation offered an opportunity to break into the U.S. science scene and to work with the next big planetary mission. Eszter and I had no idea about the purchasing value of the proposed salary. To us, it seemed like a fortune.

The invitation to go to the U.S.A. stirred all kinds of emotions in the family. My parents, Magda and János, were genuinely happy because they understood the limitations of Hungarian society and the restrictions of the Socialist system. They were also hoping that their children would get closer to one another on the other side of the ocean and eventually move the entire Gombosi family to the United States. In 1978 this was a far-fetched hope, but Magda repeatedly expressed it. Eszter's parents, however, saw the situation completely differently. They had given up their comfortable lifestyle in Pécs to be close to their daughter and grandchildren and they were terrified by the idea of being left behind. As Communists, they genuinely believed that the future of the United States was bleak and eventually communism would triumph over capitalism everywhere in the world. They did not want their children to end up on the wrong side of history.

Getting permission to work in the U.S.A., or in Western Europe, was quite difficult. While Hungary was undoubtedly the most liberal among the Soviet block countries, it was still strictly controlled by the Communist Party. The joke at the time was that "Hungary was the most joyful tent in the socialist camp." At the end of the day it was still only a tent and not a real building. Hungary was eager to show a moderate face to the outside world and the regime particularly favored high-visibility activities. In particular, Olympic sports, performing arts (especially classical music) and "hard sciences" had privileged status: these people could travel more than the general population and were allowed to keep some of the hard currencies earned abroad. These were small privileges, but they made these important groups relatively satisfied and defections from Hungary plummeted. The athletes, artists and scientists were also very efficient "ambassadors" of Hungary, underscoring the regime's liberal reputation.

It was against this backdrop that I submitted my request for a one-year leave to go to the University of Michigan and work on NASA's Pioneer Venus mission. The approval process took about three months and Eszter and I were not very hopeful that the permission would be given. After all, this was only seven years after my sister Éva had defected from Hungary, and the regime usually had long memories about family "sins."

The first positive sign came about a month after I submitted the request. My nemesis,

András Varga, was a midlevel official in the Communist Party. One day he suddenly asked if I was interested in joining the Communist Party. I was very surprised, because I had never hidden my very independent political views which were often at odds with the party line. And, I was aware that anti-semitism lingered in the Communist Party which tried to limit the number of Jews among party members. Openly and proudly Jewish, this made me a very unlikely recruit. I concluded that the invitation indicated that the authorities were inclined to approve my request to spend a year in the United States, but they wanted an "insurance policy" against defection: this was the height of the Cold War, the U.S. visa application form had a specific question about Communist Party membership and Communist Party membership was a reason to be excluded from the U.S.A. In the end I felt I had no choice and reluctantly agreed to join the Hungarian Socialist Workers Party (MSZMP, the official name of the Hungarian Communist Party).

Everybody was surprised when my request was not only approved, but I was allowed to take my family with me to the U.S.A. The paperwork took a few more months, but by early 1979 everything was in place. We left Hungary on the morning of February 1, 1979 and arrived in New York the same evening. We had a couple hundred dollars and high hopes for the future.

10 Dezső's Dream: Back to the U.S.A.

10.1. Arrival

Éva and Gyuri met us at New York's Kennedy airport. It was near midnight by the time we arrived at their recently purchased house in Stony Brook on Long Island. The children were very tired and they were put to bed immediately. Judit was so excited and tired that she threw up in the middle of the night.

The next day Éva took us to Toys-Я-Us, a symbol of American commercialism. The impact on the children was dramatic. At this time in Hungary toy stores were small and all items were kept behind the counter on shelves. Children were not allowed to touch any toys, let alone play with them in the store. When Judit and Zoli entered Toys-Я-Us they were in awe. They had never seen anything like it. So many toys and they could touch everything. Moreover, many toys were open so that children could play in the store. Éva told Judit and Zoli that she would buy one toy for each of them. Zoli broke down crying: he just was not used to seeing this many toys and could not imagine how to choose only one.

We spent ten days in Stony Brook and needed to purchase a few basic items. The most important thing was to buy a car, because we had no transportation from Stony Brook to Ann Arbor. Éva suggested that we buy a large station wagon because that would be able to accommodate the family, our belongings (we had four suitcases) and some household items that she had given us. These items included an old black-and-white television that served us during our entire stay. Since we only had about $200, we also needed to borrow money from Éva to cover our purchases.

Even before our arrival Éva had been looking at the classified section of the local newspaper and had spotted an appropriate looking car for sale. It was a 1971 Buick Estate station wagon and the asking price was $700. Eszter and I looked at the car and bought it. It never occurred to us that we could have bargained, nor did we look under the hood. In retrospect our inexperience and

The Gombosi family car in 1979, a Buick Estate Station Wagon. Judit and Zoltán Gombosi are in the backseat.

naïveté is laughable. The car was huge and very comfortable. It had an 8 liter engine, air conditioning, power steering, power windows and a huge open space behind the back seat. It got about 8 miles per gallon, but at the time gasoline was still relatively cheap, so the poor mileage was not a major concern. Finally, on February 11, 1979, Éva and my family left Stony Brook and started a 670 mile drive to Ann Arbor.

When we arrived in the U.S.A., I did not have a driver's license. I had had bad eyes since birth and, even with eye glasses, my vision could not be corrected to meet the Hungarian standards for driving. This was not a problem in Hungary where the public transportation was excellent. Eszter did have a driver's license and Eszter and I had had a car (an East German made Trabant) since 1974. The lack of a driver's license was, however, a serious problem in the U.S.

The drive from Stony Brook to Ann Arbor took two days. Éva and Eszter shared the driving while I sat in the back seat and the children had a playground at the back of the car. We stopped for the night near the Pennsylvania-Ohio border and arrived in Ann Arbor in the early afternoon of the second day.

✂ ✂

The University of Michigan has several different housing options for students and visitors. In addition to the usual student dormitories there are several housing complexes for students with families and for longer term visitors. These family housing units are concentrated near the North Campus of the university and are called Northwood I through V. The units range from studio apartments to three-bedroom townhouses. We rented a two bedroom furnished 572 square feet apartment in the Northwood-III complex. It had a tiny kitchen, a living/dining/family room, a large and a small bedroom and a single bathroom. The furniture was pretty simple: shelves, a dining table with six chairs, a convertible sofa, a coffee table, and a bed in each bedroom. There was no air conditioning. The main advantage of the apartment was that it was furnished and the rent was subsidized including heating, electricity and gas, necessities that European tenants always pay for themselves.

Eszter and I decided to give the bedrooms to the children and we slept on the convertible sofa in the living room. This was very un-American, but we were used to this since apartments were quite small in Hungary.

Éva stayed a few days helping Eszter to get started with daily life. They opened a

 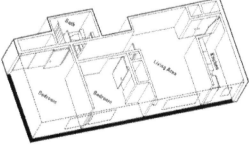

The second floor 572 sq ft apartment the Gombosi family rented during their first visit to Ann Arbor.

bank account and enrolled Judit in kindergarten. They found daycare for Zoli, since Eszter wanted to start working as soon as possible. By this time we had realized that my salary would not support a family of four and Eszter was offered a part-time programmer job by Andy Nagy. Éva gave us another few hundred dollars and returned home. When we dropped her off at the airport, Eszter and I realized that we were on our own. This was probably the scariest moment of our visit.

Surviving the first month was a challenge. We had already borrowed about $1500 from Éva, more than my monthly salary. (It took us about six months to repay the debt.) We also had unexpected expenses. The winter of 1979 was particularly harsh in Ann Arbor and we did not have appropriate clothes for the children. We had to buy snowsuits for Judit and Zoli. Since we were new in the country, we did not have anything in our pantry and we had to buy basic food stuffs. To add insult to injury, our car broke down shortly after Éva left. This was a consequence of our inexperience in buying used cars. Having never looked under the Buick, we had not spotted the red liquid leaking from the car. Every American knows that the red liquid comes from the automatic transmission, but of course Eszter and I did not know anything. When the transmission of the car broke down, it took $400 to get it fixed and broke our budget.

The Gombosi family in the summer of 1979.

Most workplaces in the U.S.A. pay at the end of the pay period. At the University of Michigan, faculty (including postdocs) are likewise paid at the end of each month. When Éva left there were still about ten days left until the first paycheck and our reserves were rapidly depleted. I was able to get a $100 loan from the office's coffee piggy bank, but this was all the help we got. Toward the end of the month we were rationing food so that we could get through until the paycheck arrived. A bittersweet story from this period is that one day I took Eszter and the kids to the North Campus Commons where there was a cafeteria. We had enough money to buy two sandwiches and Eszter and I thought that, as usual, the kids would eat a little and then we would finish the sandwiches. Judit and Zoli, however, were hungry and they ate the two sandwiches. In the end Eszter and I looked at each other and started laughing. That laugh was our meal for the day.

✂ ✂

From day one Judit loved kindergarten. She did not speak English, but proudly boarded the school bus and went to school with the other children from North Campus, most of whom came from other foreign families. The Ann Arbor school system was quite used to accommodating newcomers and there was a well-organized support network for children with limited English. In a few months Judit and Zoli started to speak English and after

Left: The Michigan Theater on Liberty Street. Right: Zingerman's deli, "the best Jewish deli outside of New York."

about half a year they already used it between themselves. In school Judit was "renamed" to the more English sounding version of her name, Judy. From this point on everyone called her Judy, even in the family.

Zoli loved daycare and though less talkative than Judy, showed clear signs that he understood the English conversations around him. One day Judy was sick and had to stay home. In the afternoon one of her friends noticed her standing at the window and called to her to come down to play in the courtyard. Judy replied, "I cannot come, I am sick." Four-year-old Zoli, playing with his toys in the room, looked up and declared, "and I am seven." Eszter and I got a good laugh and realized that our son was about to start speaking English.

10.2. Ann Arbor and the University of Michigan

Ann Arbor is located in southeast Michigan about 40 miles west of the city of Detroit. Its population is about 110,000 making it the sixth largest city in Michigan. Founded in 1824 by land speculators John Allen and Elisha Rumsey, there are various accounts concerning the origin of the settlement's name; one states that Allen and Rumsey decided to name it for their wives, both named Ann, and for the stands of burr oak in the 640 acres (260 hectares) of land they purchased for $800 from the federal government. The University of Michigan moved from Detroit to Ann Arbor in 1837, and the city showed steady growth throughout the 19th and 20th centuries. During the 1960s and 1970s, the city gained a reputation as a center for liberal politics. Ann Arbor became a focal-point for left-wing activism and served as a hub for the civil-rights movement and anti-Vietnam War movement, as well as the student movement.

Ann Arbor has a typically Midwestern humid continental climate, which is influenced by the Great Lakes. There are four distinct seasons: winters are cold with moderate to heavy snowfall, while summers are warm and often humid; in between, spring and autumn are short but mild. The area experiences "lake effect" weather, primarily in the form of increased cloudiness during late fall and early winter. Snowfall, which normally occurs from November to April and occasionally in October, averages 58 inches (147 cm) per season. It is interesting to note that the geographic latitude of Ann Arbor is 42°N, the same as Rome, Italy. However, the climate could not be more different.

Left: The Hill Auditorium and the Burton Memorial Tower on Central Campus. Center: The Law Quadrangle. Right: The Lurie Engineering Center on North Campus.

The University of Michigan (UM, U-M, or U of M), frequently referred to simply as Michigan, is one of the eight "Public Ivy" public research university systems[1] that successfully compete with the private Ivy League schools in academic rigor, attract superstar faculty and successfully compete for the best and brightest students. The University of Michigan has 6,200 faculty members and roughly 38,000 employees. The University has 18 schools and colleges with a total student population of over 43,500 (Fall 2013 enrollments are in parenthesis):

- College of Literature, Science, and the Arts (19,781)
- College of Engineering (9,107)
- Stephen M. Ross School of Business (3,298)
- School of Medicine (1,278)
- School of Law (1,098)
- School of Music, Theatre & Dance (1,105)
- School of Nursing (1,003)
- School of Public Health (967)
- School of Kinesiology (943)
- A. Alfred Taubman College of Architecture & Urban Planning (655)
- School of Dentistry (633)
- School of Social Work (630)
- School of Art & Design (607)
- School of Education (541)
- School of Information (441)
- School of Pharmacy (434)
- School of Natural Resources & Environment (335)
- Gerald R. Ford School of Public Policy (312)

Michigan has one of the world's largest living alumni groups at more than 500,000 in 2012 and one of the largest research expenditures of any American university, totaling about $1.25 billion.

The University of Michigan Medical Center, the preeminent health facility in Michigan, includes one of the best hospitals and medical schools in the U.S. The University of Michigan Health System (UMHS) employs about 12,000 people and includes the University Hospital, the C.S. Mott Children's Hospital and the Women's Hospital in its core complex.

---

[1]College of William & Mary (Williamsburg, Virginia), Miami University (Oxford, Ohio), University of California (campuses as of 1985), University of Michigan (Ann Arbor), University of North Carolina at Chapel Hill, University of Texas at Austin, University of Vermont (Burlington) and the University of Virginia (Charlottesville)

University of Michigan Medical Center.

UMHS also operates outpatient clinics and facilities throughout southeastern Michigan. The area's other major medical centers include a large facility operated by the Department of Veterans Affairs in Ann Arbor, and Saint Joseph Mercy Hospital just outside the city.

The University of Michigan's athletic teams, called the Wolverines, are members of the Big Ten Conference. The athletic program is dominated by the football program and Michigan is the winningest college football program (with over 900 victories). The football team plays in Michigan Stadium, also known as "The Big House," the largest football stadium in the world, with an official capacity of 109,901, and an actual capacity of more than 114,000.

Michigan is one of four states with public university governing boards elected directly by the people (along with Colorado, Nebraska, and Nevada). This fact puts the nine member Board of Regents level with the Michigan Legislature. The result is that the Legislature cannot set any policy for the university, even though they control the state appropriations for it. The state's contribution to the university's budget is shrinking. In 2012 the State of Michigan contributed $308 million of the nearly $6 billion annual budget (5%). In effect, Michigan operates as a "privately funded public university" with its out-of-state tuition comparable to that of Ivy League private universities and the largest endowment (about $8.5 billion) among public universities.

Michigan Stadium (the "Big House") in 2011.

10.3. Postdoc Year

The V-2 rocket (Vergeltungswaffe-2, meaning Retaliation Weapon 2) was a short-range ballistic missile developed during World War II in Nazi Germany. It was the precursor of all modern rockets, including those used by the space programs of the United States and the Soviet Union. Beginning in September 1944, over 3,000 V-2s were launched as military rockets against Allied targets during the war, mostly London and later Antwerp and Liege. The attacks resulted in the deaths of an estimated 9,000 civilians and military personnel, while 12,000 forced laborers and concentration camp prisoners were killed producing the weapons.

At the end of the war, a race began between the United States and the Soviet Union to retrieve as many V-2 rockets and engineering staff as possible. Three hundred rail-car loads of V-2s and parts were captured and shipped to the United States and 126 of the principal designers, including Werner von Braun and Walter Dornberger were in American hands. V-2 engines, fuselages, propellant tanks, gyroscopes and associated equipment were brought to the rail-yards in Las Cruces, New Mexico, so they could be placed on trucks and driven to the White Sands Proving Grounds, also in New Mexico.

It was decided at the highest political levels that the captured V-2s should be used for peaceful scien-

The V-2 rocket.

tific research – to demonstrate the contrast between the values of Nazi Germany and the United States. A committee, the Upper Atmosphere Research Panel, was formed with military and civilian scientists, to review payload proposals for the reassembled V-2 rockets. The members were Ernst H. Krause (Chair, Naval Research Laboratory), G.K. Megerian (secretary, General Electric Co.), William G. Dow (University of Michigan), M.J.E. Golay (U.S. Army Signal Corps), C.F. Green (General Electric Co.), K.H. Kingdon (General Electric Co.), Myron H. Nichols (Princeton University, who soon moved to the University of Michigan), James Van Allen (Johns Hopkins University later University of Iowa) and Fred L. Whipple (Harvard University).

Not surprisingly, the first experiments were built by members of the panel. This led to an eclectic array of experiments that flew on V-2s and paved the way for American space exploration. Rockets launched at the proving grounds were routinely fitted with instrumentation to study solar spectroscopy, cosmic rays, and the measurement of pressures and temperatures in the upper atmosphere. There were problems associated with this pioneering research, in particular because the trajectory of the V-2 allowed for only short interludes at extreme altitudes. Engineers gave careful attention to utilizing the V-2's warhead compartment to house instruments. Special access panels were created to install and adjust the variety of scientific instruments used in the program. Cameras were mounted on several V-2s launched at White Sands, taking photos of Earth from altitudes of up to 100 miles.

Thanks to the major involvement of Michigan faculty in the Upper Atmosphere Research Panel, the University of Michigan became a major player in the V-2 program. The first successful flight of a Michigan experiment on a V-2 rocket launched from White Sands on November 21, 1946, following a spectacular failure of an earlier attempt in August of that year. Following the first success, two research laboratories were founded at the University of Michigan: the High Altitude Engineering Laboratory (HAEL) in the Aeronautical Engineering Department and the Space Physics Research Laboratory (SPRL) in the Electrical Engineering Department. In the 1950s and 1960s these two laboratories carried out powerful, sometimes competing efforts that propelled Michigan to an internationally recognized position of leadership in space research. In the mid-60s, HAEL and SPRL were responsible for nearly half of the externally funded research in the College of Engineering. By the late 1970s, however, HAEL disintegrated and its remnants were integrated into SPRL. Since most of the research carried out in SPRL was related to the study of the upper atmosphere, the academic home of SPRL gradually shifted from Electrical Engineering to the newly formed Department of Atmospheric and Oceanic Sciences (AOS).

In 1974 AOS had hired a new department Chair, Thomas(Tom) Donahue, who dramatically changed the direction of AOS and SPRL. He was one of the space pioneers in the U.S.A., a leader of the first generation of space scientists. He laid the foundation for our current understanding of planetary atmospheres. From 1982 to 1988 he was Chairman of the Space Science Board of the National Research Council of the National Academy of Sciences, where he was a strong advocate for unmanned space science missions within the federal space budget.

Donahue was an expert in upper atmospheres and he brought SPRL into AOS. This move resulted in a shift in the scientific interests of AOS, since the closeness of SPRL provided the faculty with new scientific methods and opened the way to space instrumentation. This change was taking place when I arrived at AOS.

✂ ✂

When we arrived at Ann Arbor, SPRL was a semi-independent research laboratory inside AOS. The department and the laboratory were housed in the Space Research Building (SRB) that had been constructed on North Campus with NASA funds in the mid-1960s. The building was designed with a gross disrespect for human nature: hallways were placed next to the outside walls (supposedly in order to conserve energy) and no office had a window or any access to natural light. It did not present a pleasant working environment. SRB was, however, very conveniently located for me, since it was about a ten minute walk from our Northwood apartment. This was an important consideration given my lack of a driver's license.

At the time SPRL was a large operation completely dependent on external (i.e. government) funding. Most of the funding came from NASA with smaller amounts coming from the National Science Foundation (NSF) and other federal agencies. As a result of its dependence on external funding, inside SPRL money talked. Whoever had funding had control over the organization. When I arrived SPRL was a confederation of "fiefdoms" controlled by successful principal investigators (PIs). The "Lords of SPRL" were George Carignan, Paul Hays and Andy Nagy. Carignan and Hays were building instruments for various space-craft and Nagy was leading a small group that carried out theoretical investigations of upper atmospheres (including Earth and Venus). Since I was hired by Andy Nagy, I became part of the "Nagy empire." This group included a couple of postdoctoral researchers (these were a few years beyond their Ph.D. degrees), a full-time research scientist, several Ph.D. students and a secretary. The two postdocs were both working on Andy Nagy's Pioneer Venus project and shared an office. I was one of these postdocs and Thomas (Tom) Cravens was the other.

The Space Research Building.

Cravens was born and raised in New York. He attended the State University of New York at Stony Brook and obtained his Ph.D. in Astronomy from Harvard University. After two postdoctoral positions at the Universities of Colorado and Florida he came to Michigan in 1977 to work on the Pioneer Venus project with Andy Nagy. Tom is a very talented space scientist, among the best experts in the physics and chemistry of planetary upper atmospheres. Tom Cravens and I developed a very close personal relationship. I learned a lot about upper atmospheric physics from Tom and I very much liked his personality. In some respects we were polar opposites: I was outgoing, cynical, politically savvy and quick to react, while Tom was reserved, idealistic, deliberate and not very good in professional politics. I quickly understood the political landscape in SPRL, while Tom was at a loss in understanding the inner workings of the system. The two of us, however, formed a powerful intellectual nucleus that was quickly recognized by the senior people in the Laboratory.

During our visit I continued numerical modeling of Venus's plasma environment. In collaboration with Cravens, I developed several interesting ideas – some of which turned out to be correct, while others were dead ends. Because Andy Nagy was an active member of the Pioneer Venus project, I immediately gained access to the inner circles of the U.S. planetary science community. This was a huge opportunity, since the U.S. science community at this time was operating like an "old boys" network. Most decisions were made over drinks and dinner and being a good drinking partner was almost as important as being a good scientist (there are always more good scientists than dinner partners). I was talented enough to stand on my own at the science meetings. By the end of our visit I was considered by the inner circles of the U.S. planetary science community one of the very promising young space scientists in the world.

Another promising young scientist was hired about the same time as Tom and I. Timothy (Tim) Killeen was born in Wales and educated at the University College London (UCL). He

George Carignan   Paul Hays   Tom Donahue

Andy Nagy   Tim Killeen   Tom Cravens

My colleagues during my postdoc year in Ann Arbor.

had joined SPRL in the summer of 1978 just a few months before our arrival. He lived with his wife and small daughter, Myra, in the same North Campus apartment building where we lived. Tim was working for Paul Hays and focusing his research on the upper atmosphere of Earth. At this time there was little professional interaction between Tim and I, since we were members of different "fiefdoms," but later our scientific careers became quite intertwined.

✂ ✂

The visit of a "Soviet trained" scientist did not go unnoticed. Shortly after my arrival in the U.S.A. my sister was visited by the FBI. At the time Éva was already working at Brookhaven National Laboratory (BNL), one of the sixteen facilities associated with nuclear weapon and energy programs. Even though Éva's work was completely unclassified, the facility was considered sensitive and my appearance in the U.S.A. raised flags at the FBI. They wanted to know if I had shown any interest in the details of Éva's work and if I had visited BNL during our visit with my sister. Fortunately, I had been far too busy with moving to Ann Arbor and did not show much interest in Brookhaven, or any other laboratory.

The situation became even more interesting when I was given access to one of the biggest supercomputers of the times. I needed powerful computers for my simulations and Andy Nagy obtained an account for me at the Cray-1 supercomputer operating at the

National Center for Atmospheric Research (NCAR). (In 1979 the Cray-1 was considered an exceptionally powerful machine, but today any respectable smartphone outperforms it by a factor of about 100.) When I was given an account on the Cray-1, I had to sign a document certifying that I would not use the computer to do three things: simulate nuclear explosions, simulate airfoils and generate large prime numbers. The first requirement seems obvious to everyone, but the other two might seem strange to non-experts. Airfoil simulations are critical for the design of high performance military aircraft and large prime numbers are the mathematical underpinnings of modern encryption methods. Needless to say that I was more than willing to certify that I had no intention to design nuclear weapons, military jets or new encryption techniques. I used my Cray-1 account to simulate the upper atmosphere and ionosphere of Venus. In the end, these simulations produced several important scientific papers that were crucial for my career.

Sometime in the summer of 1979 an FBI agent visited me in my office and asked a few questions. His first question was, "Are you a spy?" I was so surprised that for a second I did not know what to say. Finally I said, "Of course I am not." The agent nodded and took note of the answer. He followed up with a series of questions about my self-assessment ("Are you the best space scientist in Hungary?") and my family. Interestingly he did not ask questions about my experience in the Soviet Union nor about my professional work. In any case, this interview left me rattled, because this was the first time any security or intelligence agency overtly interviewed me (I am sure that there were covert checks in Hungary and the Soviet Union before).

In in my office in 1979. In the background Judy is drawing on the blackboard. Note the huge stacks of computer printouts on the shelves.

✂ ✂

Andy Nagy had been born in Budapest in 1932 as András Nagy. His father was a successful lawyer. Sometime in the early 1940s the family converted to Catholicism, but even this conversion did not protect them from the anti-Jewish laws. They survived the fascist terror under the protection of Raoul Wallenberg who saved many thousands of Hungarian Jews. In 1949 the family managed to escape from the Communist regime and moved to Australia. Since his father's law license was not valid in Australia, the family had financial difficulties and Andy had to work to earn a living. He attended evening school and earned a bachelor's degree in engineering. With the help of a Fulbright scholarship, Andy came to the U.S.A. where he earned his M.Sc. degree in electrical engineering from the University of Nebraska (1959) and his Ph.D. from the University of Michigan (1963). His Ph.D. research was to work on space instrumentation in SPRL and he gained considerable experience in measuring charged particle properties in the ionosphere. After graduation he joined the Electrical Engineering department at the University of Michigan as an Assistant Professor. In the early 1970s he had moved from Electrical Engineering to Atmospheric and Oceanic Science becoming one of the "Lords" of SPRL.

Andy became a very successful scientist through a combination of his ability to schmooze, understand political winds and undercurrents, collaborate with the right people, and most importantly, recognize talent. I was his last discovery, but several of Andy's earlier postdocs emerged as leaders in the field. Nagy's most successful postdoc, Ralph Cicerone (he is presently president of the U.S. National Academies), left Michigan just a short time before my arrival. Andy not only gave full political support to his talented postdocs, but more importantly, he gave them scientific freedom (within reasonable limits) to pursue whatever relevant question they became interested in. This approach was quite atypical among leading scientists, who usually kept pretty tight control over the problems their postdocs were working on. By giving nearly unprecedented freedom to his talented people Andy himself became very successful because he was led into new and exciting areas of space science. For example, Ralph Cicerone together with Richard Stolarski (another Nagy postdoc) played a seminal role in understanding the chemistry of the Antarctic ozone hole, Tom Cravens pioneered the understanding of the hot oxygen corona of Venus, and I later put Michigan on the map of comet research. In short, it was an unusually rewarding experience to work for Andy Nagy and I took full advantage of the opportunity.

✂ ✂

In May 1980 we returned to Hungary. By this time Judy and Zoli were speaking fluent English and Judy had finished first grade. The family had had a great experience in Ann Arbor and Eszter and I had become quite adjusted to life in the United States. In fact, Eszter became so adjusted that she did not want to go back to Budapest. I, however, was convinced that there was a huge difference between being a visitor and a competitor, and I was very uncertain about my job prospects if we decided to stay in the U.S.A. As history showed, Eszter was right that we should stay in America, and I was correct in my assessment that I needed more experience to compete for good jobs in the U.S.A.

10.4. Halley's Comet

Less than a month after our return to Hungary the Committee on Space Research (COSPAR) held its 23rd annual general assembly in Budapest. After the USSR launched its first Earth satellite in 1957 starting the Space Age, the International Council of Scientific Unions (ICSU) established COSPAR in 1958. COSPAR's main objective is to promote peaceful scientific research in space. During the Cold War COSPAR represented one of the main venues in which U.S. and Soviet scientists could meet and exchange results and ideas. Having the COSPAR meeting in Budapest was a very big deal for Hungary, offering an opportunity to showcase Hungarian involvement in space research. For me this was a special event since I had a chance to host my Soviet and American colleagues and bring them together to initiate some joint projects.

Left: The 1066 apparition of Halley's comet is represented on the Bayeux Tapestry as a fiery star. Right: The 1301 apparition has been painted by the artist Giotto di Bondone as a fire-colored comet in the Nativity section of his Arena Chapel cycle (The Adoration of the Magi), completed in 1305.

The results of the meeting exceeded all expectations. The scientific program was interesting, but the most important events took place outside the meeting rooms. It was customary for the local scientists to organize small receptions in their homes during large international meetings. Eszter and I invited about 30 colleagues to our small condo for a wine and cheese reception. Among the invitees were my Soviet mentors Sagdeev and Gringauz, my American friends including Andy Nagy, and several well known European colleagues. One of these was Jaques Blamont, a colorful French space scientist who was a driving force behind the successful Franco-Soviet cooperation in space research. At the time France and the Soviet Union were negotiating French involvement in a Venus mission that would deploy long-lived scientific balloons in Venus's atmosphere to study its properties. Sagdeev and Blamont were the leaders of this planned mission.

The two men had a very important discussion on the balcony of the Nagyenyed Street apartment. Shortly before the COSPAR meeting engineers at IKI realized that the trajectory of the planned Franco-Soviet Venus mission (called Venera) could be modified so that it would intercept Halley's comet in March 1986. Sagdeev suggested that the mission be modified and in addition to delivering scientific balloons to Venus it should also be instrumented to investigate the vicinity of this very famous comet. As a result of the change in mission, the French balloon payload had to be downsized and the two Venera spacecraft would no longer be placed into orbit to support them. Blamont liked the idea but in the end the French decided to walk away from the balloon program, leaving the Soviets to build their own balloon payload instead. The French, however, became major participants in the Halley observations. In short, the Venus-Halley (VEGA) program was born on the Nagyenyed Street balcony.

✂ ✂

Halley's Comet, or Comet Halley, is the best-known of the short-period comets and is visible from Earth every 75-76 years. It is the only short-period comet clearly visible to the naked eye from Earth, and the only naked-eye comet that might appear twice in a human lifetime. Other naked-eye comets may be brighter and more spectacular, but will appear only once in thousands of years. Halley's returns to the inner solar system have been observed and recorded by astronomers since at least 240 BCE. Clear records of the comet's appearances were made by Chinese, Babylonian, and medieval European chroniclers, but were not recognized as reappearances of the same object at the time. The comet's periodicity was first determined in 1705 by English astronomer Edmond Halley, after whom it is now named. Artists used the image of the comet in medieval paintings.

NASA missed the chance to visit Halley's comet. At least three initiatives for NASA to send a mission fell to budget cuts during the 1970s and early 1980s. These cuts were necessary to fund the Space Shuttle program. It is also true that the U.S. planetary science community was not willing to settle for a much cheaper fly-by mission but insisted on a rendez-vous that would have provided an opportunity to investigate changing cometary activity. Finally the combination of Shuttle overruns and the cost of a rendez-vous mission killed NASA's mission to Halley's comet.

The European Space Agency (ESA) decided to launch its first deep space mission to Halley's comet. The Giotto mission, named after the Italian Renaissance artist Giotto di Bondone, was officially approved by ESA in July 1980, shortly after the birth of the VEGA project. Giotto carried ten science instruments to study Comet Halley and its environment.

Japan also decided that they would attempt a much more modest but still scientifically useful mission to Comet Halley. During the 1970s Japanese scientists and engineers began studies for a probe to be launched using their own launch vehicle. In 1979 the Japanese Halley mission was approved with six years to complete the project. It was decided to launch two spacecraft: the Planet-A (later renamed to Suisei) probe that would make the close pass of the comet and a technology demonstrator (later called Sakigake), launched seven months earlier in order to test the launch vehicle and the probe design as well as to allow distant observations of the interplanetary environment upstream of the comet.

By the fall of 1980 the international Halley armada had taken shape: the Soviets would launch two VEGA spacecraft, ESA would launch Giotto and Japan their two probes. Coordination efforts between ESA, JAXA (Japan Aerospace Exploration Agency) and IKI started in late 1980 and gradually accelerated as time went on. Even though NASA did not have a dedicated Halley mission they did not want to be left out of the international cooperation and joined the informal coordinating group.

✂ ✂

Almost by chance, I found myself in the middle of international activities associated with the planned Halley armada. I was well known by IKI scientists and my scientific reputation had greatly benefited from my work in the U.S.A. During the COSPAR meeting in Budapest Sagdeev invited me to participate in the new VEGA mission. The fact that at this time I did not know much about comets was not an obstacle, since around 1980 cometary science was in its infancy. Everyone had to learn the little we knew about comets and eventually a new area of space research emerged from the Halley missions. By luck, I was at the forefront of this emerging field and in a few years became one of the world's leading experts of the physics of comets.

The VEGA mission offered a great opportunity for Hungarian scientists and engineers
to participate in a world class science project.
This participation, however, needed significant
resources. At the end of the hardware phase of
the VEGA mission nearly a hundred scientists
and engineers were working on the project at
KFKI. This was a significant fraction of the institute's manpower and this much involvement
could not have been done without the full support of the upper management of the institute.
The Director General of KFKI at the time was
Ferenc Szabó who quickly understood the opportunity and became a strong supporter of the
Hungarian VEGA project. The day-to-day management was delegated to Károly Szegő, director of one of the five research institutes that con-
stituted KFKI. This institute, the Institute for
Particle and Nuclear Research (RMKI) carried
out most of the engineering work. The Cosmic

Ferenc Szabó and me in 1982.

Ray Division was one of the scientific units in RMKI and headed by Antal Somogyi (see
Section 9.2). Somogyi, as well as my nemesis, András Varga, became active members of
the Hungarian VEGA team.

Károly Szegő in 2011.

Károly Szegő had been trained as an elementary particle theorist. In the early 1970s he was
the leader of the KFKI branch of the Hungarian Communist youth movement (KISZ) when
the director of RMKI suffered a massive heart
attack and had to resign. The Director General
at the time, Lénárd Pál, was so impressed by
the young Szegő that he appointed Károly to be
new director of RMKI. At the time Szegő was
not even 30 years old and his appointment created quite a stir among the more senior scientific
staff. Szegő turned out to be a good administrator and a shrewd politician and soon most of the
skepticism and criticism subsided. The high administrative post, however, interrupted Szegő's
scientific career, since his administrative duties
pretty much took up all of his time. He made
an effort to set aside some time for scientific research, but he could not keep up with his peers
who did scientific research full time. By the
early 1980s Szegő realized that he needed a different track if he ever wanted to earn the highest

level of scientific credential, the Doctor of Science (D.Sc.) degree (see Section 9.5).

The VEGA project offered Szegő the opening he needed for his D.Sc. degree. Since he was managing the Hungarian VEGA project, he was in the position to take credit for the success of the mission and to reap its scientific fruits. To his credit, he educated himself in cometary science and developed a good understanding of the main scientific issues. He also received a lot of support from a group of leading IKI plasma physicists lead by Galeev and Shapiro.

Szegő's decision to become a "comet expert" created a strained situation with me. Since the entire Hungarian VEGA participation was my initiative and I worked hard to make the entire VEGA mission a success, I did not like to be pushed aside. I was a fighter and resisted Szegő's efforts to take over the scientific leadership of the Hungarian effort. The situation was made even murkier by the constant efforts of András Varga to undermine me any way he could.

The top leadership of IKI and KFKI recognized the situation and tried to create room for both Szegő and myself in the project. This was possible because the VEGA project was really large and there was room to grow for several people. Sagdeev and Ferenc Szabó created the position of "VEGA Project Scientist for Hungary" for me and Szegő became "VEGA Project Manager for Hungary." This move diffused the situation to some extent, but the relationship between Szegő and myself was never better than a distant and cautious mutual respect. We tried to manage the conflict, but could not entirely resolve it.

✂ ✂

In 1980 the Cold War was still going on, even though some cooperation was taking place between the superpowers. The multinational Halley coordinating group offered a good opportunity to have some behind the scenes contacts between American and Soviet scientific leaders. This, however, could not be done overtly: they needed an intermediary to organize contacts at a somewhat neutral venue. Roald Sagdeev was a major driving force of this scientific opening. He was a personal friend of Mikhail Gorbachev, who would become the leader of the Soviet Union five years later and who already had tremendous influence on Soviet policy in the early 1980s (see Section 9.4). Sagdeev's main partner in this effort was the Science Director of the European Space Agency, Ernst Trendelenburg.

Ernst Trendelenburg was a German scientist who, as a young conscript during World War II, was captured by the Soviet Red Army and kept in prisoner of war camps. Interestingly, his wartime experience did not make him hostile towards the Soviet Union. Rather, he had a grudging and cynical respect for Soviet space science and scientific accomplishment. He was a very good politician and a good manger, even though he was quite controversial. He was marginally alcoholic, had some personal scandals (he married his secretary after she became pregnant while working for him) and loved to play the political maverick. He was a strong supporter of East-West cooperation and the driving force behind ESA's Giotto mission. Sagdeev and Trendelenburg had a special personal relationship based on mutual respect and shared scientific and political interests.

Sagdeev introduced me to Trendelenburg sometime in late 1980. We developed an instant affinity for each other: my cynicism and irreverence was a great fit with Trendelenburg's style. Trendelenburg also liked the fact that I could keep up with him in drinking, and could even drink him under the table when it came to that (I was nearly thirty years younger, so I had a great advantage). He also liked my irreverent humor. When I explained to Trendelenburg my theory that NATO was very lucky not to have Hungary as its member, since Hungary had not been on the winning side of any war in more than 500 years, Trendelenburg just exclaimed: "You must be Jewish!" To which I said that of course I was.

Ernst Trendelenburg in 1983 in the way I best remember him: a little drunk and with his mischievous smile.

By 1981 I had become an important intermediary between Sagdeev and Trendelenburg. This fact gave me visibility, not only in Hungarian and Eastern European science, but also in Western Europe. And within a year, I was quite well known in space science circles in Eastern and Western Europe, the Soviet Union and the U.S.A.

In late 1982 two opportunities increased my international visibility. The first successful planetary probe, Mariner-2, encountered Venus on December 14, 1962. The Planetary Society, a U.S. nonprofit organization founded by Carl Sagan to promote the exploration of the solar system, organized a major event in Washington D.C. to commemorate the 20th anniversary of the Mariner-2 flyby and to advocate for further exploration of Venus. The event was attended by politicians, NASA officials and many luminaries. In the afternoon there was a symposium in one of the largest auditoriums in the city and it was followed by a large fundraising dinner. For the symposium Sagan scheduled three presentations: one by himself talking about the inspiration of planetary exploration, one by the famous science fiction writer Isaac Asimov who talked about his vision for humanity moving beyond Earth, and the last one by Roald Sagdeev, who was supposed to talk about the VEGA mission.

Even though the VEGA project was well under way, there had never been a public lecture about it. The Soviets were notorious for keeping their space missions under wraps until they were successfully launched. Sagan was eager to break this practice and wanted Sagdeev to talk publicly about the upcoming VEGA mission.

Sagdeev very much liked Sagan's idea and agreed that a public lecture about VEGA at a high profile event would be very useful. For some reason, however, he did not want to give this lecture himself and he suggested me instead. People at the Planetary Society had never heard of me before and they were quite surprised by this suggestion. Their puzzlement was further deepened by the fact that Sagdeev did not recommend a Soviet scientist but a Hungarian one. These facts aroused both Sagan's and Asimov's curiosity and they gave me a royal reception. There was a press conference with the three speakers before the public lectures, and the speakers posed with the President of the National Academies, Frank Press, at dinner.

My lecture was a huge success. I was at ease and unintimidated by the fact that I was following two famous speakers. I even joked that Sagan and Asimov had just given the introduction and now I would give the "real" lecture. In some respects this was true, since

Clockwise from top left: Isaac Asimov, Carl Sagan and I at the press conference; Isaac Asimov and I; Frank Press, Isaac Asimov, Carl Sagan and I; Carl Sagan and I.

the main attraction of the event was the introduction of the VEGA project to the American public.

One of the more interesting tidbits of the event was that after the talks were finished the science attaché of the Soviet Embassy came over and congratulated me for the job well done. The Hungarian Embassy was not represented, even though one of the main speakers was representing Hungary.

After this event Carl Sagan stayed in touch with me and we occasionally got together until his untimely death. I had the highest respect for Sagan who accomplished something that very few scientists do: he made people interested and excited about basic science, especially about the exploration of the solar system.

The other event was not public, but it brought together the space science elite of the Soviet Union with the leadership of ESA. The occasion was the ending of Trendelenburg's term and his replacement by Roger Bonnet, a French solar physicist. Sagdeev decided to

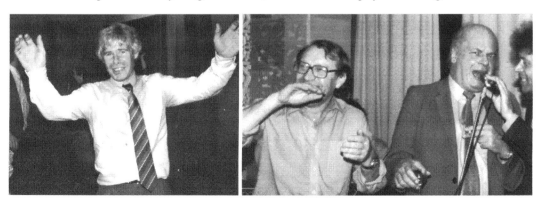

Farewell party for Ernst Trendelenburg. Left panel: Roger Bonnet. Right panel: Roal Sagdeev and Ernst Trendelenburg.

organize an event to honor Trendelenburg and welcome Bonet to the East-West collaboration. Sagdeev selected picturesque Samarkand, Uzbekistan as the venue and invited the cream of Soviet astrophysics and space science to attend. There was a scientific symposium and an unforgettable party to which Sagdeev also invited Károly Szegő and myself. It is interesting to note that we were the only invitees from Eastern Europe (outside the Soviet Union).

✂ ✂

While I was having a professionally very successful period between 1980 and 1983, the family had a more challenging time. Shortly after returning to Hungary Eszter and I bought a car. A Russian made Lada (based on a successful Fiat design), it was underpowered and unreliable. Nevertheless, having a car helped a lot with transporting the children around town and we were very fortunate to have a convenient mode of transportation. I still did not have a driver's licence, so Eszter did all the driving.

Eszter washing the windshield of the new Lada in 1980.

In 1980 the Hungarian educational system was completely unprepared for children who came from different countries. Immigration to Hungary was not allowed and all children were expected to go through the very rigid Hungarian school system.

Judy and Zoli leaving for school in the fall of 1981.

Judy had finished first grade in Ann Arbor where a significant fraction of children learned English as a second language. She was a good student and she loved school. When Eszter and I tried to enroll her in second grade in Budapest, the school tested her in Hungarian reading and writing; a test she obviously failed. At first the school wanted her to repeat first grade and only after a long back and forth did they agree to give Judy a second chance. She had to go through private tutoring during the summer and only when she successfully passed a second test was she allowed to enroll in second grade. School in Hungary was very different from the U.S. school system in that kids were not encouraged at all. There was harsh criticism for every little mistake and Judy quickly lost all interest in school. Second and even third grade was a painful and joyless experience for her.

Zoli started school in the fall of 1981 and he had a better experience than Judy did. He was not a very good student, but did well enough not to be a problem in class. He liked school and his teachers liked him.

After life in the U.S.A. Eszter could not return to Hungarian reality. Part of the problem was that she had never really experienced life outside of Hungary and had been raised with Communist ideology by a very strong and smart mother. Never before had she questioned her mother's judgment or disagreed with her opinion. She had been convinced that socialism was far superior to capitalism and that life in the West, especially in the U.S.A., was overall less satisfying than that in Socialist Hungary. The year in the U.S.A. not only opened her eyes, but also made her suspicious of anything her mother and Hungarian propaganda claimed. This awakening had a dramatic effect on Eszter and she revolted against everything Hungarian. Her only desire was to return to the U.S.A. and she refused to accept the daily compromises and humiliations that came with Hungarian reality.

I had never been a believer in Communism, so I did not go through a similar trauma. I was very happy with my exciting work. Eszter, on the other hand, was unhappy to the point of borderline depression.

In spite of the difficulties, there were happy moments in our family life as well. Judy and Zoli were happy children adored by their parents and grandparents. We four were able to spend the summers of 1981 and 1982 back in Ann Arbor, where I continued my comet work. Cometary physics was so interesting that gradually Andy Nagy and Tom Cravens also joined me in this field of research.

✂ ✂

By the middle of 1983 the hardware phase of the VEGA mission was winding down. My situation in KFKI was becoming more and more challenging, since I was squeezed between Károly Szegő's ambitions, András Varga's badmouthing and the growing jealousy of senior people at the institute. I also felt that this was the right moment to move from being a big fish in a small pond to the open seas. I was pretty sure that I could swim with the sharks. In retrospect it is amazing how naïve and arrogant this assumption was, but at the age of 36 I was still very self-confident. In addition, Eszter was so visibly unhappy in Hungary that returning to the U.S.A. became inevitable.

I had two more tasks before I was able to leave Hungary, though. First I had to defend my Doctor of Science (D.Sc.) thesis to obtain the highest possible scientific qualification (see Section 9.4) and I had to participate in the organization of the annual International Astronautical Congress (IAC) organized by the International Astronautical Federation (IAF) to be held in Budapest in the fall of 1983.

The IAF was created in 1951 with the aim of encouraging the advancement of knowledge about space and the development and application of space assets for the benefit of humanity. Usually, the IAC focused on space technology and space travel. It was a tradition for both the Soviet and the American human space flight programs to showcase their astronaut corps. Because I was fluent both in Russian and English I was put in charge of the special programs the IAC provided for astronauts and cosmonauts.

The first American female astronaut, Sally Ride, had completed her space flight aboard the Space Shuttle earlier in 1983. She was the star of the U.S. delegation participating in the activities of the IAC in Budapest. The Soviets did not want to fall behind in the publicity competition. They sent the second Soviet female cosmonaut, Svetlana Savitskaya (who flew 19 years after Valentina Tereshkova became the first woman to have flown in space), to the conference. Since the IAC was about peaceful cooperation in space, the two women were supposed to make several joint appearances and they both were very much looking

Clockwise from top left: Eszter, Tamás, Judy and Zoli in 1982.

forward to meeting each other.

World events, however, can interfere even with the best laid plans. On September 1, 1983, just a few days before the start of the IAC, Korean Air Lines Flight 007 was shot down by a Soviet interceptor west of Sakhalin Island, in the Sea of Japan. All 269 passengers and crew aboard were killed. The aircraft was en route from New York City to Seoul via Anchorage when it flew through prohibited Soviet airspace around the time of a U.S. reconnaissance mission. The Soviet Union claimed that the aircraft was on a spy mission and that it was a deliberate provocation by the United States to test the Soviet Union's air defenses. The incident was one of the tensest moments of the Cold War and resulted in an escalation of anti-Soviet rhetoric in the United States. The political climate during the IAC was very tense and the U.S. delegation cancelled all joint appearances of American and Soviet astronauts and cosmonauts. This was a huge disappointment for Sally Ride and Svetlana Savitskaya, who were very much looking forward to their meeting.

Astronauts and cosmonauts are selected from very large groups of strong individuals good at overcoming obstacles. Sally Ride quickly realized that I was not a KGB agent and did not care much about rules and regulations. She approached me and told me about her desire to meet with Svetlana Savitskaya in spite of the official position that there be no meeting between them. I had 24 hours to arrange a "secret" meeting because of the tight schedule of the astronauts.

I enlisted the help of the Hungarian cosmonaut, Bertalan Farkas, and the KFKI leadership. Farkas approached the Soviet delegation who were actually quite pleased by the idea of a private meeting between the two women. They, however, insisted that Svetlana should not go alone but be accompanied by the commander of the mission she flew on.

The next evening there was a reception at the U.S. embassy, after which Sally sneaked out of her hotel room and was picked up by me in a private car that took us to the apartment of Bertalan Farkas. Svetlana and her chaperon arrived about the same time. A group of about ten people, including spouses, gathered, and the two women chatted for six or seven hours, until the early morning. I translated for them and by the end was quite exhausted. Not the women. They were as perky at five in the morning as they had been at the beginning of their meeting. It is interesting to note that Sally Ride remained forever grateful to me for organizing this meeting. She regularly kept in touch with me and we occasionally got together at various meetings until her untimely death in 2012.

10.5. Back to America

I had a standing invitation from Andy Nagy to come back to the University of Michigan. By the spring of 1983, I had several opportunities to continue my research at leading institutions in Western Europe, but I wanted to get back to the U.S.A. Eszter did not want to hear about any other place but Ann Arbor, so I asked my institute, KFKI, to let me go to the University of Michigan for two years. Károly Szegő supported the idea, since he knew that I would not be around to compete with him when the "glory" of the VEGA mission would be harvested.

The Director General of KFKI, Ferenc Szabó, really liked me and was also very supportive of the idea of letting me return to the U.S.A. for a few years. He was hoping to

Left: Sally Ride, Bertalan Farkas, Svetlana Savitskaya and Tamás. Right: Sally Ride and Svetlana Savitskaya.

raise a group of world-class scientists with strong international reputations to enhance the standing of KFKI. He was also hoping that some day I would assume scientific leadership in the institute. Even though Eszter and I were talking between ourselves about staying in the U.S.A. forever, I was smart enough not to indicate this plan to anyone – at a time when defection was still treated as treason by the government. By the late summer of 1983 we obtained all documents and we were ready to return to the U.S.A. After I defended my D.Sc. degree and the IAF congress ended with success, I was ready for the next phase of my life.

Eszter and the children arrived in Ann Arbor in late September 1983 because school in Ann Arbor started right after Labor Day and we wanted to minimize the number of school days Judy and Zoli missed. I followed them about six weeks later, after defending my D.Sc. thesis.

Eszter rented a 3 bedroom unfurnished apartment in the Traver apartment complex about two miles from the Space Research Building. The apartment complex contained several hundred apartments and was commercially managed. Our apartment was a second floor, 1200 square feet unit with two bathrooms, about 50% larger than the Nagyenyed Street apartment in Budapest. Eszter collected some spare furniture from friends and purchased a few basic items. In spite of the simplicity of the living conditions, the family had much more space than we were used to. Most importantly, there were three bedrooms so that

External view of an apartment building in the Traver apartment complex.

not only Judy and Zoli had their own rooms, but Eszter and I no longer had to sleep in the livingroom. When I arrived life was already pretty well organized: we had an apartment, the children were attending school and Eszter had purchased a used car – in good condition.

Since the apartment was about 2 miles from my office I realized that I had to solve my transportation problem. I could not rely on Eszter, even though she worked in the same building. Her work schedule was flexible, but she had to look after the children and she was not always available to give me a ride when I needed one. So, shortly after my arrival I went to the local office of the Michigan Secretary of State and applied for a driver's license. In the State of Michigan a driver's license can be issued to an individual who has visual acuity of 20/40 and a peripheral field of vision of 140 degrees. With my glasses I met these requirements and I walked out of the Secretary of State's office with a learner's permit entitling me to drive a car as long as an adult with a valid driver's license was sitting next to me. Later I joked that the vision requirements were much stricter in Hungary because that country had only 10 million people and killing even one would be noticed. In the U.S.A., however, there were close to 300 million people and nobody would notice if I killed one or two.

Learning to drive at the age of 36 was challenging. We had an Oldsmobile station wagon with automatic transmission that made driving somewhat easier, but Eszter was very concerned about my driving and refused to teach me. A family friend came to the rescue. István T.-Szűcs was an engineer from KFKI working in SPRL at the time; he volunteered. István and I spent quite a bit of time on the roads together. I was not a natural in driving. It took me a long time to reach a proficiency level that promised I could pass the driving test. Which I finally did, on my first attempt, in early December. However, according to Eszter, I am still the worst driver in the family.

Our Oldsmobile in 1983.

Life in Ann Arbor was quite pleasant. Judy and Zoli enjoyed school and soon became typical American kids. Eszter and I worked full time and had a very busy life. The rental apartment was big enough so that the grandparents could visit every year. These visits usually required some coordination because Magda and János split their time between Stony Brook and Ann Arbor, while Juci and Pista spent most of their time in Ann Arbor. For instance, in 1985 Magda and János arrived in New York and spent the first half of their visit with the Bozokis. Simultaneously Juci and Pista were in Ann Arbor visiting our family. At some point we drove to Stony Brook with Juci and Pista and stayed there for a week or so. This was a broad family reunion filled with joy and some tension between the sparring grandmothers.

In 1984 Eszter took an open-ended position in the Space Physics Research Laboratory working for Tim Killeen's data analysis project. This position came with full benefits, including vacation, sick time, health insurance and a generous contribution to her 401(k) retirement plan (Eszter had to contribute 5% of her income and the University matched it with an additional 10%). This was our first tangible step toward establishing a new life in the U.S.A.

I obtained an open-ended research position with full benefits in 1985 when I became Associate Research Scientist in SPRL. Just like for Eszter, this was a big demotion from my position in Hungary, but it is fairly typical for new immigrants to start well below their old positions. I was supported by Andy Nagy and had no independent funding. The transition from visitor to an open-ended position was a big step, the start of the transition from being a big fish in Eastern Europe to the open ocean of American science.

That same year we applied for permanent residency, known by the term "green card," in the U.S.A. This was a difficult process for several reasons. First of all, we both had exchange visitor (J-1) visa status and it was challenging to change it to permanent residency.

The extended family in 1985. From left to right: István Gárdos, Juci Bíró, Eszter, Zoli, Judy, Éva, Gyuri, Magda and János.

Second, U.S. law at the time did not allow members of Communist parties to obtain visas, let alone green cards, unless they obtained a waiver from the Immigration and Naturalization Service (INS). INS waivers required an explanation for the reason the applicant had joined a Communist party in the first place. This was a complicated process and I had to work with an immigration lawyer to navigate it. It was time consuming and stressful. I felt humiliated and stressed through much of the process.

Things became more complicated and frightening shortly after we filed our green card applications. At the time U.S. intelligence agencies were barred from recruiting foreign visitors on U.S. university campuses. At the same time, there was an increase of intelligence activities during the Reagan years. A few weeks after we submitted our green card applications I received a phone call from the same FBI agent who had interviewed me during my first visit to Ann Arbor five years earlier. He invited me for a meeting in a local off-campus hotel. I was very apprehensive, but felt that I had no choice but to attend.

When I arrived at the designated hotel room I was greeted by the familiar FBI agent who introduced a colleague. This colleague showed a badge and introduced himself as a representative of the National Security Agency (NSA). He did not beat around the bush: his agency wanted to recruit me, send me back to Hungary and eventually to the Space Research Institute in Moscow to spy for the U.S.A. I was speechless. I worked in a politically sensitive field. I knew that the Hungarian intelligence services kept an eye on me. I knew that the Soviet KGB was watching me. But, nobody had ever tried to recruit me before to spy. I was given a short time to think about this offer and warned that if I refused, as a Hungarian Communist, I would have no future in the U.S.A.

It is hard to describe how frightened I was after this interview. I did not know what to do. I was certain that I did not want to be a spy under any circumstances. At the same time, I was worried about the future of my family if I refused the offer. After a sleepless night I decided to act. I went to the University's leadership and asked for their help. I told the story to the chair of the department, Bill Kuhn, who in turn went to the Dean of the College of Engineering, James Duderstadt.[2] The Dean called the FBI liaison who had been present at the meeting and told him in no uncertain terms that the University was very upset and this whole recruitment must stop.

The story, however, did not end there. I was in effect put on a list of "excludable aliens" and I had to go through extra scrutiny every time I left the country. This caused quite a bit of anxiety since there was no guarantee that an overzealous border agent would not put me back on the first plane every time I returned to the U.S.A. from a professional conference or from Hungary. Many years later, after I'd become a U.S. citizen, I met again with the FBI liaison who apologized for this incident. He said that he had no idea what the intelligence agent wanted when he asked for a meeting, and that he was taken aback by the entire episode. This, however, was too little, too late.

Looking back, I wonder about the strange nature of this episode. Was this a real recruitment attempt, or just a test or provocation? As far as I know, the NSA is a signal intelligence agency not involved in human intelligence. Was the guy just using NSA as a cover? Was he from the CIA, or some other intelligence agency? I guess I will never know, and actually, I want to forget the entire episode as much as I can.

Left: Judy is showing off her split in her future bedroom during the construction of the new family home. Right: front view of the new house with the two family cars in the driveway. The blue Honda Accord was Eszter's car and the burgundy Honda Civic was mine.

By early 1986 we had saved enough money to buy a house. At first we looked at the neighborhood around the Traver apartment complex, but did not find anything suitable. Finally, we started to look at new construction and found a new subdivision being developed just south of the center of town. We purchased a 1/3 acre lot and selected a popular model from the builder's portfolio. The builder allowed us to make some minor changes and finally we settled on a two story, four bedroom colonial model with 2,000 square feet of above-ground living area and an unfinished basement. The house was built on Crestland Avenue just next to one of the elementary schools. It took about six months to finish and we moved into our new home in December 1986.

Home ownership presented new and somewhat unexpected challenges. Eszter and I

---

[2]James Duderstadt received a PhD in 1967 from California Institute of Technology. He joined the University of Michigan in 1969 as an Assistant Professor of nuclear engineering. In 1981 he became Dean of the College of Engineering and in 1988 was appointed as President of the University. Since 1996 he is President Emeritus of the University of Michigan.

Apple picking in 1986. Left: Tamás and Judy. Right: Tamás and Zoli.

were responsible for cleaning the snow from the driveway and the sidewalk. Shoveling snow was not something we'd really considered. It also turned out that a new house always has problems that the builder has to fix. These problems included a leaky roof, adjustments of cabinets and other issues. It took about a year or so to "shake out" all the initial problems. Creating a lawn, watering and mowing was also new to me and I did not relish it. Overall, however, the family very much enjoyed the new home and our "American dream."

✂ ✂

In March 1986 our family was granted permanent residency status in the U.S.A. and our immigration ordeal was pretty much over. Six years later, in October 1992, we were sworn in as new citizens of the United States.

10.6. Professor Gombosi

Before 1980 there were only a handful of scientists working on the study of comets. Most of them were traditional astronomers who observed comets with ground based telescopes and were mainly interested in phenomenological descriptions of their observations. The physical understanding was at a fairly elementary level. It was only in 1950 that the "father" of comet research, Fred Whipple, realized that comets were "dirty iceballs" containing ordinary water ice and dust grains. As cometary nuclei approach the Sun, water vapor evaporates from the surface generating a rapidly expanding cloud of dust and gas. This gas-dust mixture forms the "head' and the tail of the comet. An active comet, like Halley, can have a tail almost as long as the Sun-Earth distance.

After work started on the Soviet, European and Japanese Halley missions, a highly experienced group of space physicists "invaded" the field of comet research. In a few years the area of cometary physics was transformed from the "backwaters" of astronomy to the forefront of modern space physics. This influx of newcomers created some resentment among the "cometary old timers," but these tensions were minor irritations compared to the delight the old timers felt when their research topic was suddenly propelled to the center of interest.

I was among the leaders of the "invaders" and worked on many aspects of cometary science. I became one of the pioneers who developed the theory of cometary plasma physics and laid the groundwork for a new area of space plasma physics that later turned out to be the key to the understanding of many interesting phenomena in the solar system and beyond (for more details see Appendix B).

Most of the funding for Andy Nagy's group came from two NASA missions and from a broadly defined grant from the National Science Foundation (NSF). The NASA missions were Pioneer Venus (see Section 10.3) and Dynamics Explorer (DE). Dynamics Explorer was launched in 1981 and operated for a decade. The mission consisted of two satellites, DE-1 and DE-2, whose purpose was to investigate the upper atmosphere and ionosphere. Nagy was an interdisciplinary scientist on DE and active in the modeling and interpretation of the observations. Since Tom Cravens was focusing on the Pioneer Venus mission it fell on me to start theoretical investigations in support of the DE mission.

There were two SPRL instruments onboard of the DE-2 spacecraft: the Neutral Atmosphere Composition Spectrometer (Principal Investigator was George Carignan) and the Fabry-Perot Interferometer (Principal Investigator was Paul Hays). The third Michigan investigation was Andy Nagy's interdisciplinary modeling effort. Altogether, SPRL had a leading role in this very interesting space mission.

As happens in most space missions, most of the work was carried out by young scientists, while the senior leaders provided general direction and looked after funding. Hays and Carignan relied on another young and ambitious scientist, Tim Killeen, to lead the actual data analysis of the two Michigan instruments, while Nagy relied on me (and to a lesser extent on Tom Cravens) to carry out supporting modeling. It became a family affair when Eszter was hired by Kileen to work on the data analysis project.

I already had considerable experience with modeling the transport of fast particles and Nagy asked me to model the terrestrial "polar wind," a supersonic outflow of ions and electrons from the polar ionosphere. Its existence was theoretically predicted in the late 1960s and one of the goals of the DE mission was to observe it. In about a year, I developed a novel method that was not only able to model the stationary polar wind (as other models did at this time), but also described transient behaviors that developed in response to disturbances in the ionosphere. This model was an important advance in the area.

Just like any new idea, my model ran into resistance from the established modeling groups. It took all of Nagy's political skills to smooth the situation and overcome the natural hostility of the established groups. In the end, however, the model gained wide acceptance and contributed to my growing reputation as an up-and-coming space physics modeler.

The Cravens-Gombosi-Killeen trio soon emerged as a highly promising group in the space sciences. By late 1985 we had attracted national attention and other universities started to consider raiding Michigan, recruiting us to fill tenure-track faculty positions. The increased national visibility changed the dynamics in SPRL and in AOS.

As has been noted, atmospheric research started in the Department of Civil Engineering in the mid-1950s. This was the time when nuclear power plants were built in the Midwest and understanding the dispersion of potential radioactive releases was an important question. A small group of faculty started research in atmospheric diffusion and air pollution. In 1958 the University of Michigan and 12 other universities established the University Corporation for Atmospheric Research (UCAR). The meteorology group had become interested in adding an oceanography component at an early stage. In July 1963 the Department of Meteorology and Oceanography was formally established within the College of Engineering by the University Regents.

The increasing visibility of SPRL in the area of global measurements of atmospheric composition had been key in luring Tom Donahue[3] to Michigan in 1974 to chair the AOS department. His six years as chair were marked by achievement in space science and in stratospheric chemistry. His presence at Michigan, together with the strengths of the AOS Department and SPRL, attracted an outstanding group of young scientists to Michigan. At one time in the late 1970s, James Anderson[4], William Chameides[5], Ralph Cicerone[6], John Fredrick[7], Shaw Liu[8], Don Stedman[9] and Rich Stolarski[10] were all working in SPRL on stratospheric studies. They made major contributions to the understanding of the origin of the atmospheric ozone hole that is a consequence of climate change due to human activities. Members of this group have since defined the field and are now members of the scientific elite of the nation. As a matter of fact, in the late 1970s, AOS was probably the world's best atmospheric chemistry department.

As has also been noted, in the fall of 1974, AOS and SPRL were merged and the newly expanded department moved to the NASA funded Space Research Building. The department has always been somewhat divided over the three central topics of its portfolio. At first it was meteorology versus oceanography. By the early 1970s the study of the upper

---

[3]Born in Oklahoma in 1921, he grew up in Kansas City, Missouri, and graduated from Rockhurst College with degrees in both classics and physics. He obtained his Ph.D. degree in atomic physics from Johns Hopkins University in the fall of 1947. In 1951 he joined the Physics Department of the University of Pittsburgh where he organized a program in atomic physics and atmospheric science that led to experimental and theoretical studies of the upper atmosphere of the Earth and the other planets of the solar system with instruments flown on sounding rockets and spacecraft. In 1974 he joined AOS as Chair, a position he held until 1980. Donahue participated as an experimenter or as an interdisciplinary scientist on the Orbiting Geo- physical Observatory (OGO) missions, Apollo-17, Apollo-Soyuz, Voyager, Pioneer Venus, Galileo, Comet Rendezvous Asteroid Flyby (CRAF), and the international Cassini mission to Saturn and Titan. He laid the foundation for our current understanding of planetary atmospheres.

[4]Philip S. Weld Professor of Atmospheric Chemistry at Harvard University

[5]Dean, Nicholas School of the Environment of Duke University, member, National Academy of Sciences

[6]Chancellor of UC Irvine (1998–2005), President of the National Academy of Sciences (2005–present).

[7]Professor, University of Chicago

[8]Director, Research Center for Environmental Changes, Chinese Academy of Sciences

[9]Professor Emeritus, University of Denver

[10]Emeritus Research Scientist, NASA Goddard Space Flight Center

atmosphere – mainly associated with SPRL – gained strength and traditional meteorology and air pollution studies lost ground.

During Donahue's chairmanship, this division was especially acute, with much bickering among the groups. The balance of power shifted even more when Paul Hays moved the space-based optical spectroscopy group to SPRL, where it soon became a major force. The combination of *in situ* and remote measurements was very powerful and kept Michigan at the forefront of space exploration and upper atmospheric science. Hays was a brilliant experimentalist with no social skills and a short temper that often resulted in outright bullying. He quickly alienated most of his colleagues and the engineering and administrative staff. However, at the time he was very successful and the upper administration did not want to lose him (or the research funding he brought to Michigan).

The divided department was not able to present a unified front to the leadership of the College of Engineering and by the late 1970s had lost all talented young atmospheric chemists. Even when AOS had an opportunity to hire someone to a tenure track position, the majority of the faculty voted for third-rate meteorologists over emerging superstars like Jim Anderson and Ralph Cicerone.

In the early 1980s a nasty internal split emerged on the oceanography side of the department. Eventually, part of the oceanography faculty left AOS and joined the Department of Geological Sciences. And in 1984 Paul Hays "deposed" the long-time SPRL director, George Carignan, to take over the directorship so that he could ensure all engineering resources could be focused on his space instruments.

It was in this divided department that the young trio of Cravens, Gombosi and Killeen emerged. At the time the AOS department had 18 tenure track faculty, four of whom were associated with upper atmospheric and/or planetary research. The three senior people were Donahue, Hays and Nagy. They were determined that the mistake of the late 1970s, losing emerging stars, should not be repeated. In this effort they got help from Deans of Engineering, James Duderstadt and later, Charles (Chuck) Vest[11] who transformed the College from a sleepy old boys club to a prominent research institution. In this process they often clashed with the old guard and ruffled many feathers. They greatly valued research excellence and international recognition. Duderstadt and Vest were the right leaders to recognize the opportunity offered by the emerging stars in AOS.

As part of his coup to take over SPRL, Paul Hays obtained a tenure-track faculty "hunting license." His intent was to offer the position to Killeen. However, according to University rules, the position had to be advertised nationally, creating an opening for Cravens and myself who also applied for the position. This resulted in an internal power struggle between Hays, Nagy and Donahue, who all felt that they had very strong candidates. Nagy promoted Cravens and myself, while Donahue supported me and an outside candidate who specialized in planetary astronomy.

In the end, the three warring faculty members approached the College and recommended that it hire three people for the single open spot. Hays picked Killeen, Nagy and Donahue picked me, and Donahue picked the outside planetary astronomer. I do not know the specifics of the negotiations, but in the end Killeen and I emerged victorious from this

---

[11]A mechanical engineer by training, he became Dean of Engineering in 1986 and served in this capacity until 1988 when he became Provost of the University of Michigan. In 1990 he was inaugurated as President of the Massachusetts Institute of Technology (MIT) and served in this capacity until 2004.

struggle, but Tom Cravens was left behind.[12] He left Michigan a few years later accepting a tenure-track position at the University of Kansas.

In the autumn of 1987 I was appointed as a tenure-track Associate Professor[13] in AOS. In September I started to teach my first course, the kinetic theory of gases. I spent an enormous amount of time with the course and was rewarded by excellent student evaluations. The course was quite innovative and challenging. After a few years I turned the course material into a graduate level textbook, *Gaskinetic Theory*, published by one of the main academic publishers, Cambridge University Press.

From left to right: Tom Cravens, Tamás Gombosi and Tim Killeen in 2010.

Shortly after my appointment as a tenure-track faculty member I wrote a letter to KFKI asking for permission to stay indefinitely in the United States. The letter did not come as a surprise, almost everyone at KFKI was expecting me to stay in the U.S.A. But, at the end of 1987 Hungary was still under Communist rule and in the waning days of the Kádár regime. Various people reacted pretty predictably. My mentors showed understanding and tried to cool the rhetoric of my distractors. Sagdeev and Gringauz were supportive and conveyed the message that I might become even more useful for international cooperation in space research in my new capacity as an American Professor. As usual, András Varga fanned the flames telling everyone, "I told you he was a traitor." Somogyi was silent, Szegő went with the flow, and Ferenc Szabó was disappointed that I had not informed him about my ambitions, since he had great plans for me.

History, however, was on my side. 1988 was a turbulent year in Eastern Europe. The collapse of the Soviet Union was rapidly approaching and Eastern European countries, including Hungary, were gradually moving toward ending the one-party system. My "defection" was the smallest problem of the Kádár regime and it took a long time for it to officially respond to my request. Finally, in the spring of 1989 I received a letter from the Hungarian Embassy in Washington D.C. with a stern message: return to Hungary within 30 days or the government will initiate "appropriate action."

---

[12]An interesting note about this triple hire is that in the early 1990s Killeen and Hays were competing against each other with mission proposals submitted to NASA. Hays designed an innovative mission to study the middle atmosphere, while Killeen was promoting a mission to the upper atmosphere of Mars. In the end neither of them won, but their relationship soured. Hays could not tolerate dissent and took Killeen's different priorities as treason. Soon after the loss of his mission proposal Hays suffered a massive heart attack. He eventually retired from the department.

[13]Academic tenure is similar to the lifetime tenure that protects some judges from external pressure. The intent of tenure is to allow original ideas to be more likely to arise, by giving scholars the intellectual autonomy to investigate the problems and solutions about which they are most passionate, and to report their honest conclusions. In U.S. universities and colleges, the tenure track has long been a defining feature of employment.

The timing of the letter could not have been any better. In May 1989 the Hungarian government dismantled the "iron curtain" by opening the border for hundreds of thousands of East Germans who immediately fled to Austria. Shortly thereafter, the Kádár regime collapsed and a new, democratically elected government took over.

In the fall of 1989, I received a thick envelope from the Hungarian Embassy in Washington D.C. It contained four passports for my family and a cover letter signed by the same Embassy official who had sent the stern letter earlier. The Hungarian Embassy wished us a pleasant stay in the U.S.A. I enjoyed the irony of the situation and decided to move on.

Sometime in the mid-1980s the Department of Atmospheric and Oceanic Sciences changed its name to "Department of Atmospheric, Oceanic and Space Sciences (AOSS)." This change reflected the evolving dynamics of a faculty that included an increasing number of space and planetary scientists. I had been the first space plasma physicist in the department. My hire represented a dramatic turning point in the department and later was followed by a large number of other hires in the area. Today, about 20% of the tenure-track faculty are space plasma physicists.

In 1991 I was promoted to Professor with tenure. This promotion gave me stability and crowned my efforts to establish roots in the United States.

✂ ✂

1992-93 was an emotionally difficult period for us. My father, János Gombosi, passed away in February. He was 83 years old. At the time he was hospitalized with atrial fibrillation, the most common cardiac arrhythmia (heart rhythm disorder). While in the hospital his arrhythmia turned into heart failure and he died after a short struggle. Tragically, nobody was at his side, since he was supposedly getting better at the time. My father's sudden death devastated my mother who never fully recovered from the loss.

Eszter's mother, Juci Bíró, died in October 1992. She was 76 years old. She had had serious health problems for years. She was a heavy smoker and suffered from heart disease, emphysema (a type of chronic obstructive pulmonary disease), and polycystic kidney disease (cysts take the place of the normal tissue and make the kidneys work poorly). Her kidneys deteriorated to the point that she needed dialysis. She suffered a massive heart attack while her veins were being prepared for dialysis and died a couple of days later. Eszter was just landing in Budapest when her mother died and did not get to say goodbye.

Eszter's father, Pista Gárdos, passed away nine months later, in July 1993. He was 86 years old. He suffered from inoperable colon cancer and after the passing of his wife lost his will to live. In the last few months he lived in a Jewish hospice. Again, Eszter was not able to be there when he passed away.

My mother, Magda Róna, survived her husband by 14 years. In the beginning she was in good health and she spent long periods of time in the U.S. visiting my sister, Éva, and us. Éva even obtained a green card for her, so that she could travel with relative ease. Sometime around 2000, however, her health started to deteriorate. As a complication from a flu infection she developed congestive heart failure and it was obvious for us that she needed help. At the same time she remained fiercely independent and resisted the idea of either moving to an assisted living facility or even hiring part time help.

In the end Éva and I decided that we had no choice but to hire somebody to be with our mother at least a few hours every day helping her with shopping, cooking, cleaning and

The graves of our parents in the Budapest Jewish cemetery.

similar chores. This decision turned into a battle of wills. First, Magda fought the idea with any means she had: obstruction, delay, giving us the run-around, and so on. Her most powerful weapon was playing the guilt-trip card (Jewish mothers are particularly good in this game).

Finally, Éva and I managed to hire a lady who was supposed to spend about four hours a day with our mother. However Magda made her life so miserable that, after about a week or so, she quit. "You see, I do not need anybody," Magda gloated. Éva was hopping mad, and I just laughed. Soon we hired another lady, and Éva made it crystal clear that if this failed, we would look into assisted living. This threat gave us a few months before our mother managed to get rid of the next lady.

By the early 2000s Magda had difficulty climbing the stairs to her apartment. She only left the house a few times a week and even then only in the company of her helper. Occasionally, she nearly fainted while walking on the streets and her helper had to support her to prevent collapsing. Once she actually fainted on the street and was taken by ambulance to a nearby hospital. Various tests were performed and eventually she was transferred to a neurosurgery hospital where it was determined that she had a fairly large, but benign, cyst in her brain causing the fainting episodes. Magda was around 90 years old at the time but doctors recommended an invasive procedure in which a needle would be inserted into the cyst enabling the doctors to "suck out" the fluid from the cyst. This would have resulted in the collapse of the cyst so that it could be removed from the brain. Needless to say, the procedure was not without risk, especially for a 90 year old.

Magda flatly refused the proposed treatment. "I want to die sane and in one piece" she said. At this point the doctors decided to transfer her from the special neurosurgery hospital to a regular one. She was put in an ambulance and off they went.

This was, however, already the era of mobile phones. Éva and I were able to talk to our mother while she was in the hospital and she knew that both of us were already on the plane rushing to Budapest. When Magda realized that she was just being transferred from one hospital to another she revolted. "I will not get out of this ambulance until you take me home!" she declared. The paramedics were in a bind and had no idea what to do. They conferred with their dispatcher and got permission to take the old lady home. I arrived some five hours later and rushed to the Izabella Street apartment from the airport. My mother opened the door with her sweetest smile asking, "What took you so long?" I almost cried and just hugged my stubborn, strong willed mother.

My mother passed away in her sleep in the summer of 2006, one week before her 94th birthday, exactly the way she wanted it to happen.

✂ ✂

In an interesting twist of fate my niece, Andi, moved to Ann Arbor in the 1990s. She had attended Cornell University in Ithaca, New York where she met her future husband, David Annis. They both majored in biology. After graduating from Cornell, Andi and my sister Éva were at loggerheads about Andi's future. Andi was a talented opera singer (she took lessons in New York City) and wanted to follow her artistic dreams. Her mother insisted that Andi should go to medical school and become a physician. (This reminds me of the old Jewish joke: When is the Jewish fetus viable? When it graduates from medical school.) Medicine was Andi's second choice, but she was young, idealistic and did not want to give up her dreams. In the end they made a compromise; for one year Andi took singing lessons and devoted all her time to developing her singing skills. I do not know the details, but after the trial year Andi enrolled in the medical school of the State University of New York at Brooklyn. She did an internship at Beth Israel Medical Center in Manhattan and then moved to Ann Arbor to pursue a residency in neurology at the University of Michigan.

Andrea arrived in Ann Arbor in 1994. She finished a 2 year clinical fellowship in Geriatric Neurology and then joined the Institute of Gerontology and trained in memory disorders of aging and early Alzheimers disease. In 2001 she joined the faculty of the Department of Neurology and Neuro-ophthalmology at Michigan State University. Andi and David now live in Okemos (a suburb of Michigan's capitol city) and have three sons: Joshua Dylan (1998), Ari Janos (2001) and Zachary Logan (2005). Andi is an ardent feminist and decided that boys should have a family name that comes neither from their father or mother. They combined the two last names (BOZoki and ANNis) into a new name, Bozann. So in this family, the mother is Andrea Bozoki, the father is David Annis and the children are Joshua, Ari and Zahary Bozann. I think this solution fits a TV show just like "Modern Family."

✂ ✂

I had a very successful career at the University of Michigan. In 1993 the International Academy of Astronautics elected me to be Corresponding Member and in 1997 I became a full, lifetime member. In 1996 I was elected Fellow of the American Geophysical Union (AGU), a very high professional recognition. Every year 0.1% of the membership can be elected Fellow, so the numbers are quite limited. Ten years later I was named as the Rollin M. Gerstacker Endowed Professor of Engineering, a major distinction at the University of Michigan. In 2013 I was awarded AGU's inaugural "Space Weather" Prize.

Left: Andy Nagy and I at my AGU Fellowship induction. Right: The Rollin M. Gerstacker endowed chair and I.

I served as Editor-in-Chief of the *Journal of Geophysical Research – Space Physics* for five years (1992–1997), a role that is very important for the space science community. I served as Chair of AOSS (2003–2011) and revitalized the department. I played a leading role in the very successful Cassini mission to the Saturn system. I served on several important NASA and NSF advisory committees and mentored many students and postdoctoral researchers (see Appendix B).

Throughout my scientific career I followed a small number of guiding principles. These principles helped me not to take myself too seriously and to overcome setbacks and disappointments.

1. Science is like sex. Sure, it may have some practical results, but that's not why we do it. (Richard Feynman)
2. In planetary missions half the fun is just being in orbit. (Fred Scarf)
3. Old ideas never die. Scientists do. (another version: Science progresses one funeral at a time) (Max Planck paraphrased)
4. If we knew what we were doing, it wouldn't be called research. (Albert Einstein)
5. Nothing is so firmly believed as what we least know. (Michel de Montaigne)
6. All great truths begin as blasphemies. (George Bernard Shaw)
7. Everything is forgiven when the pictures come back. (NASA's "motto")
8. He who can, does. He who cannot, teaches. (George Bernard Shaw)
9. Academic arguments are vicious because the stakes are so small. (Henry Kissinger)
10. If anything can go wrong, it already has. You just do not know it yet. (Jewish Murphy's law)

11. An optimist thinks that things cannot get any worse. A pessimist knows they will. (old Russian truism)
12. If we always accepted our parents' advice, we would still be living in caves. (I do not know where I heard this)
13. No good deed goes unpunished (Clare Boothe Luce)
14. Life is too short for bad wine. (Old truism)
15. A government that robs Peter to pay Paul can always depend on the support of Paul. (George Bernard Shaw)

Part III

The Future is Here

11 | The XXIst Century

11.1. Judy

Our daughter Judy attended the University of Michigan, majoring in psychology. A good student, she graduated with distinction. During her university years she had an active social life. She joined the Alpha Omicron Pi (AOΠ) sorority and lived in the sorority house for two years.

In 1995, after receiving her B.A. degree, she moved to Chicago with two of her friends. The three women shared an apartment in the downtown area, in Lincoln Park. After a short search Judy found her first full time job at TMP Worldwide, a company selling Yellow Pages advertisements. TMP was also the parent company of Monsters.com, the dominant career website at the time. At first she had an entry level job, but smart, eager and ambitious, she rapidly moved up the ladder. In 1999 she transferred to the sales side of the company and became a Director of New Business Development (a fancy name for sales). In this position

Judy Gombosi's wedding in Ann Arbor.

she was very successful and very well compensated. She, however, did not like sales and wanted to return to marketing.

In 2001 Judy enrolled in the Kellogg School of Management at Northwestern University while working full time. She graduated in 2003 with a Master of Business Administration (MBA) degree in marketing. The same year she joined the Chicago office of the Anglo-Dutch multinational consumer goods company, Unilever. Unilever products include foods, beverages, cleaning agents and personal care products. It is the world's third-largest con-

Top panel: The Pomerantz family in the spring of 2013. In front of Steve and Judy are the three boys, Jake (left), Sam (center) and Ben (right). Bottom panels: the Pomerantz boys: Ben (left), Jake (center) and Sam (right).

sumer goods company (after Procter & Gamble and Nestlé) and the world's largest maker of ice cream. Judy worked in the personal care product division managing products like Suave hair care, Dove, and later all personal care items for men. In 2010 Unilever closed its Chicago office and moved all personal care marketing to its North American headquarters in New Jersey. Judy was offered a job at the new location, but she already had a family and they decided not to move.

In 2011 Judy became a private marketing consultant and works on and off while raising her three sons (see below). She mainly consults for Unilever, but occasionally she also works for other companies.

In September 2002 Judy married Steven Pomerantz whom she had known for a while, but they came together on a trip to Israel sponsored by a Jewish youth organization.

Steve has an MBA degree from Washington University in St. Louis. For a long time he worked for GE Capital, the financial arm of GE that provides commercial lending and leasing. Recently he joined the Bank of America Merrill Lynch team as Senior Vice President in the corporate landing division.

Judy and Steve have three sons: Benjamin Miklos (Ben) born in December 2006, Jacob Arnold (Jake) born in August 2008, and Samuel Noah (Sam) born in April 2012.

11.2. Zoli

Our son Zoltan also attended the University of Michigan. Since childhood he had been interested in computers (especially in computer games) and he majored in mathematics and computer science. He graduated with a double major in 1997. After graduation he enrolled in the Masters program and in 1999 earned a Master of Science in Computer Science and Engineering from the University of Michigan.

While in graduate school Zoli worked part time as a software engineer for the pharmaceutical company Park-Davis (later acquired by Pfizer) at their Ann Arbor research complex. After graduation he joined a small local company creating medical software for the University of Michigan Health System. After a year with this

Zoli's wedding in Maui in March 2007.

startup company he was recruited to ArborText, an Ann Arbor based company producing publishing software. While working at ArborText he married his college girlfriend, Suzanne Kowalczyk, but the marriage lasted only nine months. After the collapse of the marriage Zoli moved to the San Jose (California) area where in 2002 he joined the software giant Oracle Corporation. The move to the San Francisco area took him to Silicon Valley, the Mecca of modern information technology.

Zoli did not like the highly compartmentalized culture of Oracle's software development and in 2006 left the company and joined a software startup, Siperian. In the more free-wheeling environment of a startup he throve becoming a very successful software engineer. In early 2010 Siperian was acquired by Informatica, a mid-size software company. Informatica's main product is a toolset for establishing and maintaining enterprise-wide data warehouses. Zoli is very successful at Informatica. He started as a software developer and later was promoted to software development manager. More recently he moved to product management, an area where technical expertise and user interactions merge. He has a bright future in this area.

In March 2007 Zoli married Alison Hoffman (the family calls her Ali). Ali worked at the Gordon Biersch restaurant in Palo Alto and they met through some friends. Ali was first introduced to the family in the summer of 2004. The outdoor wedding took place in Maui on a beautiful afternoon. In the background one could see the ocean with whales jumping out of the water.

Ali and Zoli have two daughters: Grace Julianna (born in May 2009) and Leah Madeleine (born in January 2012).

The younger Gombosi family. Left panel: Leah, Ali, Grace and Zoli. Center panel: Grace. Right panel: Leah.

11.3.   Grandparents

As often happens to new immigrants, Eszter and I had no family or close friends in the vicinity and had to balance work and family. Since at the beginning I was relatively poorly paid (as also often happens to new immigrants) Eszter had to work to make sure that the family stayed financially sound. Actually, it never occurred to her that she could stay-at-home and raise the children. The concept of stay-at-home mothers was alien to Eszter and me, since in Hungary both parents had to work to support a family. However, Eszter made a conscious choice to put the family first and her career second. She had already made this choice back in Hungary when she did not pursue a Ph.D. degree. Eszter's choice made it possible for me to focus on my scientific career, leaving the problems of day-to-day life to her.

Eszter left SPRL in 1988 and started work at the Medical Center of the University of Michigan. She worked on a research project in pediatric endocrinology where she designed, implemented and maintained a database for a newborn hypothyroid screening program. She very much enjoyed this job and her work was much appreciated by her supervisor. Unfortunately, the research project ended in the early 1990s and Eszter needed to look for a new job.

In the early 1990s Michigan had a very strong research program in neurology. One of the focus areas was Alzheimer's disease, the most common form of dementia. There is no cure for the disease, which worsens as it progresses, and eventually leads to death. In the late 1980s the research of neurodegenerative diseases gained increasing importance and a small number of national research centers were established by the National Institutes of Health (NIH). The University of Michigan was the site of one of these centers and the Michigan Alzheimer Disease Research Center (MADRC) was established in 1989.

Eszter was hired to design and implement the database system for the Center in collaboration with physicians and researchers in 1989 and she worked there until her retirement in

Eszter and I with our five grandchildren in the fall of 2012. I am holding Sam, Eszter is holding Leah, while Jake, Grace and Ben are standing in the middle.

2010. During the first fifteen or so years on the project Eszter very much enjoyed her work and was very much appreciated by the leadership. She actively participated in the activities of the national coordinating center of Alzheimer research centers and in 2003 was elected for a three-year term to serve on the National Alzheimer's Coordinating Center (NACC) Steering Committee.

Around 2005 MARDC lost a number of its top researchers and gradually declined. In 2010 it lost its NIH funding and downsized its activities significantly. In this process Eszter was laid off in the summer of 2010. Rather than starting a job search at age 62 she decided to officially retire from the University of Michigan.

If anyone thinks that retirement means less work for Eszter, you are mistaken. By the time she retired we had two grandsons in Chicago, about four hours driving from Ann Arbor, and a granddaughter in the San Francisco area, four hours flying from Ann Arbor.

I do not keep statistics, but on average Eszter goes to Chicago to care for the boys about once a month. Most of the time she is just asked to come and help when the nanny is not available, but a couple of times a year Judy and Steve leave town (to have some rest) and leave the three boys with Grandma. Eszter loves to care for her grandchildren, but she is not 20 years old anymore, and when she comes back to Ann Arbor she is usually exhausted and needs a few weeks to fully recover. By the time she feels rested there is another phone call asking her to come again. I bet that overall she works more hours than she did when she was employed full time.

Eszter would love to give the same support to her granddaughters, but the situation is different with Ali and Zoli. First of all, it is much easier to drive to Chicago (or take the train) than to buy a plane ticket to San Francisco. Second, Ali's mother lives just a few miles away and there is less need for Eszter's help. Nevertheless, we see our granddaughters five or six times a year. Zoli and his family typically visit Ann Arbor about two or three times every year, and we visit them about three times a year.

The birth of the grandchildren had a dramatic effect on me. I love and adore them, and I realized that the most important thing in life is to ensure continuity. I was so affected by the grandchildren that my priorities shifted. Through my entire life work was ahead of everything else, including family. Now I put the grandchildren ahead of (almost) everything. I was present at the birth of all five of them and never miss a birthday. I am even willing not to attend important meetings to make sure that I can be at the birthdays of Ben, Jake, Grace, Leah and Sam.

12 Epilogue

We covered the history of our families over the last two centuries. We came from humble origins in Hungary and our families were nearly exterminated during the Holocaust. We rose from the ashes like a Phoenix and multiplied. We established life in the land of freedom and we witnessed the birth of a new generation who will never know oppression or be persecuted for who they are. Our hope is that for the lifespan of a Phoenix our descendants will multiply, be safe and prosperous.

I would like to conclude this book with a beautiful Yom Kippur payer written by Rabbi Alvin Fine:

> Birth is a beginning and death a destination;
> But life is a journey.
> A going, a growing from stage to stage:
> From childhood to maturity and youth to old age.
>
> From innocence to awareness and ignorance to knowing;
> From foolishness to discretion and then perhaps, to wisdom.
> From weakness to strength or strength to weakness and often back again.
> From health to sickness and back we pray, to health again.
>
> From offense to forgiveness, from loneliness to love,
> From joy to gratitude, from pain to compassion.
> From grief to understanding, from fear to faith;
> From defeat to defeat to defeat, until, looking backward or ahead:
>
> We see that victory lies not at some high place along the way,
> But in having made the journey, stage by stage, a sacred pilgrimage.
> Birth is a beginning and death a destination;
> But life is a journey, a sacred pilgrimage,
> Made stage by stage...To life everlasting.

"Life everlasting" is the continuity of generations, not the immortality of an individual. This is what this book is all about.

A | Hungary, Jews and Anti-semitism

Our family's history is intimately intertwined with the history of Hungary, central and eastern Europe, and the changing face (but persistent existence) of anti-semitism in the region. Here, I try to give my perspective of the history of Hungary in general, and on the history of Hungarian Jews and their relationship to the rest of the population.

I am not a historian and my views are not always correct, and certainly not politically correct. I do not claim scientific evidence to support my conclusions and interpretations; these are strictly my own opinions. As you will see my views of Hungarian history are a bit cynical and irreverent, but I hope they will help the reader to understand my worldview and how this history affected our families' lives.

In order to help the reader to put my historical remarks into perspective I briefly list the rulers of Hungary beginning with the Conquest (see Appendix A.2) and ending with the oppressive regime of Admiral Horthy (see Appendix A.11). In the "remarks" column I point to the section where the relevant events are discussed.

Timeline of Hungarian Rulers

Ruler	From–To	Remarks
Grand Princes of Hungary		
Árpád	c895–c907	Led the Home Conquest (see Appendix A.2)
Zoltán	c907–c947	Son of Árpád
Fajsz	c947–c955	Grandson of Árpád. Hungarian raiding party is defeated and this puts an end to the Western raids (see Appendix A.2)
Taksony	c955–c972	Son of Zoltán
Géza	c972–997	Son of Taksony
Vajk	997–1000	Son of Géza. In 1000 converted to Christianity and took the name István (Stephen) (see Appendix A.3)
Kings of the Árpád Dynasty		
István I (St. Stephen)	1000–1038	The first King of Hungary
Péter & Sámuel	1038–1047	Fight between Géza's grandson and son-in-law
András (Andrew) I	1047–1061	Descendent of Taksony
Béla I	1061–1063	Brother of András I
Salamon	1063–1074	Son of András I
Géza I	1074–1077	Son of Béla I
László I (St. Ladislaus)	1077–1095	Son of Béla I (see Appendix A.3)

Continued on next page

Table A.1 – *Continued from previous page*

Ruler	From-To	Remarks
Kálmán (Coloman)	1095–1116	Son of Géza I
István II (Stephen)	1116–1131	Son of Kálmán
Béla II	1131–1141	Nephew of Kálmán
Géza II	1141–1162	Son of Béla II
István (Stephen) III	1162–1171	Son of Géza II
Béla III	1172–1196	Younger brother of István III
Imre (Emerich) I	1196–1204	Son of Béla III
László (Ladislaus) III	1204–1205	Son of Imre
András (Andrew) II	1205–1235	Brother of Imre. Was forced to issue the Golden Bull (see Appendix A.3)
Béla IV	1235–1270	Son of András II Mongol invasion, Battle of Muhi (1241) (see Appendix A.4)
István (Stephen) V	1270–1272	Son of Béla IV
László (Ladislaus) IV	1272–1290	Son of István V
András (Andrew) III	1290–1301	Grandson of András II Last king of the Árpád dynasty (see Appendix A.5)
Kings of Different Dynasties		
Vencel (Wenceslaus)	1301–1305	King of Bohemia
Otto	1305–1308	Duke of Lower Bavaria
Károly (Charles) I	1308–1342	House of Anjou
Lajos (Louis) I	1342–1382	House of Anjou. Also became King of Poland in 1370
Mária (Mary) I	1382–1385	House of Anjou. Married Zsigmond (Sigismund) of Luxemburg in 1385.
Zsigmond (Sigismund) I	1387–1437	Husband of Mária. Also Roman-German King (1410), Holy Roman Emperor (1433)
Albert I	1437–1439	Son-in-law of Zsigmond I., also Roman-German King, Duke of Austria (see Appendix A.5)
Ulászló (Vladislaus) I	1440–1444	Also King of Poland
László V	1444–1457	Hapsburg Dynasty. János Hunyadi stops the Ottoman invasion at Nándorfehérvár (see Appendix A.5)
Mátyás (Matthias) I	1458–1490	Son of János Hunyadi, also King of Bohemia. The last ethnic Hungarian King (see Appendix A.5)
Ulászló (Vladislaus) II	1490–1516	Also King of Bohemia
Lajos (Louis) II	1516–1526	Also King of Bohemia, killed in the Battle of Mohács. Ottoman invasion (see Appendix A.6)
Hapsburg Dynasty		
Ferdinánd (Ferdinand) I	1526–1564	During this period Hungary was effectively split into three parts: Royal Hungary in the north and west, Ottoman Hungary in the south, and the Principality of Transylvania in the east. Hungary was reunited after the defeat of the Ottoman Empire in 1699. (see Appendix A.6)
Miksa (Maximilian) I	1563–1576	
Rudolf I	1576–1608	
Mátyás (Matthias) II	1608–1619	
Ferdinánd (Ferdinand) II	1618–1637	
Ferdinánd (Ferdinand) III	1637–1657	
Lipót (Leopold) I	1657–1705	

Continued on next page

Table A.1 – *Continued from previous page*

Ruler	From-To	Remarks
József (Joseph) I	1705–1711	
Károly (Charles) III	1711–1740	
Mária Terézia (Maria Theresa) II	1740–1780	Resettlement (see Appendix A.7)
József (Joseph) II	1780–1790	
Lipót (Leopold) II	1790–1792	
Ferenc (Francis) I	1782–1835	
Ferdinánd (Ferdinand) V	1835–1848	
Ferenc József (Franz Joseph) I	1848–1916	Uprising of 1848-49 (see Appendix A.8), Compromise of 1867 (see Appendix A.9) and World War I (see Appendix A.11)
Károly (Charles) IV	1916–1918	
Regency		
Miklós (Nicholas) Horthy	1920–1944	Anti-Jewish laws (see Appendix A.11), World War II and Holocaust (see Appendix A.12)

A.1. Origin

The Hungarian language belongs to the Ugrian branch of the Finno-Ugrian group of Uralic languages. The common homeland of the Ob-Ugrians and the ancient Hungarians is believed to be somewhere along the central Volga. The closest languages to present day Hungarian are Mansi and Khanty – two Siberian tongues spoken by very few people. Among the "larger" related languages are Estonian and Finnish, both spoken by a few million people. Though many claim that Hungarian is closely related to Finnish, present day Hungarian is as close to Finnish as Italian is to German: speakers of neither language understand one another.

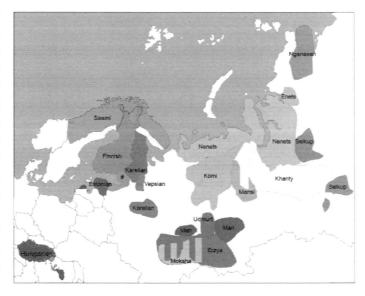

Distribution of Finno-Ugrian languages and peoples (from Wikipedia)

Some 2500 years ago the ancestors of the Hungarians moved southward, joining the Onogur tribes of Bulgar-Turkic origin and living with them along the northern shore of the Black Sea. About 1500 years ago the Onogurs and Hungarians came under the rule of the Khazar Empire which was at its peak at this time. The Turkic Khazars were quite unusual:

they were Jewish. The Khazars used Jewish personal names, spoke and wrote in Hebrew, were circumcised, had synagogues and rabbis, studied the Torah and Talmud, and observed Hanukkah, Pesach, and the Sabbath. They were an advanced civilization with one of the most tolerant societies of the medieval period and extensive trade relations with Europe and Asia.

Around the middle of the first millenium most of the Onogurs moved on and eventually settled in the Bulgarian homeland near the Danube delta. There were, however, some Onogur tribes left behind who eventually integrated into the Hungarian tribes. The strongest tribe of the alliance was the Megyer tribe and as time went on, the entire alliance started to use this name to identify themselves. Eventually this name morphed into "Magyar" and this is the origin of the present-day name Magyarország. The names used by other nations, such as Hungary, Ungarn, Ungheria, Hongrie, etc., actually come from the other side of the alliance, the Onogurs.

A.2.   The Conquest and Western Raids

In around the 8th century Pecheneg tribes attacked the Megyers and pushed them westward. Finally, around 895 the Megyer tribes entered the defensible Carpathian Basin, where they rapidly overcame the resistance of the Slavic ethnic population. This is referred to as the "Honfoglalás" (literally *Home Conquest*). The Conquest was led by the chieftain of the strongest tribe, Árpád. There were seven Hungarian and three Khazar tribes among the conquerors. The Khazar tribes were Jewish, so Jewish roots in Hungary go back to the Conquest. This is the source of the old Jewish putdown that is used when a "real" Hungarian calls Jews *foreign elements*: "When your ancestors arrived in the Carpathian Basin, my ancestors were already selling all necessities for home conquest at the entrance."

In the 10th century the Magyars occasionally raided Western Europe. They burnt and pillaged cities and villages in lands as far away as Castile and the Omayyad Caliphate in Spain, Burgundy in France and Apulia in South-Italy, though their most common targets were Germany, northern Italy and Byzantium. These raids ended in 955 when a large Hungarian raiding army (somewhere between 10,000 and 25,000) was decimated by Conrad the Red. (He was killed while fighting and defeating the Magyars. In the height of battle he was suffering from battle fatigue caused by an unusually hot sun. He loosened the straps of his armor to catch his breath when an arrow pierced his throat and killed him instantly.) The defeated Hungarians left their booty behind and the surviving disorganized troops returned to Hungary. The sad state of the returning troops inspired the Hungarian expression "gyászmagyar" (a disorganized group that looks like a funeral procession) used to describe defeatist and demoralized attitudes.

A.3.   Christianity

In 1000 King Stephen of Hungary converted to Christianity and – following the customs of the times – the entire Hungarian nation converted with him. His crown (the Holy Crown of Hungary) was a gift from Pope Sylvester II. Even though there were a few pagan uprisings against Christianity, by the middle of the 11th century Hungary became a predominantly Christian country.

With the rise of Christianity came anti-semitism. In 1092 the Synod of Szabolcs decreed that Jews should not be permitted to have Christian wives or to keep Christian slaves. This decree had been promulgated in the Christian countries of Europe since the fifth century, and the Hungarians adopted it nearly a century after converting to Christianity.

In the early 12th century the Crusaders rampaged through Central Europe intimidating the locals and killing Jews. As a result many rich Jews moved from Bohemia (today the Czech Republic) to Hungary where they became very active in commerce and banking. They became Chamberlains (financial managers of large households), mint, salt, and tax officials. Needless to say, the Hungarian nobility did not like to see Jews in power. When King Andrew II (1205-1235) was forced by the restive nobility to issue the "Aranybulla" (literally "Golden Bull,") the Hungarian equivalent of the Magna Carta it included the following: "No Jew or Ismaelite (Muslim), can hold a public position. The Nobles of the Chamber, those working with monies, tax collectors and customs officials may only be Hungarian noblemen."

The Holy Crown of Hungary

A.4. Mongol Invasion (Tatárjárás)

The Mongol Empire existed during the 13th and 14th centuries, and was the largest contiguous land empire in human history. Beginning in the Central Asian steppes, it eventually stretched from Eastern Europe to the Sea of Japan, covering large parts of Siberia in the north and extending southward into Southeast Asia, the Indian subcontinent, and the Middle East. The Mongol Empire emerged from the unification of Mongol and Turkic tribes in the region of modern-day Mongolia under the leadership of Genghis Khan, who was proclaimed ruler of all Mongols in 1206. The empire grew rapidly under his rule and then that of his descendants, who sent invasions in every direction.

Subutai (1176-1248) was the primary military strategist and general of Genghis Khan and Ögedei Khan (the son of Genghis Khan). He directed more than twenty campaigns in which he conquered thirty-two nations and won sixty-five battles, overrunning more territory than any other commander in history. He gained victory by means of imaginative and sophisticated strategies and routinely coordinated movements of armies that were hundreds of kilometers away from each other. He is also remembered for devising the campaign that destroyed the armies of Hungary and Poland within two days of each other, by forces over five hundred kilometers apart.

Subutai is regarded in history as one of Genghis Khan's and the Mongol Empire's most prominent generals in terms of ability and tactics helping with the military campaigns in Asia and Eastern Europe. He commanded many successful attacks and invasions during his time and was rarely defeated.

The Mongol invasions of Europe under the leadership of Subutai, centered on the destruction of East Slavic principalities, such as Kiev and Vladimir. The Mongols then invaded the Kingdom of Hungary and fragmented Poland. The former invasion commanded by Batu Khan, Genghis Khan's grandson, and the latter a diversion commanded by Kadan, another grandson of Genghis Khan; both invasions were masterminded by Subutai.

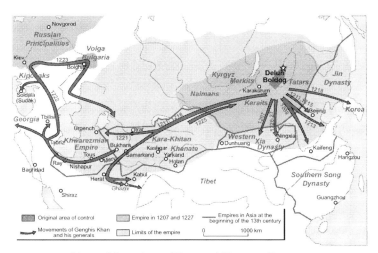

Mongol invasion of Rus and Eastern Europe.

The "Tatárjárás" (Mongol invasion) in 1241–42 followed the tragic Battle of Muhi (Muhi csata, April 1241) where most of the 60,000 strong Hungarian army was slaughtered. After this the Mongolian forces lead by Batu Khan systematically occupied and devastated the country. After the sudden death of Ögedei Khan in the spring of 1242, the Mongolians voluntarily left Hungary and Batu Khan returned home to participate in the succession process. About 40% of the Hungarian population died during the Tatárjárás leaving a lasting wound in the Hungarian psyche. Even today the Battle of Muhi is considered one of the great Hungarian tragedies, and the expression "vigyen el a tatár" (be taken by the Tatars) is an often used curse.

Jews played a prominent role in the reconstruction after the Mongolian invasion. King Béla IV (1235–1270) appointed a Jew to serve as his financial manager and also entrusted the Jews with the mint. Hebrew coins of this period have been found in Hungary. Between the Battle of Muhi and the Battle of Mohács (Mohácsi Vész, August 29, 1526) the Jews were repeatedly expelled from Hungary only to be readmitted when the country was in financial distress. For instance, in 1349 Jews were expelled from Hungary due to the Black Death. Their expulsion was decreed officially in 1360, though by 1364, they were allowed to return.

A.5.   King Mátyás and the Hapsburgs

One cannot understand the Hungarian psyche and world view without learning about the last ethnic Hungarian king, King Mátyás (Matthias Corvinus) (1458–1490). The Hungarian narrative makes Mátyás a larger than life figure exemplifying everything Hungarians would like to be (but often are not): smart, educated, heroic on the battlefield and in the workplace, and most of all bringing justice to the weak and underprivileged. The Kingdom of Hungary reached its largest geographic extent under Mátyás, and Hungarians never stopped yearning for the "glory days." Historic reality, however, is that Mátyás' successes were short lived and his strategic mistakes paved the way to the Ottoman occupation and to more than 400 years of Hapsburg rule of Hungary. In my view Mátyás is the perfect symbol of the Hungarian psyche that savors short term glory even if the price is centuries of tragedy. In the Hungarian narrative the consequences are always the result of anti-Hungarian conspiracies, while the short term glory is what this Great Nation deserves forever.

The death of King András (Andrew) III in 1301 brought an end to the Árpád dynasty. The Hungarian throne was first occupied by the French Anjou dynasty, followed by a long succession of various Western European and Polish kings.

This was the period when the Ottoman Empire evolved from a patchwork of independent states in Anatolia to a powerful entity that ruled over the Eastern Mediterranean and the Balkans. The Ottoman conquest of Constantinople (present-day Istanbul) in 1453 cemented the status of the empire as the preeminent power in southeastern Europe and the eastern Mediterranean. At this time Ottoman forces were also pushing towards Central Europe and ran into resistance from the strongest power of the region, the Kingdom of Hungary. The most successful military leader confronting the Ottoman expansion was János (John) Hunyadi (1407–1456). He displayed extraordinary military talent with the limited resources at his disposal.

The period of 1430 to 1460 was quite turbulent in Hungary. There was a rapid succession of Hungarian kings full of intrigue and murder. In some respect this period in Hungary was not unlike the era of the "wars of the roses" in England (1455–1485).

King Albert II (1438–1439) of the Hapsburg dynasty was a descendant of King Béla IV (1235–1270) (through Béla's daughter, Ilona) and became King of Hungary on January 1, 1438. He died unexpectedly in October 1439 leaving behind a five months pregnant wife, Elizabeth of Luxembourg, daughter of the Holy Roman Emperor Sigismund. Their son, László V (1440–1457) or Ladislaus Postumus was born four months after his father's death. However, there was a dispute about the Hungarian crown. The infant László's mother had the Holy Crown of Hungary stolen from its guardians at Visegrád and smuggled to Wiener Neustadt. According to legend, the cross on the crown is askew because it was damaged in transit. Elisabeth arranged for the three-month-old László to be crowned at Székesfehérvár on 15 May 1440.

As the anarchy resulting from the division became unmanageable, János Hunyadi was elected Regent of Hungary on 5 June 1446 in the name of László V. Later Hunyadi was accused of conspiracy to overthrow the King. In order to defuse the increasingly volatile domestic situation, he relinquished the title of Regent in 1453.

Meanwhile, Sultan Mehmed II was rallying his troops against Hungary. His immediate objective was Nándorfehérvár (today Belgrade) a major castle-fortress, and a gatekeeper of south Hungary. The fall of this stronghold would have opened a clear way to the heart of Central Europe. Hunyadi arrived at the siege of Nándorfehérvár at the end of 1455. On July 14, 1456 the flotilla assembled by Hunyadi on the river Danube destroyed the Ottoman fleet. On July 21, the Hungarian forces in the fortress repulsed a fierce assault by the Ottoman troops, and Hunyadi pursued the retreating forces into their camp. After fierce but brief fighting, the camp was captured, and Mehmed II lifted the siege and returned to Constantinople. Pope Callixtus III ordered the bells of every European church to be rung every day at noon, as a call for believers to pray for the defenders of Nándorfehérvár. However, in many countries (like England and the Spanish kingdoms), news of the victory arrived before the Pope's order, and the ringing of the church bells at noon thus transformed into a commemoration of the victory at Nándorfehérvár. Future Popes never withdrew the order, and churches still ring the noon bell in the Christian world to this day.

Three weeks after the lifting of the siege of Nándorfehérvár, plague broke out in Hunyadi's camp and János Hunyadi died on August 11, 1456. His legacy is still alive in Hungary and he is the most revered military commander in Hungarian history. His statue is prominently displayed in the Hungarian Millennium Monument in the center of Budapest.

After Hunyadi's death, there was a two-year struggle between Hungary's various barons

János Hunyadi (1407–1456) Governor of Hungary. Hungarian Millenium Monument (by Ede Margo, 1906).   *Mátyás Hunyadi(1443–1490), King of Hungary (1458–1490). Hungarian Millenium Monument (by György Zala, 1905).*

and László V, with treachery from all sides. Hunyadi's older son, László Hunyadi was one party attempting to gain control. In 1457, László Hunyadi was captured and beheaded, thus leaving his fourteen-year-old brother Mátyás (Matthias) as the sole surviving Hunyadi heir. When László V died suddenly in November 1457 the Hungarian barons gathered to elect a new king. There was a general dislike of foreign candidates and most of the electors assumed that the young Hunyadi would be a weak monarch. On 20 January 1458, Matthias was elected king by the Hungarian Diet (Parlament). On 24 January 1458, 40,000 Hungarian noblemen assembled on the ice of the frozen Danube, unanimously declared the fifteen-year-old Mátyás Hunyadi king of Hungary, and on 14 February the new king made his state entry into Buda. His statue is prominently displayed in the Hungarian Millennium Monument.

The new king faced a dangerous situation. The Ottomans and the Venetians threatened the country from the south, Emperor Frederick III from the west, and Casimir IV of Poland from the north, both Frederick and Casimir claiming the Hungarian throne. Matthias imposed a tax, without the consent of the Diet, in order to hire mercenaries. His "unauthorized" taxation, however, alienated the powerful barons and most of the nobility. After a period of internal struggle, Matthias prevailed and was able to turn against the Ottoman Empire.

Mátyás formed a large royal army, the so called "Fekete Sereg" (Black Army) of professional soldiers. With the help of this army he successfully fought on all fronts and defeated his adversaries. Thus, Hungary reached its greatest territorial extent ever (including present-day southeastern Germany to the west, Dalmatia to the south, Eastern Carpathians to the east, and southwestern Poland to the north).

In 1463 a peace treaty between the Kingdom of Hungary and the Holy Roman Empire was signed in Wiener Neustadt. This treaty enabled Mátyás to secure the Western front and retrieve the Holy Crown of Hungary from the Hapsburgs, but it also included a clause that eventually ended Hungarian independence for five centuries. This critical clause said that if Mátyás died without a legitimate son or grandson, his Kingdom would pass to the Holy Roman Emperor (in effect the Hapsburg dynasty). The twenty-year-old Mátyás probably was convinced that this clause was just a formality, but it turned out that he doomed the country with this agreement for a long time to come. This again shows the power of unintended consequences.

Map of Hungary in 1490 showing the conquests of King Mátyás.

High taxes to sustain Mátyás' lavish lifestyle and the Fekete Sereg (Black Army) could imply that he was not very popular with his contemporaries. But the fact that he was elected king by an anti-Hapsburg popular movement, that he kept the barons in check, persistent rumors about him sounding public opinion by mingling among commoners incognito, and the fact that he was the last ethnic Hungarian king ensured that Mátyás' reign is considered one of the most glorious chapters of Hungarian history.

Mátyás's empire collapsed after his death (1490), since he had no children except for an illegitimate son, John Corvinus, whom the noblemen of the country did not accept as their king. After the death of Mátyás, Holy Roman Emperor Maximilian I sent an offer to the Hungarian nobles in which he submitted his claims for the throne of Hungary based upon the Wiener Neustadt treaty. He promised protection against Poland, assured the annexation of the Matthias conquests to Hungary, and pledged to keep the Hungarian clerks and counselors in their offices. Otherwise, he threatened to use force to gain the submission of the Hungarian Kingdom. Eventually, the Hapsburg dynasty inherited the Hungarian throne. They were very successful in broadening their reach to many parts of Europe, mainly by marriage, but sometimes with arms. As the irreverent Latin saying goes: "bella gerant alii, tu felix Austria nube" (let others wage war, you fortunate Austria marry).

A.6. The Ottoman Occupation

By the early sixteenth century, the power of the Ottoman Empire had increased gradually, as did the territory controlled by them in the Balkans, while the Kingdom of Hungary was weakened by a peasant uprising and internal divisions. Sultan Suleiman I (Suleiman the Magnificent) attacked the weakened Hungary and in 1521 captured Nándorfehérvár.

The road was now open to the heart of Hungary.

In the Battle of Mohács (mohácsi vész) most of the Hungarian army were killed by the superior forces of the expanding Ottoman Empire. King Lajos (Louis) II himself died while fleeing the victorious Ottoman forces. By 1550 Hungary was divided into three parts: the central part was absorbed by the Ottoman Empire, the eastern part became the pseudo-independent Transylvania (in effect a satellite country of the Ottoman empire), while the western part was Hapsburg Hungary. The ensuing two hundred years of near constant warfare between the two empires, Hapsburg and Ottoman, turned Hungary into a perpetual battlefield. The countryside was regularly ravaged by armies moving back and forth, in turn devastating the population. After the Battle of Mohács, Hungary never regained its former political power. The Battle of Mohács is still deeply instilled in the Hungarian psyche as it is obvious from the often used adage of "több is veszett Mohácsnál" (more was lost at Mohács), meaning that things need to be put in perspective.

Jews living in the Ottoman and Transylvanian parts of Hungary were treated far better than those living under the Hapsburgs. There were strong anti-Jewish sentiments and laws in Hapsburg Hungary. Jews were to be taxed double the amount imposed upon other citizens, were forbidden to be customs and tax collectors, and in general were excluded from the privileges of the citizenry.

At the end of the 17th century the "Holy League" of Western Europe defeated the Ottoman Empire which, in 1699, was forced to sign the Treaty of Karlowitz in which most of Hungary, devastated and depopulated from 150 years of constant warfare, was given to the Hapsburgs.

The Ottoman Empire treated non-muslims as second-class citizens. They followed the Koranic principle of "convert, submit or die." Very few Hungarians converted, most had no choice but submit to Islamic rule, and those who resisted were mercilessly killed. The animosity against Islam is still deeply rooted in the Hungarian psyche. This is reinforced by such literary classics as the *Eclipse of the Crescent Moon* by Géza Gárdonyi (the original Hungarian title is *Egri Csillagok* or the *Stars of Eger*). Hungarians are deeply suspicious of political Islam (or Islamism, if you wish) which still reminds them of 150 years of Ottoman occupation.

A.7. Resettlement

Around 1700, Hungary had a population of about 6 million, a fraction of the population of comparable Western European countries. The Hapsburgs started an agressive repopulation program and invited settlers from neighboring countries. In the course of the 18th century some 400,000 Serb, 1,200,000 German and 1,500,000 Romanian immigrants moved to Hungary, dramatically lowering the portion of ethnic Hungarians from about 80% before the Ottoman conquest to approximately 40% by the end of the 18th century. The new Jewish population mainly arrived from Germany and Poland, but some Jews immigrated from as far as France. In 1735 there were about 12,000 Jews in Hungary. Their numbers grew to ~125,000 by 1800, ~250,000 by 1825, ~400,000 by 1850, and to nearly a million by the beginning of World War I.

In 1726 Charles III (1711-1740) decreed that in the Austrian provinces only one male member in each Jewish family be allowed to marry. This decree, restricting the natural growth of the Jewish population, had a great impact on the Jewish communities of Hungary, since many Austrian Jews who were not allowed to marry in Austria moved to Hungary to marry and start families.

The rule of Maria Therese (1740-1780) was a very interesting period in Hungarian history. Shortly after her coronation many Western European rivals attacked Austria expecting little resistance from a "weak woman." In this desperate situation she took the unprecedented step of visiting the Hungarian Diet (legislature) in Pozsony (today Bratislava) and with her newborn son in her arms she appealed for help. Seeing the tears flowing down the face of their beautiful Queen the Hungarian nobles did what every man would do when confronted by a weeping woman. All those present unsheathed their swords and broke out in one voice with the cry: "Vitam et sanguinem pro Regina nostra!" (Our life and blood for our Queen!) Hungarian legend, however, also tells us that right after offering their life and blood, they added: "sed avinam non!" ("But we will not give oats," meaning no new taxes). Sound familiar?

An interesting tidbit of history is the Military Order of Maria Therese created by the Empress in 1757. It was specifically given for "successful military acts of essential impact to a campaign that were undertaken on [the officer's] own initiative, and might have been omitted by an honorable officer without reproach." This medal demonstrates the prevailing mentality in the Hungarian culture: we reward the lack of discipline if it brings success. This reminds me of the attitude at NASA's Jet Propulsion Laboratory: "everything is forgiven when the pictures come back." The Military Order of Maria Therese remained a highly regarded military honor in the Austro-Hungarian armed forces until the end of World War I when the Hapsburg empire came to a crushing end.

My opinion is that the mentality embodied in the high esteem of the Military Medal of Maria Therese is one of the reasons why Hungary lost every single war since the 13th century (Battle of Muhi). This is not to say that there were no battles won by Hungary, but in the end they always managed to end up on the losing side. This inspired me to make the irreverent comment during Communism that knowing Hungarian history the Russians were crazy to include Hungary in the Warsaw Pact. Had they been smart they would have forced Hungary to join NATO. No wonder the Soviet Union collapsed. Now that Hungary is a member of NATO and an ally of the United States we know that NATO and the U.S. are doomed.

It is very likely that our families immigrated to Hungary sometime in the second half of the 18th or early in the 19th century. As the Hungarian Jewish population exploded during the second half of the 18th and the first part of the 19th century, a grand bargain started to emerge between the Hungarian majority and the Jewish minority: if the Jews were willing to adopt the Hungarian language they would be given equal rights with other Hungarian citizens. As a consequence, late in the 19th century many Jews changed their names to Hungarian sounding ones. Additionally, early in the 19th century all Jewish citizens of the Austrian Empire were forced to adopt German names. This is the reason many Jews have German sounding names even today. All our families mentioned in this book had German names at the middle of the 19th century.

A.8. The 1848 Uprising

1848 witnessed a series of revolts against European monarchies, beginning in Sicily, and spreading to France, Germany, Italy, and the Austrian Empire. Eventually, they all ended in failure and repression. Within the Austrian Empire the nationalities subjected to the imperial rule fought for national governments with Hungary actually succeeding in its secession from the Hapsburg Empire. The Hungarian revolution was eventually defeated in 1849 with the help of the Russian army. By the end of 1849 absolute monarchy was reestablished in Hungary.

By the time of the Hungarian revolution a large fraction of Jews spoke Hungarian and identified with the uprising. There were many among the army volunteers and Jews also played important roles in financing the national government and army. After the uprising was defeated the Jews were severely punished for having taken part. Field Marshal Julius Jacob von Haynau, the new governor of Hungary, imposed heavy war-taxes upon them. Some Jews were executed or imprisoned, while others sought refuge in emigration.

The decade of absolutism in Hungary (1849-1859) forced the Jews to establish their own school system. Most schools were led by well-educated teachers. Teacher education also became an important part of this process.

A.9. Compromise (Kiegyezés) and Hungarian Nationalism

In 1866, Austria was completely defeated in the Austro-Prussian War and its position as the leading state of German speaking Europe ended forever. The German principalities were soon absorbed into the German Empire created by Prussia. Austria also lost almost all of her remaining claims and influence in Italy, which had been her chief foreign policy interest. In the wake of Austria's defeat the Hungarians saw an opportunity for separation. To avoid this, Emperor Franz Joseph I suggested a dual monarchy between Austria and Hungary. At this time the leading politician of Hungary was Ferenc (Franz) Deák who broke with the secessionist movement and also advocated a dual monarchy under the Hapsburgs. Emperor Franz Joseph and Ferenc Deák signed The Compromise, and it was ratified by the Hungarian Legislature (Diet) on March 30, 1867.

Map of the Austro-Hungarian Empire. The map also shows the post-Trianon borders.

Under The Compromise, Austria and Hungary each had separate parliaments which met in Vienna and Buda (later Budapest), respectively. Each state had its own government, headed by its own prime minister. The "joint monarchy" consisted of the emperor/king, and the ministers of foreign affairs, defense, and finance in Vienna. This arrangement lasted until the end of World War I when the Austro-Hungarian Empire collapsed.

The concept of a "nation" developed differently in Hungary than in Western Europe or the United States. In Hungary nationalism was based on cultural and linguistic exclusiveness. Many Hungarians believed that the Magyar "nation" was a living organism comprised of all the individual Magyars. This living entity was thought to be vulnerable to contamination and even ruin from other languages and cultures. In 1867, the Hungarian *Nationalities Act* defined Hungarian citizens as part of the "united Magyar nation." Inclusion in the "nation" was determined by cultural identification and the ability to speak Hungarian, not political boundaries. For many decades, the ability to speak Hungarian would determine if one was seen as a "true" Hungarian or a foreigner, regardless of how long one's family had resided within the borders of Hungary.

Ethnic Hungarians did not make up the majority of the population of Hungary. Most inhabitants on the Kingdom of Hungary were ethnic Croats, Serbs, Germans, Slovaks and Romanians. The fact that ethnic Hungarians were outnumbered increased their paranoia that the "Magyar nation" was vulnerable. After 1874 Hungary developed an official policy of "Magyarositás" (Hungarianization) thereby forcing ethnic minorities to adopt the Hungarian language and culture. However, the ethnic minorities, with the exception of Jews, resisted Hungarianization. On the other hand, Hungarian peasants saw the inclusion of ethnic minorities and Jews as an assault on their culture. Resisting changes to their feudal way of life became an expression of "Magyar pride" (and it still is).

Jews made up only 5% of the Hungarian population, but as they embraced Hungarianization, they helped to tilt the ethnic balance in favor of Hungarians. Before World War I Hungarian Christians valued their Jewish neighbors not only for the commercial skills

Hungarian!provinces before the collapse of the Austro-Hungarian empire.

and entrepreneurial talents, but also for their intense Hungarian patriotism. More than any other group, Hungarian Jews embraced the chance to show their patriotism and love of their homeland by learning the language. By 1910, although Jews made up only 5% of the overall population, more Hungarian Jews (76%) spoke Hungarian than did Hungarian Catholics (55%).

The emancipation of Jews in the Dual Monarchy lifted the lid from the Jewish community. Hungarian Jews increasingly integrated and assimilated into the Hungarian society. Professions that had long been closed to Jews suddenly became available. Jews could enter higher education, commerce, and various guilds. This was the time when many Hungarian Jews changed their foreign sounding names to Hungarian sounding ones.

It is interesting to note that most of our family branches, the Glaubers, Rothmüllers and Strauszers, changed their names to Hungarian sounding ones: Gombosi, Róna and Bíró (the Günsbergers changed their name to Gárdos between the two world wars). Tthe turn of the century was the time when anti-semitism was below the surface and every self-respecting gentile family had to have a "house-Jew" (Jewish friend).

There was, however, anti-semitism below the surface, an intrinsic contradiction of the political reality of the Dual Monarchy: Jews were emancipated and increasingly assimilated into society, while an official "anti-semitic party" was formed in 1880. Later the famous Hungarian writer, Kálmán Mikszáth wrote that "an anti-Semite is someone who hates the Jews more than is necessary." The most infamous anti-semitic incident was associated with the "Tiszaeszlár affair."

On April 1, 1882, Eszter Solymosi, a fourteen-year-old Christian peasant girl was sent on an errand from which she did not return. When she was not found, a rumor was circulated that the girl had become the victim of Jewish ritual murder, and nationwide incitement followed. It was claimed that Jews killed the girl in order to use her blood to prepare matzoh for the approaching Passover. The investigators intimidated the five-year-old son of the local sexton (a synagogue officer charged with the maintenance of its buildings and the surrounding graveyard) who claimed that he had observed the girl's ritual murder. On June 18 a badly decomposed body was found in the nearby river wearing Eszter's clothes. By this time the locals were so convinced about the guilt of the Jews that they claimed that another corpse was dressed in the girl's clothes in order to provide an alibi for the sexton and his friends. A long trial followed attracting national attention. The more open-minded press and politicians openly sided with the Jews pointing out the many contradictions of the accusations. There was, however, a strong wave of anti-semitism whipped by some politicians. In the end, the court acquitted the sexton and the other defendants, but the accusation darkened the atmosphere for a long time.

A.10.   The "Martians"

In 1868, a year after The Compromise, Baron József Eötvös, the Minister of Religious Affairs and General Education submitted to the National Assembly a new National Education Act, which, after a stormy debate, was passed by both the Chamber of Representatives and the Upper House. This revolutionized the Hungarian education system and half a century later produced the "Martians."

Here are the highlights of the Act which created a state funded national school system and 30 teacher colleges, gave the state control of the curriculum, and specified the subjects every school must teach. The list of subjects was the following:

- speech and comprehension exercises;
- reading/writing;
- religious knowledge;
- arithmetic/geometry;
- geography/history/civics;
- natural history/physics;
- singing/drawing/physical culture;
- practical farming and gardening experience.

It is interesting to note that a century later, when I attended school in Hungary the only changes in the curriculum were the replacement of farming experience with industrial practicum and religious knowledge was replaced by Communist indoctrination.

The new school system emphasizing science dramatically changed Hungary. Combined with the emancipation of Jews, it opened the dam for talented Jewish and non-Jewish students unable to get a science based education before. This system was well ahead of its time and resulted in a disproportionate number of prominent Hungarian scientists and engineers. It also gave rise to the myth of "Martians."

The myth of the Martian origin of Jewish Hungarian scientists who entered world history during World War II probably originated in Los Alamos. Leon Lederman[1] wrote in his 1993 book *The God Particle: If the Universe Is the Answer, What Is the Question?*:

> The production of scientists and mathematicians in the early 20th century was so prolific that many otherwise calm observers believe Budapest was settled by Martians in a plan to infiltrate and take over the planet Earth.

These "suspicious" Jewish Hungarians included Tódor (Theodore von) Kármán[2], János (John von) Neumann[3], Leo Szilárd[4], Jenő (Eugene) Wigner[5], Ede (Edward) Teller[6] and others. *Yankee* magazine [March 1980] reported this landing in detail:

---

[1]Leon Max Lederman is an American experimental physicist who received the Wolf Prize in Physics in 1982 and the Nobel Prize for Physics in 1988 for his research on neutrinos. He is Director Emeritus of Fermi National Accelerator Laboratory (Fermilab) in Batavia, Illinois, U.S.A.

[2]Theodore von Kármán was a Hungarian-American mathematician, aerospace engineer and physicist active primarily in the fields of aeronautics and astronautics. He is responsible for many key advances in aerodynamics, notably his work on supersonic and hypersonic airflow characterization. He is regarded as the outstanding aerodynamic theoretician of the twentieth century. In 1944 he founded the Jet Propulsion Laboratory (JPL) at Caltech.

[3]John von Neumann was a Hungarian-born American mathematician and polymath. He made major contributions to a number of fields, including mathematics, physics, economics, computer science, and statistics. He was a principal member of the Manhattan Project and the Institute for Advanced Study in Princeton and a key figure in the development of game theory and the digital computer.

[4]Leó Szilárd was a Hungarian-born American physicist. He conceived the nuclear chain reaction in 1933, patented the idea of a nuclear reactor with Enrico Fermi, and in late 1939 wrote the letter for Albert Einstein's signature that resulted in the Manhattan Project which built the atomic bomb. He also conceived the electron microscope, the linear accelerator and the cyclotron. Szilárd never received the Nobel Prize, but others were awarded the Prize as a result of their work on two of his inventions.

[5]Eugene Paul Wigner was a Hungarian-American theoretical physicist and mathematician. He received a share of the Nobel Prize in Physics in 1963 "for his contributions to the theory of the atomic nucleus and the elementary particles, particularly through the discovery and application of fundamental symmetry principles."

[6]Edward Teller was a Hungarian-born American theoretical physicist, known colloquially as "the father of the hydrogen bomb."

Gábor[7], von Kármán, Kemény[8], von Neumann, Szilárd, Teller, and Wigner were born in the same quarter of Budapest. No wonder the scientists in Los Alamos accepted the idea that well over one thousand years ago a Martian spaceship crashlanded somewhere in the center of Europe. There are three firm proofs of the extraterrestrial origins of the Hungarians: they like to wander about (like gypsies radiating out from the same region). They speak an exceptionally simple and logical language which has not the slightest connection with the language of their neighbors. And they are so much smarter than the terrestrials. (In a slight Martian accent John G. Kemény added an explanation, namely, that it is so much easier to learn reading and writing in Hungarian than in English or French, that Hungarian kids have much more time left to study mathematics.)

My explanation of the "Martians" goes back to the father of Theodore von Kármán, Mór Kármán. He was a Professor of Philosophy who in 1871 founded the "Minta Gimnázium" (model high school) that focused on the physical sciences. The intent was to create a Hungarian Eaton, a school for future scientific leaders. Among its graduates were Theodore von Kármán, Leo Szilárd, George Hevesy, Edward Teller and many others. It is safe to say that the Minta Gimnázium fulfilled its founder's dreams many times over. There was a second science focused gimnázium in Budapest, the "Fasor Gimnázium." It got its name from its location; it was built at the corner of Bajza Street and the "Fasor" – Hungarian for "esplanade"). Among the graduates of the Fasor Gimnázium were János (John) von Neumann, Jenő (Eugene) Wiegner, János (John) Harsányi[9] and many others.

Altogether, as of 2013, there have been 14 Nobel Laureates of Hungarian origin, 10 of them Jewish. No wonder, the myth of Martians is still alive.

A.11.   Between World War I and World War II

World War I was long, bloody and dramatically changed Hungary and the lives of Hungarian Jews. Altogether about 17 million people died, 1.5 million of whom were from Austro-Hungary (about 350,000 of the dead were from present-day Hungary). About 3% of the Hungarian war dead were Jewish, roughly proportional to their numbers in the population. It is safe to say that Hungarian Jews fully supported the government and participated in the war effort.

Over 70% of Hungary was lost to neighboring countries by the Trianon Peace Treaty that also ended the rule of the Hapsburg dynasty. This generated a huge wave of dissatisfaction in humiliated Hungary which eventually gave rise to a Communist Revolution (Tanácsköztársaság) on March 21, 1919. Most of the leaders of the Communist Revolution

---

[7] Dennis Gabor was a Hungarian-British electrical engineer and physicist, most notable for inventing holography, for which he later received the 1971 Nobel Prize in Physics.

[8] John George Kemény was a Hungarian-American mathematician, computer scientist, and educator best known for co-developing the BASIC programming language in 1964. Kemény served as the 13th President of Dartmouth College from 1970 to 1981 and pioneered the use of computers in college education. He chaired the presidential commission that investigated the Three Mile Island accident in 1979.

[9] John Charles Harsanyi was a Hungarian-American economist and Nobel Memorial Prize in Economic Sciences winner. He is best known for his contributions to the study of game theory and its application to economics, specifically for his developing the highly innovative analysis of games of incomplete information, so-called Bayesian games.

Nobel Laureates of Hungarian origin (as 2013).

Year	Name	Field	Jewish?
1905	Fülöp von Lénárd	Physics	no
1914	Róbert Bárány	Medicine	yes
1925	Richard Adolf Zsigmondy	Chemistry	no
1937	Albert Szent-Györgyi	Medicine	no
1943	György (George) Hevesy	Chemistry	yes
1961	György (George) Békésy	Medicine	no
1963	Jenő (Eugene) Wigner	Physics	yes
1971	Dénes (Dennis) Gábor	Physics	yes
1986	John Charles Polányi	Chemistry	yes
1986	Elie Wiesel	Peace	yes
1994	John Harsányi	Economics	yes
1994	George Andrew Oláh	Chemistry	yes
2002	Imre Kertész	Literature	yes
2004	Avram Hershko	Chemistry	yes

were of Jewish origin (such as Béla Kún, Tibor Szamuely and Jenő Landler). The presence of Jews in positions of revolutionary leadership helped foster the notion of a "Judeo-Communist" conspiracy.

The Communist regime lasted only three months, but it greatly contributed to the resurfacing of anti-semitism in post World War I Hungary. The new regime was led by Admiral Miklós Horthy. He remained the "Regent" of Hungary until October 1944, when a putsch of Hungarian fascists deposed him.

Since the Hungarians did not need Jews for ethnic majority anymore and they were unhappy about the excesses of the Communist regime, there was no more reason to suppress anti-Jewish sentiments. This was reinforced by resentment of Jewish successes.

In 1921, 88 percent of the members of the stock exchange and 91 percent of the currency brokers in Hungary were Jews, many of them ennobled. In interwar Hungary, more than half and perhaps as much as 90 percent of Hungarian industry was owned or operated by a few closely related Jewish banking families. Jews represented one-fourth of all university students and 43 percent percent at Budapest Technical University. In 1920, 60 percent of Hungarian doctors, 51 percent of lawyers, 39 percent of all privately employed engineers and chemists, 34 percent of editors and journalists, and 29 percent of musicians identified themselves as Jews by religion.

Resentment of this Jewish trend of success was widespread: Admiral Horthy himself declared that he was "an anti-Semite," and remarked in a letter to one of his prime ministers, "I have considered it intolerable that here in Hungary everything, every factory, bank, large fortune, business, theater, press, commerce, etc. should be in Jewish hands, and that the Jew should be the image reflected of Hungary, especially abroad." There is a shocking resemblance in these words to today's accusations of a "worldwide Jewish conspiracy." Some things never change.

In the new Hungary, Jews became the most visible minority remaining in Hungary. The other large "non-Hungarian" populations (including Slovaks, Slovenes, Croats, and Romanians, among others) were removed from Hungary by the territorial losses at Trianon leaving Hungary's Jews as the one ethnically separate group which could serve as a scapegoat for the nation's ills. The scapegoating began shortly after the defeat of the short-lived Communist regime. Horthy's government passed the law of "Numerus clausus," restricting minority (primarily Jewish) enrollment at universities to the percentage of that minority in the general population.

Anti-Jewish policies grew more repressive in the interwar period as Hungary's leaders, who remained committed to regaining the lost territories of "Greater Hungary," aligned themselves (albeit warily) with the fascist governments of Germany and Italy. The inter-war years also saw the emergence of Hungarian fascist groups, such as the Hungarian National Socialist Party and the Nyilaskeresztes (Arrow Cross) Party.

Starting in 1938, Hungary passed a series of specifically anti-Jewish measures similar to Germany's Nuremberg Laws. The first, introduced on May 29, 1938, restricted the number of Jews in each commercial enterprise, in the press, among physicians, engineers and lawyers to twenty percent. The second anti-Jewish law (May 5, 1939) for the first time, defined Jews by birth and by religion: people with 2, 3 or 4 Jewish-born grandparents were declared Jewish. Their employment in government at any level was forbidden, they could not be editors of newspapers, their numbers were restricted to 6% among theater and movie actors, physicians, lawyers and engineers. Private companies were forbidden to employ more than 12% Jews. The "Third Jewish Law" (August 8, 1941) prohibited intermarriage and penalized sexual intercourse between Jews and non-Jews.

A.12.   World War II and the Holocaust

In 1941, 6.2% of the population of Hungary, about 850,000 people, was considered Jewish. From this number, 725,000 were Jewish by religion (184,000 in Budapest, 217,000 in the pre-1938 country, and 324,000 in the reunited Northern Transylvania, Carpatho-Ruthenia and southern Slovakia), while the others were identified as Jews by the Nuremberg style law.

At the end of 1919, Hungary established the "Munkaszolgálat" or as it was usually referred to "MUSZ" (Military Forced Laborer Service) for people who were either unwilling or unable to serve in the regular army. This institution was unique to Hungary and was not originally directed at Jews. In 1938, however, the Labor Service was transformed into a forced labor institution directed solely at Jews. As the war progressed, the situation of the Jews in these labor companies became extremely difficult, and many did not survive. They were brought to the Russian front to clean up minefields and other dangerous work. They were not allowed to carry arms.

Operation Margarethe I was the occupation of Hungary by German forces on 19 March 1944. Even though the Hungarian government was an ally of Nazi Germany, Horthy had been discussing an armistice with the Allies. Hitler found out about these discussions and, feeling betrayed by the Hungarians, ordered German troops to implement Operation Margarethe and occupy Hungary. The occupation was a complete surprise and was quick and bloodless. According to some German memoirs, the invading Germans were greeted with flowers. This invasion was remembered by many of the German invaders as their last war

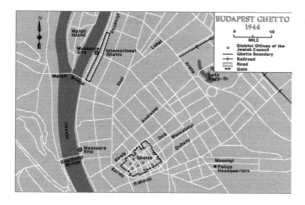

Location of the Budapest Ghetto. The map also shows the location of a major massacre of Jews who were shot into the Danube. (From the U.S. Holocaust Museum)

Deatiled map of the Budapest Ghetto. (from Balázs Mihályi)

with flowers (Blumenkrieg). The joke in Hungary after the invasion was that while planning Operation Margerethe I, Hitler asked his generals how long would Hungary's invasion take. "If there is resistance it will take a day, if there is no resistance, it will take a week" was the answer. "Why?" – asked the surprised Hitler. "Because if there is no resistance we have to listen to the welcoming speeches" – was the answer.

The day after German forces took over Hungary, Adolf Eichmann arrived to oversee the process of deporting the Hungarian Jews to Auschwitz. After a few weeks orders were issued to completely disenfranchise the Jews, to put them into Ghettos and deport them. The whole action's sole aim was to murder all Jews living in Hungary.

The order of 5 April 1944 to wear the yellow star was the beginning of publicly humiliating and dehumanizing all Jews. On 3 May orders were issued to register apartments and houses in Budapest belonging to Jews, to prepare to concentrate Jews in selected buildings within the town. These were called "sárga csillagos házak" (yellow star houses). The order to concentrate Jews living in Budapest was issued on 16 June 1944. It regulated labeling the houses with a yellow Star of David in order to easily identify them.

Each Jewish family was allocated only one room. Up to 200,000 Jews were moved into about 2,000 houses where living conditions deteriorated rapidly. Most of the Jews had to leave their belongings in their former apartments, leaving them without basic furnishings so that they often had to sleep on the bare floor. They were only allowed to leave their houses between 2 p.m. and 5 p.m. On 22 April 1944 food rations for the Jews were drastically reduced and often they could not even obtain this inadequate ration. After the 16th of October provisions were reduced even further. Many Budapest Jews died of starvation.

The first transports to Auschwitz began on May 15, 1944 less than two months after the Nazi occupation. By July 8, nearly 450,000 Jews had been deported from the countryside in 150 trains. By the end of the summer very few Jews remained outside of Budapest. During the summer of 1944, the Germans under Eichmann continued their preparations to deport Budapest's Jews to Auschwitz and other concentration camps. The deportation of the Jews of Budapest, scheduled for July 5, was halted before Admiral Horthy finally ordered the suspension of all deportations on July 8, and as a result almost 100,000 Jews of Budapest survived. The decision to end the transport was opposed by the Germans. To forestall a Nazi coup d'état, Horthy ordered the remaining parts of the army and the gendarmerie still loyal to him to Budapest. Nonetheless, another 30,000 Jews were deported from the Trans-Danubian region and the outskirts of Budapest.

On October 15, 1944 Horthy was deposed by a Nazis supported coup of the Hungarian fascist Nyilaskeresztes (Arrow Cross) Party. In November 1944, the nyilas (Arrow Cross) government ordered the remaining Jews in Budapest into a closed Ghetto. In the three months between November 1944 and February 1945, the Arrow Cross shot 10,000 to 15,000 Jews on the banks of the Danube. After the Nyilas takeover deportations also resumed.

Jews were also rounded up for forced labor. Many Jews from the yellow star houses were made to dig trenches around Budapest. Those who could not carry

The Holocaust emlékfa (memorial tree) behind the main synagogue in Dohány utca by Imre Varga (1990). The leaves contain names of Hungarian Holocaust victims. My grandfather, Dezső Gombosi, is remembered on the lowest leaf of branch CLVII.

out the heavy physical work were often shot. In October 1944 about 50,000 Jews from Budapest were forced to march over 125 miles to the German Reich where they were to do forced labor. By the time they reached the western Hungarian border up to 7,000 had been shot and an additional 2,000 had died from exhaustion. A further 11,000 of the estimated 35,000 Jews deployed along the fortification line died within six months. Almost every third Jew deported from Budapest died in forced labor. A very moving memorial to the Hungarian victims of the Holocaust stands in the courtyard of the main Synagogue of Budapest.

A.13. The Cold War

Soviet troops liberated the Budapest Ghetto on January 18, 1945. By the end of World War II only about 250,000 Hungarian Jews survived from the prewar population of ∼850,000. The survival rate in Budapest was quite a bit higher (about 50%) due to the short time between the start of deportations and the arrival of the Red Army. Compared to other Eastern European countries, such as Poland, the survival rate in Hungary was "high," even though it is impossible to describe the human suffering.

A major wave of emigration of Hungarian Jews occurred after the Holocaust. Many chose to emigrate to the U.S.A. and Palestine (present day Israel), others returned to Hungary to search for missing family members. In 1949, four years after the end of the war, about 100,000 Jews lived in Budapest (total population ∼2 million). Before the war Budapest's Jewish population was about 250,000, so 2 out of every 5 Jews were either killed or left the country. The number of Jews in the provinces was much smaller due to their lower survival rates, migration to Budapest or emigration. This number is a fraction of the approximately 350,000 Jews who lived in post-Trianon Hungary outside of Budapest before the Holocaust.

The social structure of Jews who survived the Holocaust changed radically after World War II. Traditionalist, religious Jewry, who had formed a major segment of Hungarian Jews before the war, was almost completely annihilated, and those who did survive gradually left the country. However, those who remained in Budapest encountered new opportunities for social mobility. Most of the remaining Jews came from assimilated, middle-class families; they found opportunities to advance, as they were highly educated, possessed professional qualifications and – since they were victims of the previous regime – were considered politically trustworthy. After the war, many Jews earned university diplomas or started new careers in public administration, as civil servants, in politics, or in state security organizations. Needless to say, this generated additional resentment.

The Hungarian Communist Party gradually took over power using the so called "salami tactic" (one slice at a time). The takeover was complete in late 1949.

In the 1945-49 period a considerable number of Hungarian Jews supported the antifascist left-wing and social democratic parties. Support for Zionist organizations grew greatly, too. In 1948, more than 10% of all Jews were members of Zionist organizations. In March 1949, however, the Hungarian Zionist Alliance was forced to dissolve after the Communist Party seized power.

By the late 1940s the "iron curtain" hermetically separating Soviet dominated Eastern Europe from the West was in place and Hungarian emigration came to an end until the borders were temporarily opened in 1956.

The Communist government of Mátyás Rákosi included a large number of Jews in prominent and influential decision-making positions. Jews among the Communist leadership included Rákosi, Prime Minister Ernő Gerő, József Révai (Minister of Culture), General Péter Gábor (head of the dreaded ÁVH, the internal security agency), and many others. This heavy Jewish participation in the very unpopular Hungarian Communist regime also contributed to the amber of anti-semitism.

At the same time, during the first half of the 1950s, a considerable portion of the Jewish middle class and small bourgeoisie fell victim to the antireligious and anticapitalist policies of the Communist government. In 1951 members of the "former ruling classes" were interned (resettled outside Budapest) by the Hungarian government. Among them some 2,000 to 3,000 Jews who had been entrepreneurs, merchants, and higher-ranking bureaucrats were deprived of their apartments and private property and forcibly moved to the provinces.

The Communist regime also introduced a class background check for all university admissions and promotion to higher positions. There were three classes: "workers" (including landless peasants), "intellectuals" (this included almost everyone who did not do physical work and was not hostile to the regime) and "x-class" later renamed "egyéb" (other). The "x-class" designed "osztályidegen" (not part of the previously "oppressed" classes). If someone was in the "x-class" it was very difficult to gain university admission or job promotion.

On 23 October 1956 a popular uprising broke out against the Communist regime. While many of the leaders were not Jewish, the heavy Jewish involvement in the hated Rákosi regime still gave an anti-semitic undertone to the uprising. The uprising was defeated by the Soviet Red Army in less than a month. The western border of Hungary (toward Austria) was opened and was not entirely closed again until early 1957. During this short period about 200,000 people (among them ~20,000 Jews) left the country and resettled in the U.S., Western Europe and Israel.

After the defeat of the revolution János Kádár established a more "humane" Communist regime. There was more tolerance, and by the mid 1960s the class background check was abolished together with many other elements of overt dictatorship. This regime was called "Gulash Socialism" and it was the most liberal system in Eastern Europe. We jokingly said at that time that Hungary was the most livable tent in the Socialist Camp. However, it was still a tent and not a house.

While overt anti-semitism was not allowed during the Kádár regime, there was a state supported covert discrimination. This was partly caused by political considerations, since Hungary – together with the Soviet block – was openly anti-Israel and pro-Arab. Strangely enough, this generated some positive feelings for Israel (and by extension towards Jews) among the population; people disliked the Soviets so much, that anything the Soviets were against must have been a good thing.

A.14.   Hungary in the 21th Century

The iron curtain and the Soviet block fell in 1989. Hungary played a very important role by opening its western border to masses of East Germans fleeing toward Austria. The first free parliamentary election was held in March 1990 and resulted in the formation of a center-right government. This government introduced dramatic changes that eventually transformed Hungary to a Western style democracy. The Soviet occupying forces finally left Hungary in 1991 and eventually Hungary joined NATO (1999) and the European Union (2004). Power was peacefully transitioned between center-right and center-left coalitions between 1990 and 2010.

In April 1997, the Hungarian parliament passed a Jewish compensation act that returned property stolen from Jewish victims during the Nazi and Communist eras. Under this law, properties were given back and monetary payments were made to the Jewish public heritage foundations and to Jewish victims of the Holocaust. The amounts, however, were trivial, representing nothing more than a symbolic gesture which many international observers have deemed too little, too late.

Most estimates about the number of Jews in Hungary today range from 50,000 to 150,000. This population is generally highly assimilated and intermarriage rates are around 60%. In the 2001 census there were only 13,000 people identifying themselves as "Jewish by religion." At the same time, Hungary has a number of active synagogues, including the Dohány Street Synagogue, which is the second largest synagogue in the world. Jewish education is well organized: there are three Jewish high schools (Lauder Javne, Wesselényi and Anna Frank), all in Budapest. Hungary is also home to the Jewish Theological Seminary - University of Jewish Studies.

Overt anti-semitism has been a problem in Hungary since the fall of Communism. After the outbreak of the worldwide economic crisis in 2007 extreme elements established an extreme right wing party, called "Movement for a Better Hungary" or Jobbik,[10] with a paramilitary organization complete with Nyilas-like uniforms and armbands.

In the 2010 Hungarian elections the center-right FIDESZ (Fiatal Demokraták Szövetsége, Alliance of Young Democrats) won a 2/3 majority in the Hungarian parliament enabling it to change the Constitution over the objections of the opposition. They have done this several times in the last few years raising concerns in Western democracies that Hungary is moving towards an authoritarian regime. It would be a true (and sad) irony if Hungary turned back the time and returned to a Horthy style regime. Only time will tell.

I found a very telling photograph symbolizing the situation in post-Cold War Hungary. The picture, taken from the Castle Hill, shows the Lánchíd (Chain Bridge) in the foreground, representing tradition (it was built in 1849), the new Four Seasons Hotel

This picture symbolises post-Cold War Hungary. It shows the Lánchíd (Chain Bridge) in the foreground, representing tradition, the new Four Seasons Hotel (former Grescham Palace) in the middle, representing Capitalism, and the dominating Szent István Bazilika (St. Stephen Cathedral) in the background, representing the influence of the Catholic Church.

(former Grescham Palace) in the middle, representing Capitalism, and the dominating Szent István Bazilika (St. Stephen Cathedral) in the background, representing the influence of the Catholic Church.

A.15. Code Words

I would like to devote this short section to an explanation of some code words that have political and emotional undertones. To someone not familiar with Hungarian history and politics some of these words or expressions might seem harmless, but they actually carry

---

[10]the name originally comes from "Jobboldali Ifjúsgi Közösség" (Right-wing Youth Organization) that was abbreviated as JOBBIK. Later it became a national party but kept the name, which is in fact a play on words. The word "Jobb" in Hungarian has two meanings, the adjective for "better" and the direction "right," the comparative Jobbik therefore means both 'the more preferable choice' and 'more to the right'. This is similar to the English "Right Choice" meaning both Conservative and Proper.

very powerful messages and stir raw emotions.

Let us start with the word anti-semitism. The term "Anti-Semitism" has its origin in the ethnological theory that the Jews, as Semites, are entirely different from the Hungarian populations and can never be integrated. The word implies that the Jews are not opposed on account of their religion, but on account of their racial characteristics such as greed, a special aptitude for money-making, taking advantage of others, aversion to hard work, clannishness and obtrusiveness, lack of social tact, and especially of patriotism. Finally, the term is used to justify resentment for every crime or objectionable act committed by any individual Jew.

In Hungarian politics the adjective "Christian" means non-Jewish. "Christian nation" refers to ethnic Hungarians with no Jewish blood. "Christian gentleman" refers to non-Jewish intellectuals who value knowledge and learning, are moderately right wing, but at the same time are tolerant against other views. A Christian gentleman does not socialize with Jews, but can accept them as colleagues or even neighbors.

Indirectly (and always derogatively) referring to Jews is becoming an art in present-day Hungary. "Non-Hungarian elements," "global financial circles," "cosmopolitans," "liberals," are the more indirect synonyms. The cruder ones include "parasites," "Zionists," or "Israel firsters." More recently international financial and political institutions also became synonyms of global Jewish conspiracies against Hungary. These include the International Monetary Fund (IMF), the European Union (especially the EU Central Bank), the "New York - Tel Aviv axis," and many other variations. More extreme opinions are also freely expressed. Before the 2010 elections a right wing newspaper wrote: "Given our current situation, anti-Semitism is not just our right, but it is the duty of every Hungarian homeland lover, and we must prepare for armed battle against the Jews."

The present ruling party, FIDESZ, merged anti-globalization views with coded popular anti-semitism, support of Christian values, Hungarian nationalism, and attacks on ethnic minorities. Serving both radical nationalists and disillusioned voters, the government's economic policies are primarily directed against "the neoliberal ideology dominated policies," capitalizing on increasing joblessness, corruption crises, and social unrest caused by the global economic crisis. In light of widespread economic and cultural fears, the party mobilizes political and cultural resentments not only against pro-European and pro-cosmopolitan elites and minorities but also against multinational corporations, America, and Israel – i.e. globalism, imperialism, and international institutions (supposedly all of these are dominated by Jews). A popular quote by Oszkár Molnár, a FIDESZ member of the Hungarian Parliament states: "I love Hungary, I love Hungarians, and I prefer Hungarian interests to global financial capital, or Jewish capital, if you like, which wants to devour the whole world, but especially Hungary."

Another important code word in present-day Hungary is "war for economic independence." This expression builds on the word "szabadságharc" referring to two aborted wars of independence: the Rákóczi uprising (1703-1711) and the Hungarian revolution of 1848. Both uprisings were defeated by the Hapsburg forces, but today are symbols of Hungarian national pride and independence from foreign influence. According to present Prime Minister Viktor Orbán, the Hungarians of today are descendants of the 1848 warriors of freedom. According to Orbán, the program of 2012, just as the one in 1848, is that "we will not be a colony!" Furthermore, Hungarians are strong enough to achieve "a free Hungarian life" and therefore don't need "unsolicited foreign help" that comes "from people in well-tailored suits and not from men in shoulder-strapped uniforms" which is just another way of comparing the (supposedly Jewish dominated) EU and IMF to the Soviet Union.

Orbán gets even more specific. In a speech given on 15 March 2012 (the anniversary of the uprising of 1848) he said: "Modern colonizers stalk their prey patiently. They lull their vital instincts and their resistance .... This is what happened to Hungary after 2002 when people didn't even notice that they were being captured by comfortable loans. It was in the last minute that we managed to avert disaster." He also had some more harsh words for the EU: "the European Union is not an alliance of saints but they cannot watch with folded arms while some political and intellectual trend forces an unholy alliance on Europe." Here he is referring to the "liberal pestilence" (i.e. Jews) that "is taking hold of Europe."

B | Tamás Gombosi's Scientific Biography (November 2013)

B.1. Education

- Ph.D. (Physics), Loránd Eötvös University, Budapest, Hungary, 1974.
- M.S. (Physics), Loránd Eötvös University, Budapest, Hungary, 1970.
- *Post-PhD Degrees*
  - Candidate of Science (Physics), Hungarian Academy of Sciences, 1979.
  - Doctor of Science (Physics), Hungarian Academy of Sciences, 1983.

B.2. Employment

- *Rollin M. Gerstacker Endowed Professor of Engineering*, University of Michigan, 2007–present.
- *Chair*, Department of Atmospheric, Oceanic and Space Sciences, University of Michigan, 2003–2011.
- *Director*, Space Physics Research Laboratory, University of Michigan, 2003–2006.
- *Director*, Center for Space Environment Modeling, University of Michigan, 2002–present.
- *Associate Professor and Professor*, University of Michigan, 1987–2007.
- *Associate Research Scientist*, University of Michigan, 1985–87.
- *Associate Research Scientist, Research Scientist, Senior Research Scientist, Scientific Advisor*, Central Research Institute for Physics, Hungarian Academy of Sciences, 1970–85.

B.3. Awards & Recognitions

- Recipient of the American Geophysical Union's (AGU) inaugural Space Weather Prize, 2013.
- Rollin M. Gerstacker Endowed Professor of Engineering, The University of Michigan, 2007.
- Elected Full Member, International Academy of Astronautics (Corresponding Member 1993, Full Member 1997)
- Fellow of the American Geophysical Union (elected in 1996)
- *Awards*
  - NASA Group Achievement Award (Cassini Interdisciplinary Scientists), 2009.
  - NASA Public Service Group Achievement Award (Rosetta), 2007.
  - Steven S. Attwood Award (the highest faculty achievement award in the College of

Engineering), College of Engineering, The University of Michigan, 2002.

– Team Excellence Award, College of Engineering, The University of Michigan, 1999.
– NASA Group Achievement Award (Cassini Orbiter), 1998.
– Research Excellence Award, College of Engineering, The University of Michigan, 1992.
– Lajos Jánossy Award (the highest science award of the research center), Central Research Institute for Physics, Hungary, 1987.
– László Detre Award (young scientist award), Lóraánd Eötvös Physical Society, Hungary, 1982.
– KFKI Award, Central Research Institute for Physics, Hungary, 1978.
– KFKI Award, Central Research Institute for Physics, Hungary, 1976.
– Albert Fonó Award (young scientist award), Hungarian Astronautical Society, 1976.

B.4.   Scientific Biography

A native of Hungary, Professor Gombosi was educated in theoretical physics. In the mid-1970s he was the first foreign national to do postdoctoral research at the Space Research Institute (IKI) in Moscow, where he participated in theoretical studies of the solar wind interaction with Venus and in data interpretation of the first Venus orbiters, Venera-9 and Venera-10. At IKI he worked under the direction of Konstantin Gringauz, Roald Sagdeev, Albert Galeev and Vitalii Shapiro. A few years later he came to the U.S. to participate in theoretical work related to NASA's Venus exploration.

In the early 1980s he played a leading role in the planning and implementation of the international VEGA mission to Venus and Halley's comet. As project scientist for Hungary he actively participated in the design of several *in situ* and remote sensing instruments (such as the imaging system, the energetic particle detector, and the plasma spectrometer). In addition to his involvement in cometary missions he also carried out pioneering theoretical work in the emerging field of cometary plasma physics.

In the mid 1980s he permanently moved to the U.S., and in 1987 he joined the faculty of the University of Michigan, where presently he is Rollin M. Gerstacker Professor of Engineering, Professor of Space Science and Professor of Aerospace Engineering. In addition, he is the founding Director of the Center for Space Environment Modeling.

At Michigan he established close interdisciplinary collaborations with computational fluid dynamics and computational science faculty and formed a tightly integrated group of faculty and students that pioneered high performance simulation technology of space plasmas extending from the solar surface to cometary and planetary magnetospheres and ionospheres, to the outer edges of the solar system.

His present research includes:

• Development of the first generation of first-principles-based predictive global space weather simulation codes,
• Physics of planetary space environments (including Earth, planetary satellites and comets),
• Theoretical investigations of plasma transport in various regions of the heliosphere,
• Fundamental kinetic theory of gases and plasmas, and
• Multi-scale MHD simulations of solar system plasmas on solution adaptive unstructured grids.

He also continues to participate in the exploration of the space environment and the solar system. He is Interdisciplinary Scientist of the international Cassini/Huygens mission to Saturn and its moon, Titan. He is Chair of Working Group X (providing modeling support for the mission) and Co-Investigator of the ROSINA ion-neutral mass spectrometer on the international Rosetta mission presently en route to comet Churyumov-Gerasimenko. Professor Gombosi is Co-Investigator of the IMPACT plasma instrument on NASA's STEREO mission to explore solar storms, and member of the science team of the Magnetospheric Multiscale (MMS) mission. In addition, he is Principal Investigator of several large interdisciplinary research efforts.

B.5. Main Scientific Accomplishments

His scientific contributions span across many areas of space and planetary physics. Here is an incomplete list of his most important scientific contributions:

- He was first author of the paper published in *Nature* that first established the directional anisotropy of $\sim 10^{14}$ eV galactic cosmic rays. In order to prove the existence of a 0.1% directional anisotropy, the arrival directions of over 100 million extensive air shower events were analyzed.
- Using theoretical calculations and plasma observations by the Venera-9 and -10 Venus orbiters he and his Russian colleagues were the first to establish that during solar minimum conditions energetic electrons originating from the solar wind are responsible for the maintenance of the nighttime ionosphere of Venus.
- He played a pioneering role in the development of modern cometary plasma physics. He made major contributions to the theoretical description of the cometary ion pick-up process, which essentially controls the cometary plasma environment. Also, he was among the first scientists to explain the acceleration of pick-up ions by self-generated low frequency MHD waves.
- He was a pioneer of modeling the complicated physical processes controlling the interface region between the comet nucleus and the continuously escaping cometary coma. His "friable sponge" model of cometary surface layers and his "icy-glue" model of cometary nuclei were essentially confirmed by spacecraft and remote optical observations. He was a leader in the development of the first detailed numerical model describing the strongly coupled dusty gas flow near cometary nuclei.
- He developed the first time-dependent model of the terrestrial polar wind, which accounted for the dynamics and energetics of the transonic ion outflows from the high-latitude ionosphere. His model calculations were the first to predict the solar cycle dependence of the H^+ outflow, the origin of O^+ in polar wind transients, and the effects of low-altitude frictional heating on the polar wind.
- He derived new transport equations from higher-order velocity moments of the Boltzmann equation using a non-isotropic Gaussian base-function. These equations are stable, hyperbolic, and ensure positivity of the velocity distribution function. These features make the new moment closures both tractable and well-suited for today's sophisticated numerical algorithms.
- Over the last 15 years he has been leading a group of faculty and students pioneering the development of a new generation of high-performance 3D MHD numerical simulation models using solution adaptive grids. This group has also developed the Space Weather

Modeling Framework that couples state-of-the-art models describing the complex Sun-Earth system.

B.6.   Management Experience

Department Chair. From 2003 to 2011 Professor Gombosi was Chair of the Department of Atmospheric, Oceanic and Space Sciences (AOSS), College of Engineering, University of Michigan. Under his leadership AOSS grew significantly, while maintaining a balanced budget. When he took over the department, AOSS had 12 Full Professors and 3 tenured Associate Professors. When he stepped down as Chair of AOSS, the department had 16 Full Professors, 2 Associate Professors and 6 Assistant Professors, a 60% increase in tenure track faculty. He created a world-class climate program, hiring 7 new tenure track faculty in this area. He rejuvenated the space & planetary science side of the department by hiring 4 tenure track faculty in this field. In addition, the research faculty grew from 25 to 35. At the end of Professor Gombosi's chairmanship there were 45 undergraduates (a 250% increase), 60 Ph.D. students (a 20% increase), 50 professional Masters students (a 300% increase) enrolled and 12 postdoctoral researchers (100% increase) trained in AOSS. At the same time departmental administration remained nearly constant (at 25 full time equivalent positions) and professional engineering support staff slightly increased (to 25). Today, AOSS is one of the top departments in the world in space and planetary science, and is among the best in climate science.

Center Director. In 2002 Professor Gombosi founded the Center for Space Environment Modeling (CSEM) in cooperation with Professors Kenneth Powell (Aerospace Engineering) and Quentin Stout (Computer Science). This multidisciplinary center integrates the activities of space and planetary scientists, applied mathematicians and computer scientists. The collaboration resulted in the development and application of modern numerical algorithms and software practices to challenging space science problems. Under Professor Gombosi's leadership CSEM became the leading center of first-principles-based space weather modeling. Presently, CSEM includes about ten tenure track and an equal number of research faculty, several postdocs and approximately fifteen Ph.D. students.

Project Scientist. During the first part of the 1980s Professor Gombosi was Project Scientist for Hungary in the international VEGA (Venus-Halley) mission lead by the Soviet Union. In this capacity he played a critical role in establishing East-West collaborations. In effect, he was the mission's "ambassador" to ESA and NASA and provided behind-the-scenes communication channels between the Soviet space program and NASA and ESA during the height of the Cold War (these were the "Evil Empire" years). At the same time he played a critical role in instrument and mission design of theVEGA mission. He worked on optical tracking strategies, nucleus and coma models, and was a leader of the plasma and energetic particle instruments.

B.7.   Books, Publications & Presentations

Gaskinetic Theory. Professor Gombosi's first graduate level textbook was published by Cambridge University Press in 1994. *Gaskinetic Theory* was written based on the course he taught at the University of Michigan to aerospace engineers and space scientists. It is an introductory text on the molecular theory of gases and on modern transport theory suitable for upper division undergraduates in physics and first year graduate students in aerospace engineering, upper atmospheric science and space research. The first part introduces basic concepts, including the distribution function, classical theory of specific heats, binary collisions, mean free path, and reaction rates. Transport theory is used to express coefficients such as viscosity and heat conductivity in terms of molecular properties. The second part of the book covers advanced transport theory. Generalized transport equations are derived from the Boltzmann equation. The Chapman-Enskog and the Grad methods are discussed to obtain higher order transport equations for low density gases. The aerodynamics of solid bodies is explored and the book concludes with the kinetic description of shock waves. The book is widely used by aerospace departments around the world.

Physics of the Space Environment. Professor Gombosi's second graduate level textbook was published in 1998 by Cambridge University Press. *Physics of the Space Environment* provides a comprehensive introduction to the physical phenomena that result from the interaction of the Sun and the planets -often termed space weather. It explores the basic processes in the Sun, in the interplanetary medium, in the near-Earth space, and down into the atmosphere. The first part of the book summarizes fundamental elements of transport theory relevant for the atmosphere, ionosphere and the magnetosphere. This theory is then applied to physical phenomena in the space environment. The fundamental physical processes are emphasized throughout, and basic concepts and methods are derived from first principles. This book is unique in its balanced treatment of space plasma and aeronomical phenomena. It is used by several universities with graduate programs in space science.

Publications. At this time Professor Gombosi has written two textbooks, edited four scientific monographs and authored or co-authored over 300 peer reviewed publications. Of these, 8 were published in *Science* and 5 in *Nature*, the most prestigious periodicals in planetary and space science. Most of the other papers were published in the *Journal of Geophysical Research*, the *Astrophysical Journal*, *Icarus* or *Geophysical Research Letters*. Professor Gombosi's work has been cited more than 6800 times and his h-index is 43.

Presentations. Professor Gombosi gave or significantly contributed to more than 150 invited and 550 contributed presentations at major national and international conferences. The majority of these more than 700 presentations were given at meetings of the American Geophysical Union (AGU), Committee of Space Resaerch (COSPAR), International Association of Geomagnetism and Aeronomy, part of the International Union of Geodesy and Geophysics (IAGA/IUGG), the European Geophysical Union (EGU) and the Division of Planetary Sciences of the American Astronomical Society (DPS/AAS). In addition, he gave over a hundred colloquia at major universities and research centers around the world. Professor Gombosi also gave a number of public lectures about space exploration at all levels, from elementary schools to high schools, to large national public events.

B.8. Professional Activities

Space Missions.

- Worked on the interpretation of particles and fields data obtained by the first Venus orbiters, Venera–9 and –10.
- Participated in the scientific analysis of particles and fields data returned by NASA's Pioneer–Venus Orbiter.
- Played an active role in the VEGA mission to comet Halley, and in international activities related to the 1986 apparition of Halley's comet. In 1982–83 he served as Project Scientist

for Hungary in the International Venus–Halley (VEGA) Mission.
- Interdisciplinary Scientist (Magnetosphere and Plasma) of the Cassini mission to Saturn.
- Co-Investigator, Rosetta Ion-Neutral Analyser (ROSINA) and the Plasma Investigation on the Rosetta comet rendezvous mission.
- Co-Investigator, IMPACT instrument, STEREO mission.
- Co-Investigator, MMS/SMART mission.

Research Funding. Presently he is Principal Investigator (PI) or Co-PI of research grants totalling over $2M per year. His research is, or has been supported by several major awards, including

- Two NASA High Performance Computing and Communications (HPCC) awards to develop modern high performance adaptive MHD codes and the Space Weather Modeling Framework (SWMF).
- A DoD Multidisciplinary University Initiative (MURI) grant to develop a physics-based Sun-to Earth space weather model chain.
- An NSF Knowledge and Distributed Intelligence (KDI) award to develop high performance coupled ionosphere-thermospehere-magnetosphere codes.
- a NSF Information Technology Research (ITR) award supporting further development of the Space Weather Modeling Framework, research in grid computing and data assimilation.
- a NASA-NSF-AFOSR grant to develop a comprehensive model of the heliosphere for the Living with a Star and the National Space Weather Program,
- An NSF Cyber-Enabled Discovery and Innovation (CDI) award to develop new data assimilation and tomographic methods for space weather applications.

Editorial Experience. He was Senior Editor of the *Journal of Geophysical Research – Space Physics* (1992-1997). This journal publishes about 600 papers annually, and is the word's leading publication in the area of aeronomy, magnetospheric physics, and solar system astrophysics. Additional editorial experience includes:

- Member, Publishing Policy Committee, American Institute of Physics (AIP), 1998–2000.
- Editor of four scientific monographs.
- Associate Editor, *Icarus*, 1991–1997.
- Member, Translation Journals Board, American Institute of Physics (AIP), 1993–1997.
- Member, Publications Committee, American Geophysical Union, 1990–1992.
- Associate Editor, *Geophysical Research Letters*, 1986–1988.

B.9.   Ph.D. Thesis Supervision

1. John Haiducek (Atmospheric and Space Science, AOSS, expected to graduate in 2018)
2. Judit Szente (Atmospheric and Space Science, AOSS, expected to graduate in 2018)
3. Doğa Can Sur Özturk (Atmospheric and Space Science, AOSS, expected to graduate in 2018)
4. Dimitriy Borovikov (Atmospheric and Space Science, AOSS, expected to graduate in 2017)
5. Yuxi Chen (Atmospheric and Space Science, AOSS, expected to graduate in 2017)
6. Jonathan Nickerson (Atmospheric and Space Science, AOSS, expected to graduate in 2016)
7. Sidney Ellington (Applied Physics, AOSS, expected to graduate in 2015)

8. Zhenguang Huang (Atmospheric and Space Science, AOSS, expected to graduate in 2014)
9. Meng Jin (Atmospheric and Space Science, AOSS, expected to graduate in 2014)
10. Rona Oran (Atmospheric and Space Science, AOSS, expected to graduate in 2014)
11. Xing Meng (Ph.D. 2013, postdoc at NASA JPL)
12. Fang Fang (Ph.D. 2012, postdoc at NCAR HAO)
13. Alex Glocer (Ph.D. 2008, scientist at NASA GSFC)
14. Daniel Welling (Ph.D. 2008, Assistant Research Scientist in AOSS)
15. Ofer Cohen (Ph.D. 2008, researcher at Harvard-Smithonian)
16. Noé Lugaz (Ph.D. 2006, Research Scientist at University of New Hampshire)
17. Kenneth C. Hansen (Ph.D. 2001, Associate Research Professor in AOSS)
18. Konstantin Kabin (Ph.D. 2000, Professor at Royal Military College, Canada)
19. Timur Linde (Ph.D. 1998, financial analyst on Wall Street)
20. Madai Frey (Ph.D. 1997, spacecraft designer at Northrop-Grumman)
21. Michael Liemohn (Ph.D. 1996, Professor in AOSS)
22. Nathan A. Schwadron (Ph.D. 1996, Professor at the University of New Hampshire)
23. Claudia J. Alexander (Ph.D. 1993, scientist at NASA JPL)
24. Kenneth M. Chick (Ph.D. 1993, scientist at the Carnegie Institution for Science)
25. Steven M. Guiter (Ph.D. 1992, scientist in Canada)
26. Richard W. Cannata (Ph.D. 1990, deceased)
27. Ákos Kőrösmezey (Ph.D. 1984, software engineer at Ericsson, Hungary)
28. Mihály Horányi (Ph.D. 1982, Professor at the University of Colorado)
29. Erzsébet Merényi (Ph.D. 1980, Professor at Rice University)

B.10.   Postdoc Supervision

1. André Bieler, Postdoc in cometary physics, University of Michigan, 2013–present
2. Lars Daldorff, Postdoc in computational space physics, University of Michigan, 2010–present
3. Xienzhe Jia (2009–10), Presently Assistant Research Scientist, AOSS, University of Michigan
4. Martin Rubin (2006–08), Presently Associate Professor of Physics, University of Bern, Switzerland
5. Merav Opher (2001–04), Presently Associate Professor of Astronomy, Boston University
6. Ilia Roussev (2001–02), Presently Program Director, National Science Foundation (NSF)
7. Ward Manchester (2000–01), Presently Associate Research Professor, AOSS, University of Michigan
8. Roman Häberli (1996–97), Presently works in Swiss industry
9. Clinton Groth (1995–96), Presently Professor of Aerospace Engineering, University of Toronto
10. Darren De Zeeuw (1992–93), Presently Associate Research Scientist, AOSS, University of Michigan

B.11. Service

National/International Organizations and Committees. Served on a large number of NASA and NSF selection committees. An incomplete list of other committee service is:

- Chair (2005–2007) and Member (2004–2005, 2012–2013, 2013–2014), NASA Living with a Star Targeted Research and Technology Stearing Committee.
- Member, NRC Decadal Survey of Heliophysics, R2O/O2R Subcommittee, 2010–2011.
- Chair, NSF Advisory Subcommittee for Atmospheric and Geospace Sciences, 2009–2010.
- Member, NSF Advisory Committee for Geosciences, 2008–2010.
- Chair, Committee of Visitors, NSF Upper Atmosphere Section, 2008.
- Co-Chair, NASA Advanced Modeling & Simulation Technology Capability Roadmap team, 2004–2005.
- Member, NSF Petascale Computing for Geosciences Committee, 2004–2005.
- Member, NSF Steering Committee for Cyberinfrastructure Research and Development in the Atmospheric Sciences (CyRDAS), 2003–2004.
- Chair, Committee on Space Research (COSPAR) Commission D (Space Plasmas including Planetary Magnetospheres), 1996–2000.
- Member, Committee on Solar and Space Physics, Space Studies Board, U.S. National Research Council, 1996–1999.
- Member, NASA Planetary Atmospheres Management Operations Group, 1991–93.
- Member, Plasma Science and Halley Environment Working Groups, Inter-Agency Consultative Group (IACG), 1982–86.
- Chair (1987–91) and Co-Chair (1979–87), International Association of Geomagnetism and Aeronomy (IAGA) Division IV (Solar Wind and Interplanetary Magnetic Field).

University of Michigan Committees. An incomplete list of his committee service is:

- Member, Russel Awards Faculty Advisory Committee, 2006–2008.
- Member, AOSS Departmental Review Committee, 1998.
- Chair, SPRL Review Committee, 1998.
- Program Advisor, Interdepartmental Graduate Program in Space and Planetary Physics, 1996–2006.
- Program Advisor, Master of Engineering in Space Systems, 1995–2003.
- Member, Aerospace Engineering Department Chair Search Committee, 1995-1996.
- Chair, Honors and Awards Committee, College of Engineering, 1993–94.
- Co-Chair, Space Physics Research Laboratory (SPRL) Director Search Committee, 1989–90.
- Member, SPRL Review Committee, 1989.

B.12. Memberships in Scientific Societies

- American Association for the Advancement of Science.
- American Geophysical Union.
- American Physical Society.
- Division for Planetary Sciences, American Astronomical Society.
- European Geophysical Union.

B.13.   Theses

1. T. Gombosi, *A napszél szerepe a Vénusz körüli részecskeáramok kialakitásában (The role of solar wind in the formation of particle fluxes in the vicinity of Venus)*, Thesis for the Degree of "Doctor of Physics", Hungarian Academy of Sciences, 1983.

2. T. Gombosi, *Flare részecskék és a bolygóközi tér kölcsönhatása (Interaction of flare particles with the interplanetary medium)*, Thesis for the Degree of "Candidate of Physics", Hungarian Academy of Sciences, 1978.

3. T. Gombosi, *Részecskeeloszlások vizsgálata a sugárzási övek alatt az INTERKOZMOSZ-3 mesterséges hold segitségével (Investigation of particle distributions below the radiation belts with the INTERCOSMOS-3 satellite)*, Ph.D. Thesis, Roland Eötvös University, Budapest, Hungary, 1974.

B.14.   Books and Edited Books

1. T. I. Gombosi, *Physics of the Space Environment*, Cambridge University Press, Cambridge, UK, 1998.

2. T. I. Gombosi, *Gaskinetic Theory*, Cambridge University Press, Cambridge, UK, 1994.

3. T. I. Gombosi (ed.), *Plasma Environments of Non-Magnetic Planets*, Pergamon Press, Oxford, United Kingdom, 1993.

4. T. I. Gombosi, S. K. Atreya, E. Grün and M. S. Hanner (eds.), *Cometary Environments*, Pergamon Press, Oxford, United Kingdom, 1989.

5. T. I. Gombosi (ed.), *Cometary Exploration*, KFKI Press, Budapest, Hungary, 1983.

B.15.   Articles in Peer Reviewed Journals[1]

2013

1. Oran, R., B. van der Holst, E. Landi, M. Jin, I. V. Sokolov, and T. I. Gombosi, A global wave-driven magnetohydrodynamic solar model with a unified treatment of open and closed magnetic field topologies, **Astrophys. J.**, **778**, 176–195, doi:10.1088/0004-637X/778/2/176, 2013. [PDF]

2. Meng, X., G. Toth, A. Glocer, M.-C. Fok, and T. I. Gombosi, Pressure Anisotropy in Global Magnetospheric Simulations: Coupling with Ring Current Models, **J. Geophys. Res.**, **118**, 5639–5658, doi:10.1002/jgra.50539, 2013. [PDF]

3. Jin, M., W.B. Manchester, B. van der Holst, R. Oran, I. Sokolov, G. Toth, Y. Liu, X.D. Sun, and T. I. Gombosi, Numerical simulations of coronal mass ejection on 2011 March 7: One-temperature and two-temperature model comparison, **Astrophys. J.**, **773**, 50, doi:10.1088/0004-637X/773/1/50, 2013. [PDF]

4. Pulkkinen, A., L. Rastätter, M. Kuznetsova, H. Singer, C. Balch, D. Weimer, G. Tóth, A. Ridley, T. Gombosi, M. Wiltberger, J. Raeder and R. Weigel, Community-wide validation of geospace model ground magnetic field perturbation predictions to support model transition to operations, **Space Weather**, **11**, 369–385, doi:10.1002/swe.20056, 2013. [PDF]

5. Sokolov, I.V., B. van der Holst, R. Oran, C. Downs, I.I. Roussev, M. Jin, W.B.

---

[1]Bibliographic citations are in the following format: authors, title, journal, volume, pages, doi (digital object identifier), year of publication.

Manchester, R.M. Evans, and T.I. Gombosi, Magnetohydrodynamic waves and coronal heating: Unifying empirical and MHD turbulence models, **Astrophys. J.**, **764**, 23, doi:10.1088/0004-637X/764/1/23, 2013. [PDF]

2012

6. Vidotto, A.A., R. Fares, M. Jardine, J.-F. Donati, M. Opher, C. Moutou, C. Catala and T.I. Gombosi, The Stellar wind cycles and planetary radio emission of the tau Boo system, **Mon. Not. R. Astron. Soc.**, **423**, 3285–3298, doi:10.1111/J.1365-2966.2012.21122.X, 2012. [PDF]

7. Manchester, W.B., B. van der Holst, G. Tóth, and T.I. Gombosi, The coupled evolution of electrons and ions in coronal mass ejection-driven shocks, **Astrophys. J.**, **756**, 81, doi:10.1088/0004-637X/756/1/81, 2012. [PDF]

8. Meng, X., G. Tóth, M. W. Liemohn, T. I. Gombosi, and A. Runov, Pressure anisotropy in global magnetospheric simulations: A magnetohydrodynamics model, **J. Geophys. Res.**, **117**, A08216, doi:10.1029/2012JA017791, 2012. [PDF]

9. Jia, Y.-D., Y-J. Ma, C.T. Russell, H.R. Lai, G. Tóth, T.I. Gombosi, Perpendicular flow deviation in a magnetized counter-streaming plasma, **Icarus**, **218**, 895–905, doi:10.1016/j.icarus.2012.01.017, 2012. [PDF]

10. Huang, Z., R.A. Frazin, E. Landi, W.B. Manchester, A.M. Vásquez and T.I. Gombosi, Newly Discovered Global Temperature Structures in the Quiet Sun at Solar Minimum, **Astrophys. J.**, **755**, 86–97, doi:10.1088/0004-637X/755/2/86, 2012. [PDF]

11. Combi, M.R., V.M. Tenishev, M. Rubin, N. Fougere, and T.I. Gombosi, Narrow dust jets in a diffuse gas coma: A natural product of small active regions on comets, **Astrophys. J.**, **749**, 29, doi:10.1088/0004-637X/749/1/29, 2012. [PDF]

12. Glocer, A., N. Kitamura, G. Tóth, T. Gombosi, Modeling solar zenith angle effects on the polar wind, **J. Geophys. Res.**, **117**, A04318, doi:10.1029/2011JA017136, 2012. [PDF]

13. Jia, X., K.C. Hansen, T.I. Gombosi, M.G. Kivelson, G. Tóth, D.L. DeZeeuw, A.J. Ridley, Aaron J., Magnetospheric configuration and dynamics of Saturn's magnetosphere: A global MHD simulation, **J. Geophys. Res.**, **117**, A05225, doi:10.1029/2012JA017575, 2012. [PDF]

14. Rubin, M., K. C. Hansen, M. R. Combi, L. K. S. Daldorff, T. I. Gombosi, and V. M. Tenishev, Kelvin-Helmholtz instabilities at the magnetic cavity boundary of comet 67P/Churyumov-Gerasimenko, **J. Geophys. Res.**, **117**, A06227, doi:10.1029/2011JA017300, 2012. [PDF]

15. Jia, X., M. G. Kivelson, and T. I. I. Gombosi, Driving Saturn's magnetospheric periodicities from the upper atmosphere/ionosphere, **J. Geophys. Res.**, **117**, A04215, doi:10.1029/2011JA017367, 2012. [PDF]

16. Evans, R. M., Opher, M., Oran, R., van der Holst, B., Sokolov, I. V., Frazin, R., Gombosi, T. I., Vasquez, A., Coronal heating by surface Alfvén wave damping: Implementation in a global magnetohydrodynamics model of the solar wind, **Astrophys. J.**, **756**, 155, doi:10.1088/0004-637X/756/2/155, 2012. [PDF]

17. Meng, X., G. Tóth, I.V. Sokolov, T.I. Gombosi, Classical and Semirelativistic Magnetohydrodynamics with Anisotropic Ion Pressure, **J. Computational Phys.**,

231, 3610–3622, doi:10.1016/j.jcp.2011.12.042, 2012. [PDF]

18. Tóth, G., B. van der Holst, I. V. Sokolov, D. L. De Zeeuw, T. I. Gombosi, F. Fang, W. B. Manchester, X. Meng, D. Najib, K. G. Powell, Q. F. Stout, A. Glocer, Y.-J. Ma, M. Opher, Adaptive Numerical Algorithms in Space Weather Modeling, **J. Computational Phys.**, **231**, 870–903, doi:10.1016/j.jcp.2011.02.006, 2012. [PDF]

19. Jin, M., W.B. Manchester, B. van der Holst, J.R. Gruesbeck, R.A. Frazin, E. Landi, A.M. Vasquez, P.L. Lamy, A. Llebaria, A. Fedorov, G. Tóth and T.I. Gombosi, A global two-temperature corona and inner heliosphere model: A comprehensive validation study, **Astrophys. J.**, **745**, 6, doi:10.1088/0004-637X/745/1/6, 2012. [PDF]

2011

20. Lugaz, N., Roussev, I.I.; Gombosi, T.I., Determining CME parameters by fitting heliospheric observations: Numerical investigation of the accuracy of the methods, **Adv. Space Res.**, **48**, 292–299, doi:10.1016/J.Asr.2011.03.015, 2011. [PDF]

21. Liu, Y. C., M. Opher, Y. Wang, T. I. Gombosi, Downstream structure and evolution of a simulated CME-driven sheath in the solar corona, **Astronomy and Astrophysics**, **527**, A46, doi:10.1051/0004-6361/201014384, 2011. [PDF]

22. Das, I., M. Opher, R. Evans, C. Loesch, T.I. Gombosi, Evolution of piled up compressions in modeled CME sheaths and the resulting sheath structures, **Astrophys. J.**, **729**, 112, doi:10.1088/0004-637X/729/2/112, 2011. [PDF]

23. Evans, R. M., M. Opher and T. I. Gombosi Learning from the outer heliosphere: Interplanetary coronal mass ejection sheath flows and the ejecta orientation in the lower corona **Astrophys. J.**, **728**, 41, doi:10.1088/0004-637X/728/1/41, 2011. [PDF]

24. Sterenborg, M.G., O. Cohen, J.J. Drake, T.I. Gombosi, Modeling the young sun's solar wind and its interaction with earth's paleomagnetosphere, **J. Geophys. Res.**, **116**, A01217, doi:10.1029/2010JA016036, 2011. [PDF]

25. Rubin, M., V.M. Tenishev, M.R. Combi, K.C. Hansen, T.I. Gombosi, K. Altwegg, H. Balsiger, Monte Carlo modeling of neutral gas and dust in the coma of Comet 1P/Halley, **Icarus**, **213**, 655–677, doi:10.1016/J.Icarus.2011.04.006, 2011. [PDF]

26. Lugaz, N., C. Downs, K. Shibata, I. I. Roussev, A. Asai, T. I. Gombosi, Numerical investigation of a coronal mass ejection from an anemone active region: Reconnection and deflection of the 2005 August 22 eruption, **Astrophys. J.**, **738**, 127, doi:10.1088/0004-637X/738/2/127, 2011. [PDF]

27. Vidotto, A.A., M. Jardine, M. Opher, J.F. Donati, and T.I. Gombosi, Powerful winds from low-mass stars: V374 Peg, **Mon. Not. R. Astron. Soc.**, **412**, 351–362, doi:10.1111/j.1365-2966.2010.17908.x, 2011. [PDF]

28. Drake, R.P. F.W. Doss, R.G. McClarren, M.L. Adams, N. Amato, D. Bingham, C.C. Chou, C. DiStefano, K. Fidkowski, B. Fryxell, T.I. Gombosi, M.J. Grosskopf, J.P. Holloway, B. van der Holst, C.M. Huntington, S. Karni, C.M. Krauland, C.C. Kuranz, E. Larsen, B. van Leer, B. Mallick, D. Marion, W. Martin, J.E. Morel, E.S. Myra, V. Nair, K.G. Powell, L. Rauchwerger, P. Roe, E. Rutter, I.V. Sokolov, Q. Stout, B.R. Torralva, G. Toth, K. Thornton, A.J. Visco, Radiative effects in radiative shocks in

shock tubes **High Energy Density Physics**, **7**, 130–140, doi:10.1016/J.Hedp.2011.03.005, 2011. [PDF]

29. Tóth, G., X. Meng, T. I. Gombosi, A. J. Ridley, Reducing numerical diffusion in magnetospheric simulations, **J. Geophys. Res.**, **116**, A07211, doi:10.1029/2010JA016370, 2011. [PDF]

30. Downs, C., I.I. Roussev, B. van der Holst, N. Lugaz, I.V. Sokolov, T.I. Gombosi, Studying extreme ultraviolet wave transients with a digital laboratory: Direct comparison of extreme ultraviolet wave observations to global magnetohydrodynamic simulations, **Astrophys. J.**, **728,**, 2, doi:10.1088/0004-637X/728/1/2, 2011. [PDF]

31. Cohen, O., V. L. Kashyap, J. J. Drake, I. V. Sokolov and T. I. Gombosi, The dynamics of stellar coronae harboring hot Jupiters. II. A space weather event on a hot Jupiter, **Astrophys. J.**, **738**, 166, doi:10.1088/0004-637X/738/2/166, 2011. [PDF]

32. Cohen, O., V. L. Kashyap, J. J. Drake, I. V. Sokolov, C. Garraffo and T. I. Gombosi, The dynamics of stellar coronae harboring hot Jupiters. I. A time-dependent magnetohydrodynamic simulation of the interplanetary environment in the HD 189733 planetary system, **Astrophys. J.**, **733**, 67, doi:10.1088/0004-637X/733/1/67, 2011. [PDF]

2010

33. Cohen, O., J.J. Drake, V.L. Kashyap, H. Korhonen,D. Elstner, T.I. Gombosi, Magnetic structure of rapidly rotating FK comae-type coronae, **Astrophys. J.**, **719**, 299, doi:10.1088/0004-637X/719/1/299, 2010. [PDF]

34. Jia, Y.-D., C. T. Russell, K. K. Khurana, Y. J. Ma, W. Kurth, and T. I. Gombosi, Interaction of Saturn's magnetosphere and its moons: 3. Time variation of the Enceladus plume, **J. Geophys. Res.**, **115**, A12243, doi:10.1029/2010JA015534, 2010. [PDF]

35. van der Holst, B., W.B. Manchester, R.A. Frazin, A.M. Vasquez, G. Tóth, T.I. Gombosi, A data-driven, two-temperature solar wind model with Alvén waves, **Astrophys. J.**, **725**, 1373–1383, doi:10.1088/0004-637X/725/1/1373, 2010. [PDF]

36. Cohen, O., J. J. Drake, V. L. Kashyap, I. V. Sokolov, and T. I. Gombosi, The impact of hot Jupiters on the spin-down of their host stars, **Astrophys. J. Lett.**, **723**, L64–L67, doi:10.1088/2041-8205/723/1/L64, 2010. [PDF]

37. Ridley, A. J., T. I. Gombosi, I. V. Sokolov, G. Tóth, and D. T. Welling, Numerical considerations in simulating the global magnetosphere, **Ann. Geophys.**, **28**, 1589–1614, doi:10.5194/angeo-28-1589-2010, 2010. [PDF]

38. Rae, I. J., K. Kabin, J.Y. Lu, R. Rankin, S. E. Milan, F. R. Fenrich, C. E. J. Watt, J. C. Zhang, A. J. Ridley, T. I. Gombosi, C. R. Clauer, G. Tóth, and D.L. DeZeeuw, Comparison of the open-closed separatrix in a global magnetospheric simulation with observations: The role of the ring current., **J. Geophys. Res.**, **115**, A08216, doi:10.1029/2009JA015068, 2010. [PDF]

39. Vidotto, A.A., M. Opher, V. Jatenco-Pereira, and T. I. Gombosi, Simulations of Winds of Weak-lined T Tauri Stars. II. The effects of a tilted magnetosphere and planetary interactions, **Astrophys. J.**, **720**, 1262–128, doi:10.1088/0004-637X/720/2/1262, 2010. [PDF]

40. Jia, Y.-D., C. T. Russell, K. K. Khurana, Y. J. Ma, D. Najib, and T. I. Gombosi, Interaction of Saturn's magnetosphere and its moons: 2. Shape of the Enceladus plume, **J. Geophys. Res.**, **115**, A04215, doi:10.1029/2009JA014873, 2010. [PDF]

41. Jia, Y.-D., C. T. Russell, K. K. Khurana, G. Tóth, J. S. Leisner, and T. I. Gombosi, Interaction of Saturn's magnetosphere and its moons: 1. Interaction between corotating plasma and standard obstacles, **J. Geophys. Res.**, **115**, A04214, doi:10.1029/2009JA014630, 2010. [PDF]

42. Watanabe, M., K. Kabin, G. J. Sofko, R. Rankin, T. I. Gombosi, and A. J. Ridley, Dipole tilt effects on the magnetosphere-ionosphere convection system during IMF B_y-dominated periods: MHD modeling, **J. Geophys. Res.**, **115**, A07218, doi:10.1029/2009JA014910, 2010. [PDF]

43. Cohen, O., Attrill, G.D.R., Schwadron, N.A., Crooker, N.U., Owens, M.J., Downs, C., Gombosi, T.I., Numerical simulation of the 12 May 1997 CME Event: The role of magnetic reconnection, **J. Geophys. Res.**, **115**, A10104, doi:10.1029/2010Ja015464, 2010. [PDF]

44. Zieger, B., K.C. Hansen, T.I. Gombosi and D.L. De Zeeuw, Periodic plasma escape from the mass-loaded Kronian magnetosphere, **J. Geophys. Res.**, **115**, A08208, doi:10.1029/2009JA014951, 2010. [PDF]

45. Cohen, O., J.J. Drake, V.L. Kashyap, G.A.J. Hussain, and T.I. Gombosi, The Coronal Structure of AB Doradus, **Astrophys. J.**, **721**, 80–89, doi:10.1088/0004-637X/721/1/80, 2010. [PDF]

46. Downs, C., I.I. Roussev, B. van der Holst, N. Lugaz, I.V. Sokolov and T.I. Gombosi, Toward a realistic thermodynamic model of the global solar corona, **Astrophys. J.**, **712**, 1219–1231, doi:10.1088/0004-637X/712/2/1219, 2010. [PDF]

47. Gombosi, T.I. and A.P. Ingersoll, Saturn: Atmosphere, ionosphere, and magnetosphere, **Science**, **327**, 1476–1479, doi:10.1126/science.1179119, 2010. [PDF]

2009

48. Glocer, A., G. Tóth, Y. Ma, T.I. Gombosi, J.-C. Zhang, and L.M. Kistler, Multifluid Block-Adaptive-Tree Solar wind Roe-type Upwind Schememe: Magnetospheric composition and dynamics during geomagnetic storms – Initial results, **J. Geophys. Res.**, **114**, A12203, doi:10.1029/2009JA014418, 2009. [PDF]

49. Opher, M., F. Alouani Bibi, G. Tóth, J.D. Richardson, V.V. Izmodenov, and T.I. Gombosi, A strong, highly-tilted interstellar magnetic field near the Solar System, **Nature**, **462**, 1036–1038, doi:10.1038/nature08567, 2009. [PDF]

50. Cohen, O., J.J. Drake, V.L. Kashyap, S.H. Saar, I.V. Sokolov, W.B. Manchester, K.C. Hansen, and T.I. Gombosi, Interactions of the magnetospheres of stars and close-in giant planets, **Astrophys. J. Lett.**, **704**, L85–L88, doi:10.1088/0004-637X/704/2/L85 , 2009. [PDF]

51. Vidotto, A.A., M. Opher, V. Jatenco-Pereira, and T.I. Gombosi, Simulations of winds of weak-lined T Tauri stars: The magnetic field geometry and the influence of the wind on giant planet migration, **Astrophys. J.**, **703**, 1734–1742, doi:10.1088/0004-637X/703/2/1734, 2009. [PDF]

52. Glocer, A., G. Toth, M. Fok, T. Gombosi, M. Liemohn, Integration of the radiation

belt environment model into the space weather modeling framework, **J. Atmospheric and Solar-Terrestrial Physics**, **71**, doi:10.1016/j.jastp.2009.01.003, 2009. [PDF]

53. Evans, R.M., M. Opher, V. Jatenco-Pereira, and T.I. Gombosi, Surface Alfvén wave damping in a three-dimensional simulation of the solar wind, **Astrophys. J.**, **703**, 179–186, doi:10.1088/0004-637X/703/1/179, 2009. [PDF]

54. Cohen, O., J.J. Drake, V.L. Kashyap, and T.I. Gombosi, The effect of magnetic spots on stellar winds and angular momentum loss, **Astrophys. J.**, **699**, 1501–1510, doi:10.1088/0004-637X/699/2/1501, 2009. [PDF]

55. Vidotto, A.A., M. Opher, V. Jatenco-Pereira, and T.I. Gombosi, Three-dimensional numerical simulations of magnetized winds of solar-like stars, **Astrophys. J.**, **699**, 441–452, doi:10.1088/0004-637X/699/1/441, 2009. [PDF]

56. Gombosi, T.I., T.P. Armstrong, C.S. Arridge, K.K. Khurana, S.M. Krimigis, N. Krupp, A.M. Persoon and M.F. Thomsen, Saturn's magnetospheric configuration, in *Saturn from Cassini-Huygens*, edited by M. Dougherty, L. Esposito, and T. Krimigis, Springer, pp. 203–256, doi:10.1007/978-1-4020-9217-6_9, 2009. [PDF]

57. Opher, M., J.C. Richardson, G. Tóth, T. I. Gombosi, Confronting observations and modeling: The role of the interstellar magnetic field in Voyager 1 and 2 asymmetries, **Space Science Reviews**, **143**, 43–55, doi:10.1007/s11214-008-9453-x, 2009. [PDF]

58. Jia, Y.-D., Russell, C.T., Jian, L.K., Manchester, W.B., Cohen, O., Vourlidas, A., Hansen, K.C., Combi, M., R., Gombosi, T.I., Study of the 2007 April 20 CME-comet interaction event with an MHD model, **Astrophys. J. Lett.**, **696**, L56–L60, doi:10.1088/0004-637X/696/1/L56, 2009. [PDF]

59. Zieger, B., K.C. Hansen, O. Cohen, T.I. Gombosi, T.H. Zurbuchen, B.J. Anderson and H. Korth, Upstream conditions at Mercury during the first MESSENGER flyby: Results from two independent solar wind models, **Geophys. Res. Lett.**, **36**, L10108, doi:10.1029/2009GL038346, 2009. [PDF]

60. Glocer, A., G. Tóth, T. Gombosi, and D. Welling, Modeling Ionospheric Outflows and Their Impact on the Magnetosphere: Initial Results, **J. Geophys. Res.**, **114**, A05216, doi:10.1029/2009JA014053, 2009. [PDF]

61. van der Holst, B., W.B. Manchester, I.V. Sokolov, G. Tóth, T.I. Gombosi, D.L. DeZeeuw, O. Cohen, Breakout coronal mass ejection or streamer blowout: The bugle effect, **Astrophys. J.**, **693**, 1178–1187, doi:10.1088/0004-637X/693/2/1178, 2009. [PDF]

62. Sokolov, I.V., I.I. Roussev, M. Skender, T.I. Gombosi, and A.V. Usmanov, Transport equation for MHD turbulence: Application to particle acceleration at interplanetary shocks, **Astrophys. J.**, **696**, 261–267, doi:10.1088/0004-637X/696/1/261 , 2009. [PDF]

63. Rubin M, K.C. Hansen, T.I. Gombosi, M.R. Combi, K. Altwegg, H. Balsiger, Ion composition and chemistry in the coma of Comet 1P/Halley – A comparison between Giotto's Ion Mass Spectrometer and our ion-chemical network, **Icarus**, **199**, 505–519, doi:10.1016/j.icarus.2008.10.009, 2009. [PDF]

2008

64. Liu, Y.C.-M., M. Opher, O. Cohen, P.C. Liewer, and T.I. Gombosi, A simulation of a coronal mass ejection propagation and shock evolution in the lower solar corona, **Astrophys. J.**, **680**, 757–763, doi:10.1086/587867, 2008. [PDF]

65. Tóth, G., Y. Ma, T.I. Gombosi, Hall magnetohydrodynamics on block-adaptive grids, **J. Comp. Phys.**, **227**, 6967-6984, doi:10.1016/j.jcp.2008.04.010, 2008. [PDF]

66. André, N., M. Blanc, S. Maurice, P. Schippers, E. Pallier, T. I. Gombosi, K. C. Hansen, D. T. Young, F. J. Crary, S. Bolton, E. C. Sittler, H. T. Smith, R.E. Johnson, R. A. Baragiola, A. J. Coates, A.M. Rymer, M. K. Dougherty, N. Achilleos, C. S. Arridge, S. M. Krimigis, D. G. Mitchell, N. Krupp, D. C. Hamilton, I. Dandouras, D.A. Gurnett, W. S. Kurth, P. Louarn, R. Srama, S. Kempf, H. J. Waite, L. W. Esposito, and J. T. Clarke, Identification of Saturn's magnetospheric regions and associated plasma processes: Synopsis of Cassini observations during orbit insertion, **Rev. Geophys.**, **46**, RG4008, doi:10.1029/2007RG000238, 2008. [PDF]

67. Evans, R.M., M. Opher, W.B. Manchester, T.I. Gombosi, Alfvén profile in the lower corona: Implications for shock formation, **Astrophys. J.**, **687**, 1355–1362, doi:10.1086/592016, 2008. [PDF]

68. Kabin, K., M.H. Heimpel, R. Rankin, J.M. Aurnou, N. Gomez-Perez, J. Paral, T.I. Gombosi, T.H. Zurbuchen, P.L. Koehn, D.L. DeZeeuw, Global MHD modeling of Mercury's magnetosphere with applications to the MESSENGER mission and dynamo theory, **Icarus**, **195**, 1–15 doi:10.1016/j.icarus.2007.11.028, 2008. [PDF]

69. Lugaz, N., W.B. Manchester, I.I. Roussev, T.I. Gombosi, Observational evidence of CMEs interacting in the inner heliosphere as inferred from MHD simulations, **J. Atmospheric and Solar-Terrestrial Physics**, **70**, 598–604, doi:10.1016/j.jastp.2007.08.033, 2008. [PDF]

70. Taktakishvili, A., Kuznetsova, M.M., Hesse, M., Fok, M.-C., Rastätter, L., Maddox, M., Chulaki, A., Tót, G., Gombosi, T. I., De Zeeuw, D. L., Role of periodic loading-unloading in the magnetotail versus interplanetary magnetic field Bz flipping in the ring current buildup **J. Geophys. Res.**, **113**, A03206, doi:10.1029/2007JA012845, 2008. [PDF]

71. Manchester W.B., A. Vourlidas, G. Tót, N. Lugaz, I. I. Roussev, I. V. Sokolov, T. I. Gombosi, D. L. De Zeeuw, and M. Opher, Three-dimensional MHD simulations of the 2003 October 28 coronal mass ejection: comparison with LASCO coronagraph observations, **Astrophys. J.**, **684**, 1448-1460, doi:10.1086/590231 , 2008. [PDF]

72. Cohen, O., I. V. Sokolov, I. I. Roussev, and T. I. Gombosi, Validation of a synoptic solar wind model, **J. Geophys. Res.**, **113**, A03104, doi:10.1029/2007JA012797, 2008. [PDF]

73. Cohen, O., I.V. Sokolov, I.I. Roussev, N. Lugaz, W.B. Manchester, T.I. Gombosi, C.N. Arge, Validation of a global 3D heliospheric model with observations for the May 12, 1997 CME event, **J. Atmospheric and Solar-Terrestrial Physics**, **70**, 583–592, doi:10.1016/j.jastp.2007.08.065, 2008. [PDF]

74. Aschwanden, M.J., L.F. Burlaga, M.L. Kaiser, C.K. Ng, D.V. Reames, M.J. Reiner, T.I. Gombosi, N. Lugaz, W. Manchester, I.I. Roussev, T.H. Zurbuchen, C.J. Farrugia, A.B. Galvin, M.A. Lee, J.A. Linker, Z. Mikic, P. Riley, D. Alexander, A.W. Sandman, J.W. Cook, R.A. Howard, D. Odstrcil, V.J. Pizzo, J. Kota, P.C. Liewer, J.G. Luhmann, B. Inhester, R.W. Schwenn, S.K. Solanki, V.M. Vasyliunas, T. Wiegelmann, L. Blush,

P. Bochsler, I.H. Cairns, P.A. Robinson, V. Bothmer, K. Kecskemety, A. Llebaria, M. Maksimovic, M. Scholer and R.F. Wimmer-Schweingruber, Theoretical modeling for the STEREO mission, **Space Sci. Rev.**, **136** 565–604, doi:10.1007/s11214-006-9027-8, 2008. [PDF]

2007

75. Ma, Y.-J., A. F. Nagy, G. Tóth, T. E. Cravens, C. T. Russell, T. I. Gombosi, J.-E. Wahlund, F. J. Crary, A. J. Coates, C. L. Bertucci, and F. M. Neubauer, 3D global multi-species Hall-MHD simulation of the Cassini T9 flyby, **Geophys. Res. lett.**, **34**, L24S10, doi:10.1029/2007GL031627, 2007. [PDF]

76. Kuznetsova, M.M., M. Hesse, L. Rastätter, A. Taktakishvili, G. Tóth, D.L. De Zeeuw, A.J. Ridley, T.I. Gombosi, Multiscale modeling of magnetospheric reconnection, **J. Geophys. Res.**, **112**, A10210, doi:10.1029/2007JA012316, 2007. [PDF]

77. Watanabe, M., G.J. Sofko, K. Kabin, R. Rankin, A.J. Ridley, C.R. Clauer, and T.I. Gombosi, The origin of the interhemispheric potential mismatch of merging cells for IMF-By dominated periods, **J. Geophys. Res.**, **112**, A10205, doi:10.1029/2006JA012179, 2007. [PDF]

78. Taktakishvili, A., M.M. Kuznetsova, M. Hesse, M.-C. Fok, L. Rastätter, M. Maddox, A. Chulaki, T.I. Gombosi, and D.L. De Zeeuw, Buildup of the ring current during periodic loading-unloading cycles in the magnetotail driven by steady southward interplanetary magnetic field, **J. Geophys. Res.**, **112**, A09203, doi:10.1029/2007JA012317, 2007. [PDF]

79. Fairfield, D.H., M.M. Kuznetsova, T. Mukai, T. Nagai, T.I. Gombosi, and A.J. Ridley, Waves on the dusk flank boundary layer during very northward interplanetary magnetic field conditions: Observations and simulation, **J. Geophys. Res.**, **112**, A08206, doi:10.1029/2006JA012052, 2007. [PDF]

80. Tóth, G., D.L. De Zeeuw, T.I. Gombosi, W.B. Manchester, A.J. Ridley, I.V. Sokolov, and I.I. Roussev, Sun-to-thermosphere simulation of the 28-30 October 2003 storm with the Space Weather Modeling Framework, **Space Weather**, **5**, S06003, doi:10.1029/2006SW000272, 2007. [PDF]

81. Opher, M., E.C. Stone, and T.I. Gombosi, The Orientation of the Local Interstellar Magnetic Field, **Science**, **316**, 875–878, doi:10.1126/Science.1139480, 2007. [PDF]

82. Lugaz, N., W.B. Manchester, I.I. Roussev, G. Tóth, and T.I. Gombosi, Numerical Investigation of the Homologous CME Events from Active Region 9236, **Astrophys. J.**, **659**, 788–800, doi:10.1086/512005, 2007. [PDF]

83. Zhang, J., M.W. Liemohn, D.L. De Zeeuw, J.E. Borovsky, A.J. Ridley, G. Tóth, S. Sazykin, M.F. Thomsen, J.U. Kozyra, T.I. Gombosi, and R.A. Wolf, Understanding storm-time ring current development through data-model comparisons of a moderate storm, **J. Geophys. Res.**, **112**, A04208, doi:10.1029/2006JA011846, 2007. [PDF]

84. Cohen, O., I.V. Sokolov, I.I. Roussev, C.N. Arge, W.B. Manchester, T.I. Gombosi, R.A. Frazin, H. Park, M.D. Butala, F. Kamalabadi, and M. Velli, A Semiempirical Magnetohydrodynamical Model of the Solar Wind, **Astrophys. J. Lett.**, **654**, L163–L166, doi:10.1086/511154, 2007. [PDF]

85. A. Glocer, T. I. Gombosi, G. Tóth, K. C. Hansen, A. J. Ridley, and A. Nagy, The Polar

Wind Outflow Model: Saturn Results, **J. Geophys. Res.**, **112**, A01304, doi:10.1029/2006JA011755, 2007. [PDF]

86. H. Balsiger, K. Altwegg, P. Bochsler, P. Eberhardt, J. Fischer, S. Graf, A. Jäckel, E. Kopp, U. Langer, M. Mildner, J. Müller, T. Riesen, M. Rubin, S. Scherer, P. Wurz, S. Wüthrich, E. Arjis, S. Delanoye, J. de Keyser, E. Neffs, D. Nevejans, H. Réme, C. Aostin, C. Mazelle, J.-L. Médale, J.A. Sauvaud, J.-J. Berthelier, J.-L. Bertaux, L. Duvet, J.-M. Illiano, S.A. Fuselier, A.G. Ghielmetti, T. Magnocelli, E.G. Shelley, A. Korth, K. Heerlein, H. Lauche, S. Livi, A. Loose, U. Mall, B. Wilken, F. Gliem, B. Fiethe, T.I. Gombosi, B. Block, G.R. Carignan, L.A. Fisk, J.H. Waite, D.T. Young and H. Wollnik, ROSINA - Rosetta orbiter spectrometer for ion and neutral analysis, **Space Sci. Rev.**, **128**, 745-801, doi:10.1007/S11214-006-8335-3, 2007. [PDF]

87. K. C. Hansen, T. Bagdonat, U. Motschmann, C. Alexander, M. R. Combi, T. E. Cravens, T. I. Gombosi, Y.-D. Jia and I. P. Robertson, The Plasma Environment of Comet 67P/Churyumov-Gerasimenko Throughout the Rosetta Main Mission, **Space Sci. Rev.**, **128**, 133-166, doi:10.1007/S11214-006-9142-6, 2007. [PDF]

88. Y.-D. Jia, M. R. Combi, K. C. Hansen, and T. I. Gombosi, A global model of cometary tail disconnection events triggered by solar wind magnetic variations, **J. Geophys. Res.**, **112**, A05223, doi:10.1029/2006JA012175, 2007. [PDF]

2006

89. I. V. Sokolov, K. G. Powell, T. I. Gombosi, aand I. I. Roussev, A TVD Principle and Conservative TVD Schemes for Adaptive Cartesian Grids, **J. Comp. Phys.**, **220**, 1-5, doi:10.1016/J.Jcp.2006.07.021, 2006. [PDF]

90. O. Cohen, L. A. Fisk, I. I. Roussev, G. Tóth, and T. I. Gombosi, Enhancement of Photospheric Meridional Flow by Reconnection Processes, **Astrophys. J.**, **645**, 1537-1542, doi:10.1086/504402, 2006. [PDF]

91. W. B. Manchester, A. J. Ridley, T. I. Gombosi, and D. L. De Zeeuw, Modeling the Sun-to-Earth propagation of a very fast CME, **Advances in Space Research**, **38**, 253-262, doi:10.1016/J.Asr.2005.09.044, 2006. [PDF]

92. G. Tóth, D. L. De Zeeuw, T. I. Gombosi, and K. G. Powell, A parallel explicit/implicit time stepping scheme on block-adaptive grids, **J. Comput. Phys.**, **217**, 722-758, doi:10.1016/J.Jcp.2006.01.029, 2006. [PDF]

93. I. V.Sokolov, I. I.Roussev, L. A.Fisk, M.A.Lee, T. I.Gombosi and J. I.Sakai, Diffusive Shock Acceleration Theory Revisited, **Astrophys. J.**, **642**, L81-L84, doi:10.1086/504406, 2006. [PDF]

2005

94. G. Tóth, I. V. Sokolov, T. I. Gombosi, D. R. Chesney, C. R. Clauer, D. L. De Zeeuw, K. C. Hansen, K. J. Kane, W. B. Manchester, R. C. Oehmke, K. G. Powell, A. J. Ridley, I. I. Roussev, Q. F. Stout, O. Volberg, R. A. Wolf, S. Sazykin, A. Chan, and B. Yu, Space Weather Modeling Framework: A new tool for the space science community,**J. Geophys. Res.**, **110**, A12226, doi:10.1029/2005JA011126, 2005. [PDF]

95. R.A. Wolf, S. Sazykin, X. Xing, R.W. Spiro, F.R. Toffoletto, D. L. De Zeeuw, T.I. Gombos, and J. Goldstein, Direct effects of the IMF on the inner magnetosphere, in

Global Physics of the Coupled Inner Magnetosphere, **Inner Magnetosphere Interactions**, **AGU Monograph**, **159**, 127–139, doi:10.1029/159Gm09, 2005. [PDF]

96. I.V. Sokolov, T.I. Gombosi, and A.J. Ridley, Non-potential electric field model of ionosphere-magnetosphere coupling, in **Global Physics of the Coupled Inner Magnetosphere**, **Inner Magnetosphere Interactions**, **AGU Monograph**, **159**, 141–152, doi:10.1029/159Gm10, 2005. [PDF]

97. N. Lugaz, W. B. Manchester, and T. I. Gombosi, Numerical simulation of the interaction of two coronal mass ejections from sun to earth, **Astrophys. J.**, **634**, 651-662, doi:10.1086/491782, 2005. [PDF]

98. K. C. Hansen, A. J. Ridley, G. B. Hospodarsky, N. Achilleos, M. K. Dougherty, T. I. Gombosi and G. Tóth, Global MHD simulations of Saturn's magnetosphere at the time of Cassini approach, **Geophys. Res. Lett.**, **32**, L20S06, doi:10.1029/2005GL022835, 2005. [PDF]

99. J.G. Luhmann, D.W. Curtis, R.P. Lin, D. Larson, P. Schroeder, A. Cummings, R.A. Mewaldt, E.C. Stone, A. Davis, T. von Rosenvinge, M.H. Acuna, D. Reames, C. Ng, K. Ogilvie, R. Mueller-Mellin, H. Kunow, G.M. Mason, M. Wiedenbeck, A. Sauvaud, C. Aoustin, P. Louarn, J. Dandouras, A. Korth, V. Bothmer, V. Vasyliunas, T. Sanderson, R.G. Marsden, C.T. Russell, J.T. Gosling, J.L. Bougerel, D.J. McComas, J.A. Linker, P. Riley, D. Odstrcil, V.J. Pizzo, T. Gombosi, D. De Zeeuw and K. Kecskemety, IMPACT: Science goals and firsts with STEREO, **Adv. Space Res.**, **36**(8), 1534-1543, doi:10.1016/J.Asr.2005.03.033, 2005. [PDF]

100. K. A. Keller, M.-C. Fok, A. Narock, M. Hesse, L. Rastätter, M. M. Kuznetsova, T. I. Gombosi and D. L. DeZeeuw, Effect of multiple substorms on the buildup of the ring current, **J. Geophys. Res.**,**110**, A08202, doi:10.1029/2004JA010747, 2005. [PDF]

101. L. Rastätter, M. Hesse, M. Kuznetsova, J. B. Sigwarth, J. Raeder, and T. I. Gombosi, Polar cap size during 14-16 July 2000 (Bastille Day) solar coronal mass ejection event: MHD modeling and satellite imager observations, **J. Geophys. Res.**, **110**, A07212, doi:10.1029/2004JA010672, 2005. [PDF]

102. M. Watanabe, K. Kabin, G. J. Sofko, R. Rankin, T. I. Gombosi, A. J. Ridley, and C. R. Clauer, Internal reconnection for northward interplanetary magnetic field, **J. Geophys. Res.**, **110**, A06210, doi:10.1029/2004JA010832, 2005. [PDF]

103. N. Lugaz, W. B. Manchester, and T. I. Gombosi, The Evolution of CME Density Structures, **Astrophys. J.**, **627**, 10191030, doi:10.1086/430465, 2005. [PDF]

104. W. B. Manchester, T. I. Gombosi, D. L. De Zeeuw, I. V. Sokolov, I. I. Roussev, K. G. Powell, J. Kóta, G. Tóth, and T. H. Zurbuchen, Coronal Mass Ejection Shock and Sheath Structures relevant to particle acceleration, **Astrophys. J.**, **622**, 1225-1239, doi:10.1086/427768, 2005. [PDF]

105. T. I. Gombosi and K. C. Hansen, Saturn's variable magnetosphere, **Science**, **307**, 1224–1226, doi:10.1126/Science.1108226, 2005. [PDF]

2004

106. K. Kabin, R. Rankin, G. Rostoker, R. Marchand, I.J. Rae, A.J. Ridley, T.I. Gombosi, C.R. Clauer, D.L. De Zeeuw, Open-closed field line boundary position: A parametric study using an MHD model, **J. Geophys. Res.**, **109**, A05222,

doi:10.1029/2003JA010168, 2004. [PDF]

107. J. Vogt, B. Zieger, A. Stadelmann and K.-H. Glassmeier, T. I. Gombosi, K. C. Hansen, and A. J. Ridley, MHD simulations of quadrupolar paleomagnetospheres, **J. Geophys. Res.**, **109**, A12221, doi::10.1029/2003JA010273, 2004. [PDF]

108. D.L. De Zeeuw, S. Sazykin, R.A. Wolf, T.I. Gombosi, A.J. Ridley, and G. Tóth, Coupling of a Global MHD Code and an Inner Magnetosphere Model: Initial Results, **J. Geophys. Res.**, **109**, A12219, doi:10.1029/2003JA010366, 2004. [PDF]

109. G. Tóth, D. Kovács, K. C. Hansen, and T. I. Gombosi, Three-dimensional MHD simulations of the magnetosphere of Uranus, **J. Geophys. Res.**, **109**, A11210, doi:10.1029/2004JA010406, 2004. [PDF]

110. I. V. Sokolov, I. I. Roussev, T. I. Gombosi, M. A. Lee, J. Kóta, T. G. Forbes, W. B. Manchester, and J. I. Sakai, A new field line advection model for solar particle acceleration, **Astrophys. J.**, **616**, L171-L174, doi:10.1086/426812, 2004. [PDF]

111. A. J. Lovell, N. Kallivayalil, F. P. Schloerb, M. R. Combi, K. C. Hansen, and T. I. Gombosi, On the effect of electron collisions in the excitation of cometary HCN, **Astrophys. J.**, **613**, 615-621, doi:10.1086/422900, 2004. [PDF]

112. A.J. Ridley, T.I. Gombosi, D.L. De Zeeuw, Ionospheric control of the magnetosphere: Conductance, **Ann. Geophys.**, **22**, 567-584, doi:10.5194/Angeo-22-567-2004, 2004. [PDF]

113. M. Opher, P.C. Liewer, M. Velli, L. Bettarini, T.I. Gombosi, W. Manchester, D.L. De Zeeuw, G. Tóth, and I. Sokolov, Magnetic effects at the edge of the solar system: MHD instabilities, the De Laval nozzle effect, and an extended jet, **Astrophys. J.**, **611**, 575-586, doi:10.1086/422165, 2004. [PDF]

114. W.B. Manchester, T.I. Gombosi, D.L. De Zeeuw, and Y. Fan, Eruption of a Buoyantly Emerging Magnetic Flux Rope, **Astrophys. J.**, **610**, 588-596, doi:10.1086/421516, 2004. [PDF]

115. T.E. Cravens, and T.I. Gombosi, Cometary magnetospheres: A tutorial, **Adv. Space Res.**, **33**(11), 1968-1976, doi:10.1016/S0273-1177(04)00020-1, 2004. [PDF]

116. T. H. Zurbuchen, P. Koehn, L. A. Fisk, T. Gombosi, G. Gloeckler and K. Kabin, On the space environment of Mercury, **Adv. Space Sci.**, **33**(11), 1884-1889, doi:10.1016/J.Asr.2003.04.048, 2004. [PDF]

117. B. Zieger, J. Vogt, K.-H. Glassmeier, T.I. Gombosi, Magnetohydrodynamic simulation of an equatorial dipolar paleomagnetosphere, **J. Geophys. Res.**, **109**, A07205, doi:10.1029/2004JA010434, 2004. [PDF]

118. T.I. Gombosi, K.G. Powell, D.L. De Zeeuw, C.R. Clauer, K.C. Hansen, W.B. Manchester, A.J. Ridley, I.I. Roussev, I.V. Sokolov, Q.F. Stout, and G. Tóth, Solution Adaptive MHD for Space Plasmas: Sun-to-Earth Simulations, **Computing in Science and Engineering**, **6**, 14–35, doi:10.1109/Mcise.2004.1267603, 2004. [PDF]

119. I.I. Roussev, I.V. Sokolov, T.G. Forbes, T.I. Gombosi, M.A. Lee, J.I. Sakai, A numerical model of a coronal mass ejection: Shock development with implications for the acceleration of GeV protons, **Astrophys. J.**, **605**, L73-L76, doi:10.1086/392504, 2004. [PDF]

120. W.B. Manchester, T.I. Gombosi, A.J. Ridley, I.I. Roussev, D.L. De Zeeuw, I.V. Sokolov, K.G. Powell, G. Tóth, Modeling a space weather event from the Sun to the Earth: CME generation and interplanetary propagation **J. Geophys. Res.**, **109**,

A02107, doi:10.1029/2003JA010150, 2004. [PDF]

121. W.B. Manchester, T.I. Gombosi, I. Roussev, D.L. De Zeeuw, I.V. Sokolov, K.G. Powell, G. Tóth, and M. Opher, Three-dimensional MHD simulation of a flux-rope driven CME, **J. Geophys. Res.**, **109**, A01102, doi:10.1029/2002JA009672, 2004. [PDF]

122. Sazykin, S., R.A. Wolf, R.W. Spiro, T.I. Gombosi, D.L. DeZeeuw, M.F. Thomsen, Interchange Instability in the Inner Magnetosphere Associated With Geosynchronous Particle Flux Decreases, **Geophys. Res. Lett. 31**, doi:10.1029/2003Gl019191, 2004 [PDF]

123. I.J. Rae, K. Kabin, R. Rankin, F.R. Fenrich, W. Liu, J.A. Wanliss, A.J. Ridley, T.I. Gombosi, and D.L. De Zeeuw, Comparison of Photometer and Global MHD determination of the Open-Closed Field Line Boundary, **J. Geophys. Res.**, **109**, A01204, doi:10.1029/2003JA009968, 2004. [PDF]

2003

124. T.E. Cravens, J.H. Waite, T.I. Gombosi, and N. Lugaz, G.R. Gladstone, B.H. Mauk, R.J. MacDowall, Implications of Jovian X-Ray Emission for Magnetosphere-Ionosphere Coupling, **J. Geophys. Res.**,**108**(A12), 1465, doi:10.1029/2003JA010050, 2003. [PDF]

125. I.I. Roussev, T.I. Gombosi, I.V. Sokolov, M. Velli, W. Manchester, D.L. DeZeeuw, P. Liewer, G. Tóth, and J.G. Luhmann, A Three-Dimensional Model of Solar Wind Incorporating Solar Magnetogram Observations, **Astrophys. J.**, **595**, L57-L61, doi:10.1086/378878, 2003. [PDF]

126. M. Verigin, J. Slavin, A. Szabo, T. Gombosi, G. Kotova, O. Plochova, K. Szegö, M. Tátrallyay, K. Kabin, and F. Shugaev, Planetary bow shocks: Gasdynamic analytic approach, **J. Geophys. Res.**, **108**(A8), 1323, doi:10.1029/2002JA009711, 2003. [PDF]

127. Verigin, M., J. Slavin, A. Szabo, G. Kotova, and T. Gombosi, Planetary Bow Shocks: Asymptotic MHD Mach Cones, **Earth Planets And Space**, **55**, 33–38, 2003. [PDF]

128. A.J. Ridley, T.I. Gombosi, D.L. De Zeeuw, C.R. Clauer, A.D. Richmond, Ionospheric control of the magnetospheric configuration: Thermospheric neutral winds, **J. Geophys. Res.**, **108**(A8), 1328, doi:10.1029/2002JA009464, 2003. [PDF]

129. M. Opher, P.C. Liewer, T.I. Gombosi, W. Manchester, D. L. DeZeeuw, I. Sokolov, G. Tóth, Probing the Edge of the Solar System: Formation of an Unstable Jet-Sheet, **Astrophys. J.**, **591**, L61-L65, doi:10.1086/376960, 2003. [PDF]

130. T.I. Gombosi, D.L. De Zeeuw, K.G. Powell, A.J. Ridley, I.V. Sokolov, Q.F. Stout, and G. Tóth, Adaptive Mesh Refinement MHD for Global Space Weather Simulations, in "**Space Plasma Simulation**", edited by J. Büchner, C. T. Dum, M. Scholer, **Lecture Notes in Physics**, **615**, 247-274, Springer, Berlin-Heidelberg-New York, doi:10.1109/Mcise.2004.1267603, 2003. [PDF]

131. K. Kabin, R. Rankin, R. Marchand, T.I. Gombosi, C.R. Clauer, A.J. Ridley, V.O. Papitashvili, D.L. De Zeeuw, Dynamic response of the Earth's magnetosphere to By reversals, **J. Geophys. Res.**, **108**(A3), 1132, doi:10.1029/2002JA009480, 2003. [PDF]

132. I. Roussev, T.G. Forbes, T.I. Gombosi, I.V. Sokolov, D.L. De Zeeuw, and J. Birn, A Three-Dimensional Flux Rope Model for Coronal Mass Ejections Based on a Loss of Equilibrium, **Astrophys. J.**, **588**, L45–L48, doi:10.1086/375442, 2003. [PDF]

133. P.L. Israelevich, A.I. Ershkovich, T.I. Gombosi, F.M. Neubauer and O. Cohen, Fine structure of the diamagnetic cavity boundary in comet Halley, **J. Geophys. Res.**, **108**(A2), 1097, doi:10.1029/2002JA009622, 2003. [PDF]

2002

134. M. Blanc, S. Bolton, J. Bradley, M. Burton, T.E. Cravens, I. Dandouras, M.K. Dougherty, M.C. Festau, J. Feynman, R.E. Johnson, T.G. Gombosi, W.S. Kurth, P.C.Liewer, B.H. Mauk, S. Maurice, D. Mitchell, F.M. Neubauer, J.D. Richardson, D.E. Shemansky, E.C. Sittler, B.T. Tsurutani, Ph. Zarka, L.W. Esposito, E. Grün, D.A. Gurnett, A.J. Kliore, S.M. Krimigis, D. Southwood, J.H. Waite and D.T. Young, Magnetospheric and Plasma Science with Cassini-Huygens, **Space Science Reviews**, **104**, 253-346, doi:10.1023/A:1023605110711, 2002. [PDF]

135. A.J. Ridley, K.C. Hansen, G. Tóth, D.L. De Zueew, T.I. Gombosi, K.G. Powell, University of Michigan MHD results of the GGCM metrics challenge, **J. Geophys. Res.**, **107**(A10), 1290, doi:10.1029/2001JA000253, 2002. [PDF]

136. M.R. Combi, T.I. Gombosi, and K. Kabin. Plasma Flow Past Cometary and Planetary Satellite Atmospheres, in "**Atmospheres in the Solar System: Comparative Aeronomy**", **Geophysical Monograph**, **130**, 151-167, doi:10.1029/130Gm10, AGU, Washington D.C., 2002. [PDF]

137. Y. Ma, A.F. Nagy, K.C. Hansen, D.L. De Zeeuw, T.I. Gombosi, and K.G. Powell, Three-dimensional multispecies MHD studies of the solar wind interaction with Mars in the presence of crustal fields, **J. Geophys. Res.**, **107**(A10), 1282, doi:10.1029/2002JA009293, 2002. [PDF]

138. S. Sazykin, R.A. Wolf, R.W. Spiro, T.I. Gombosi, D.L. De Zeeuw, and M.F. Thomsen, Interchange instability in the inner magnetosphere associated with geosynchronous particle flux decreases, **Geophys. Res. Lett.**, **29**(10), doi:10.1029/2001GL014416, 2002. [PDF]

139. L. Rästatter, M. Hesse, M. Kuznetsova, T.I. Gombosi, and D.L. De Zeeuw, Magnetic field topology during July 14-16, 2000 (Bastille Day) solar CME event, **Geophys. Res. Lett.**, **29**(15), doi:10.1029/2001GL04136, 2002. [PDF]

140. K.A. Keller, M. Hesse, M. Kuznetsova, L. Rästatter, T. Moretto, T.I. Gombosi, and D.L. De Zeeuw, Global MHD modeling of the impact of a solar wind pressure change, **J. Geophys. Res.**, **107**(A7), doi:10.1029/2001JA000060, 2002. [PDF]

141. T.I. Gombosi, G. Tóth, D.L. De Zeeuw, K.C. Hansen, K. Kabin, and K. G. Powell, Semi-relativistic magnetohydrodynamics and physics-based convergence acceleration, **J. Computational Phys.**, **177**, 176–205, doi:10.1006/Jcph.2002.7009, 2002. [PDF]

2001

142. A.J. Ridley, D.L. De Zeeuw, T.I. Gombosi, and K.G. Powell, Using steady-state MHD

results to predict the global state of the magnetosphere-ionosphere system, **J. Geophys. Res.**, **106**, 30,067-30,076, doi:10.1029/2000Ja002233, 2001. [PDF]

143. M. Verigin, G. Kotova, A. Szabo, J. Slavin, T. Gombosi, K. Kabin, F. Shugaev, and A. Kalinchenko, Wind observations of the terrestrial bow shock: 3D shape and motion, **Earth Planets Space**, **53**, 1001-1009, 2001. [PDF]

144. M. I. Verigin, G. A. Kotova, J. Slavin, A. Szabo, M. Kessel, J. Safrankova, Z. Nemecek, T. I. Gombosd, K. Kabin, F. Shugaev and A. Kalinchenko, Analysis of the 3-D shape of the terrestrial bow shock by Interball/Magion 4 observations, **Adv. Space Res.**, **28**(6), 857–862, doi:10.1016/S0273-1177(01)00502-6, 2001. [PDF]

145. P.L. Israelevich, T.I. Gombosi, A.I. Ershkovich, K.C. Hansen, C.P.T. Groth, D.L. De Zeeuw, and K.G. Powell, MHD simulation of the three-dimensional structure of the heliospheric current sheet, **Astron. Astrophys.**, **376**(1), 288–291, 2001. [PDF]

146. Y. Liu, A.F. Nagy, T.I. Gombosi, D.L. De Zeeuw, and K.G. Powell, The solar wind interaction with Mars: Results of three-dimensional three-species MHD studies, **Adv. Space Res.**, **27**(11), 1837–1846, doi:10.1016/S0273-1177(01)00301-5, 2001. [PDF]

147. P. Song, D. L. DeZeeuw, T. I. Gombosi, J. U. Kozyra and K. G. Powell, Global MHD simulations for southward IMF: a pair of wings in the flanks, **Adv. Space Res.**, **28**(12), 1763-1771, doi:10.1016/S0273-1177(01)00544-0, 2001. [PDF]

148. P. Song, T.I. Gombosi and A.J. Ridley, Three-fluid Ohm's law, **J. Geophys. Res.**, **106**, 8149-8156, doi:0.1029/2000Ja000423, 2001. [PDF]

149. T.I. Gombosi, D.L. De Zeeuw, C.P.T. Groth, K.G. Powell, C.R. Clauer, and P. Song, From Sun to Earth: Multisclae MHD simulations of Space Weather, in **Space Weather**, edited by P. Song, H.J. Singer and G.L. Siscoe, **Geophys. Monograph**, **125**, 169–176, AGU, Washington D.C., doi:10.1029/GM125p0169, 2001. [PDF]

150. A.F. Nagy, Y. Liu, K.C. Hansen, K. Kabin, T.I. Gombosi, M.R. Combi, D.L. De Zeeuw, K.G. Powell, and A.J. Kliore, The interaction between the magnetosphere of Saturn and Titan's ionosphere, **J. Geophys. Res.**, **106**, 6151-6160, doi:10.1029/2000Ja000183, 2001. [PDF]

151. K. Kabin, M.R. Combi, T.I. Gombosi, D.L. De Zeeuw, K.C. Hansen, and K.G. Powell, Io's magnetospheric interaction: an MHD model with day-night asymmetry, **Planetary and Space Sci.**, **49**, 337-344, doi:10.1016/S0032-0633(00)00155-0, 2001. [PDF]

2000

152. C.R. Clauer, T.I. Gombosi, D.L. De Zeeuw, A.J. Ridley, K.G. Powell, B. van Leer, Q.F. Stout, C.P.T. Groth, and T.E. Holzer, High-performance computer methods applied to predictive space weather simulations, **IEEE Trans. Plasma Sci.**, **28**, 1931-1937, doi:10.1109/27.902221, 2000. [PDF]

153. D.L. De Zeeuw, T.I. Gombosi, C.P.T. Groth, K.G. Powell, and Q.F. Stout, An Adaptive MHD Method for Global Space Weather Simulations, **IEEE Trans. Plasma Sci.**, **28**, 1956-1965, doi:10.1109/27.902224, 2000. [PDF]

154. P.L. Israelevich, T.I. Gombosi, A.I. Ershkovich, D.L. De Zeeuw, and K.G. Powell, Magnetic field structure at the diamagnetic cavity boundary (numerical simulations)

Geophys. Res. Lett., **27**, 3817-3820,
doi:10.1029/2000Gl000110, 2000. [PDF]

155. R. Bauske, A.F. Nagy, D.L. De Zeeuw, T.I. Gombosi, and K.G. Powell, 3D multiscale mass loaded MHD simulations of the solar wind interaction with Mars, **Adv. Space Res.**, **26**(10), 1571-1575,
doi:10.1016/S0273-1177(00)00105-8, 2000. [PDF]

156. M. Tátrallyay, M.I. Verigin, K. Szegö, T.I. Gombosi, K.C. Hansen, K. Schwingenschuh, M. Delva, I. Apáthy, A.P. Remizov, and T. Szemerey, On the distribution of pickup ions as observed by the VEGA spacecraft at Comet Halley, **Adv. Space Res.**, **26**(10), 1565-1568, doi:10.1016/S0273-1177(00)00102-2, 2000. [PDF]

157. M. Tátrallyay, M.I. Verigin, K Szegö, T.I. Gombosi, K.C. Hansen, D.L. De Zeeuw, K. Schwingenshuh, M. Delva, A.P. Remizov, I. Apáthy, and T. Szemerey, Interpretation of VEGA observations at Comet Halley applying three-dimensional MHD simulations, **Phys. Chem. Earth** (**C**), **25**, 153-156,
doi:10.1016/S1464-1917(99)00059-8, 2000. [PDF]

158. K.C. Hansen, T.I. Gombosi, D.L. De Zeeuw, C.P.T. Groth, and K.G. Powell, A 3D global MHD simulation of Saturn's magnetosphere, **Adv. Space Res.**, **26**(10), 1681-1690, doi:10.1016/S0273-1177(00)00078-8, 2000. [PDF]

159. K. Szegö, K.-H. Glassmeier, R. Bingham, A. Bogdanov, C. Fischer, G. Haerendel, A. Brinca, T. Cravens, E. Dubinin, K. Sauer, L. Fisk, T. Gombosi, N. Schwadron, P. Isenberg, M. Lee, C. Mazelle, E. Möbius, U. Motschmann, V.D. Shapiro, B. Tsurutani and G. Zank, Physics of mass loaded plasmas, **Space Sci. Rev.**, **94**, 429-671,
doi:10.1023/A:1026568530975, 2000. [PDF]

160. Y. Liu, A.F. Nagy, K. Kabin, M.R. Combi, D.L. De Zeeuw, T.I. Gombosi, and K.G. Powell, Two species, 3D, MHD simulation of Europa's interaction with Jupiter's magnetosphere, **Geophys. Res. Lett.**, **27**, 1791, doi:10.1029/1999Gl003734, 2000. [PDF]

161. P.L. Israelevich, A.I. Ershkovich, and T.I. Gombosi, Does the solar wind affect the solar cycle?, **Astron. Astrophys.**, **362**, 379-382, 2000. [PDF]

162. T.I. Gombosi, D.L. De Zeeuw, C.P.T. Groth, K.G. Powell, and Q.F. Stout, Multiscale MHD simulation of a coronal mass ejection and its interaction with the magnetosphere-ionosphere system, **J. Atmos. Solar Terrestrial Phys.**, **62**, 1515-1525, doi:10.1016/S1364-6826(00)00091-2, 2000. [PDF]

163. C.P.T. Groth, D.L. De Zeeuw, T.I. Gombosi, and K.G. Powell, Global 3D MHD simulation of a space weather event: CME formation, interplanetary propagation, and interaction with the magnetosphere, **J. Geophys. Res.**, **105**, 25,053-25,078,
doi:10.1029/2000Ja900093, 2000. [PDF]

164. T.I. Gombosi, K.G. Powell, and B. van Leer, Comment on "Modeling the magnetosphere for northward interplanetary magnetic field: Effects of electrical resistivity" by Joachim Raeder, **J. Geophys. Res.**, **105**, 13, 141-13,147,
doi:10.1029/1999Ja000342, 2000. [PDF]

165. T.I. Gombosi, D.L. De Zeeuw, C.P.T. Groth, K.C. Hansen, K. Kabin, and K.G. Powell, MHD simulations of current systems in planetary magnetospheres: Mercury and Saturn, in **Magnetospheric Current Systems**, AGU Monograph, **118**, 363-370,
doi:10.1029/GM118p0363, 2000. [PDF]

166. T.J. Linde, and T.I. Gombosi, Interstellar dust filtration at the heliospheric interface, **J. Geophys. Res.**, **105**, 10,411-10,417, doi:10.1029/1999Ja900149, 2000. [PDF]

167. K. Kabin, P.L. Israelevich, A.I. Ershkovich, F.M. Neubauer, T.I. Gombosi, D.L. De Zeeuw, and K.G. Powell, Titan's magnetic wake: Atmospheric or magnetospheric interaction, **J. Geophys. Res.**, **105**, 10,761-10,770, doi:10.1029/2000Ja900012, 2000. [PDF]

168. C.P.T. Groth, D.L. De Zeeuw, T.I. Gombosi, and K.G. Powell, Three-Dimensional MHD Simulation of Coronal Mass Ejections, **Adv. Space Res.**, **26**(5), 793-800, doi:10.1016/S0273-1177(00)00008-9, 2000. [PDF]

169. T.I. Gombosi, D.L. De Zeeuw, C.P.T. Groth, and K.G. Powell, Magnetospheric configuration for Parker-spiral IMF conditions: Results of a 3D AMR MHD simulation, **Adv. Space Res.**, **26**(1), 139-149, doi:10.1016/S0273-1177(99)01040-6, 2000. [PDF]

170. Kabin, K., K.C. Hansen, T.I. Gombosi, M.R. Combi, T.J. Linde, D.L. DeZeeuw, C.P.T. Groth, K.G. Powell, A.F. Nagy, Global MHD Simulations of Space Plasma Environments: Heliosphere, Comets, Magnetospheres of Planets and Satellites, **Astrophysics and Space Science**, **274**, 407–421, doi:10.1023/A:1026513921198, 2000. [PDF]

171. K. Kabin, T.I. Gombosi, D.L. De Zeeuw, and K.G. Powell, Interaction of Mercury with the solar wind, **Icarus**, **143**, 397-406, doi:10.1006/Icar.1999.6252, 2000. [PDF]

172. P. Song, T.I. Gombosi, D.L. De Zeeuw, and K.G. Powell, A model of solar wind - magnetosphere - ionosphere coupling for northward IMF, **Planet. Space Sci.**, **48**, 29-39, doi:10.1016/S0032-0633(99)00065-3, 2000. [PDF]

1999

173. P.L. Israelevich, T.I. Gombosi, A.I. Ershkovich, D.L. De Zeeuw, F.M. Neubauer, and K.G. Powell, The induced magnetosphere of comet Halley, 4.: Comparison of *in situ* observations and numerical simulations, **J. Geophys. Res.**, **104**, 28,309 - 28,319, doi:10.1029/1999Ja900371, 1999. [PDF]

174. P. Song, D.L. De Zeeuw, T.I. Gombosi, C.P.T. Groth, and K.G. Powell, A numerical study of solar wind-magnetosphere interaction for northward IMF, **J. Geophys. Res.**, **104**, 28,361 - 28,378, doi:10.1029/1999Ja900378, 1999. [PDF]

175. P. Song, C. T. Russell, T. I. Gombosi, J. R. Spreiter, S. S. Stahara, and X. X. Zhang, On the processes in the terrestrial magnetosheath 1. Scheme development, **J. Geophys. Res.**, **104**, 22,345-22,355, doi:10.1029/1999Ja900247, 1999. [PDF]

176. P. Song, C. T. Russell, X. X. Zhang, J. R. Spreiter, S. S. Stahara, and T. I. Gombosi, On the processes in the terrestrial magnetosheath 2. Case study, **J. Geophys. Res.**, **104**, 22,357-22,373, doi:10.1029/1999Ja900246, 1999. [PDF]

177. C.P.T. Groth, D.L. De Zeeuw, T.I. Gombosi, and K.G. Powell, A parallel adaptive 3D MHD scheme for modeling coronal and solar wind plasma flows, **Space Sci. Rev.**, **87**, 193-198, doi:10.1023/A:1005136115563, 1999. [PDF]

178. K.G. Powell, P.L. Roe, T.J. Linde, T.I. Gombosi, and D.L. De Zeeuw, A Solution-Adaptive Upwind Scheme for Ideal Magnetohydrodynamics, **J. Computational Phys.**, **154**, 284-309, doi:10.1006/Jcph.1999.6299, 1999. [PDF]

179. K. Kabin, M.R. Combi, T.I. Gombosi, A.F. Nagy, D.L. De Zeeuw, and K.G. Powell,

On Europa's magnetospheric interaction: an MHD simulation of the E4 flyby, **J. Geophys. Res., 104**, 19,983–19,992, doi:10.1029/1999Ja900263, 1999. [PDF]

180. Y. Liu, A.F. Nagy, C.P.T. Groth, D.L. De Zeeuw, T.I. Gombosi, and K.G. Powell, 3D Multi-fluid MHD studies of the solar wind interaction with Mars, **Geophys. Res. Lett., 26**, 2689-2692, doi:10.1029/1999Gl900584, 1999. [PDF]

181. K. Kabin, T.I. Gombosi, D.L. De Zeeuw, K.G. Powell, and P.L. Israelevich, Interaction of Saturnian magnetosphere with Titan: Results from a 3D MHD simulation, **J. Geophys. Res., 104**, 2451-2458, doi:10.1029/1998Ja900080, 1999. [PDF]

1998

182. H. Balsiger, K. Altwegg, A. Arjis, J.-L. Bertaux, P. Bochsler, C.R. Carignan, P. Eberhard, L.A. Fisk, S.A. Fuselier, A.G. Ghielmetti, F. Gliem, T.I. Gombosi, E. Kopp, A. Korth, S. Livi, C. Mazelle, H. Rème, J.A. Sauvaud, E.G. Shelley, J.H. Waite, B. Wilken, J. Woch, H. Wollnik, P. Wurz, and D.T. Young, Rosetta orbiter spectrometer for ion and neutral analysis – ROSINA, **Adv. Space Res., 21**(11), pp 1527-1535, doi:x10.1016/S0273-1177(97)00945-9, 1998. [PDF]

183. T.I. Gombosi, D.L. De Zeeuw, C.P.T. Groth, K.G. Powell, and P. Song, The length of the magnetotail for northward IMF: Results of 3D MHD simulations, **Phys. Space Plasmas (1998), 15**, 121–128, 1998. [PDF]

184. Bauske, R., A.F. Nagy, T.I. Gombosi, D.L. De Zeeuw, K.G. Powell, J.G. Luhmann, A three-dimensional MHD study of solar wind mass loading processes at Venus: Effects of photoionization, electron impact ionization, and charge exchange, **J. Geophys. Res., 103**, 23625-23638, doi:10.1029/98Ja01791, 1998. [PDF]

185. Combi, M.R., K. Kabin, T.I. Gombosi, D.L. De Zeeuw, and K.G. Powell, Io's plasma environment during the Galileo flyby: Global three-dimensional MHD modeling with adaptive mesh refinement, **J. Geophys. Res., 103**, 9071-9081, doi:10.1029/98Ja00073, 1998. [PDF]

186. T.J. Linde, T.I. Gombosi, P.L. Roe, K.G. Powell, D.L. De Zeeuw, The heliosphere in the magnetized local interstellar medium: Results of a 3D MHD simulation, **J. Geophys. Res., 103**, 1889-1904, doi:10.1029/97Ja02144, 1998. [PDF]

1997

187. M.R. Combi, K. Kabin, D.L. De Zeeuw, T.I. Gombosi, and K.G. Powell, Dust-gas interaction in comets: Observations and theory, **Earth, Moon and Planets, 79**, 275-306, doi:10.1023/A:1006257922294, 1997. [PDF]

188. T.I. Gombosi, K.C. Hansen, D.L. De Zeeuw, M.R. Combi, and K.G. Powell, MHD simulation of comets: The plasma environment of comet Hale-Bopp, **Earth, Moon and Planets, 79** 179-207, doi:10.1023/A:1006289418660, 1997. [PDF]

189. R. Häberli, M.R. Combi, T.I. Gombosi, D.L. De Zeeuw,and K.G. Powell, Quantitative analysis of H_2O^+ coma images using a multiscale MHD model with detailed ion chemistry, **Icarus, 130**, 373-386, doi:10.1006/Icar.1997.5835, 1997. [PDF]

190. R.M. Häberli, T.I. Gombosi, M.R. Combi, D.L. De Zeeuw, and K.G. Powell,

Modeling of cometary X-rays caused by solar wind minor ions, **Science**, **276**, 939-942, doi:10.1126/science.276.5314.939, 1997. [PDF]

191. K. G. Powell, P. L. Roe, D. L. DeZeeuw, T. I. Gombosi and M. Vinokur, A computational approach for modeling solar-wind physics, in **Lecture Notes in Physics**, vol. **490**, Springer, doi:10.1007/BFb0107154, 1997. [PDF]

192. M. Tátrallyay, T.I. Gombosi, D.L. De Zeeuw, M.I. Verigin, A.P. Remizov, and I. Apáthy, Plasma flow in the cometosheath of comet Halley, **Adv. Space Res.**, **20**(2), 275–278, doi:10.1016/S0273-1177(97)00546-2, 1997. [PDF]

1996

193. T.I. Gombosi, D.L. De Zeeuw, R. Häberli, and K.G. Powell, A 3D multiscale MHD model of cometary plasma environments, **J. Geophys. Res.**, **101**, 15,233-15,253, doi:10.1029/96Ja01075, 1996. [PDF]

194. D.L. De Zeeuw, T.I. Gombosi, A.F. Nagy, K.G. Powell, and J.G. Luhmann, A new axisymmetric MHD model of the interaction of the solar wind with Venus, **J. Geophys. Res.**, **101**, 4,547-4,556, doi:10.1029/95Je03363, 1996. [PDF]

1995

195. R.H. Miller, C.E. Rasmussen, M.R. Combi, T.I. Gombosi, and D. Winske, Ponderomotive acceleration in the auroral region: A kinetic simulation, **J. Geophys. Res.**, **100**, 23,901–23,916, doi:10.1029/95Ja01908, 1995. [PDF]

196. S. Guiter, C. Rasmussen, T. Gombosi, J. Sojka, and R. Schunk, What is the Source of Observed Annual Variations in Plasmaspheric Density?, **J. Geophys. Res.**, **100**, 8013–8020, doi:10.1029/94Ja02866, 1995. [PDF]

197. Guiter, S.M.; Gombosi, T.I.; Rasmussen, C.E., Two-Stream Modeling of Plasmaspheric Refilling, **J. Geophys. Res.**, **J100**, 9519–9526, doi:10.1029/95Ja00081, 1995. [PDF]

1994

198. N. Schwadron and T.I. Gombosi, A unifying comparison of nearly scatter free transport models, **J. Geophys. Res.**, **99**, 19,301-19,323, doi:10.1029/94Ja01737, 1994. [PDF]

199. T.I. Gombosi, K.G. Powell and D.L. De Zeeuw, Axisymmetric modeling of cometary mass loading on an adaptively refined grid: MHD results, **J. Geophys. Res.**, **99**, 21,525-21,539, doi:10.1029/94Ja01540, 1994. [PDF]

200. T. I. Gombosi and K. G. Powell, Axisymmetric modeling of cometary mass loading on an adaptively refined grid: hydrodynamic results, in **Solar System Plasmas in Space and Time**, Geophys. Monogr. Ser., vol. 84, edited by J. L. Burch and J. H. Waite Jr., pp. 237–246, doi:10.1029/GM084p0237, AGU, Washington, D. C., 1994. [PDF]

201. G. Khazanov, C. Rasmussen, Y. Konikov, T. Gombosi, and A. Nagy, Effect of Magnetospheric Convection on Thermal Plasma in the Inner Magnetosphere, **J. Geophys. Res.**, **99**, 5923–5934, doi:10.1029/93JA02778, 1994. [PDF]

202. V.G. Khazanov, T.I. Gombosi, O.A. Gorbachev, A.A. Trukhan and R.H. Miller, Thermodynamic effect of the ion-sound instability in the ionosphere, **J. Geophys.**

Res., **99**, 5721–5726, doi:10.1029/93JA02783, 1994. [PDF]

1993

203. G.V. Khazanov, M.W. Liemohn, T.I. Gombosi and A.F. Nagy, Non-steady-state transport of superthermal electrons in the plasmasphere, **Geophys. Res. Lett.**, **20**, 2821–2824, doi:10.1029/93Gl03121, 1993. [PDF]

204. R.H. Miller, C.E. Rasmussen, T.I. Gombosi and D. Winske, Hybrid simulations of plasmaspheric refilling including convection and injection, **Adv. Space Res.**, **13**, (4)117–(4)120, doi:10.1016/0273-1177(93)90321-2, 1993. [PDF]

205. K.V. Gamayunov, G.V. Khazanov, E.N. Krivorutsky, T.I. Gombosi and V.N. Oraevskii, Plasma hydrodynamics in view of quasilinear effects, **Planet. Space Sci.**, **41**, 27–33, doi:10.1016/0032-0633(93)90014-S, 1993. [PDF]

206. K.V. Gamayunov, G.V. Khazanov, A.A. Veryaev and T.I. Gombosi, The effect of the hot, anisotropic magnetospheric protons on the dispersion relation, **Adv. Space Res.**, **13**, (4)121–(4)126, doi:10.1016/0273-1177(93)90322-3, 1993. [PDF]

207. K.M. Chick and T.I. Gombosi, Multiple scattering of light in a spherical cometary atmosphere with an axisymmetric dust jet II., Image simulation, **Icarus**, **104**, 167–184, doi:10.1006/Icar.1993.1093, 1993. [PDF]

208. L.L. Williams, N. Schwadron, J.R. Jokipii and T.I. Gombosi, A unified transport equation for both cosmic rays and thermal particles, **Astrophys. J.**, **405**, L79–L81, doi:10.1086/186770, 1993. [PDF]

209. G. Ye, T.E. Cravens and T.I. Gombosi, Pickup protons and water ions at comet Halley: Comparison with Giotto observations, **J. Geophys. Res.**, **98**, 1311–1323, doi:10.1029/92Ja02035, 1993. [PDF]

210. R.H. Miller, C.E. Rasmussen, T.I. Gombosi, V.G. Khazanov and D. Winske, Kinetic simulation of plasma flows in the inner magnetosphere, **J. Geophys. Res.**, **98**, 19,301–19,313, doi:10.1029/93JA01292, 1993. [PDF]

211. A. Körösmezey, C.E. Rasmussen, T.I. Gombosi and B. van Leer, Transport of gyration dominated space plasmas of thermal origin II.: Numerical solution, **J. Computational Phys.**, **109**, 16–29, doi:10.1006/Jcph.1993.1195, 1993. [PDF]

212. T.I. Gombosi, J.R. Jokipii, J. Kóta, K. Lorencz and L.L. Williams, The telegraph equation in charged particle transport, **Astrophys. J.**, **403**, 377–384, doi:10.1086/172209, 1993. [PDF]

1992

213. K.M. Chick and T.I. Gombosi, Multiple scattering of light in a spherical cometary atmosphere with an axisymmetric dust jet, **Icarus**, **98**, 179-194, doi:10.1016/0019-1035(92)90088-O, 1992. [PDF]

214. G.V. Khazanov, A.F. Nagy, T.I. Gombosi, M.A. Koen and S.J. Cariglia, Analytic description of the electron temperature behavior in the upper ionosphere and plasmasphere, **Geophys. Res. Lett.**, **19**, 1915–1918, doi:10.1029/92GL01940, 1992. [PDF]

215. G.V. Khazanov, T.I. Gombosi, A.F. Nagy and M.A. Koen, Analysis of the ionosphere -

plasmasphere transport of superthermal electrons: 1. Transport in the plasmasphere, **J. Geophys. Res.**, **97**, 16,887 - 16,895, doi:10.1029/92Ja00319, 1992. [PDF]

216. A. Körösmezey, C.E. Rasmussen, T.I. Gombosi and G.V. Khazanov, Anisotropic ion heating and parallel O^+ acceleration in regions of rapid $E \times B$ convection, **Geophys. Res. Lett.**, **19**, 2298-2292, doi:10.1029/92GL02489, 1992. [PDF]

217. T.I. Gombosi, L.K. Kerr, A.F. Nagy and R. W. Cannata, Helium in the polar wind, **Advances of Space Research, 12**, (6)183-(6)186, doi:10.1016/0273-1177(92)90054-2, 1992. [PDF]

1991

218. N. M. Shutte, P. Király, T.E. Cravens, A. V. Dyachkov, T.I. Gombosi, K. I. Gringauz, A.F. Nagy, W. F. Sharp, S. M. Sheronova, K. Szegö, I. Szemerey, Energy distribution of <800 eV electrons in the aeromagnetosphere, **Planet. Space Sci., 39**, 147-151, doi:10.1016/0032-0633(91)90137-Y, 1991. [PDF]

219. P. Király. R. Loch, K. Szegö, I. Szemerey. I. T.-Szü, M. Tátrallyay, N. M. Shutte. A. V. Dyachkov, K. 1. Gringauz, S. Sheronova, M. I. Verigin, T. E. Cravens. T. I. Gombosi, A. F. Nagy and W. Sharp, The HARP plasma experiment on-board the Phobos 2 spacecraft: Preliminary results, **Planet. Space Sci., 39**, 139-145, doi:10.1016/0032-0633(91)90136-X, 1991. [PDF]

220. T. I. Gombosi, Multidimensional dusty gasdynamical models of inner cometary atmospheres, in **Comets in the Post-Halley Era**, edited by R. L. Newburn, M. Neugebauer and J. Rahe, 991-1001, Kluwer Academic Publishers, 1991. [PDF]

221. S. M. Guiter and T. I. Gombosi, Modelling of plasmaspheric flows with an equatorial heat source for electrons, in "**Modeling Magnetospheric Plasma Processes**," edited by G. R. Wilson, 157, AGU, Washington, D.C., doi: 10.1029/GM062p0157, 1991. [PDF]

222. T.I. Gombosi, M. Neugebauer, A. D. Johnstone, A. J. Coates and D. E. Huddleston, Cometary ion distributions near the pickup energy outside comet Halley's bow shock, **Advances of Space Research, 11**, (9)275-(9)278, doi:10.1016/0273-1177(91)90047-N, 1991. [PDF]

223. R. H. Miller, T.I. Gombosi, D. Winske and S. P. Gary, The directional dependence of cometary magnetic energy density in the quasi-parallel and quasi-perpendicular regimes, **Advances of Space Research, 11**, (9)78-(9)82, doi:10.1016/0273-1177(91)90015-C, 1991. [PDF]

224. A.F. Nagy, A. Körösmezey, J. Kim and T.I. Gombosi, A two-dimensional, shock capturing, hydrodynamic model of the Venus ionosphere, **Geophys. Res. Lett., 18**, 801-804, doi:10.1029/91Gl00362, 1991. [PDF]

225. M. I. Verigin, K. I. Gringauz, N. M. Shutte, S. A. Haider, K. Szegö, P. Király, A.F. Nagy and T.I. Gombosi, On the possible source of the ionization in the nighttime Martian ionosphere. 1. Phobos-2/HARP electron spectrometer measurements, **J. Goephys. Res., 96**, 19,307-19,313, doi:10.1029/91Ja00924, 1991. [PDF]

226. T.I. Gombosi, An analytic solution to the double adiabatic equations, **Gephys. Res. Lett., 18**, 1181-1184, doi:10.1029/91Gl01614, 1991. [PDF]

227. T.I. Gombosi, The plasma environment of comets, **Rev. Geophys. Suppl., 29**, 976–984, 1991. [PDF]

228. R. H. Miller, T.I. Gombosi, S. P. Gary and D. Winske, The directional dependence of magnetic fluctuations generated by cometary ion pick-up, **J. Geophys. Res.**, **96**, 9479, doi:10.1029/91Ja00158, 1991. [PDF]

229. R. H. Miller, S. P. Gary, D. Winske and T.I. Gombosi, Pitch-angle scattering of cometary ions into monospherical and bispherical distributions, **Geophys. Res. Let.**, **18**, 1063-1066, doi:10.1029/91Gl01047, 1991. [PDF]

230. T.I. Gombosi, M. Neugebauer, A. D. Johnstone, A. J. Coates and D. E. Huddleston, Comparison of observed and calculated implanted ion distributions outside comet Halley's bow shock, **J. Geophys. Res.**, **96**, 9467, doi:10.1029/90Ja02750, 1991. [PDF]

231. S. M. Guiter, T.I. Gombosi and C.E. Rasmussen, Diurnal variations on a plasmaspheric flux tube: Light ion flows and F region temperature enhancements, **Geophys. Res. Lett.**, **18**, 813-816, doi:10.1029/91Gl00139, 1991. [PDF]

232. T.I. Gombosi and C.E. Rasmussen, Transport of gyration dominated space plasmas of thermal origin I.: Generalized transport equations, **J. Geophys. Res.**, **96**, 7759–7778, doi:10.1029/91Ja00012, 1991. [PDF]

233. R. H. Miller, T.I. Gombosi, S. P. Gary and D. Winske, Directional dependence of magnetic field fluctuations in the quasi-parallel and quasi-perpendicular regimes generated by cometary ion pick-up, **Adv. Space Res.**, **11**, (9)79–(9)82, doi:10.1016/0273-1177(91)90015-C, 1991. [PDF]

1990

234. I. T.-Szücs, I. Szemerey, P. Király, S. Szendrö, M. Tátrallyay, A. Tóth, T.E. Cravens, T.I. Gombosi, A.F. Nagy, W. E. Sharp, V. V. Afonin, K. I. Gringauz, S.M. Sheronova, N. M. Shutte and M. I. Verigin, The HARP electron and ion sensor on the Phobos mission, **Nuclear Instruments and Methods in Phys. Res.**, **A290**, 228–236, doi:10.1016/0168-9002(90)90366-E, 1990. [PDF]

235. A.F. Nagy, T.I. Gombosi, K. Szegö, R.Z. Sagdeev, V.D. Shapiro, V.I. Shevchenko, Venus mantle - Mars planetosphere: What are the similarities and differences, **Geophys. Res. Lett.**, **17**, 865–868, doi:10.1029/Gl017I006P00865, 1990. [PDF]

236. N. M. Shutte, P. Király, T.E. Cravens, A. V. Dyachkov, T.I. Gombosi, K. I. Gringauz, A.F. Nagy, W. F. Sharp, S. M. Sheronova, K. Szegö, I. Szemerey, I. T.-Szücs, M. Tátrallyay and M. I. Verigin, Observations of electron and fluxes near Mars with the HARP instrument on board the Phobos-2 spacecraft, **Letters to Astronomicheskii Zhurnal** (in Russian), **16**, 154–156, 1990.

237. S. M. Guiter and T.I. Gombosi, The role of high-speed plasma flows in plasmaspheric refilling, **J. Geophys. Res.**, **95**, 10,427–10,440, doi:10.1029/Ja095Ia07P10427, 1990. [PDF]

238. A. Körösmezey and T.I. Gombosi, A time dependent dusty-gas dynamic model of axisymmetric cometary jets, **Icarus**, **84**, 118–153, doi:10.1016/0019-1035(90)90162-3, 1990. [PDF]

1989

239. N. M. Shutte, P. Király, T.E. Cravens, A. V. Dyachkov, T.I. Gombosi, K. I. Gringauz, A.F. Nagy, W. E. Sharp, S. M. Sheronova, K. Szegö, I. Szemerey, I. T.-Szücs, M. Tátrallyay, A. Tóth and M. I. Verigin, Observation of electron and ion fluxes in the vicinity of Mars with the HARP spectrometer, **Nature**, **341**, 614-616, doi:10.1038/341614A0, 1989. [PDF]

240. T. I. Gombosi and A. Köorösmezey, Cometary dusty gas dynamics, in "**Solar System Plasma Physics**", edited by J. H. Waite, J. L. Burch and R. L. Moore, 433-439, AGU, Washington, D.C., doi:10.1029/GM054p0433, 1989. [PDF]

241. T.I. Gombosi and A. Körösmezey, Modeling of the cometary nucleus - coma interface region, **Adv. Space Res.**, **9**(3), 41-51, doi:10.1016/0273-1177(89)90239-1, 1989. [PDF]

242. R. W. Cannata and T.I. Gombosi, Modeling the solar cycle dependence of quiet-time ion upwelling at high geomagnetic latitudes, **Geophys. Res. Lett.**, **16**, 1141-1144, doi:10.1029/Gl016I010P01141, 1989. [PDF]

243. T.I. Gombosi and A.F. Nagy, Time-dependent modeling of field-aligned current-generated ion transients in the polar wind, **J. Geophys. Res.**, **4**, 359-369, doi:10.1029/Ja094Ia01P00359, 1989. [PDF]

244. K. Kecskeméty, T.E. Cravens, V. V. Afonin, G. Erdös, E. G. Eroshenko, L. Gan, T.I. Gombosi, K. I. Gringauz, E. Keppler, I. N. Klimenko, R. Marsden, A.F. Nagy, A. P. Remizov, A. K. Richter, W. Riedler, K. Schwingenschuh, A. J. Somogyi, M. Tátrallyay, A. Varga, M. I. Verigin and K. P. Wenzel, Pickup ions in the unshocked solar wind at comet Halley, **J. Geophys. Res.**, **94**, 185-196, doi:10.1029/Ja094Ia01P00185, 1989. [PDF]

245. T.I. Gombosi, K. Lorencz and J. R. Jokipii, Combined first and second order Fermi acceleration in cometary environments, **J. Geophys. Res.**, **94**, 15,011-15,023, doi:10.1029/Ja094Ia11P15011, 1989. [PDF]

246. T.I. Gombosi, K. Lorencz and J. R. Jokipii, Combined first and second order Fermi acceleration at comets, **Adv. Space Res.**, **9**(3), 337-341, doi:10.1016/0273-1177(89)90285-8, 1989. [PDF]

1988

247. R. W. Cannata, T. L. Killeen, T.I. Gombosi, A. G. Burns and R. G. Roble, Modeling of time-dependent ion outflows at high geomagnetic latitudes, **Adv. Space Res.**, **8**(8), 89–92, doi:10.1016/0273-1177(88)90267-0, 1988. [PDF]

248. T.I. Gombosi and A.F. Nagy, Time-dependent polar wind modeling, **Adv. Space Res.**, **8**(8), 59–68, doi:10.1016/0273-1177(88)90264-5, 1988. [PDF]

249. T. I. Gombosi, Second order Fermi acceleration of implanted cometary ions, in "**Cometary and Solar Plasma Physics**", edited by B. Buti, 183–220, World Scientific, Singapore, 1988. [PDF]

250. T.I. Gombosi and R. W. Schunk, A comparative study of plasma expansion events in the polar wind, **Planet. Space Sci.**, **36**, 753-764, doi:10.1016/0032-0633(88)90081-5, 1988. [PDF]

251. T.I. Gombosi, Preshock region acceleration of implanted cometary H^+ and O^+, **J. Geophys. Res.**, **93**, 35-47, doi:10.1029/Ja093Ia01P00035, 1988. [PDF]

1987

252. T.I. Gombosi, Dusty cometary atmospheres, **Adv. Space Res.**, **7**(12), 137–145, doi:10.1016/0273-1177(87)90211-0, 1987. [PDF]

253. O. M. Belotserkovskii, T. K. Breus, A. M. Krymskii, V. Y. Mitnitskii, A.F. Nagy and T.I. Gombosi, The effect of the hot oxygen corona on the interaction of the solar wind with Venus, **Geophys. Res. Lett.**, **14**, 503-506, doi:10.1029/Gl014I005P00503, 1987. [PDF]

254. T. K. Breus, A. M. Krymskii, V. Y. Mitnitskii, T.I. Gombosi and A.F. Nagy, The role of the hot oxygen corona in the interaction of the solar wind with Venus, **Kosmicheskie Issledovaniya**, **25**, 626-634, 1987.

255. K. Kecskeméty, T.E. Cravens, V. V. Afonin, A. Varga, K.-P. Wenzel, M. I. Verigin, L. Gan, T. Gombosi, K. I. Gringauz, E. G. Eroshenko, E. Keppler, I. P. Klimenko, P. Marsden, A.F. Nagy, A. P. Remizov, W. Riedler, A. K. Richter, K. Szegö, M. Tátrallyay, K. Schwingenschuh, A. Somogyi and G. Erdös, Energetic cometary ion measurements upstream of the comet Halley bow shock, **Kosmicheskie Issledovaniya**, **25**, 932-942, 1987.

256. K. I. Gringauz, A. P. Remizov, M. I. Verigin, A. K. Richter, M. Tátrallyay, K. Szegö, I. N. Klimenko, I. Apáthy, T. Gombosi and T. Szemerey, Electron component of the plasma environment of comet Halley as measured by PLAZMAG-1 onboard of the VEGA-2 spacecraft, **Kosmicheskie Issledovaniya**, **25**, 927-931, 1987.

257. K. I. Gringauz, M. I. Verigin, A. Richter, T. Gombosi, K. Szegö, M. Tátrallyay, A. P. Remizov and I. Apáthy, Cometary ion region in the coma of comet Halley as measured by VEGA-2, **Kosmicheskie Issledovaniya**, **25**, 914-919, 1987.

258. M. I. Verigin, K. I. Gringauz, A. Richter, T. Gombosi, A. P. Remizov, K. Szegö, K. Apáthy, T. Szemerey, M. Tátrallyay and L. A. Lezhen, Characteristics of the comet Halley plasma transition region (cometosheath) as measured by VEGA-1 and VEGA-2, **Kosmicheskie Issledovaniya**, **25**, 907-913, 1987.

259. A. A. Galeev, B. E. Gribov, T. Gombosi, K. I. Gringauz, S. I. Klimov, P. Obercz, A. P. Remizov, W. Riedler, R. Z. Sagdeev, S. P. Savich, A. Y. Sokolov, V. D. Shapiro, V. I. Shevchenko, K. Szegö, M. I. Verigin and E. G. Eroshenko, Location and structure of the comet Halley shock wave as observed by VEGA-1 and VEGA-2, **Kosmicheskie Issledovaniya**, **25**, 900-906, 1987.

260. A. P. Remizov, M. I. Verigin, K. I. Gringauz, I. Apáthy, T. Szemerey, T. Gombosi and A. K. Richter, Plasmag-1 measurements of neutral particle densities at comet Halley onboard the VEGA-1 and VEGA-2 spacecraft, **Kosmicheskie Issledovaniya**, **25**, 895-899, 1987.

261. T.E. Cravens, J. U. Kozyra, A.F. Nagy, T.I. Gombosi and M. Kurtz, Electron impact ionization in the vicinity of comets, **J. Geophys. Res.**, **92**, 7341-7353, doi:10.1029/Ja092Ia07P07341, 1987. [PDF]

262. A. Körösmezey, T.E. Cravens, T.I. Gombosi, A.F. Nagy, D. A. Mendis, K. Szegö, B. E. Gribov, R. Z. Sagdeev, V. D. Shapiro and V. I. Shevchenko, A new model of cometary ionospheres, **J. Geophys. Res.**, **92**, 7331, doi:10.1029/Ja092Ia07P07331, 1987. [PDF]

263. T. M. Donahue, T.I. Gombosi and B. R. Sandel, Cometesimals in the inner solar system, **Nature**, **30**, 548-550, doi:10.1038/330548A0, 1987. [PDF]

264. T.I. Gombosi and T. L. Killeen, Effects of thermospheric motions on the polar wind: A time-dependent numerical study, **J. Geophys. Res.**, **92**, 4725-4729, doi:10.1029/Ja092Ia05P04725, 1987. [PDF]

265. T.I. Gombosi, Charge exchange avalanche at the cometopause, **Geophys. Res. Lett.**, **14**, 1174–1177, doi:10.1029/Gl014I011P01174, 1987. [PDF]

266. M. I. Verigin, K. I. Gringauz, A. K. Richter, T.I. Gombosi, A. P. Remizov, K. Szegö, I. Apáthy, I. Szemerey, M. Tátrallyay and L. A. Lezhen, Characteristic features of the cometosheath of comet Halley: VEGA-1 and VEGA-2 observations, **Astron. Astrophys.**, **187**, 121–124, 1987. [PDF]

267. K. I. Gringauz, M. I. Verigin, A. K. Richter, T.I. Gombosi, K. Szegö, M. Tátrallyay, A. P. Remizov and I. Apáthy, Quasi-periodic features and the radial distribution of cometary ions in the cometary plasma region of comet P/Halley, **Astron. Astrophys.**, **187**, 191–194, 1987. [PDF]

268. K. I. Gringauz, A. P. Remizov, M. I. Verigin, A. K. Richter, M. Tátrallyay, K. Szegö, I. N. Klimenko, I. Apáthy, T.I. Gombosi and I. Szemerey, Analysis of the electron measurements from the Plasmag-1 experiment on board Vega 2 in the vicinity of comet P/Halley, **Astron. Astrophys.**, **187**, 287-289, 1987. [PDF]

1986

269. N. Divine, H. Fechtig, T.I. Gombosi, M. S. Hanner, H. U. Keller, S. M. Larson, D. A. Mendis, R. L. Newburn, R. Reinhard, Z. Sekanina and D. K. Yeomans, The Comet Halley dust and gas environment, **Space Sci. Rev.**, **43**, 1-104, doi:10.1007/BF00175326, 1986. [PDF]

270. T.I. Gombosi and M. Horanyi, Time-dependent modeling of dust halo formation at comets, **Astrophys. J.**, **311**, 491-500, doi:10.1086/164789, 1986. [PDF]

271. K. I. Gringauz, T.I. Gombosi, M. Tátrallyay, M. I. Verigin, A. P. Remizov, A. K. Richter, I. Apáthy, I. Szemerey, A. V. Dyachkov, O. V. Balakina and A.F. Nagy, Detection of a new "chemical" boundary at comet Halley, **Geophys. Res. Lett.**, **13**, 613-616, doi:10.1029/Gl013I007P00613, 1986. [PDF]

272. A. A. Galeev, B. N. Gribov, T.I. Gombosi, K. I. Gringauz, S. I. Klimov, P. Oberz, A. P. Remizov, W. Riedler, R. Z. Sagdeev, S. P. Savin, I. A. Sokolov, V. D. Shapiro, V. I. Shevchenko, K. Szegö, M. I. Verigin and E. G. Eroshenko, The position and structure of comet Halley bow shock: VEGA-1 and VEGA-2 measurements, **Geophys. Res. Lett.**, **13**, 841, doi:10.1029/Gl013I008P00841, 1986. [PDF]

273. A. J. Somogyi, K. I. Gringauz, K. Szegö, L. Szabó, G. Kozma, A. P. Remizov, J. Erö Jr., I. N. Klimenko, I. T-Szücs, M. I. Verigin, J. Windberg, T.E. Cravens, A. Dyachkov, G. Erdös, M. Faragó, T.I. Gombosi, K. Kecskeméty, E. Keppler, T. Kovács Jr., A. Kondor, Y. I. Logachev, L. Lohonyai, R. Marsden, R. Redl, A. K. Richter, V. G. Stolpovskii, J. Szabó, I. Szentpétery, A. Szepesváry, M. Tátrallyay, A. Varga, G. A. Vladimirova, K.-P. Wenzel and A. Zarándy, First observations of energetic particles near comet Halley, **Nature**, **321**, 285-288, doi:10.1038/321285A0, 1986. [PDF]

274. Gringauz, K.I., Gombosi, T.I., Remizov, A.P. Apathy, I. Szemerey, T . Denshchikova, L.I., Dyachkov, A.V., Keppler, E . Klimenko, I.N., Richter, A.K., Somogyi, A.J., Szegö, K., Szendrö, S., Tátrallyay,, M., Varga, A., Verigin, M.I., Vladimirova, G.A.,

First in-situ plasma and neutral-gas measurements near comet Halley – Preliminary VEGA results, **Soviet Astronomy Letters**, **12**, 279–282, 1986. [PDF]

275. K. I. Gringauz, T.I. Gombosi, A. P. Remizov, I. Apáthy, I. Szemerey, M. I. Verigin, L. I. Denchikova, A. V. Dyachkov, E. Keppler, I. N. Klimenko, A. K. Richter, A. J. Somogyi, K. Szegö, S. Szendrö, M. Tátrallyay, A. Varga and G. A. Vladimirova, First in situ plasma and neutral gas measurements at comet Halley, **Nature**, **321**, 282-285, doi:10.1038/321282A0, 1986. [PDF]

276. T. I. Gombosi, T. E. Cravens, A. F. Nagy and J. H. Waite Jr., Time-dependent numerical simulation of hot ion outflow from the polar ionosphere, in *Ion Acceleration in the Magnetosphere and Ionosphere*, 366-371, American Geophysical Union, Washington, D.C., doi:10.1029/GM038p0366, 1986. [PDF]

277. T.I. Gombosi and M. M. Horanyi, Modeling of dust halo formation following comet outbursts: Preliminary results, **Geophys. Res. Lett.**, **13**, 299-301, doi:10.1029/Gl013I003P00299, 1986. [PDF]

278. T.I. Gombosi and H. L. F. Houpis, An icy-glue model of cometary nuclei, **Nature**, **324**, 43–44, doi:10.1038/324043A0, 1986. [PDF]

279. T.I. Gombosi, A.F. Nagy and T.E. Cravens, Dust and neutral gas modeling of the inner atmospheres of comets, **Rev. Geophys.**, **24**, 667, doi:10.1029/Rg024I003P00667, 1986. [PDF]

1985

280. A. A. Galeev, T.E. Cravens and T.I. Gombosi, Solar wind stagnation near comets, **Astrophys. J.**, **289**, 807, doi:10.1086/162945, 1985. [PDF]

281. T.I. Gombosi, T.E. Cravens and A.F. Nagy, A time-dependent theoretical model of the polar wind: Preliminary results, **Geophys. Res. Lett.**, **12**, 167-170, 1985. [PDF]

282. T.I. Gombosi, T.E. Cravens and A.F. Nagy, Time dependent dusty gas dynamical flow near cometary nuclei, **Astrophys. J.**, **293**, 328, doi:10.1029/Gl012I004P00167, 1985. [PDF]

1984

283. M. Horanyi, T.I. Gombosi, T.E. Cravens, A. Körösmezey, K. Kecskeméty, A. Nagy and K. Szegö, The friable sponge model of a cometary nucleus, **Astrophys. J.**, **278**, 449, doi:10.1086/161810, 1984. [PDF]

1983

284. A. F. Nagy, T. E. Cravens and T. I. Gombosi, Basic theory and model calculations of the Venus ionosphere, in *Venus*, edited by D. M. Hunten, L. Colin, T. M. Donahue and V. I. Moroz, 841-872, Univ. of Arizona Press, Tucson, Arizona, 1983. [PDF]

285. L. H. Brace, J. Taylor H.A., T. I. Gombosi, A. J. Kliore, W. C. Knudsen and A. F. Nagy, The ionosphere of Venus: observations and their interpretation, in *Venus*, edited by D. M. Hunten, L. Colin, T. M. Donahue and V. I. Moroz, 779-840, The University of Ariozona Press, Tucson, Arizona, 1983. [PDF]

286. T.E. Cravens, S. L. Crawford, A.F. Nagy and T.I. Gombosi, A two dimensional model

of the ionosphere of Venus, **J. Geophys. Res.**, **88**, 5595-5606, doi:10.1029/Ja088Ia07P05595, 1983. [PDF]

287. C. T. Russell, T.I. Gombosi, M. Horanyi, T.E. Cravens and A.F. Nagy, Charge exchange in the magnetospheres of Venus and Mars: a comparison, **Geophys. Res. Lett.**, **10**, 163-164, doi:10.1029/Gl010I002P00163, 1983. [PDF]

288. T.I. Gombosi, M. Horanyi, K. Kecskeméty, T.E. Cravens and A.F. Nagy, Charge exchange in solar wind - cometary interactions, **Astrophys. J.**, **268**, 889-898, doi:10.1086/161011, 1983. [PDF]

1982

289. J. Kóta, E. Merényi, J.R. Jokipii, T.I. Gombosi and A.J. Owens, A numerical study of the pitch-angle scattering of cosmic rays, **Astrophys. J.**, **254**, 398-404, doi:10.1086/159744, 1982. [PDF]

1981

290. A.K. Richter, M.I. Verigin, V.G. Kurt, V.G.Stolpovskii, K.I. Gringauz, E. Keppler, H. Rosenbauer, F. M. Naubauer, T. Gombosi and A. Somogyi, The 3 January 1978 interplanetary shock event as observed by energetic particle, plasma, and magnetic field devices on board of HELIOS-1, HELIOS-2 and PROGNOZ-6, **J. Geophysics**, **50**, 101-109, 1981. [PDF]

291. T.E. Cravens, T.I. Gombosi and A.F. Nagy, Model calculations of the dayside ionosphere of Venus, **Advances in Space Research**, **1**, (9)33-(9)36, doi:10.1016/0273-1177(81)90216-7, 1981. [PDF]

292. T.I. Gombosi and A.J. Owens, Numerical study of solar flare particle propagation in the heliosphere, **Advances in Space Research**, **1**, (3)115-(3)120, doi:10.1016/0273-1177(81)90029-6, 1981. [PDF]

293. V.G. Kurt, Y.I. Logachev, V.G. Stolpovskii, G.A. Trebukhovskaya, T.I. Gombosi, K. Kecskeméty and A.J. Somogyi, Long lasting energetic particle injection from a weak flare, **Advances in Space Research**, **1**, (3)69-(3)72, doi:10.1016/0273-1177(81)90019-3, 1981. [PDF]

294. T.I. Gombosi, M. Horanyi, T.E. Cravens, A.F. Nagy and C.T. Russell, The role of charge exchange in the solar wind absorption by Venus, **Geophys. Res. Lett.**, **8**, 1265-1268, doi:10.1029/GL008i012p01265, 1981. [PDF]

295. A.J. Owens and T.I. Gombosi, The inapplicability of spatial diffusion models for solar cosmic rays, **Astrophys. J.**, **245**, 328-334, doi:10.1086/158812, 1981. [PDF]

1980

296. T.I. Gombosi, T.E. Cravens, A.F. Nagy, R.C. Elphic and C.T. Russell, Solar wind absorption by Venus, **J. Geophys. Res.**, **85**, 7747-7759, doi:10.1029/JA085iA13p07747, 1980. [PDF]

297. T.E. Cravens, T.I. Gombosi and A.F. Nagy, Hot hydrogen in the exosphere of Venus, **Nature**, **283**, 178-180, doi:10.1038/283178a0 , 1980. [PDF]

298. T.I. Gombosi and A.J. Owens, The interplanetary transport of solar cosmic rays, **Astrophys. J.**, **241**, L129-L132, doi:10.1086/183375 , 1980. [PDF]

299. T.E. Cravens, T.I. Gombosi, J. Kozyra, A.F. Nagy, L.H. Brace and W.C. Knudsen, Model calculations of the dayside ionosphere of Venus: Energetics, **J. Geophys. Res.**, **85**, 7778-7786, doi:10.1029/JA085iA13p07778, 1980. [PDF]

300. A.J. Owens and T.I. Gombosi, Cosmic ray scattering in simulated interplanetary magnetic field fluctuations, **Astrophys. J.**, **235**, 1071, doi:10.1086/157711, 1980. [PDF]

1979

301. A.J. Kliore, I.R. Patel, A.F. Nagy, T.E. Cravens and T.I. Gombosi, Initial observations of the nightside ionosphere of Venus from Pioneer Venus Orbiter radio occultations, **Science**, **205**, 99-102, doi:10.1126/science.205.4401.99, 1979. [PDF]

302. T. Gombosi, T.E. Cravens, A.F. Nagy, L.H. Brace and A.J. Owens, Plasma diffusion into the wake of Venus, **Geophys. Res. Lett.**, **6**, 349-352, doi:10.1029/GL006i005p00349, 1979. [PDF]

303. T. Gombosi, K. Kecskeméty and S. Pinter, On the connection of interplanetary shock wave parameters and energetic storm particle events, **Geophys. Res. Lett.**, **6**, 313-316, doi:10.1029/GL006i004p00313, 1979. [PDF]

304. K.I. Gringauz, M.I. Verigin, T.K. Breus and T. Gombosi, The interaction of the solar wind electrons in the optical umbra of Venus with the planetary atmosphere - the origin of the nighttime ionosphere, **J. Geophys. Res.**, **84**, 2123-2127, doi:10.1029/JA084iA05p02123, 1979. [PDF]

1978

305. M.I. Verigin, K.I. Gringauz, T. Gombosi, T.K. Breus, V.V. Bezrukikh, A.P. Remizov and G.I. Volkov, Plasma near Venus from the VENERA-9 and -10 wide-angle analyzer data, **J. Geophys. Res.**, **83**, 3724–3728, doi:10.1029/JA083iA08p03721, 1978. [PDF]

1977

306. N.N. Volodichev, N.L. Grigorov, G.Y. Kolesov, O.M. Kovrizhnik, M.I. Kudryavtsev, B.M. Kuzhevskii, V.G. Kurt, Y.I. Logachev, N.F. Pissarenko, I.A. Savenko, A.A. Suslov, L.M. Chupova, V.F. Shesterikov, I.P. Shestopalov, T. Gombosi, J. Kóta and A. Somogyi, Solnechnye kosmicheskie luchi i mezhplanetnye udarnye volny 29-30 IV 1973g (Solar cosmic rays and interplanetary disturbances during April 29-30, 1973), **Izvestiya Akademii Nauk SSSR, Seriya Fizicheskaya**, **41**, 1794–1807, 1977.

307. K.I. Gringauz, M.I. Verigin, T.K. Breus and T. Gombosi, Elektronnye potoki izmerennye v opticheskoi teni Venery na sputnikakh VENERA-9 i VENERA-10 - osnovnoi istochnik ionizatsii v nochnoi ionosphere Venery (Electron flows, measured in optical shadow Of Venus aboard Venera-9 and Venera-10 sattelites, as a main source of ionization in Venusian nocturnal ionosphere), **Doklady Akademii Nauk SSSR**, **232**, 1039-1042, 1977.

308. T. Gombosi, J. Kóta, V.G. Kurt, B.M. Kuzhevskii, Y.I. Logachev and A. Somogyi, Analysis of the complex solar particle event on 29-30 April, 1973, **Solar Physics**, **54**, 441-456, doi:10.1007/BF00159935, 1977. [PDF]

1976

309. K.I. Gringauz, V.V. Bezrukikh, T.K. Breus, M.I. Verigin, G.I. Volkov, T. Gombosi and A.P. Remizov, Predvaritel'nye rezul'taty izmerenii plazmy pri pomoshchi shirokougol'nykh priborov na sputnikakh VENERA-9 i VENERA-10, **Kosmicheskie Issledovaniya**, **14**, 839-851, 1976.

310. Gringauz, K.I., V.V. Bezrukikh, T.K. Breus, T. Gombosi, A.P. Remizov, M.I. Verigin and G.I. Volkov, Plasma observations near Venus onboard the VENERA-9 and -10 satellites by means of wide-angle plasma detectors, in "**Physics of Solar Planetary Environments**", edited by D. J. Williams, 918–932, American Geophysiscal Union, Washington, D.C., doi:10.1029/SP008p0918, 1976. [PDF]

1975

311. Gombosi, T., J. Kóta, A. Somogyi, A. Varga, B. Betev, L. Katsarski, S. Kavlakov and I. Khirov, Anisotropy of cosmic radiation in the Galaxy, **Nature**, **255**, 687-689, doi:10.1038/255687a0, 1975. [PDF]

1974

312. Bano, M., P.V. Vakulov, L. Vanicsek, S.N. Vernov, T. Gombosi, N.L. Grigorov, J. Dubinsky, A.V. Zakharov, S.N. Kuznetsov, V.A. Kuznetsova, V.N. Lutsenko, S. Pinter, N.F. Pissarenko, I.A. Savenko, A. Somogyi, A. Holba and S. Fischer, Issledovanie raspredeleniya potokov zaryazhennykh chastits pod radiatsionnymi poyasami po dannym sputnika INTERCOSMOS-3 (Investigation of charged particle distributions below the radiation belts using INTERCOSMOS-3 observations), **Kosmicheskie Issledovaniya**, **12**, 566-571, 1974.

C

Family Trees

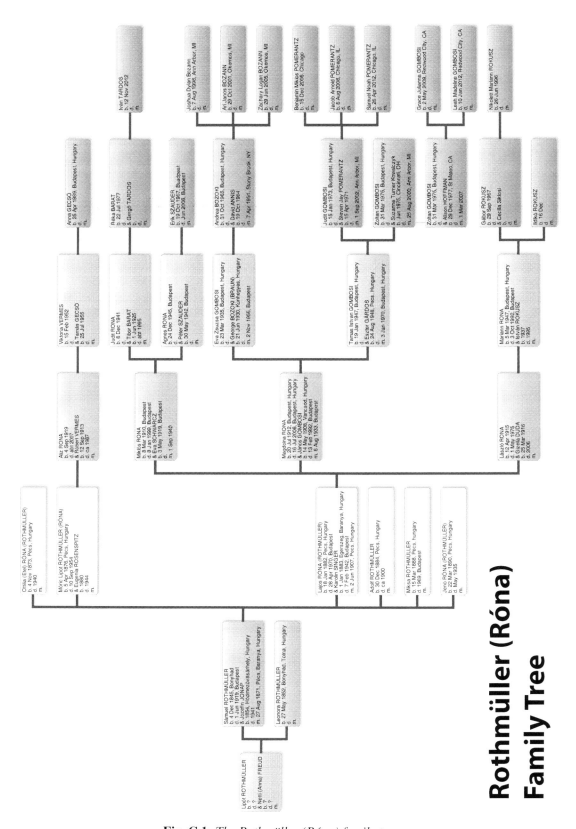

Fig. C.1: *The Rothmüller (Róna) family tree.*

Mühlhoffer/Singer Family Tree

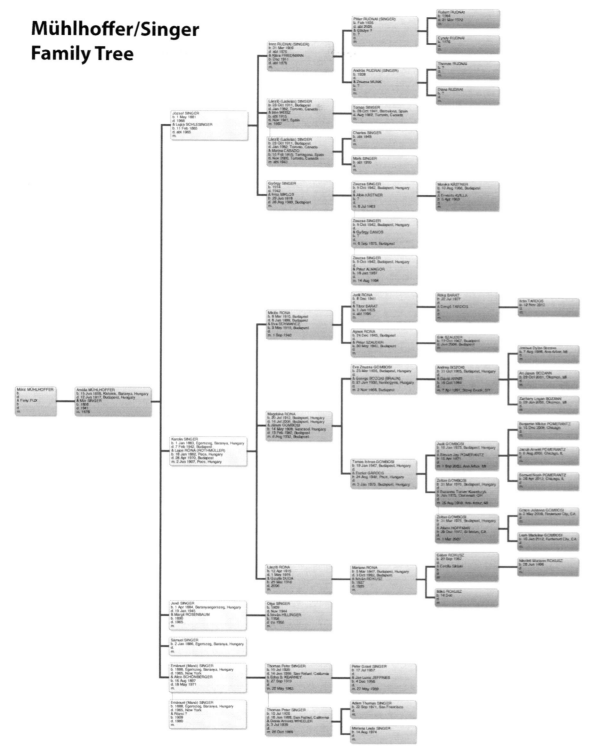

Fig. C.2: *The Mülhoffer (Singer) family tree.*

Glauber (Gombosi) Family Tree

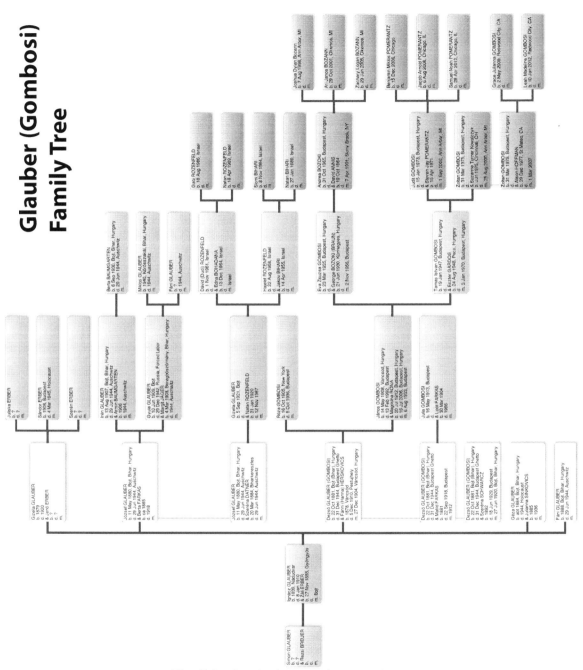

Fig. C.3: *The Glauber (Gombosi) family tree.*

Erber Family Tree

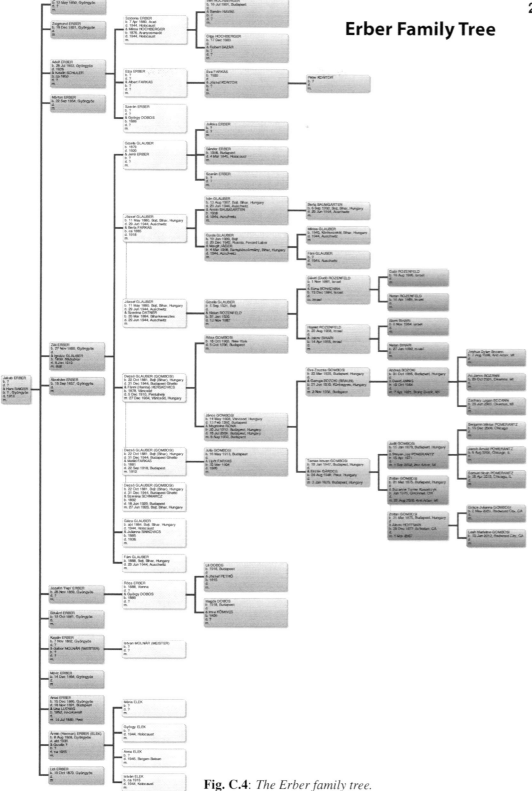

Fig. C.4: *The Erber family tree.*

Günsberger (Gárdos) Family Tree

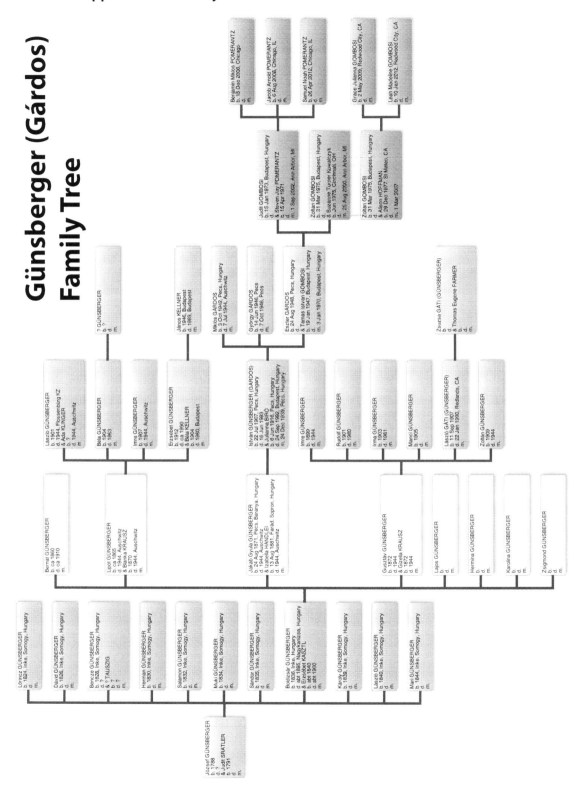

Fig. C.5: *The Günsberger (Gárdos) family tree.*

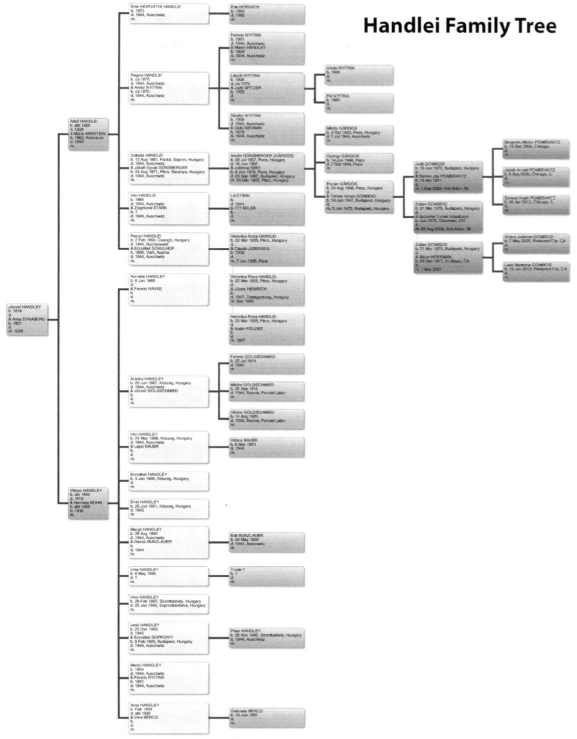

Handlei Family Tree

Fig. C.6: *The Handlei family tree.*

Strauszer (Bíró)
Family Tree

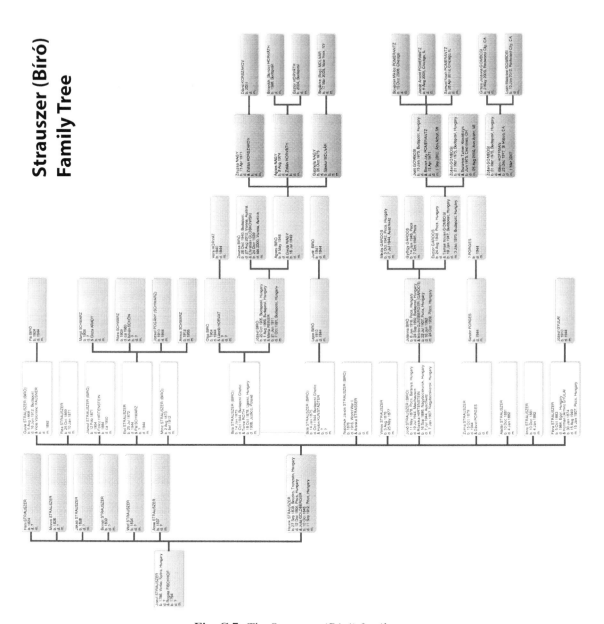

Fig. C.7: *The Strauszer (Bíró) family tree.*

Hirtenstein Family Tree

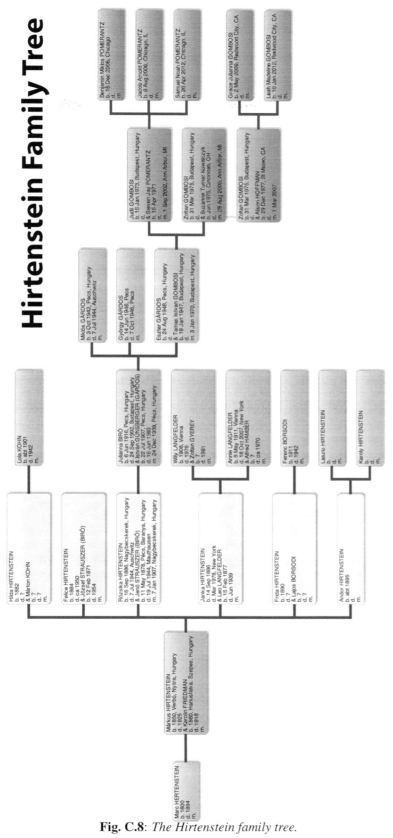

Fig. C.8: *The Hirtenstein family tree.*

Index

Made in the USA
Charleston, SC
03 December 2013